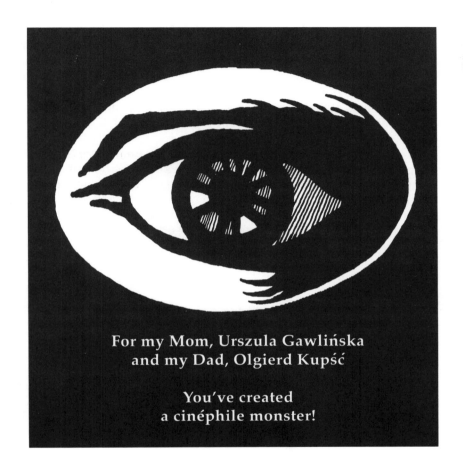

For my Mom, Urszula Gawlińska
and my Dad, Olgierd Kupść

You've created
a cinéphile monster!

Cinema for Beginners is designed to serve as an informative introductory text on the history of narrative film and as a reference guide for those who seek basic information on interesting movies. The book spans over one hundred years of film history; it begins with the events leading to the invention of the medium, chronicles the early struggle of the pioneers, introduces the people behind and in front of the camera, presents all major achievements of the silent and sound periods, and once and for all makes the most tangled film theories easily digestible.

The most unique aspect of **Cinema for Beginners** is its global approach to the subject of film history. The author introduces us to such significant developments as the Soviet montage, Italian neorealism, the French New Wave, the British "kitchen sink" cinema, and the New German Film while providing a comprehensive coverage of such American genre films as slapstick comedy, the western, film noir or science-fiction.
In addition, **Cinema for Beginners** invites the reader to delve into the lesser known regions of World cinema: Eastern Europe, South-East Asia, South America, and others.

Every key figure in the vast world of cinema is presented here with detailed information on his or her background, technique, and major accomplishments. Some, like D.W. Griffith, Sergei Eisenstein, or Orson Welles are given an opportunity to present us their unique approach to moviemaking in a lighthearted, humorous manner. The book's main goal is to make learning about movies as entertaining as it is watching them.

THE HISTORY OF
CINEMA

This book is to be returned on or before

last date stamped below or you will be
charged a fine

New City College – Redbridge campus
Library and Learning Centre
Barley Lane
Romford RM6 4XT
https://towham.cirqahosting.com
Redbridge: 020 8548 7118

Writers and Readers Publishing Inc.
PO Box 461, Village Station
New York, NY 10014

Writers and Readers Ltd.
35 Britannia Row
London N1 8QH
e-mail: begin@writersandreaders.com
web site: writersandreaders.com

A Writers and Readers Documentary Comic Book
Copyright © 1998
ISBN -0-86316-275-4

Manufactured in Finland by WSOY

Beginners Documentary Comic Books are published by Writers and Readers Publishing Inc. and Writers and Readers Ltd. Its trademark, consisting of the words "For Beginners™, Writers and Readers Documentary Comic Books" and the Writers and Readers logo, is registered in the U.S. Patents and Trademark Office and other countries.

CONTENTS

Cinema of the 1950s

Cinema of the 1960s

Cinema of the 1970s

1970s Cont.

Cinema of the 1980s

1980s–Present

1980–Present Cont.

USA in the 1990s

INTRODUCTION

The purpose of *Cinema for Beginners* is to make learning about motion pictures as pleasurable as it is watching them.

The book invites the reader to embark on a fantastic journey across the first one hundred years of film history. Any colorful trip of such magnitude would not be complete without a responsible guide – in this case we leave you in the competent hands of **Professor Elmo Flicker**, a once-respected film scholar who had fallen out of grace with the academic crowd. His crime: teaching about film with a benevolent and humorous attitude; his punishment: banishment from lecture halls across the nation.

Undaunted, Professor Flicker has taken to the streets and backroads of America in his VW van and continues preaching to the needy about Cinema, the one and only art deprived of its own Muse.

His lectures were meticulously transcribed over the years by Jarek Kupść, one of his most devoted followers, and constitute the body of this book.

Prof. Elmo Flicker

JAREK KUPŚĆ?

NEVER HEARD OF THE GUY.

The Not So Humble Beginnings

Persistence of vision—an ability of the human brain to retain images perceived by the eye for a brief period of time after they disappear from the filed of vision. Persistence of vision was known since the time of the ancient Egyptians, but it is not until the mid 19th century when entrepreneurs exploit this phenomenon for its optical entertainment value. Toys of various quality and complexity are produced, providing viewers with an illusion of movement.

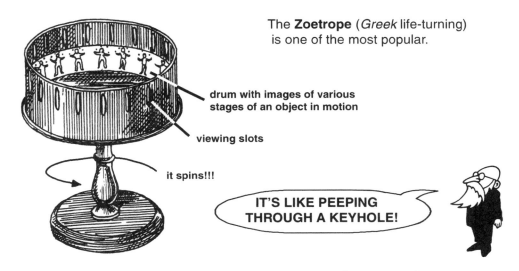

The **Zoetrope** (*Greek* life-turning) is one of the most popular.

drum with images of various stages of an object in motion

viewing slots

it spins!!!

IT'S LIKE PEEPING THROUGH A KEYHOLE!

Using multiple still cameras which capture consecutive stages of movement, Briton **Eadweard Muybridge** (1830-1904) becomes the first man in history to record continuous live action.

It is called **Series Photography**.

1877 Muybridge helps the former governor of California **Leland Stanford** win a substantial bet when his series of photographs depicting a galloping horse prove that at one stage of motion all four hooves are off the ground (not pictured below).

Expanding his studies of animal movement, Muybridge takes candid pictures of people performing athletic feats while nude.

1882   Etienne-Jules Marey (1830-1904), a French physiologist, replaces Muybridge's multiple camera setup with the **chronophotographic gun** —a single camera capable of taking consecutive pictures of live action.

Marey also designs a **paper roll film** to substitute for the clumsy photographic glass plates.

1887   George Eastman (1854-1932) appropriates the invention of celluloid roll film from the Reverend **Hannibal Goodwin.** Eastman begins to mass produce it in 1889, targeting the booming photography market.

G. Eastman

Thomas Alva Edison (1847-1931) fancies an added visual accompaniment to the music of his tremendously successful phonographic parlors.

William Kennedy Laurie Dickson (1860-1935), a young Edison Laboratories assistant is assigned to develop a camera which would be able to capture movement by allowing for more extensive sequences than the chronophotographic gun.

Synthesizing Muybridge's and Marey's accomplishments, Dickson designs a motion picture camera which uses the Eastman celluloid stock.

Edison patents the invention under the name **Kinetograph** (*Greek* motion writer).

He hesitates, however, to apply the 17th century **Magic Lantern** principle of image projection to motion pictures. His Kinetoscope apparatus allows only one person at a time to watch his short films through a peephole.

WHY PROJECT A MOVIE FOR HUNDREDS OF PEOPLE AT A TIME IF I CAN MAKE A NICKEL EACH TIME A PERSON VIEWS IT IN MY KINETOSCOPE?

T.A. Edison

SAVVY

In the meantime, a brilliant German film pioneer **Oskar Messter** (1866-1943) designs a movie projector which provides a steady motion of the film roll.

In France, brothers **Auguste** and **Louis Lumière** (1862-1954; 1864-1948) develop the **Cinematographe** (*Greek* "motion recorder"), an apparatus which combines the functions of movie camera, film printer and film projector.

MARCH 22, 1895

The Lumière Brothers conduct the first successful projection of a motion picture, **Workers Leaving the Lumière Factory** (*La Sortie des ouviers de l'usine Lumière*).

On December 28, 1895, the Lumières open the first movie theatre in history, showing several short films to a paying audience.

Among the selected films is the amusing comic sketch, **The Sprinkler Sprinkled** (*L'Arrouseur arrosé*), widely considered to be the first narrative motion picture ever made.

On the other side of the Atlantic, **Thomas Armat** (1866-1948), a young inventor, perfects a method of projecting the Kinetograph film shorts. In 1896, impressed by the new invention and success of the Lumières, Edison decides to abandon his own research and buys Armat's projection machine.

He calls it **Vitascope** (*Greek* life-viewing).

I'LL TAKE THE CREDIT, YOU GET A PLAQUE WITH YOUR NAME ON THE BACK OF EACH VITASCOPE.

FAIR ENOUGH, I THINK.

T.ARMAT DESIGNER

The first Vitascope projection for an audience takes place in New York on **April 23,1896** as one of the acts in a vaudeville bill.

A well established Parisian stage magician **Georges Méliès** (1861-1938) recognizes the illusionist potentials of the film medium. Between 1897 and 1913, at **Montreuil**, the first movie studio in Europe, Méliès produces about five hundred films, most of which he directs, photographs, and acts in.

Méliès most popular work becomes *A Trip to the Moon* (*Le Voyage dans la Lune*, 1902), a thirty-scene comical fantasy about the conquest of the Earth's satellite.

Méliès calls his filmed scenes "**tableaux**." The shots are static, but the action within each tableaux is full of movement. Some of Méliès' innovations include **multiple exposure**, **slow motion**, **time-lapse photography**, **dissolves** and **hand-tinting** of the film strip.

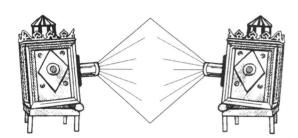

Méliès' *The Magic Lantern* (1903) becomes the first film to self-reflect upon cinema's origins and infinite possibilities.

In 1917, 400 of Méliès' films are destroyed to produce boot heels for the French Army.

WAR IS *SO* WRONG.

GREAT BRITAIN

George Albert Smith (1864-1959), **James Williamson** (1855-1933), and **Cecil Hepworth** (1873-1953), the most innovative filmmakers of the 1896-1906 period, propel the medium toward new territories. Because of sophisticated editing techniques, Hepworth's *Rescued by Rover* (1905) remains the most well structured narrative film before D.W. Griffith's more mature work.

Rover takes five

4

Highly impressed with the storytelling ability of Méliès and the editing rhythms of the English pioneers, a former Kinetoscope operator **Edwin Stanton Porter** (1869-1941) combines staged scenes with stock footage in his entertaining six-minute film *Life of an American Fireman* (1903). Porter's innovation is development of **parallel action**— telling separate stories in a simultaneous, overlapping fashion. Explored further in Porter's most successful film, *The Great Train Robbery* (1903), parallel action becomes the foundation of narrative filmmaking.

At the conclusion of the lengthy (12 min.) *Robbery*, a bandit fires his pistol directly at the audience. The viewers try to dodge the bullet in panic.

George Barnes in *The Great Train Robbery*

One of the first effective close-ups

A young unsuccessful writer and a former encyclopedia salesman named **David Wark Griffith** (1875-1948) makes his leading man debut in Porter's *Rescued From an Eagle's Nest* (1907).

JUNE 1905

A comfortable permanent movie theatre is opened in Pittsburgh. It provides its nickel-paying customers with an hour-long program of motion pictures accompanied by live piano music. It is the first **nickelodeon**, a type of movie theatre which will soon mushroom all across America.

1908   In order to fight the rampant movie copyright piracy and curtail the anarchy of distributors, nine of the most vital film companies (under Edison's leadership) form the **Motion Picture Patents Company**.

Film business goes corporate.

Thanks to a legal action initiated by such independent film companies as **Paramount**, **Fox** and **Universal**, the MPPC is disbanded in 1917 as an illegal trust.

1908 FRANCE

The stately called **Société Film d'Art** begins to produce films based on classical plays and novels. Despite the fact that these productions are basically a filmed theatre and possess no merit in terms of advancing the syntax of cinema language, **film d'art** becomes an international success. It proves once and for all that audiences will sit through a film over 15 minutes long.

Sarah Bernhardt (1844-1923) triumphs in **Queen Elizabeth** (*La Reine Elizabeth*, 1912), which runs about 50 minutes (yes, it is silent).

1906 Frenchman **Charles Pathé** (1863-1957) begins a worldwide expansion of his thriving film industry. By 1908, in the U.S. alone, **Pathé Frères** distributes double the number of films produced by American companies.

SOIT.

By 1918, over fifty percent of <u>all movies</u> are shot with Pathé's patents.

One of the most gifted and prolific talents working for Pathé is **Max Linder** (1883-1923).

HI, I'M **MAX**. I'M GOING TO DIRECT AND STAR IN ABOUT 400 SILENT COMEDIES. MY STYLINGS WILL INFLUENCE THE WORK OF **MACK SENNETT** AND HIS MOST FAMOUS PERFORMER – **CHARLIE CHAPLIN**.

GO FOR IT, MAX.

SEE IF ANYONE REMEMBERS YOU.

1907-1913 USA

Mass migration of the East Coast-based film companies to Southern California.

1905-1906 ITALY

Filotea Alberini (1865-1937) establishes the Cines film studio in Rome, which is responsible for the first Italian costume film, **The Capture of Rome** (*La presa di Roma*, 1905). Turin's Ambrosia Films follows with **The Last Days of Pompeii** (*Gli ultimi giorni di Pompei* , 1908), a movie which initiates the influx of historical spectacle. The most lavish and innovative movies of that genre are **Enrico Guazzoni**'s **Quo Vadis** (1913) and **Giovanni Pastrone**'s *Cabiria* (1914).

D.W. GRIFFITH

OR THE COMING OF AGE OF THE NARRATIVE FILM

After appearing in a string of Porter-produced one-reelers, Griffith moves to Biograph where he directs his first film, ***The Adventures of Dollie*** (1908), a blunt remake of *Rescued by Rover*.

> LET'S TURN ROVER INTO A BITCH. THE LAST-MOMENT RESCUE ALSO NEEDS SOME WORK.

Producing and directing hundreds of short films, Griffith develops a unique sense of shot composition.

> THE CAMERA SHOULD OBEY THE ACTION, NOT THE OTHER WAY AROUND.

> IF I COULD BREAK THE THEATRICAL SCENE INTO A SERIES OF SHOTS AND STILL PRESERVE THE UNITY OF ACTION, I COULD INCREASE THE DRAMATIC INTENSITY OF MY FILMS.

I SHOULD INTRODUCE THE ACTION WITH AN **ESTABLISHING SHOT**...

THEN CUT TO A **MEDIUM SHOT** FOR MORE CLARITY.

THEN I COULD GO TO A **CLOSE-UP** FOR SPECIFIC DETAIL OR DRAMATIC EFFECT.

THAT'LL DO, **D.W.**

Crosscutting between the subplots in **A Corner in Wheat** (1909) doesn't go over well with the Biograph management.

In his approach to actors, Griffith is just as specific.

Angry at Biograph's reluctance to make feature length (multiple-reel) films, Griffith leaves the studio for an independent California company, **Mutual/Reliance-Majestic**. He takes his personal cameraman **G.W. "Billy" Bitzer** and his entire acting ensemble along for the ride.

After several feature-length movies, Griffith is ready to take on his own independent project, **The Birth of a Nation** (1915).

WE IN THE SOUTH SEE THINGS DIFFERENTLY.

NO KIDDING.

Despite its blatant racism and historical inaccuracies, *The Birth of a Nation* remains a milestone cinematic achievement.

IT'S LIKE WRITING HISTORY WITH LIGHTNING!

Woodrow Wilson on *Birth*.

Cinema finally gains artistic prestige and is universally proclaimed the most powerful medium of expression.

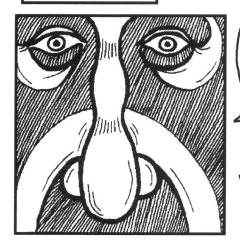

I'M GOING TO PRODUCE A PICTURE SO GRAND AND EXTRAVAGANT, SO EXCESSIVE AND LAVISH, THAT IT WILL DWARF EVERYTHING I'VE DONE THUS FAR, EVEN IF...

EVEN IF WHAT, MR. GRIFFITH?

EVEN IF IT MEANS THE END OF MY CAREER AND LIFELONG DEBTS.

Intolerance (1916) means exactly that.

Costing nearly forty times as much as an average feature film, *Intolerance* tells four parallel stories set in four separate time periods: 6th century B.C. Babylon, Judea in the times of Jesus, 16th century Reformation France, and Modern Day America. The movie runs approximately eight hours.

Unfortunately, the audiences don't care for *Intolerance*'s complexity and grandeur. The movie, although a brilliant example of continuity storytelling, lacks the human touch of *The Birth of a Nation*. It is a financial disaster and marks the beginning of Griffith's decline as the preeminent figure in the world's cinema.

14

GERMANY

Andreas Hofer (1909) is the first feature film produced by the German pioneer **Oskar Messter**. His studio is responsible for introducing such movie stars as **Emil Jannings** and **Conrad Veidt**.

Stellan Rye's ***The Student of Prague*** (*Der Student von Prag*, 1913) becomes the first German film to break out of theatrical conventions. The movie displays highly stylized lighting techniques which mirror the morbid, mysterious theme of the film.

The **German Expressionist** cinema is born.

Paul Wegener as The Student

Paul Wegener as Doppelgänger

The most memorable German film dealing with unearthly phenomena is **Robert Wiene**'s ***The Cabinet of Dr. Caligari*** (*Das Kabinett des Dr. Caligari*, 1919).

Influenced by Cubist art, the sets of *Caligari* provide more than just beautiful backdrops for the story—they shape the inner states of the protagonists and reflect the psychology of the action.

Conrad Veidt as Cesare the Somnambulist

15

SCANDINAVIA

Denmark's **Nordisk Films Kompagni** produces one of the best film adaptation of literary works to date—***Atlantis*** (1913). This visually spectacular film, based on a novel by **Gerhart Hauptmann** and directed by **August Blom** (1869-1947), serves as an inspiration to many a filmmaker, including D.W. Griffith.

Victor Sjöström (1879-1960) directs a moving drama ***Ingeborga Holm*** (1913) for **AB Svenska Biografteatren**, the Swedish chapter of Biograph, and receives international acclaim for ***The Phantom Chariot***, (*Kørkarlen*, 1921), a solemnly poetic supernatural tale which remains one of the most accomplished films of the silent era.

**Writer-director-actor
Victor Sjöström
in *The Phantom Chariot***

AB Svensk filmindustry (formerly AB Svenska Biografteatern) finances the masterful ***Witchcraft Through the Ages*** (*Häxan*, 1921) by **Benjamin Christensen** (1879-1959), a Danish writer-director with a skill for combining extravagant scenery with realistic narration.

Mauritz Stiller's *Erotikon* (1920) is an elegant and insightful romantic comedy whose sensuality will influence the future work of **Ernst Lubitsch** (1892-1947).

In Stiller's ***The Saga of Gösta Berling*** (*Gösta Berlings Saga*, 1924) makes one of her first screen appearances a young actress named **Greta Garbo** (1905-1994)

Danish director **Carl-Theodor Dreyer** (1889-1968) makes his first mark with ***Master of the House*** (*Du skal aere din hustru*,1925), a petit-bourgeoisie comedy-drama which enjoys great success in France.

USA

SEPTEMBER 1912

Mack Sennett (1880-1960) founds **Keystone Film Company** in New Jersey. Sennett, who worked as a writer-director-actor for Griffith at Biograph, incorporates the famous director's methods into his own genre of film—**slapstick comedy**, a hybrid of vaudeville, burlesque, circus and Max Linder's brand of humor.

Slapstick films introduce the world to the talents of Charlie Chaplin, Harry Langdon, Fatty Arbuckle, Gloria Swanson, and Ben Turpin and serve as a training ground for such notable directors as Buster Keaton, George Stevens, Frank Capra, and Chaplin.

Sennett in
Race for a Life

As a movie studio, Keystone patterns itself after "Inceville" (see next page), with Sennett overseeing every aspect of production. American dominance of world cinema begins with the immense success of Sennett's silent comedies.

Thomas Harper Ince (1882-1924), a former actor-director at American Biograph, establishes **"Inceville"**, a highly organized movie studio at Santa Ynez in California (later relocated to Culver City). Completely modernized by 1918, "Inceville" employs teams of writers, directors and production staff simultaneously working on multiple individual projects, all supervised by Ince himself. "Inceville" becomes a prototype for every other Hollywood-style film studio to come around in the next forty years.

✳ ✳ ✳

Charlie Chaplin (1889-1977), working under a Keystone contract, begins to develop his popular sad clown persona. But it is **Essanay Company** that allows him to make longer and more mature pictures like *The Tramp* (1915), which launches Chaplin into international stardom.

His best movies for **Mutual**, *The Immigrant* (1917) and *Easy Street* (1917), establish Chaplin not only as a master of silent physical comedy, but also as a brilliant observer of social injustice and a champion of all underdogs.

Under an unprecedented multimillion dollar contract with **First National**, Chaplin directs his most popular picture to date, *The Kid* (1921), a incisive semi-autobiographical comedy-drama about a custody battle over a five year old child (**Jackie Coogan**).

Contradicting the anonymity of the MPPA trust actors, independent studios begin to give their performers full screen credit. By 1917, with the staggering contracts of **Mary Pickford** (1893-1979) and Chaplin, the status of screen actors increases tremendously. The movie star system becomes the key component of the golden era of Hollywood.

Mary Pickford

Douglas Fairbanks (1883-1939) moves from the benevolent parodies of genre films onto extravagant costume spectacles, elaborate both in decor and acrobatic activity of the star.

It is films like *The Mark of Zorro* (1920), *Robin Hood* (1922), and *The Thief of Bagdad* (1924) which establish Fairbanks as the first action movie star in the history of cinema.

Fairbanks in *The Thief of Bagdad*

The most powerful studios to emerge after the disbandment of the MPPA in 1917 are **Paramount Pictures**, founded by **Adolph Zukor** (1873-1976), **Metro-Goldwyn-Mayer**, assembled by **Marcus Loew** and run by **Louis B. Mayer**, and **First National**. Polish-born **Samuel Goldwyn** (1882-1974) becomes one of the most influential independent producers in Hollywood.

Zukor develops the **"block booking"** system of film distribution: if theatre owners want to show movies featuring Paramount's stars (Pickford, William S. Hart), they have to rent them with groups ("blocks") of other, less commercially viable films.

1919 Taking matters into their own hands, Pickford, Fairbanks, Chaplin and Griffith create the **United Artist Corporation**, designed exclusively for distribution of their movies.

✳ ✳ ✳

The Garage

Between 1917 and 1919, **Roscoe "Fatty" Arbuckle** (1881-1933) and his sidekick **Buster Keaton** (1895-1966) appear in about fifteen slapstick two-reelers.

Subsequently, Keaton embarks on a solo career which leads him to international stardom equal only to that of Chaplin.

1923   Keaton and **Eddy Cline** (1892-1961) film *The Three Ages*, a parody of Griffith's *Intolerance*. The same year Keaton and **Jack Blystone** (1892-1939) co-direct *Our Hospitality*. Both features become huge commercial hits.

Sherlock Jr. (1924), Keaton's first solo effort as a director, remains one of the most unusual and visually inventive movies of its time. Keaton's character, a film projectionist, falls asleep at his post while his dream image enters the film being projected in the theatre.

Keaton's trademark is the **trajectory gag**:

IT INVOLVES PERFECT TIMING OF DIRECTING, EDITING AND ATHLETIC SKILLS WHICH NAVIGATE A SEQUENCE OF LOGISTICALLY CONNECTED GAGS THROUGH AN EXTENDED SCENE.

The only other silent comic who for a brief time surpasses the American box-office success of Keaton and Chaplin is **Harold Lloyd** (1893-1971).

After a string of **Hal Roach**-produced shorts patterned after Chaplin's tramp films, Lloyd goes on to develop the character of an archetypical American who beneath a competitive and success-driven façade hides a decent and compassionate soul.

Never as poignant as Chaplin's or Keaton's work, Lloyd's **"comedy of thrills"** is pure entertainment, offering a dizzying combination of elaborate sight gags and a well-structured narrative.

High and Dizzy (1920),
Safety Last (1923),
and *The Freshman* (1925)
are Lloyd's most popular of the
hysterically kinetic comedies.

The shortest span of popularity in silent burlesque belongs to **Harry Langdon** (1884-1944).

Honing his subtle pantomimic skills at Sennett's Keystone, Langdon develops his famous man-child persona: a baby-faced, naive grown-up confronted with the complexities and cruelties of the adult world.

Langdon success is based on only three features: ***Tramp, Tramp, Tramp*** (1926), ***The Strong Man*** (1926), and ***Long Pants*** (1927). The last two are directed by **Frank Capra** (1897-1991).

Stan Laurel (1890-1965) and **Oliver Hardy** (1892-1957) are paired by **Hal Roach** (1892-) in ***Putting the Pants on Philip*** (1927), directed by **Clyde Bruckman**, and become cinema's first important comedy team.

Laurel

Hardy

Chaplin continues to explore his tramp misadventures in ***The Gold Rush*** (1925). This comedy is created from such depressing issues as hunger, avarice and unrequited love.

In 1927, Buster Keaton creates his comic masterpiece, ***The General***. Co-directed with Clyde Bruckman, this Civil War epic is constructed as one long trajectory gag. It incorporates breathtaking sight jokes woven into the narrative with impeccable timing and sense of continuity. The picture's grand climax contains the most expensive single shot ever filmed to date—the collapse of a railroad bridge and the spectacular plunge of a Union locomotive into Rock River.

The General

GERMANY

Expressionist cinema approaches its heyday. Obsession with death and decline of moral values are present in every film of the **Weimar Period** (1919-1929). **Friedrich Wilhelm Murnau** (1888-1931) makes *Januskopf* (1920), his version of Stevenson's *Dr. Jeckyll and Mr. Hyde*; inspired by Dostoyevsky's *Crime and Punishment*, Robert Wiene creates a highly stylized and moody *Raskolnikov* (1923). Both films are produced by **UFA** (Universum Film Aktiengesellschaft), a government-subsidized film company which after WW I becomes the largest and most prominent movie studio in Europe.

Fritz Lang (1890-1976) directs *Destiny* (*Der müde Tod*, 1921)—a romantic and metaphysical tale of a lost love and triumph over Death. Within the frame of the main narrative, Lang and his co-writer **Thea von Harbou** (1888-1954) introduce a triptych of fantastic tales set in exotic locations—Arabia, Venice, and China. The movie's elaborate set design is provided by the former *Caligari* artists, **Walter Röhrig** and **Herman Warm**, in collaboration with **Robert Herlth**.

I WONDER WHAT WILL DOUGLAS FAIRBANKS THINK OF THE CHINESE EPISODE OF *DESTINY*... AND THAT BAGDAD SET DOESN'T LOOK SHABBY EITHER.

Lang's last important silent film, *Metropolis* (1926), offers a terrifying vision of the future at the zenith of industrialism. Workers are reduced to dehumanized geometrical blocks while the ruling class enjoys the privileges of wealth. Despite the heavy-handed metaphorical plot, *Metropolis* succeeds because of its sheer visual glory —Lang, a trained architect, masterfully orchestrates the relationship between rigid design of the city and human beings who, stripped of the last shreds of dignity, become one with the Moloch machine.

F.W. Murnau continues to explore the theme of love and death in **Nosferatu, a Symphony of Horrors** (*Nosferatu, eine Symphonie des Grauens*, 1922), a loose adaptation of Bram Stoker's *Dracula*. Photographed by **Fritz Arno Wagner** in stark, high-contrast black and white, with exaggerated shadows and **low angles,** *Nosferatu* exemplifies Expressionist cinema in its purest form.

None of the silent movies does as much to advance the mobility of the film camera as Murnau's **The Last Laugh** (*Der letzte Mann*, 1926).

A simple story of a scorned porter in Berlin develops into a poignant psychological study of the German society at large. Under Murnau's meticulous guidance, **Karl Freund** keeps his camera in constant motion, **tracking** sideways, back and forth, and, in some parts, allowing his lens to become the protagonist's eyes.

Emil Jannings
in
The Last Laugh

SUBJECTIVE CAMERA PROVIDES MULTIPLE POINTS OF VIEW WHICH ENRICH THE NARRATIVE.

The Last Laugh belongs to a new genre of German cinema—the **Kammerspiel** film ("intimate theatre").

Karl Grune's *Der Strasse* (*The Street*, 1923) initiates yet another movement of German film—**die neue Sachlichkeit** ("the new objectivity"), which deals with the postwar economical depression in a cynical, realistic manner. In the second half of the decade, "street films" (Strassenfilme) begin to dominate German screens. The most innovative picture of that genre is *The Joyless Street* (*Die freudlose Gasse*, 1925), directed by **Georg Wilhelm Pabst** (1885-1967).

To provide the viewer with an illusion of uninterrupted action, Pabst develops the concept of **continuity editing**—a seamless combination of cutting and fluid camera movement.

✳✳✳

USA

After a string of suspicious deaths, sexual scandals, and other unfortunate events, Hollywood decides to clean up its act. All major film companies finance the **MPPDA** (The Motion Picture Producers and Distributors of America), an organization regulating the moral outlook of the industry. Created to keep federal censorship out of the film business, the MPPDA counters Hollywood's negative publicity with a new-and-improved image of self-control and restraint.

Will H. Hays (1879-1954), a (disgruntled?) Postmaster General of the U.S., ultraconservative Republican and obsessively religious man becomes the head of the MPPDA.

Cecil B. DeMille's (1881-1959) *The Ten Commandments* (1923) is the first major motion picture to embody the **Hays Office** principles of censorship: as long as the sin is punished in the last reel, there is no need to restrain its depiction.

The Ten Commandments is virtually all sex and violence, shot with unsurpassed extravagance of decor and very little substance.

Erich von Stroheim (1885-1957), an immigrant from Austria and a former assistant to Griffith, makes his impressive directorial debut in 1918 with **Blind Husbands**, one of the first Hollywood films to depict sexuality in a mature manner.

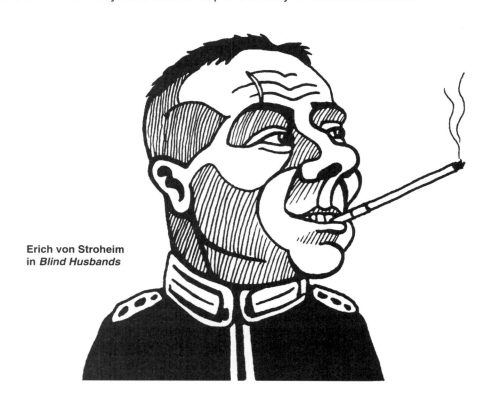

Erich von Stroheim
in *Blind Husbands*

After his critically acclaimed **Foolish Wives** (1921), Stroheim directs an adaptation of **Frank Norris**' novel, **McTeague**. Severely recut by **MGM** and renamed **Greed**, the movie still remains a masterpiece of psychological cinema, albeit a butchered one.

Greed

Always meticulous in detail reconstruction and complex in their shot composition (**mise-en-scène**), Stroheim's films go over budget every single time, causing the director's premature retirement. Stroheim continues, however, to appear in films as an actor, developing his famous "man you love to hate" persona.

JAPAN

Shochiku Cinema Institute produces the first great Japanese film, *Souls on the Road* (*Rojo no Reikon*, 1921). Directed by **Minoru Murata**, this social drama intercuts between two parallel stories: one depicts a contrite prodigal son and the other chronicles a journey of two freshly released convicts. Rather than dealing with the constrains of linear narrative, Murata focuses on creating an intense emotional atmosphere which dominates the picture. The **mood film** becomes a quintessential genre of Japanese cinema.

Souls on the road

Teinosuke Kinugasa's ***A Page of Madness*** (*Kurutta ippeiji*, 1926), a disturbing portrait of insanity, is a brilliant exercise in the Japanese version of Expressionism and displays editing techniques equal to the European standards.

THE FRENCH IMPRESSIONIST AVANT-GARDE OF THE 20's

Louis Delluc (1890-1924), an early film theorist, sets out to develop an inherently French cinema—a counterpart to Germany's Kammerspiel. Delluc's ***Fever*** (*Fièvre*, 1921) and ***The Woman from Nowhere*** (*La Femme de nulle part*, 1922*)* maintain the structure and mood adherent to his new program.

One of the first female directors, **Germaine Dulac** (1882-1942), shoots ***The Smiling Madame Beudet*** (*La Suriante Madame Beudet*, 1923), an impressionist portrait of an unhappy housewife.

29

The atmospheric *Faithful Heart* (*Coeur fidéle*, 1923) by **Jean Epstin** (1897-1953) continues the impressionist tradition of depicting middle-class life in its natural setting.

Fernand Léger and **Robert Mallet-Stevens** design avant-garde sets for **Marcel L'Herbier**'s (1890-1979) *The Inhuman* (*L'Inhumaine*, 1924), a lavishly impressionist apocalyptic science-fiction film.

R. Clair

A big fan of Méliès', **René Clair** (1898-1981) experiments with fantasy genre in *The Crazy Ray* (*Paris qui dort*, 1924), transforming the French capital into a still life. A mad scientist puts Paris to sleep via an invisible ray, allowing only six people to roam through the frozen-in-the-moment city.

After a series of visually polished melodramas, **Abel Gance** (1889-1981), makes the best anti-war drama to date, *I Accuse* (*J'accuse*, 1919).

In *The Wheel* (*La Roue*, 1922), his first picture of epic proportions, Gance explores the tragic fate of a locomotive engineer and his son. At the request of Pathé, this nine-hour film is edited down to less than four, but it still maintains its brilliance thanks to such technical innovations as rapid editing, Griffith-influenced close-ups, and stark location settings which contribute to the consistency of the picture's dark yet romantic mood.

Following the vein of *Intolerance* and *Greed*, Gance embarks on a gigantic project about the life of Napoleon. Even in its truncated eight-reel version, ***Napoleon as Seen by Abel Gance: First Part: Bonaparte*** (*Napoléon vu par Abel Gance: première époque: Bonaparte*, 1927) contains enough dazzling camera movements, metaphorical use of intercutting and complex superimpositions to be regarded as one of the greatest achievements of silent cinema.

Several parts of *Napoléon* are presented in **Polyvision**—a visual effect which relies on multiple superimposition of images displayed simultaneously from three projectors and forming a **widescreen** effect.

Inspired by Gance's *La Roue*, **Dmitri Kirsanoff** (1899-1957), a Russian expatriate living in France, shoots *Ménilmontant* (1924), a sad tale of two country women who move to a Paris suburb. Kirsanoff's use of fast editing and natural settings anticipates the achievements of the Soviet filmmakers.

✳ ✳ ✳

RUSSIA AND SOVIET UNION

The prerevolutionary Russian cinema offers two unique films by the famous stage director **Vsevolod Meyerhold** (1874-1940)—*The Picture of Dorian Grey* (*Portret Doriana Greia*, 1915), based on Oscar Wilde's novel and *The Strong Man* (*Silnyi Chelovek*, 1917), an adaptation of the Polish writer **Stanislaw Przybyszewski**'s book.

Yakov Protazanov (1881-1945) films yet another literary classic—**Leo Tolstoy**'s *Father Sergius* (*Otets Sergei*, 1918), which becomes the most mature movie of the early Russian cinema.

V. Meyerhold

After the **October Revolution** of 1917, the Soviet government faces a daunting task of unifying the new multi-cultural, multi-ethnic nation of 160 million people.

CINEMA IS FOR US THE MOST IMPORTANT OF THE ARTS.

V.I. Lenin

Soviet cinema is nationalized in 1919 and headed by the **Cinema Committee**, with **Nadezhda Krupskaya** (1869-1939), Lenin's wife, serving as its secretary. The Committee becomes responsible for creating the world's first film school, the **VGIK** (The All-Union Institute of Cinematography).

Dziga Vertov (1896-1954) is one of the first cameramen and editors of the Committee-sponsored propaganda newsreels—**agitki**. Vertov's theory of capturing the absolute reality of life on film is reflected in a series of technically dazzling documentaries collectively called **Kino-pravda** (Cinema-truth).

In 1924, Vertov directs *Cinema-eye* (*Kino-glaz*), a non-narrative feature film depicting the new reality of the Soviet Russia. The movie implements an elaborate use of montage, multiple exposure, animation and microphotography.

Portraying a summer day in the life of Moscow, Vertov's *The Man with a Movie camera* (*Chelovek s kinoapparatom*, 1929) is a virtual lexicon of cinematic techniques and becomes the most famous example of self-reflexive cinema.

✳✳✳

Lev Kuleshov (1899-1970) and his radical VGIK students, including **Sergei Eisenstein** (1898-1948) and **Vsevolod Pudovkin** (1893-1953), obtain a copy of Griffith's *Intolerance* and study its editing structure relentlessly. During a series of workshops at VGIK, Kuleshov demonstrates the power of **montage** as a tool of emotional and geographic manipulation.

SERGEI EISENSTEIN

OR THE BIRTH OF DIALECTIC MONTAGE

After his parents' departure for Western Europe, the young Sergei abandons his engineering studies and joins the Red Army to build bridges during the Revolutionary war.

I'D RATHER MAKE ART.

Soon, he begins to design propaganda posters and building props for amateur theater.

In 1920, Eisenstein joins Moscow's eclectic **Proletkult Theater** as a set designer.

Under the influence of Meyerhold's principles of **bio-mechanic** theater, Eisenstein develops a knack for combining specific aesthetic stimuli to create a desired emotional response in the audience. This principle, which is to become the guiding force of his future film editing strategy, serves him well during his brief career as a stage director.

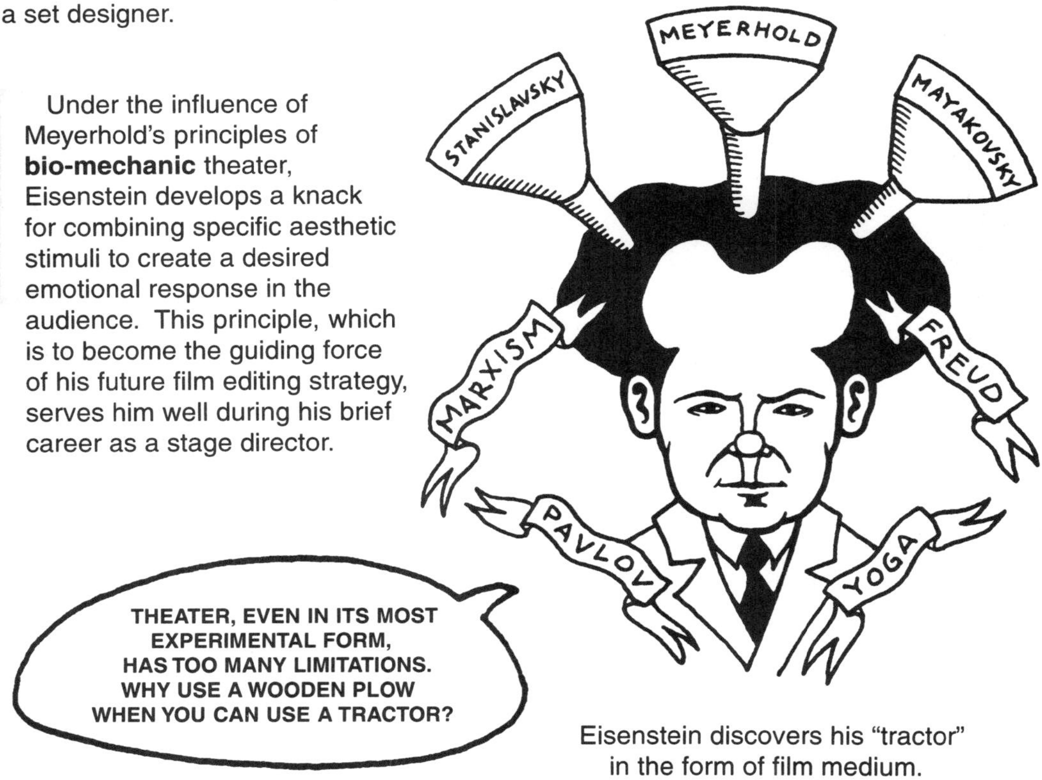

MEYERHOLD

STANISLAVSKY

MAYAKOVSKY

MARXISM

FREUD

PAVLOV

YOGA

THEATER, EVEN IN ITS MOST EXPERIMENTAL FORM, HAS TOO MANY LIMITATIONS. WHY USE A WOODEN PLOW WHEN YOU CAN USE A TRACTOR?

Eisenstein discovers his "tractor" in the form of film medium.

Lacking formal training in filmmaking, Eisenstein attends the VGIK's Kuleshov workshop and assists **Esther Shub** (1894-1959) during her "politically progressive" recutting of Fritz Lang's ***Dr. Mabuse, the Gambler*** (*Doktor Mabuse, der Spieler*, 1921). He also enjoys the multiple screenings of *Intolerance* as well as American slapstick comedies and German Expressionist classics.

In 1924, Eisenstein is invited to direct a Proletkult project called ***Strike*** (*Stachka*).

WITH ITS SHOCK-STIMULI MONTAGE* AND TACTICALLY PLACED DISSOLVES SUPPORTED BY CAREFULLY COMPOSED IMAGES, ***STRIKE*** IS LIKE THE OCTOBER REVOLUTION OF CINEMA.

EASY NOW, SERGEI. YOUR BEST WORK IS STILL TO COME.

*Montage—(*French* "to assemble") in Europe, a term applied to the process of film editing.

Eisenstein's next project is **Battleship Potemkin** (*Bronenosets Potyomkin*, 925), sponsored by the Jubilee Committee to commemorate the 1905 anti-tsarist revolt.

An avid fan of Asian culture, Eisenstein applies principles of the ancient Chinese nd Japanese languages to *Potemkin*'s **dialectical montage** method.

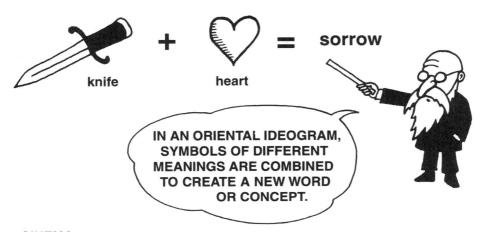

knife + heart = **sorrow**

> IN AN ORIENTAL IDEOGRAM, SYMBOLS OF DIFFERENT MEANINGS ARE COMBINED TO CREATE A NEW WORD OR CONCEPT.

CINEMA TRANSLATION: With an effective juxtaposition of shots or scenes, dialectic montage is capable of invoking any desired psychological response in the audience.

If *Strike* formulated the alphabet of montage, *Potemkin* develops the **syntax of cinema language**.

The strategy of montage splits into five categories: **metric**, **rhythmic**, **tonal**, **overtonal**, and **intellectual.**

Structure of each shot should follow the rules of classical painting composition.

Visual **counterpoints** can be provided by the **conflict** of...

...light and dark   ...small and large masses   ...movement in opposite directions.

Scenes from *Potemkin*

35

The tremendous domestic and international success of *Potemkin* leads Eisenstein to **October** (or *Ten Days That Shook the World/Oktiabr*, 1928), a movie commissioned by the Bolshevik government to honor the 10th anniversary of the 1917 revolution.

October becomes Eisenstein's private lab for further visual experimentation. His intellectual montage reaches here almost abstract levels.

Consequently, the film is deemed too **"formalistic"** by the Communist Party and dramatically recut.

In its mutilated form, just like Gance's *Napoleon* or Stroheim's *Greed*, *October* remains a striking example of a fragmentary masterpiece.

Old and New (*Staroe i novoie*, 1929) is Eisenstein's last silent film.

Its poetic rhythms and pure visual beauty come as a direct effect of the **overtonal montage** principle.

OVERTONAL MONTAGE **?**

IT MEANS THAT THE MOOD OF A FILM IS NOT A RESULT OF ISOLATED EDITING CHOICES, BUT EMERGES FROM THEIR SYNTHESIS DURING PROJECTION.

All of Eisenstein movies are photographed by the incomparable **Edouard Tissé** (1897-1961), a Franco-Russian cinematographer, who is greately responsible for the director's success.

One of the first and most talented rivals of Eisenstein is **Vsevolod Pudovkin**. Trained at VGIK, Pudovkin works on *The Extraordinary Adventures of Mr. West in the Land of Bolsheviks* (1924) and *The Death Ray* (1925)—two pictures directed by his teacher Kuleshov.

Mother (*Mat*, 1926), loosely based on **Maxim Gorky**'s novel, is Pudovkin's first dramatic feature. Similarly to *Potemkin*, the tragic plot of *Mother* takes place during the revolution of 1905. Photographed by **Anatoli Golovnia** (1900-1982), who shot most of Pudovkin's films, the movie is characterized by a flawless four-part structure supported by fluid editing. Rather than emulate the epic sweep of Eisenstein, Pudovkin focuses on a lyrical portrayal of an individual family caught in the midst of the socio-political upheaval.

The End of St. Petersburg (*Koniets Sankt-Peterburga*, 1927), like *October*, is produced by the Communist Party to commemorate the 1917 revolution.

In contrast to Eisenstein, whose intellectual montage relies on psychophysiological stimuli arranged to shock the audience, Pudovkin's editing of *St. Petersburg* plays a narrative role, using individual shots as building blocks rather than counterpoints.

Eisenstein: A+B=C

Pudovkin: A+B=AB

Storm over Asia (or *Heir to Genghis Khan/ Potomok Chingis-Khana*, 1928), is Pudovkin's last silent picture in which he manages to successfully blend realistic action with symbolic imagery. Shot on location, *Storm Over Asia* is accused by Soviet critics of excessive formalism. In the West, the visual beauty and technical mastery of the film are greatly appreciated by audiences as well as the critics.

The most poetic and aesthetically advanced work of the silent Soviet Cinema belongs to **Alexander Dovzhenko** (1894-1956). A former painter and political activist, Dovzhenko brings to the screen a new sensitivity—strongly rooted in nature and its laws yet endowed with highly stylized imagery.

Structured as an extended visual metaphor, Dovzhenko's **Arsenal** (1929) paints a complex picture of the Ukraine after the October Revolution and the ensuing civil war.

Dovzhenko's next project, **Earth** (*Zemlia*, 1930), is a movie with a barely discernible plot. Like a beautifully woven tapestry, the film is composed of life-affirming poetic vignettes set in the rural Ukraine. Again, as in the case of *October* and *Storm over Asia*, *Earth* is condemned by the Soviet critics but revered outside the country.

In 1924, Iakov Protazanov directs **Aelita**, an extravagant science-fiction movie noted for its Constructivist design.

The Overcoat (*Shinel*, 1926) is a successful screen version of Nikolai Gogol's Petersburg story, adapted by **Leonid Trauberg** (1902-) and directed under strong influences of German Expressionism by **Grigori Koznitzev** (1905-1973).

Olga Preobrazhenskaia (1884-1966), an actress turned filmmaker, directs **Women of Riazan** (*Baby Riazanski*, 1927), a lyrical study of a traditional rural life in Russia.

One of the most popular Soviet films depicting modern urban reality is **Abram Room**'s (1894-1976) **Bed and Sofa** (*Tretia Meshchanskaia*, 1926). Shot virtually in one room, the film tells a tense story of a young couple whose domestic life dramatically changes after the housing authorities tag on a stranger to their small apartment.

1929   Joseph Stalin, Lenin's dictatorial successor, reforms Soviet cinema to fit the new goals of communist propaganda, thus initiating a rapid decline of quality and ingenuity of film production.

J. Stalin

CINEMA IS FOR US THE MOST IMPORTANT TOOL OF MASS AGITATION!

FRANCE

The Avant-Garde movement continues with **Salvador Dali**'s (1904-1989) and **Luis Buñuel**'s (1900-1983) *An Andalusian Dog* (*Un Chien andalou*, 1929), a short surreal film with an elusive narrative and rich, provocative imagery evoking Freud's "unconscious mind" theories.

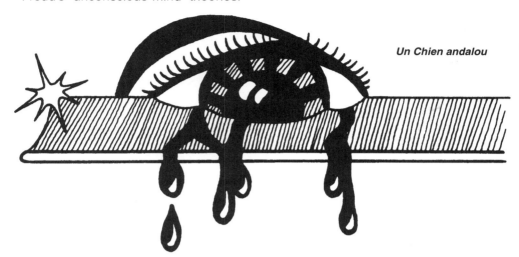

Un Chien andalou

Dali and Bunuel collaborate one more time in *The Golden Age* (*L'Âge d'or*, 1930), a non-dialogue, surreal satire of the Catholic church. The film is supported by a musical score. Also the same year, the famous avant-garde poet **Jean Cocteau** (1889-1963) makes his first film, *Blood of a Poet* (*Le Sange de un poète*).

René Clair embarks on a successful commercial career with the light fare of *The Italian Straw Hat* (*Un Chapeau de paille d'Italie*, 1927) and *Two Timid Souls* (*Les Deux timides*, 1928), both reminiscent of the **Max Linder** and **Mack Sennett** style of comedy.

The highest artistic achievement of the late silent French cinema is undoubtedly *The Passion of Joan of Arc* (*La Passion de Jeanne d'Arc*, 1928). Expertly handled by the Danish director **Carl-Theodor Dreyer** and designed by *Caligari*'s **Hermann Warm**, the movie chronicles the trial and execution of the 15th Century French heroine. Flawlessly photographed by **Rudolph Maté** (1888-1964), *Joan of Arc* offers breakthrough editing techniques and highly innovative framing as well as fluid camera movements which enhance the ever-increasing tension of this classic courtroom drama.

Renée Falconetti as Joan

The last years of silent American cinema are marked by the tremendous influence of European emigrant filmmakers.

Ernst Lubitsch (1892-1947), a German director famous for his **Kostümfilm** (a lavish period picture), arrives in Hollywood in 1922. A series of witty and visually sophisticated erotic comedies, including **Forbidden Paradise** (1924), **Kiss me Again** (1925), and **So This is Paris** (1926) establish Lubitsch as a master of suggestive detail and elegant, decorative style.

AH, THE "LUBITSCH TOUCH"!

(It means "class")

Lilian Gish (1896-1993), famous for her work with Griffith, invites **Victor Sjöström** to direct her in **The Scarlet Letter** (1926). Their collaboration reaches its pinnacle with **The Wind** (1928), a harsh story of a mismatched couple facing the adversities of nature, set in the vacuum of Texan plains.

Lillian Gish &
Lars Hanson
in *The Wind*.

Benjamin Christensen enjoys commercial success as a director of well-crafted melodramas (**The Devil's Circus,** 1926) and mysteries (**Seven Footprints of Satan**, 1929).

Less fortunate is Mauritz Stiller, whose only notable Hollywood film is **Hotel Imperial** (1926). Stiller dies two years later, disenchanted by his American experiences.

F.W. Murnau heads a long list of UFA personnel imported to Hollywood under the **Parufamet Agreement** (1926). His *Sunrise* (1927), produced by Fox, remains one of the masterpieces of silent American cinema, although most of the crew members are German.

Sunrise

In 1931, Murnau directs his last film, *Tabu*, a visually striking travelogue shot in a semi-documentary fashion. His co-director is **Robert Flaherty** (1884-1951), the famous documentary filmmaker, whose *Nanook of the North* (1920) is considered a groundbreaking etnographic film and a foreruner of independent low-budget production.

Some of the UFA actors who embark on prolific careers in Hollywood include Greta Garbo, Emil Jannings, Conrad Veidt, and personal favorite of Lubitsch's—the Polish actress **Pola Negri** (1896-1987).

The inherently American genre of adventure film enjoys great worldwide popularity in the Twenties. **Douglas Fairbanks** is still the champion at the box office with such hits as *The Black Pirate* (1926), shot in the experimental two-strip Technicolor, and *The Iron Mask* (1929).

The exotic matinee idol **Rudolph Valentino** (1895-1926) dies prematurely of peritonitis never to enjoy the commercial success of his *Son of the Sheik* (1926), a long-awaited sequel to his earlier *The Sheik* (1922).

Charles Chaplin's *The Circus* (1928) is rewarded with a special Oscar at the 1929 **Academy Awards** (est. 1927) for the extraordinary artistic versatility of its creator.

Buster Keaton completes his last two great films—*Steamboat Bill Jr.* (1928) and *The Cameraman* (1928). The latter, along with Keaton's *Sherlock Jr.*, is one of the most engaging self-referential movies and in many ways resembles the ideology behind **Vertov**'s *The Man With a Movie Camera*, coincidentally shot the same year.

The Cameraman

K. Vidor

On the dramatic scene, **King Vidor** (1894-1982) directs an enormously popular anti-war love story, *The Big Parade* (1925).

Vidor's *The Crowd* (1928), a masterful portrayal of a lower middle-class marriage may not be a blockbuster, but it establishes its director as a filmmaker with a rare sensibility toward human suffering and an impeccable eye for architectonic design.

The Advent of Sound

For a moviegoer in the silent film era, the experience of watching a motion pictures is all but soundless. It is a common practice among theatre owners to support silent movies with a live piano or organ accompaniment; often a trio of musicians or even a full-scale orchestra is brought in to enrich the projected image with a musical score. In addition, many nickelodeons begin to employ sound effect specialists and live actors who deliver dialogue from behind the screen.

In France, a person who assumes the role of a master of ceremonies at a silent film show is called a **compère**. In Japan, a **benshi**, the traditional Kabuki theater narrator becomes a staple item of the silent motion picture experience. The *benshi*'s job is to comment on the film's action as well as speak the lines of dialogue.

Benshi at work

YOU WILL KINDLY NOTICE THE THIN OUTLINE OF SPARKLING LIGHT SURROUNDING THE MOON. ALSO, OBSERVE THE LONELY CHERRY BOUGH TREMBLING IN THE MIDNIGHT CHILL. THE AUTUMN OF MAN IS NEAR.

Despite the highly sophisticated system of sound and musical accompaniment to silent pictures, the race for a sound fully synchronized with the filmed image continues from the very early days of cinema.

In the U.S., **W.K.L. Dickson** experiments with synchronization of film and sound in 1889, combining the Kinetograph and phonograph. **Léon Gaumont** is one of the first Frenchmen to successfully project sound pictures in his movie theatres.

Cecil Hepworth's **Vivaphone** is a British answer to Gaumont's **Chronophone**. The ever-innovative Oskar Messter leads the German film industry in sound-supported productions. And, of course, T.A. Edison, never one to lag behind, patents not one but two systems of sound for film: **Cinephonograph** and **Kinetophone**.

UNFORTUNATELY, THE PHONOGRAPHIC WAX CYLINDERS AND, LATER, DISKS WHICH ARE USED FOR SOUND REPRODUCTION, DO NOT PROVIDE GOOD SYNCHRONIZATION WITH THE IMAGE AND CANNOT BE AMPLIFIED FOR A LARGE AUDIENCE.

In 1886, a Polish-American pioneer of sound-on-film, **Joseph T. Tykociner**, experiments with an optical sound track on the film strip. His concept is brought to fruition in 1910 by **Eugene Augustin Lauste**, a former assistant to W.K.L. Dickson. Lauste is the first to effectively record sound on the film strip, next to the picture track. It will be years, however, before his accomplishment results in the development of the RCA Photophone sound-on-film system widely used in the first stage of sound film.

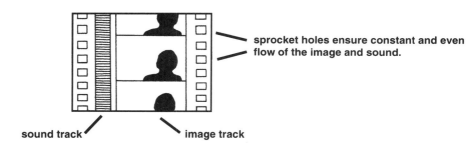

sprocket holes ensure constant and even flow of the image and sound.

sound track   image track

1926   Warner Bros. decides to invest enormous capital in Vitaphone—a highly modernized sound-on-disk system. Heavily promoted, ***Don Juan*** (dir. Alan Crosland, 1926) with **John Barrymore** (1882-1942) becomes the first feature-length motion picture with a fully synchronized orchestral score. Its projection is preceded by a filmed speech by Will Hays.

THIS IS THE BEGINNING OF A NEW ERA IN MUSIC AND MOTION PICTURES!

Hays

The Jazz Singer (dir.Alan Crosland, 1927), featuring the Russian-born star of American vaudeville **Al Jolson** (1886-1950) is originally conceived as a silent picture with musical interludes, but it accidentally develops several spontaneous "talking" scenes. Al Jolson's improvised lines attract large audiences who have never heard informal dialogue on film before. Supported by a rich orchestral score, Jewish music, and popular songs performed by Jolson, *The Jazz Singer* is a huge international success. The era of silent film is approaching its imminent end.

YOU AIN'T HEARD NOTHIN' YET!

Al Jolson

Sadly, **Sam Warner** dies one day before the premiere of *The Jazz Singer*, the movie he was the most proud of in his prolific career as a producer.

46

The German-designed **Tri-Ergon** process for recording sound directly on film dominates European movie theatres in the 1920's, rivaled only by the Danish **Petersen-Poulsen** sound-on-film method.

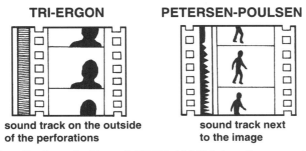

TRI-ERGON	PETERSEN-POULSEN
sound track on the outside of the perforations	sound track next to the image

In America, **Dr. Lee de Forest** (1873-1961) takes the sound-on-film system even further by solving the problem of amplification.

William Fox (1879-1952) illegally buys the rights to the Tri-Ergon Process and acquires the services of **Theodore Case**, a former de Forest collaborator. The **Fox-Case Corporation** begins to distribute short sound films and newsreels in January of 1927 under the name **Movietone**.

Warner's ***Lights of New York*** (dir. Bryan Foy, 1928) is the first all-dialogue sound film in history. Although a huge financial hit, the movie suffers from the major aesthetic and technical setbacks associated with simultaneous sound recording:

- due to the limited microphone range, acting becomes stilted and unnatural and camera movement is restricted
- the art of editing, already highly evolved, ceases to exist—the sound track cannot be broken by frequent cuts

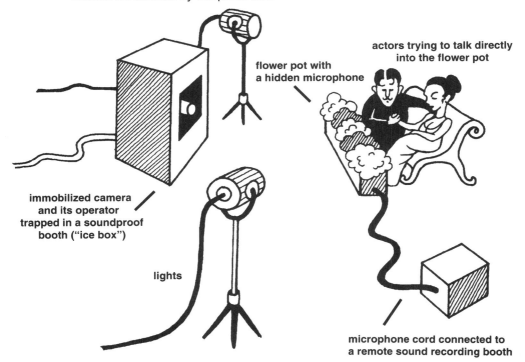

Sound Film Set — The Early Days

Sound recording creates a reactionary effect on the art of cinema and elicits outspoken criticsism from such filmmakers-theoreticians as Eisenstein, Pudovkin, and René Clair. These famous directors oppose the **naturalistic** or **synchronous** approach to sound, which allows the audience to hear only the action presented on screen.

WE OFFER THE USE OF ASYNCHRONOUS SOUND AS THE ONLY VIABLE OPTION TO ENRICH THE VISUALS OF A SOUND FILM.

V.I.Pudovkin

Asynchronous or **contrapuntal** sound theory permits the audience to experience sound effects coming from sources which are not visible (a car door slamming outside or footsteps heard off screen, etc.)

1921   The process of **postsynchronization**, also called dubbing, solves the problem of editing synchronous and asynchronous sound tracks into the same scene.

The first major motion picture to benefit from postsynchronization is **King Vidor**'s *Hallelujah!* (1929), southern drama with an all-black cast which incorporates the spiritual sounds of gospel music.

On location in Tennessee, King Vidor accidentally discovers the liberating quality of postsynchronization.

MISTER VIDOR! THE SOUND EQUIPMENT TRUCK DIDN'T SHOW UP! WHAT ARE WE GONNA DO?!

RELAX. WE'LL SHOOT THE SCENE SILENT AND ADD SOUND EFFECTS LATER IN THE STUDIO.

HALLELUJAH!

The mixing of dialogue, musical score, wild sound (recorded on location) and post-dubbed sound effects produces an audible environment which can be independent of the visuals, yet still reinforce the psychological impact of a movie.

Post-dubbing allows **Lewis Milestone** (1895-1980) for great camera mobility during the sweeping and horrifyingly realistic battle scenes of *All Quiet on the Western Front* (1930).

Lew Ayres and Raymond Griffith in *All Quiet on the Western Front*

The accomplished, Armenian-born Broadway director **Rouben Mamoulian** (1897-1987) introduces a double-channel soundtrack in his 1929 film *Applause*. The overlapping dialogue effect is achieved with the use of two microphones which record foreground sounds separately from background.

Helen Morgan in *Applause*

One of the first sound movies produced in Great Britain is **Blackmail** (1929), directed by **Alfred Hitchcock** (1899-1980), a young filmmaker with an impressive silent film resume and an art-directing background from the UFA. *Blackmail* tells a chilling story of a woman who kills a rapist painter in self-defense. Pursued by a blackmailer, she succumbs to guilt and self-doubt. The film, which was originally conceived as a silent picture, makes innovative use of postsynchronization and contains all of what the audiences will soon recognize as Hitchcock trademarks: the nightmarish atmosphere of impending doom culminating with a spectacular chase scene.

THIS CZECH ACCENT JUST KILLS ME!

On the set of *Blackmail*:
Hitch and his ideal woman,
Anny Ondra–tall, blond and deadly

The voice of **Anny Ondra**, a Czech actress, is dubbed into crisp English by **Joan Barry**.

The thrillers **Metro** (1930) and **Number Seventeen** (1931) solidify Hitchcock's prestige as the preeminent British director of the early sound era.

René Clair's **Under the Roofs of Paris** (*Sous les toits de Paris*, 1931), the first French sound picture, becomes an instant hit with audiences and critics alike. This down-to-earth musical depicts a lively Parisian working-class neighborhood. In accordance with his own contrapuntal sound theories, Clair uses dialogue sparingly and relies on postsynchronization as a way of enhancing the picture's impact.

SOUS LES TOITS DE PARIS...

The Million (*Le Million*, 1931) is the next Clair production in which the director makes strategic use of asynchronous sound effects. A brilliant musical comedy, *The Million* is also a highly entertaining adventure film, whose action revolves around a wild chase after a winning lottery ticket.

Liberty is Ours (*A nous la Liberté*, 1931) proves Clair's maturity as a serious filmmaker who is sensitive to the dehumanizing effects of industrialism. The picture's parallel stories suggest similarities between factory and prison lives.

All of Clair's early films are produced with **Tobis-Klangfilm**, the German sound company which edged **Western Electric** and **RCA** (both American companies) out of Central Europe. The Tobis movies are shot in the films' original language and in German. This bilingual practice is quickly adopted by all major studios concerned with foreign distribution.

Joseph Von Sternberg (1894-1969), the Austrian-born American director travels to Germany to film **Marlene Dietrich** (1901-92) in the truly international UFA production of *The Blue Angel* (*Der blaue Engel*, 1930). Influenced by the Kammerspiel tradition, the film tells the tragic story of an aging school teacher who falls prey to an irresistible nightclub siren.

Marlene Dietrich

The Sternberg-Dietrich collaboration continues with the visually stunning *Marocco* (1931) and the stylishly dark *Shanghai Express* (1932), whose pictorial beauty overshadows the weak story line. Both movies are photographed by **Lee Garmes** (1898-1978) and designed by **Hans Dreier**.

The recent technical developments in sound coincide with the birth of **genre film**.

> THE GENRE FILM ADHERES THEMATICALLY TO A SPECIFIC ENVIRONMENT AND FOLLOWS TRADITIONAL CONVENTIONS.

One of the first defined genres to emerge in the early thirties is the **gangster film**. It begins with **Mervyn LeRoy**'s (1900-1987) *Little Caesar* (1930), **William Wellman**'s (1896-1975) *Public Enemy* (1931), and **Howard Hawks**' (1896-1979) *Scarface* (1932). The last one remains the most accomplished gangster film of the decade, in part thanks to **Ben Hecht**'s (1894-1964) cynical and uncompromising screenplay and **Lee Garmes** (1898-1978) terrific cinematography.

MOTHER OF MERCY, IS THIS THE END OF RICO?

Edward G. Robinson
in *Little Caesar*

Paul Muni
in *Scarface*

I AIN'T RUNNIN'...
I AIN'T YELLOW...

James Cagney
in *Public Enemy*

Another tough-talking genre which flourishes with the coming of sound is the **newspaper film**. This cycle begins with Lewis Milestone's ***The Front Page***, Mervyn LeRoy's ***Five Star Final***, Frank Capra's ***Platinum Blonde***, and John Cromwell's ***Scandal Sheet***.

ALL PRODUCED IN 1931!

The British-made ***The Private Life of Henry VIII*** (1933), produced and directed by the Hungarian-born **Alexander Korda** (1893-1956), initiates the **biopic film** genre. What separates this genre from the German Kostümfilm or the Italian Superspectacle is the historical accuracy of biopics, which rely on the elaborate use of sound and dialogue in addition to the lavish decor.

Charles Laughton as the insatiable Henry VIII

The international success of *The Private Life of Henry VIII* prompts British and American studios to produce biopics on virtually every topic imaginable. The historical cycle continues with ***Queen Christina*** (dir. Rouben Mamoulian, 1933) and ***Catherine the Great*** (Paul Czinner, 1934); arts and literature are covered by ***Voltaire*** (dir. John Adolfi, 1933), ***Rembrandt*** (dir. Alexander Korda, 1936), and ***The Life of Emile Zola*** (dir. William Dieterle, 1937); science biopics include ***The Story of Louis Pasteur*** (dir. William Dieterle, 1936).

FIND THE MICROBE, KILL THE MICROBE.

Paul Muni as Louis Pasteur

The **horror** genre, originally created in Germany, enjoys resurrection on a grand scale in such Universal-produced hits as *Dracula* (dir. Tod Browning, 1931) and *Frankenstein* (dir. James Whale, 1931). *The Mummy* (1932) is directed by the German Expressionist cinematographer **Karl Freund**.

Boris Karloff in *The Mummy*

GOOD EVENING, I AM COUNT DRACULA. I BID YOU WELCOME.

Bela Lugosi in *Dracula*

Karloff in *Frankenstein*

1918-48   The African-American film pioneer **Oscar Micheaux** (1884-1951) produces, directs, and distributes movies featuring exclusively black performers and aimed strictly at African-American audiences.

　　　　Poverty Row studios produces and distributes all-black versions of genre films—horror (*The Devil's Daughter*, 1939), musical (*The Bronze Venus*, 1943), gangster (*Dark Manhattan*, 1937), and western (*Harlem on the Prairie*, 1937).

In 1928, **Walt Disney** (1907-1966) pioneers the art of image and melody synchronization in his first animated short sound film, ***Steamboat Willie***, starring **Mickey Mouse**. Disney and his lead animator, **Ub Iwerks** (1900-1971), continue to explore the infinite possibilities of sound on film with their **Silly Symphonies** cartoon series.

The early achievements of Disney pave way for the most spectacular and joyful movie genre of the 1930's—the **musical**.

> IT IS A COMMON MISCONCEPTION THAT CARTOON CHARACTERS HAVE NO INFLUENCE ON REEL LIFE.

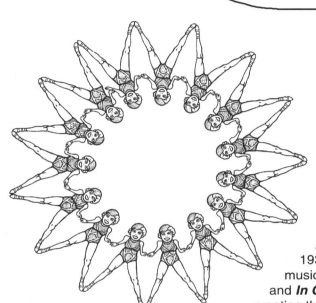

The main individual responsible for the development of the movie musical is undoubtedly **Busby Berkeley** (1895-1976), a stage choreographer from New York. Under Warners' contract, Berkeley begins to direct dance sequences for such films as ***42nd Street*** (Lloyd Bacon, 1933) and ***Gold Diggers of 1933*** (Mervyn LeRoy, 1933), and moves on to direct his own musicals—***Gold Diggers of 1935*** (1935) and ***In Caliente*** (1935). Aside from creating the extravagantly imaginative dance choreography, Berkeley liberates the camera from the laws of gravity by using a large **boom crane** for overhead shots, thus facilitating the fluid editing of picture to melody.

The **RKO** (Radio-Keith-Orpheum) studio develops its own line of highly successful musicals starring **Fred Astaire** (1899-1987). Paired with his favorite partner **Ginger Rogers** (1911-95), Astaire directs and choreographs dance numbers in such hits as ***Flying Down to Rio*** (Thornton Freeland, 1933) and ***Top Hat*** (Mark Sandrich, 1935). Camera movement in the Astaire pictures seamlessly integrates with the sophisticated dancing.

Some of the top composers of the era providing scores to Hollywood musicals include **Irving Berlin** (*Top Hat*, 1935), **Ira** and **George Gershwin** (*Shall We Dance*, 1937), **Jerome Kern** (*Swing Time*, 1936) and **Cole Porter** (*Born to Dance*, 1936).

The anarchic comedy of the **Marx Brothers** emerges naturally from the dying world of silent burlesque. Movies like *Horse Feathers* (Norman Z. McLeod, 1932), *Duck Soup* (Leo McCarey, 1933), *A Night at the Opera* (Sam Wood, 1935), and *A Day at the Races* (S. Wood, 1937) combine nonsensical, rapid-fire dialogue with the best use of physical humor since the slapstick times.

The Marx Brothers

Groucho
(Julian Marx, 1890-1977)

Harpo
(Adolph Marx, 1888-1964)

Chico
(Leonard Marx, 1887-1961)

The lesser known **Zeppo** (Herbert Marx, 1901-1979) appeared in his famous brothers' films until 1935. **Gummo** (Milton Marx, 1894-1977) left the Marx vaudeville troupe before the movies.

Another popular Paramount comedian of the 1930's is the veteran of silent film **W.C. Fields** (1879-1946). Fields screen persona—offbeat, grumpy-old-man—matches his blown-up physique perfectly.

Though the resulting films varied greatly in quality, ***It's a Gift*** (1934) and ***The Bank Dick*** (1940) remain true classics. The latter is directed by the former Buster Keaton collaborator **Eddie Cline**.

One of the many contract directors to work with Fields on his lesser films is **D.W. Griffith**, now in twilight of his career.

W.C. Fields

Mae West (1892-1980), brought by Paramount from Broadway just like the Marx Brothers, enjoys great success in such sexually charged comedies as ***She Done Him Wrong*** (1933) and ***I'm No Angel*** (1933), both co-starring **Cary Grant** (1904-86).

IT'S NOT THE MEN IN YOUR LIFE THAT COUNTS, IT'S THE LIFE IN YOUR MEN.

With major movie studios willing to sacrifice quality in order to make quick profit, the overall American film production of the 1930s resembles standardized manufacturing operation. To make matters worse, the Catholic Church and the always vigilant Hays Office lead the fight to preserve the morality and traditional American values in the entertainment industry. In 1933, Hays creates the **Production Code Administration (PCA)**. Under the strict leadership of **Joseph I. Breen**, an ardent Catholic, the PCA begins to dictate the do's and don'ts of the American film. For the next two decades no motion picture can be released without the seal of approval by the PCA.

One of the strangest films to grace the movie screens in the early sound years is the monster blockbuster of 1933, *King Kong* (dir. **Merian C. Cooper** and **Ernest B. Schoedsack**).

The picture features state-of-the-art special effects by **Willis O'Brien** (1886-1962), which include **front** and **rear projection** techniques, and combine live action with **stop-motion animation**. To produce fluid motion of the King Kong puppet, each movement is photographed in stages one frame at a time, just like in time-lapse photography. When the images are projected, the model appears to be in continuous motion.

While the big, furry ape clings to the tallest building in New York, France develops the lyrical, down-to-earth cinematic style called **poetic realism**.

One of its precursors, **Jean Vigo** (1905-1934), directs his first feature, the 45-minute *Zero for Conduct* (*Zéro du conduite*, 1933). This poetically surreal film humorously details a mutiny in a boarding school for boys. **Boris Kaufman** (1906-80), Dziga Vertov's brother, is responsible for the striking photography, while **Maurice Jaubert**'s (1900-40) unique musical score is played and recorded backwards.

The talented trio reunites the following year to work on Vigo's masterful *L'Atalante* (1934). The simple story of two newlyweds who embark on a river journey from Le Havre to Paris turns into an elaborate study of love, hate, and maturity.

L'Atalante

Jean Vigo dies at 29 of tuberculosis shortly before *L'Atalante* opens in Paris, leaving behind a small but astonishingly rich legacy of work which will influence generations of filmmakers to come.

Jean Renoir (1894-1979), son of the painter Auguste Renoir, hones his directing skills as a commercial silent filmmaker. After a series of thematically varied sound films, Renoir shoots *Toni* (1931) and *The Crime of Mister Lange* (*Le Crime de Monsieur Lange*, 1935), both of which mark his growing interest in social injustice.

Grand Illusion

Grand Illusion (*La Grande Illusion, 1937)* becomes Renoir's most accomplished work both critically and commercially. Set in a German POW camp during the last days of World War I, the film shrewdly analyzes the makeup of the French society by focusing on three prisoners—an aristocrat, a mechanic, and a Jewish banker, who unite their efforts in order to escape.

Christian Matras's (1903-77) bold **deep focus photography** allows Renoir to arrange his movie in sequences of long takes.

In **Rules of the Game** (*La Régle du jeu*, 1939), his undisputed masterpiece, Renoir continues his thorough study of contemporary cultural dynamics. The movie so realistically captures French society on the verge of self-destruction that its premiere incites a political turmoil in Paris. *Rules of the Game* is subsequently recut and re-edited for wide distribution but is banned by the end of the year by the right-wing French censors.

Jean Renoir in *La Régle du jeu*

While the films of Vigo and Clair display the lighter side of the blooming poetic realism, Renoir and **Marcel Carné** (b. 1909) delve into its darker regions. Impressed by the legacy of Kammerspiel film, Carné directs the hauntingly beautiful **Port of Shadows** (*Quai de brumes*, 1938). This melancholic film depicts an AWOL soldier awaiting his doom in the port of Havre.

Carné's **Daybreak** (*La Jour se lève*, 1939) follows a similarly gloomy path: this time a murderer hides in the attic where, after an introspective night, he takes his own life.

Both films feature the first French superstar, **Jean Gabin** (1904-76), whose talent for portraying antihero characters becomes internationally famous in **Pépé Le Moko** (dir. Julien Duvivier, 1937), an exceptional gangster movie in the tradition of *Scarface*.

Jean Gabin in *La Jour se léve*

As Stalin tightens his iron grip on the country, the freshness and boldness of the silent film experimentation comes to a halt. The early sound pictures appear hesitant, careful not to offend the despotic ruler. The seemingly safe genre that emerges during this turbulent time is the **historical biography** (**biopic**) film.

One of its most formidable examples is the highly popular *Chapaev* (1934), co-directed by two former Eisenstein students from the VGIK, **Georgi Vasiliev** (1899-1946) and **Sergei Vasiliev** (1900-56), who work as **The Vasiliev Brothers** despite being unrelated.

Chapaev

Very few of the master silent directors manage to make a smooth transition to sound. **Alexander Dovzhenko**'s *Ivan* (1932) and *Aerograd* (1935) display complexity equal to his great silent work. Unfortunately, after the striking yet enigmatic *Schors* (1939), a movie which is expected to praise the Red Army's heroic struggle in the Ukraine, Dovzhenko runs into trouble with the Party and is forced into semi-retirement.

Dziga Vertov experiments with contrapuntal sound and montage in *Enthusiasm* (*Entuziazm*, 1931) and the semidocumentary tribute to the Father of the Revolution, *Three Songs of Lenin* (*Tri pesni o Leninye*, 1934).

Dovzhenko

As with Dovzhenko, Vertov meets with a strong criticism from the establishment officials and is removed from his position as a prominent filmmaker.

Lev Kuleshov's *The Great Consoler* (*Velikij uteshitel*, 1933), based on the **O Henry** fantasy, is another early exception to the usual mediocrity of the Soviet sound film production.

After a brief and deeply discouraging stint as a Paramount employee, **Sergei Eisenstein** joins the **Mexican Film Trust**, a corporation founded by the socialist U.S. writer **Upton Sinclair** to help Eisenstein make an epic film about revolutionary Mexico. Never fully completed, ***Que Viva Mexico!***, shot between 1930-32, joins the noble circle of dismembered masterpieces like Stroheim's *Greed* and Gance's *Napoleon*.

Upon his return to the Soviet Union, Eisenstein is reluctantly greeted by the back-stabbing film community. It is not until 1938 when he is allowed to make another picture, but the long wait is well worth it.

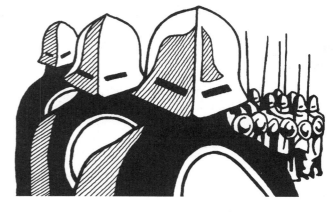

Alexander Nevsky (1938) is a true story of the heroic 13th century Novogrod prince who leads the Russian people against the invading forces of the Teutonic Knights. For this movie, which is to be his first sound film, Eisenstein secures talents of the famed Russian composer **Sergei Prokofiev**. The resulting symphonic score serves as a reference for the masterful montage of the picture.

Ivan Grozny

In the wake of the German dominance of Europe, *Alexander Nevsky* meets with the highest international and domestic praise. However, when the Soviets sign the Nonaggression Pact with the Nazis in 1939, the movie is quietly withdrawn from theatres.

Now in good standing with the establishment, Eisenstein embarks on a huge project on the life of tsar Ivan the Terrible. Envisioned as a three-part epic, Eisenstein releases ***Ivan the Terrible*** (*Ivan Grozny,* Part I) in 1945. The movie is unanimously hailed for its artistic perfection and ideological correctness. Part II, however, previewed in 1946, infuriates Stalin because of its portrayal of Ivan's increasingly paranoid behavior. This magnificently composed film is banned and the footage for Part III completely destroyed. His health deteriorating after a heart attack, Eisenstein dies in 1948, never to see his final masterpiece in its entirety.

Supported by the strong traditions of the Expressionist and Kammerspiel film, as well as technical advancements in sound, the German film industry is well equipped to prevail against the difficulties of the Depression.

Peter Lorre in *M*

Fritz Lang enters the sound period with great confidence— ***M*** (1930) is a dark story of a child murderer being hunted by the bloodthirsty mob. This moody and disturbing picture draws a very thin line between individual and collective madness and adroitly parallels German society at the gates of Nazism.

Lang's next project, ***The Testament of Dr. Mabuse*** (*Das Testament des Dr. Mabuse*, 1932), a sequel to his silent *Dr. Mabuse, der Spieler* (1922), deals with a master criminal ruling the underworld from a mental hospital. Justifiably suspecting that the insane tyranny of Dr. Mabuse has been patterned after Hitler, the Nazis ban the movie when they come to power in 1933.

Lang decides to leave Germany for France, and later America, while his wife and collaborator **Thea von Harbou** stays in the country and becomes an ardent Nazi.

Both, *M* and *Das Testament* are beautifully shot by **Fritz Arno Wagner**, the cinematographer on *Nosferatu*.

Controlled by **Josef Paul Goebbels** since 1933, German film (as well as other arts), gradually abandons the deeply rooted Jewish heritage and focuses on trivial, escapist production like ***Viktor und Viktoria*** (dir. Reinhold Schnützel, 1933), a musical comedy, or ***Hitlerjunge Quex*** (dir. Hans Steinhoff, 1933), a propaganda picture.

A REGIME MUST NOT PERMIT CINEMA TO TAKE ITS OWN COURSE.

Goebbels

Hitler commissions a young German filmmaker **Leni Riefenstahl** (b. 1902) to document the 1934 Nazi Party Rally in Nuremberg. The result, ***Triumph of the Will*** (*Triumph des Willens*, 1935), is a staged propaganda picture which endows Hitler with a mythical, godlike presence while reducing his followers to pliable geometrical masses. The movie's striking imagery proves so powerful that Britain, the U.S., and Canada prevent it from being released.

Riefenstahl's next job, also sponsored by Hitler, is ***Olympiad*** (1938), a detailed account of the 1936 Olympic Games in Berlin. The film makes an astonishing use of slow-motion photography and utilizes a wide variety of cinematic techniques which compliment the beauty of the human body in motion.

The **Italian** film situation in the 1930's resembles its German counterpart. **Benito Mussolini** develops a working relationship with the **ENIC** (Ente Nazionale Industrie Cinematografiche), a fast growing motion picture agency, which enables the Fascists to supervise all Italian film production.

After the uninspired early sound period, quality films begin to emerge. A couple of notable titles are **Alessandro Blasetti**'s historical ***1860*** (1934), and **Mario Camerini**'s social farce ***I'd Give a Million*** (*Darò un milione*, 1935), which marks the beginning of the enduring collaboration of **Vittorio De Sica** (actor-director) and **Cesare Zavattini** (screenwriter).

One of the pro-Fascist pictures of importance is the historical spectacle ***Scipio Africanus*** (dir. **Carmine Gallone**, 1937), which implies parallels between the Roman Empire's conquests in Northern Africa and Mussolini's own imperialistic tendencies.

On the average, however, the Italian cinematography provides its audiences with mindless, unchallenging movies designed to relieve pressures of the economic duress.

THE MOST POPULAR ITALIAN FILM GENRE, THE FLUFFY ROMANTIC COMEDY, BEARS THE NAME **TELEFONO BIANCO** (WHITE TELEPHONE), DERIVED FROM THE ARISTOCRATIC ENVIRONMENT IT PORTRAYS.

GREAT BRITAIN

In Britain, **The Korda Brothers** carry on the tradition of the spectacular adventure movie with **The Thief of Bagdad** (dir. Ludwig Berger, Michael Powell, Tim Whelan, 1940) and **The Jungle Book** (dir. Zoltán Korda, 1942).

Alfred Hitchcock masters his thriller skills with the Expressionistic **The Man Who Knew Too Much** (1934), featuring *M's* star Peter Lorre. **The Thirty-Nine Steps** (1935), **Secret Agent** (1936), **Sabotage** (1938), and **The Lady Vanishes** (1938), all smart and taut crime dramas, cement Hitchcock's reputation and prompt his departure for Hollywood— a move shared by a great many of his countrymen. Hitchcock invents the term **McGuffin**—a plot device that has little importance (a lost map or documents) but helps to propel the action and sustain the suspense.

The Thirty-Nine Steps

EASTERN EUROPE

The most dynamic film industry of the pre-World War II Eastern Europe belongs to **Czechoslovakia**, which remains under strong German and Austrian influences.

Gustav Machaty (1901-63), a former assistant to Griffith and Stroheim, receives worldwide recognition for his sensual and provocative **Ecstasy** (*Extase*, 1932).

Hedy Lamarr in *Ecstasy*

Martin Fric adapts for the screen the traditional Tatra folk tale about a rebellious highlander fighting social injustice in **Jánosík** (1935).

Otakár Vavra dazzles audiences and critics with **Guild of the Kutná Hora Maidens** (*Cech panen kutnohorskych*, 1938); another outstanding film of pictorial beauty is the lyrical **The River** (*Reka*, 1934) directed by **Josef Rovensky**.

The prewar cinematography of **Hungary** suffers from commercialization. To make matters worse, the most promising young filmmakers such as **Sándor Korda** (Alexander Korda), **Mihaly Kertész** (Michael Curtiz), and **Endre Tóth** (André de Toth) emigrate to America.

Pál Fejös (1898-1963), back in Hungary after a brief career in the U.S., makes the acclaimed *Spring Shower* (*Tavazsi Zápor, 1932*).

Another notable picture, *Hortobágy* (1935), directed by the German filmmaker **Georg Hoellring**, is a poignant study of the peasant life.

After the outbreak of WW II, Hungarian cinema falls under the control of the rightist **Horthy** government which sides with the Nazis.

The **Polish** cinema of the 1930's focuses on such commercially viable pictures as the comedies and musicals starring the versatile and charismatic **Adolf Dymsza** (1900-75) and his frequent partner **Eugeniusz Bodo** (1899-1941).

A. Dymsza

The most important dramatic work belongs to the filmmakers involved in the progressive **START** (Society of Devotees of Artistic Film) film society, and its direct descendant

Ghosts

SAF (Cooperative of Film Artists), founded in 1937. Among its most dynamic directors are **Alexander Ford** (1908-80), whose *Legion of the Streets* (*Legion Ulicy*) is the most popular film of 1932, **Eugeniusz Cekalski** and **Karol Szolowski**, the co-directors of the highly sophisticated drama *Ghosts* (*Strachy*, 1937), and **Wanda Jakubowska**, whose adaptation of the Polish classic novel *On the Niemen* (*Nad Niemnem*, 1939), also co-directed by Szolowski, is destroyed by the invading Nazis.

The best Polish-Jewish production, *The Dybbuk* (*Dibuk*, Michal Waszynski, 1937), is a beautifully made story of unfulfilled love, told in the cabalistic tradition.

Plagued by the lack of funds, the **Yugoslavian** cinema produces a minimal number of films between 1930-40. One of the more absorbing ones is *With Faith in God* (*S verom v boga, 1932*) by **Mihailo-Mika Popovic**.

The first **Bulgarian** sound film is *Graves Without Crosses* (*Beskrastni grobove*, 1931) by **Boris Grezhov**, a politically committed historical picture depicting the White Terror of 1923. Other noteworthy movies include the film-poem *The Cairn* (*Gramada*, Alexander Zazov, 1936) and *Strahil the Voevoda* (*Voevoda Strahil*, Yosip Novak, 1938), a folk hero tale set during the Turkish oppression.

Graves Without Crosses

The enduring tradition of **benshi** narrators extends the life of silent film to the mid 930s. Among the most interesting pictures of the early sound era is **Kenji Mizoguchi**'s 1898-1956) **Osaka Elegy** (*Nani na ereji*, 1936), a highly realistic portrayal of a young emale telephone operator's ruined life. Women are also the focus of Mizoguchi's next lm, **Sisters of Gion** (*Gion no shimai*, 1936) whose action takes place in modern day yoto.

Both films utilize the long take and sparse editing which allow Mizoguchi to depict the action unhurriedly and objectively.

Sisters of Gion

The Only Son (*Hitori Musuko*, 1936), the first talkie by **Yasujiro Ozu** (1903-63), s one of the brighter examples of the **gendai-geki** genre which deals with everyday roblems of modern Japan. Some of the gendai-geki pictures belong to the **endency-film** movement which criticizes the established norms of Japanese society.

The Only Son

The other major genre, **jidai-geki**, deals exclusively with historical topics.

Man-slashing, Horse-piercing Sword (*Zanjin zamba ken*, 1930), directed by he tendency-film theoretician **Daisuke Ito**, is one of the few jidai-geki that question the noral legacy of feudal Japan.

USA

Sound brings a premature end to such great silent film comedians as Buster Keaton and Harold Lloyd, who, despite excellent vocal skills, cannot adapt to the new cinematic standards.

Modern Times

Charlie Chaplin's first sound film, ***City Lights*** (1931) has no dialogue and makes a very limited use of sound effects, relying primarily on musical score and Chaplin's pantomime.

His next project, ***Modern Times*** (1936), is also basically a silent picture with synchronized sound except for a nonsensical song performed by Chaplin. *Modern Times*, whose visual humor and design is directly based on René Clair's *A nous la Liberté*, is an astute satire on industrialism and mechanization of the human life, and spells out Chaplin's leftist orientation.

The **screwball comedy** is another popular film genre of the 1930's. Its quick-witted dialogue is delivered with great timing, and the fast-paced action often incorporates physical humor.

YOU'RE WONDERFUL, IN A LOATHSOME SORT OF WAY.

The heroine of a screwball comedy is usually an emancipated woman of great intelligence, wit, and emotional strength, frequently acting as aggressively as her male counterpart.

Rosalind Russell in *His Girl Friday*

Three of the quintessential screwball comedies, ***Twentieth Century*** (1934), ***Bringing Up Baby*** (1938), and ***His Girl Friday*** (1940) are directed by the versatile **Howard Hawks**.

Other notable examples of screwball are Ernest Lubitsch's ***Design for Living*** (1933), Richard Boleslawski's ***Theodora Goes Wild*** (1936), and William Wellman's ***Nothing Sacred*** (1937).

Frank Capra's contributions to screwball comedy include *It Happened One Night* (1934), *Mr. Deeds Goes to Town* (1936), and the more serious *Mr. Smith Goes to Washington* (1939), which features **James Stewart** (1908-97) as a young senator trying to preserve his integrity in the scoundrel-ridden capital.

Claudette Colbert in
It Happened One Night

James Stewart
as Mr. Smith

Because of its tremendously prolific output and popularity with worldwide audiences, the period of pre-WWII American cinema can be classified as the **Golden Years of the Studio Era**.

Thanks to the Parufamet agreement, **Paramount** remains the most "continental" of the big studios. Its stylish *Blond Venus* (1932) and *The Devil Is a Woman* (1935) again unite director **Joseph von Sternberg** with his muse, **Marlene Dietrich**.

Lubitsch' success continues with Paramount's *Trouble in Paradise* (1932), *Angel* (1937) and *Ninotchka* (1939). The latter features Greta Garbo in her first comedic performance as a Soviet envoy in Paris on a mission to cash in on crown jewels.

GARBO LAUGHS!

Garbo in *Ninotchka*

The Marx Brothers, Mae West, and W.C. Fields are also among the prized Paramount possessions, as are such stars as Cary Grant, Gary Cooper, and Claudette Colbert.

Warner Bros. centers on economically safe production which involves simply told, hard-hitting movies. Warner's chief domain are gangster and biopic genres, as well as such socially conscious films as *I Am a Fugitive from a Chain Gang* (dir. Mervyn LeRoy, 1932) and *Black Fury* (dir. Michael Curtiz, 1935).

The most frequently featured Warner star is indisputably the chameleon-like Paul Muni. Other contract players of the studio include James Cagney, Humphrey Bogart, E.G. Robinson, and **Errol Flynn** (1909-59), an Australian transplant specializing in adventurous roles (***Captain Blood***, 1935, ***Robin Hood***, 1938, ***Charge of the Light Brigade***, 1938).

Flynn in *Captain Blood*

Of all major studios, **MGM** is the undisputed champion in the 1930's. Its director lineup is impressive: **King Vidor**, **Clarence Brown** (***Anna Christie***, 1930, ***Anna Karenina***, 1935), **George Cukor** (***Dinner at Eight***, 1933, ***David Copperfield***, 1935, ***Romeo and Juliet***, 1936), **Jack Conway** (***Viva Villa!***, 1934, ***Libeled Lady***, 1936, ***Too Hot to Handle***, 1938), **Sam Wood** (*A Night at the Opera*, 1935, *A Day at the Races*, 1937, ***Good-bye Mr. Chips***, 1938), and **Victor Fleming**, the director of the spectacular Southern epic, ***Gone With the Wind*** (1939).

Captain Blood

Spencer Tracy and Mickey Rooney in *Boys Town*

Fritz Lang makes his American debut with MGM's ***Fury*** (1936), a terrific gangster picture starring **Spencer Tracy** (1900-67). This popular actor is about to hit the jackpot of his career: his next two films, ***Captain Courageous*** (dir. Victor Fleming, 1936) and ***Boys Town*** (dir. Norman Taurog, 1938) win him back-to-back Oscars.

Other mega-stars with reserved parking spaces on the MGM lot are: Greta Garbo, Joan Crawford, Jean Harlow, Clark Gable, William Powell, James Stewart, and Mickey Rooney.

David O'Selznick (1902-65) and **Irwin Thalberg** (1899-1936) are two of the most sophisticated producers at MGM, which remains under the iron hand of **Louis B. Mayer** (1885-1957). In addition to such prestigious productions as ***Grand Hotel*** (1932) with Greta Garbo and ***Mutiny on the Bounty*** (1935) with Clark Gable and Charles Laughton, Thalberg is responsible for breathing new life into the sagging **Tarzan** franchise. For the 10th screen incarnation of the Apeman, Thalberg signs the Olympic swimming champion **Johnny Weismuller** (1904-84).

Color Film

As with sound, experimentation with color film dates back to the early days of cinema. The first **hand-tinted** movies appear as early as 1896; each frame is elaborately painted under a magnifying glass.

Around 1905 Pathé introduces **stencil-coloring** of film positives (**Pathécolor**). Up to six stencils are manually cut for individual colors which are to be applied in selected areas of the frame. This painstaking method is soon mechanized, but to make it profitable, about 200 copies of each film must be printed. Pathé changes its name to **Pathéchrome** in 1929 and continues to reap profits from this stencil process until well into the next decade.

THE PATHÉ STENCIL-COLORING PROCESS

stencils for three colors

final image in three colors

In 1916, **Max Handschiegl** and **Alvin Wyckoff** develop a more sophisticated color application method. Handschiegl applies his lithographic expertise to this multiple color matrix procedure, which results in a somewhat realistic rendition of natural hues. Among other films, the Handschiegl process is used for such movies as *Joan, the Woman* (dir. C.B. De Mille, 1917), *Greed* (dir. E. von Stroheim, 1924), *Phantom of the Opera* (dir. R. Julian, 1925), and *The Big Parade* (dir. K. Vidor, 1925)—one of the most successful films of the 1920s.

As an alternative to dying the already developed film, the Belgian company **Gevaert** introduces colored celluloid to be used as film base. This process gives the effect of more evenly distributed hues.

 The principles of color photography, developed in 1855 by **James Clerk Maxwell** (1831-79), the Scottish physicist, are slowly applied to cinematography. Maxwell proved that practically all natural colors may be reproduced by mixing red, green, and blue light. In 1899, Britons **F. Marshall Lee** and **Edward R. Turner** patent a color camera with rotating red, green, and blue filters placed in front or behind the lens.

1906 **Charles Urban** (1871-1942) designs a two-color system based on **G.A. Smith**'s experiments with red and green filters, which produce a wide variety of colors upon projection. The system is called **Kinemacolor**.

Other interesting methods include Gaumont's **Chronochrome** (1912), which relies on a three-lens camera filming through red, green, and blue filters, and the British-made **Cinechrome** (1914) and **Raycol** (1929).

71

In 1922, The Boston-based **Technicolor Company** invents a camera capable of splitting the incoming light into two beams which expose two negatives (two-color subtractive process). After a complex chemical procedure, two film positives are developed: one dyed orange-red, the other—green. The positives are then cemented togethe for projection resulting in a good quality color image. Some of the more prominent movies including sequences shot in this fashion are *The Ten Commandments* (dir. C.B. De Mille, 1923) and *Merry Widow* (dir. E. von Stroheim, 1925).

TO PROJECT EARLY TECHNICOLOR FILMS THE OPERATOR NEEDED TO BE A CROSS BETWEEN A COLLEGE PROFESSOR AND AN ACROBAT. THE TWO-COLOR SYSTEM SIMPLIFIES ALL THAT.

Dr. Herbert Kalmus (1891-1963), one of the founders of Technicolor, with his improved two-color camera

One of the drawbacks of the early Technicolor is the shifting registration of colors. By 1932, however, a new, **three-color** camera is developed; it is perfected by the end of the decade.

The first three-color Technicolor film is Disney's animated *Flowers and Trees* (1932). *Becky Sharp* (dir. R. Mamoulian), the first full-length live-action feature, follows in 1935.

The types of movies to benefit the most from the three-strip process are animation (Disney's *Snow White and The Seven Dwarfs*, 1937, *Fantasia*, 1940), action (*The Adventures of Robin Hood*, 1938), musical (*The Wizard of Oz*, 1939) and epic (*Gone With the Wind*, 1939).

TO BE PERFECTLY HONEST WITH YOU, HONEY, I AM NOT AT ALL CONCERNED.

SAY IT LIKE A MAN, CLARK!

Vivien Leigh and Clark Gable rehearse the first draft of dialogues on the set of *Gone With the Wind*

At age five, Orson Welles has already revealed his affinity for entertainment—he creates his own puppet theatre and learns magic tricks (once supervised by the **Great Houdini** himself).

1925 A ten-year old Orson adapts for the stage and performs *Dr. Jeckyll and Mr. Hyde*.

After leaving the **Todd Academy** at Woodstock, Illinois, where he excelled at drama, Welles travels to Ireland and joins the **Gate Theatre** of Dublin. There, only 16, he is cast in a wide range of adult roles for which he receives a uniformly rave reviews.

The boy-wonder Welles edits and illustrates the collected works of Shakespeare which are published in the form of prompt books entitled *Everybody's Shakespeare*. The books, coedited with Welles' mentor **Roger Hill**, are sold to schools nationwide and considered a great success.

1935 Already a veteran of the European and American stages, the young actor and director lands his first radio job on CBS's **The March of Time** show. A year later, he becomes the director of the **Negro Theatre Project** in New York. It is there where his talents for innovative staging and bold interpretation of classic literature come to bloom. His Harlem adaptation of *Macbeth*, influenced by the Haitian voodoo rituals, becomes legendary.

In the mean time his career in radio as a performer, writer, and director reaches a new level with the enormously popular *Shadow* series and *First Person Singular* adaptations of literary works.

1938 Welles' Mercury Theatre on the Air performs the all too realistic adaptation of **H.G. Wells'** *The War of The Worlds* . The live broadcast of the show causes panic in the streets and brings an instant national fame for the young actor-director-producer. These events, coupled with Welles' continuing success in theatre, result in an RKO contract in 1939.

AND I'M ONLY 23!

For his first movie Welles decides to adapt **Joseph Conrad**'s *Heart of Darkness*, but the studio rejects this idea in the early stages of preproduction. He is then given a green light to begin work on *American*—a movie based on the life of **William Randolph Hearst**, the newspaper magnate. After months of meticulous preparations which include Welles' crash course in film technique, the complete screenplay (written by Welles and **Herman J. Mankiewicz**) is ready to be filmed under the title of *Citizen Kane*.

73

TEN REASONS WHY *CITIZEN KANE* IS STILL CONSIDERED THE BEST MOVIE EVER MADE:

1. Structure

The story of Charles Foster Kane is told in flashbacks, through a variety of point of view. The plot-motivating metaphor (Rosebud) is introduced in the first scene of the film and explained in the last. All of the narrative elements fall into place with perfect timing and every subplot is resolved before the movie reaches its conclusion.

Gregg Toland

2. Cinematography

In the movie's final credits, cinematographer **Gregg Toland**'s name appears next to Welles to honor his influence on the breathtaking look of *Citizen Kane*. An established professional in his field (*Les Misérables*, *Grapes of Wrath*, *Wuthering Heights*), Toland brings to the project **deep-focus** photography, maturity of camera angles and framing. His **low-key** lighting technique, in the finest *Kammerspiel* tradition, gives *Kane* an unprecedented depth of space and nearly tangible atmosphere.

3. Art Design

A young, talented RKO art designer **Perry Ferguson** (*Bringing Up Baby*, *Gunga Din*) consults on daily bases with both Welles and Toland on the specifics of *Kane*'s meticulously planned art direction. His stylish sketches greatly influence the striking look of the film, as does the artwork of his colleague **Mario Larrinaga**, Kane's **matte painter** and **concept artist**.

4. Make-Up

Maurice Seiderman (*Gunga Din*, *The Swiss Family Robinson*), a Russian emigre with artistic background, is responsible for the utter realism of Kane's transition from the young, dynamic journalist to the old, overweight monster tycoon.

ROSEBUD...

Welles as the dying Kane

5. Musical Score

Bernard Hermann, a CBS composer, is brought in during the shooting to ensure complete understanding of the movie's drama. Ultimately, many scenes in *Kane* are cut to fit Hermann's score so that his music not only supports the image, but also provides transitions between scenes. In this respect, the score proves to be instrumental in shaping the movie's narrative.

WHAT I TRULY WANT IS TO WORK WITH A REAL DIRECTOR LIKE HITCHCOCK.

Bernard Hermann
in action

6. Casting

Thanks to his extremely extensive acting background, the young Welles' interpretation of Kane meets every demand of the script. His range is magnificent: in his facial expressions, body posture, and voice fluctuation there is not a single false note which might undermine the audience's acceptance of the passage of almost half a century.

The rest of the cast, mostly Welles' old collaborators from theatre and radio, is equally impressive: **Joseph Cotten**, **Everet Sloane**, **William Alland**, **George Coulouris**, **Ruth Warrick** and **Dorothy Comingore** share a collective responsibility for bringing the world of C.F. Kane to life.

Everet Sloane

7. Editing

The movie's pace is dictated by the relatively limited coverage (amount of filmed material) of the key scenes, which, as planned by Welles and Toland, are long and contain few close-ups for **reaction shots**. The editor of the picture, **Robert Wise** (b. 1914) closely adheres to Welles' directions and the precisely drawn storyboards. Nothing is left to chance.

8. Sound

As a radio genius, Welles intuitively understands how essential sound is in creating the *Kane* universe. Elaborate sound effects are created specifically for the film (the usual studio practice is to rely on stock sound library), actors are cast for their voices, and high-ceiling sets built to amplify their speeches. For greater realism, dialogue is frequently overlapped or edited according to the characters' spatial relationship. Sound recording is engineered by **James G. Stewart** and mixed by **Bailey Fesler**, a veteran of both film and radio.

9. Special Effects

The main reason for the unusually extensive use of special effects on *Citizen Kane* is financial. Many scenes require large, extravagant sets which are too expensive to build, but possible to achieve through trick photography. The key component of *Kane's* special effects is the **optical printer**—a device which enables the filmmakers to create complex images through seamless overlapping of independent components (i.e. a matte-painting of an audience blends perfectly with the footage of Kane delivering his speech). **Linwood Dunn**, the optical printer pioneer, is in charge of providing *Kane* with most of its elaborate backdrops and foregrounds (city blocks, exotic locations, crowds, complex interiors), as well as **wipes**, **fades**, **optical zoom effects**, and extreme close-ups.

> I'M GONNA HAVE TO REFER PEOPLE TO THE TERM CHART AGAIN!

10. Director

Given such unprecedented complete creative control over *Citizen Kane*, Welles manages to personally oversee every single aspect of production, lending it his unerring sense of artistic unity. His involvement in planning the movie, the actual shooting and postproduction result in an ideally balanced film— a masterpiece whose individual parts (each superb in its own right) enhance the brilliance of the whole.

> HEY, COTTEN! QUIT FOOLING AROUND OR I'LL HAVE SEIDERMAN FILL YOUR CONTACTS WITH MILK!

To make the performers' eyes lose their youthful sheen, *Kane's* make-up artists supply contact lenses filled with milk

Welles at work

Though the United States, throughout its history, has successfully warded off attempts at the subversion of its democratic principles and dictatorial rule, the powers of paranoid newspaper tycoons remained untouched. William Randolph Hearst, one such individual, decides that the despotic title character of *Citizen Kane* resembles his own persona too closely and successfully sabotages the film's domestic distribution. As a result, the picture is a financial disaster. Its instant success with the critics cannot save *Kane* from being systematically denied access to the screens across the nation.

Never again will Orson Welles have the opportunity to control his own movie project to such degree as *Citizen Kane*.

Welles' next project, ***The Magnificent Ambersons*** (1942), the turn-of-the century family saga based on **Booth Tarkington**'s novel, drives RKO into bankruptcy. Welles loses the rights to the final cut of the picture, which is truncated almost by half by the studio. Despite a new, hastily added and absurdly optimistic ending, *Ambersons* dies at the box office. Even in this truncated version, however, the film is a beautifully composed masterpiece with striking, deep-focus **low-key** cinematography (by **Stanley Cortez**) reminiscent of Kane's visual splendor.

Deep-focus photography in *The Magnificent Ambersons*

Welles comments on his career pattern:

I STARTED AT THE TOP AND WORKED MY WAY DOWN.

In 1938, **John Ford** (1895-1973) directs *Stagecoach*, the much admired western which makes wonderful use of the natural landscape of Arizona (most films of that period are shot in studio-built sets) and displays some very dramatic indoor lighting techniques. Orson Welles studies *Stagecoach* prior to the shooting of Citizen Kane.

Before Hollywood turns its attention to WWII, several socially conscious movies appear in the early 1940s. One of the most moving ones is ***The Grapes of Wrath*** (1940), directed by Ford and photographed by Gregg Toland. Based on the **John Steinbeck** novel, this depression drama portrays the poverty and desperation of migrant workers with great realism and uncompromising detail.

EVERYWHERE
YOU SEE SUFFERING...
THAT'S WHERE I AM.

Henry Fonda as Tom Joad
in *The Grapes of Wrath*

How Green Was My Valley (1941), a story of a Welsh mining village set in the last years of the 19th Century, establishes Ford as one of the most respected prewar Hollywood directors.

Charlie Chaplin's first all-dialogue feature, *The Great Dictator*, is released in October of 1940, amidst Hitler's greatest triumphs in Europe. Staunchly antifascist, the movie satirizes Hitler and his cronies, most notably Mussolini.

Perhaps *The Great Dictator*'s greatest achievement is cracking a hole in the American isolationist attitude toward the war. Very soon, all major studios become involved in producing anti-Nazi films.

Chaplin as Adenoid Hynkel

Ernst Lubitsch directs *To Be or Not to Be* (1942), the greatest anti-Nazi comedy made during the war years. The action is set in the occupied Warsaw: a Polish acting troupe becomes involved in the Resistance movement.

William Wyler (1902-81), known for his stylish literary adaptations, directs Emily Brontë's *Wuthering Heights* (1939) and Lillian Hellman's *The Little Foxes* (1941). His *Mrs. Miniver*, loosely based on Jan Struther's book, is one of the first convincing portrayals of civilians affected by WWII.

Alfred Hitchcock, now backed by major American studios (Selznick International, RKO), directs two expensive and well crafted thrillers, *Rebecca* (1940) and *Foreign Correspondent* (1940), an antifascists picture. *Suspicion* (1941), which

portrays a delusional wife, is a more modest movie, but its psychological intensity equals Hitchcock's greatest work.

Lifeboat (1944) marks Hitchcock's first direct involvement with the subject of war. The group of castaways drifting in a lifeboat epitomizes the world's social and cultural diversity struggling for collective survival.

After December 7th, 1941, through the efforts of the War Department, many documentary and narrative filmmakers join their forces in creating a series of documentaries depicting the U.S.'s involvement in WWII. Some of the most brave and prolific recruits include Frank Capra and Anatole Litvak (The *Why We Fight* series), John Huston (*Report From the Aleutians*, *The Battle of San Pietro*), John Ford and Gregg Toland (*December 7th*), William Wyler (*Memphis Belle*, *Thunderbolt*).

The Battle of San Pietro

The echoes of war resound in it only peripherally, but *Casablanca* (dir. Michael Curtiz, 1942) remains one of the most romantic and memorable films of the 1940s.

BUT WHAT ABOUT US?

WE'LL ALWAYS HAVE PARIS.

Ingrid Bergman and Humphrey Bogart
in *Casablanca*

Nöel Coward (1899-1973), the famous British theatre personality, makes the utterly patriotic *In Which We Serve* (1942), which stresses England's anti-Nazi sentiments while glorifying the Royal Navy. The film is co-directed by **David Lean** (1908-91).

Nöel Coward in
In Which We Serve

Humphrey Jennings (1907-50), one of the many documentary filmmakers working for the **Crown Film Unit**, makes the impressionistic *Fires Were Started* (1943), which praises the struggle of London firefighters during the Blitz.

The first period of the American anti-Nazi movies is characterized by exaggerated nationalism and formulaic plots. They do, however, serve their purpose of encouraging audiences to sympathize with the occupied nations of Hitler's Europe.

Lewis Milestone is one of the more prolific filmmakers on the subject of occupation and resistance: *Edge of Darkness* (1943) takes place in Norway and *North Star* (1943) in the Soviet Union. His later combat films deal with the realities of war in a more direct and unglamorous manner: *Purple Heart* (1944) revolves around the trials of American pilots shot down over Japan; *A Walk in the Sun* (1945) portrays the U.S. troops in and Italian countryside.

Other notable films which take a personal approach to combat include *Destination Tokyo* (dir. Delmer Daves, 1943), *Sahara* (dir. Zoltán Korda, 1944), and the moving *Story of G.I. Joe* (dir. William Wellman, 1945).

Robert Mitchum in *Story of G.I. Joe*

The most realistic and emotionally faithful of the war movies completed before 1945 is **Roberto Rossellini**'s (1906-77) *Rome Open City* (*Roma, città aperta*, 1945), striking in its use of newsreel-like photography and authentic locations. The film deals with the doomed attempts of Italian freedom-fighters to escape a Gestapo gridlock.

In 1944, **Laurence Olivier** (1907-89) stars in and directs the best Shakespeare adaptation to date—**Henry V**. The colorful (Technicolor) and heavily stylized sets are designed to resemble Renaissance etchings. The patriotic and militaristic glory of the film boosts British morale in the final year of the war, just as *Alexander Nevsky* had done for the Russians a few years earlier when the Germans had attacked the Soviet Union.

After the war, Olivier makes an astonishing, black and white adaptation of **Hamlet** (1948), which owes its success as much to the beauty of the Bard's language as it does to Freud's psychoanalysis.

Laurence Olivier in *Henry V*

David Lean tackles **Charles Dickens** twice in two years: the exceptionally designed and performed ***Great Expectations*** (1946) and ***Oliver Twist*** (1947) establish new cinematic canons for literary adaptations.

Oliver Twist

82

Carol Reed (1906-76) successfully brings to the screen two **Graham Greene** stories, *The Fallen Idol* (1948) and *The Third Man* (1949). Both films employ low camera angles, low-key lighting, precise composition of shots and an increasing tempo of editing—a technical arsenal openly borrowed from Orson Welles. As a tribute, Reed casts Welles in *The Third Man* in a role tailor-made to fit his screen personality—a shady character of great power whose evil ways ultimately bring him a well deserved punishment.

Trevor Howard in *The Third Man*

Dead of Night (1945) is a precursor to the increasingly popular in Britain horror genre. Composed of five disturbing tales and the "linking story" (dir. Alberto Cavalcanti, Charles Crichton, Robert Hammer and Basil Dearden), *Dead of Night* utilizes dramatic, expressionistic lighting and great sense of composition.

The most enduring partnership of the postwar period belongs to **The Archers: Michael Powell** (1905-90) and **Emeric Pressburger** (1903-88), who write, direct, and produce such great and extravagant pictures as the romantic fantasy *A Matter of Life and Death* (*Stairway to Heaven* in U.S., 1946), an exotic and unsettling tale of British nuns in a Himalayan village, *Black Narcissus* (1947), and the mature ballet drama, *The Red Shoes* (1948).

Deborah Kerr in *Black Narcissus*

Kind Hearts and Coronets (dir. Robert Hammer, 1949), a brilliantly conceived comedy, showcases the multiple talents of **Alec Guiness** (b. 1914), who plays eight different roles in the picture.

FILM NOIR

> **ARGUABLY THE MOST INFLUENTIAL AMERICAN GENRE OF THE FORTIES IS FILM NOIR.**

The name **film noir** (French *Black Film*) derives from the French-published detective novels (Série Noire—The Black Series), which include such authors a as **Raymond Chandler** and **Dashiell Hammett**. French movie critics apply the modified term film noir to a group of dark and cynical American crime movies which emerge in the first half of the 1940s.

Noir movies are almost invariably set in an urban environment and display high-contrast lighting which produces hard and unfriendly shadows. Characterized by the sense of impending disaster and utter fatalism, these pictures find their roots in the German cinema of the 1920s and the early 1930s.

Film noir contains a set of archetypical characters:
- the hero is often an outlaw, a misfit, or a jaded gumshoe (all usually emotionally perturbed)
- *femme fatale*—a mysterious woman whose seductive behavior foreshadows the hero's inevitable doom
- bad girl—dispensable and often abused woman

Double Indemnity

The stylishly murky settings of ***The Maltese Falcon*** (dir. John Huston, 1941) and ***This Gun For Hire*** (dir. Frank Tuttle, 1942) anticipate the more pessimistic outlook of such film noir classics as ***Double Indemnity*** (dir. Billy Wilder, 1944) and ***Out of the Past*** (dir. Jaques Tourneur, 1947).

The pronounced negativism of *Double Indemnity* is accentuated by the theme of moral corruption and adultery—vices never before presented on the American screen with such relentless accuracy.

Out of the Past shatters all illusions of human loyalty and trust, throwing its hapless hero into the abyss of multiple betrayal.

The low-budget ***Detour*** (dir. Edgar E. Ulmer, 1945) remains true to the noir aesthetic in its persistent adherence to the subject of nihilistic and predetermined fate.

81ˢᵀ ST.

84

In *The Postman Always Rings Twice* (dir. Tay Garnett, 1946) and *The Lady From Shanghai* (dir. Orson Welles, 1948), *femmes fatales* fulfil their murderous destiny with unprecedented premeditation.

Rita Hayworth in
The Lady From Shanghai

Ava Gardner and Burt Lancaster
in *The Killers*

The criminal world is portrayed with honest brutality in such noir movies as Robert Siodmak's *The Killers* (1946) and *Cry of the City* (1948) and Nicholas Ray's *They Live by Night*.

I'M POISON, SWEDE, TO MYSELF AND EVERYBODY AROUND ME.

James Cagney returns to his gangster film roots in *The White Heat* (dir. Raoul Walsh, 1949), portraying a psychopatic fugitive with a death wish.

Jules Dassin's masterful study of gambling addiction, *The Night and the City* (1950), takes place in the sweaty underbelly of London.

Richard Widmark in
The Night and the City

The corrupted world of boxing serves as a metaphor for good vs. evil in two excellent noir pictures—***Body and Soul*** (dir. Robert Rossen, 1947) and ***The Set-Up*** (dir. Robert Wise, 1949).

In ***Force of Evil*** (1948), **Abraham Polonsky** (b. 1910), the author of the *Body and Soul* screenplay, directs **John Garfield** in one of the most characteristic noir performances in the genre. The movie's dramatic plot serves as an indictment of the corroded capitalist society.

John Garfield in
Force of Evil

The generally negative feel of film noir counteracts with the self-deluding attitudes of the postwar American society. The great international appeal of these movies proves that mendacity is quite a universal phenomenon in a world trying to shake off the all-too-recent memory of war.

✳ ✳ ✳

On the other side of the American film spectrum, **Preston Sturges** (1898-1959) directs ***Sullivan's Travels*** (1941), a shrewd, satirical film dealing with the social dynamics of the prewar years.

In ***Hail the Conquering Hero*** (1944), Sturges questions the American stereotypes of patriotism in a playful and superficially innocent manner.

Another allegorical satire on the American perception of life is **Frank Capra**'s ***It's a Wonderful Life*** (1947). Despite its overtly comedic tone and a sentimental happy ending, the film's central section offers a very disturbing alternative vision of evil America.

John Ford's classic western ***My Darling Clementine*** (1946) analyzes the foundations of frontier community in a personal and poetic fashion.

Henry Fonda in *My Darling Clementine*

Two years after his twisted film noir, *The Big Sleep*, **Howard Hawks** makes another brilliant western of the era, the epic *Red River* (1948). This spectacular and superbly acted picture focuses on the rivalry between a father (**John Wayne**) and his adopted son (**Montgomery Clift**) during the great cattle drive of 1865.

Monty and Duke in *Red River*

John Huston directs his father **Walter** in the superior *The Treasure of Sierra Madre* (1949), a depression-era picture which singles out avarice as the main source of human decay.

Charles Chaplin's second film of the decade is *Monsieur Verdoux* (1947), a bitter and cynical satire whose central character, played by Chaplin, is a misogynist serial killer. It is by far the most cinematically advanced and intriguing of all Chaplin movies, but its lack of "chaplinesque" qualities results in a dismal box-office performance.

In **George Cukor**'s *Adam's Rib* (1949), one of the more sophisticated comedies dealing with sexual double standards in the contemporary world, **Katharine Hepburn** and **Spencer Tracy** prove that a woman and a man can develop a mutually respectful relationship .

Alfred Hitchcock recruits **Salvador Dali** to design a surreal dream sequence for his first postwar thriller, *Spellbound* (1945).

His next project, *Notorious* (1946), is a beautifully photographed spy movie set against the backdrop of Rio de Janeiro. In the intense *The Rope* (1948), Hitchcock experiments with single-take moviemaking. Shot in one room, the film contains no editing, and the necessary cuts, motivated by the length of film reels, are shrewdly masked by the actors blocking the camera's view.

William Wyler's outstanding drama **The Best Years of Our Lives** (1946), produced by Sam Goldwyn, touches on a difficult but timely problem of WWII veterans trying to claim their place in postwar society. The movie features mature, believable characters involved in realistic situations—a precedent by Hollywood standards. Gregg Toland provides the crisp deep-focus photography.

Fredric March in *The Best Years*

The first Hollywood picture to deal with race issues is **Home of the Brave** (dir. Mark Robson, 1949), a black WWII veteran story adapted from a stage play.

Macbeth

In 1948, after the commercially disappointing *The Lady From Shanghai*, **Orson Welles** is forced to accept the services of a lesser studio, **Republic Pictures**, in order to produce, direct, and star in his expressionistic adaptation of **Macbeth**. This highly theatrical movie (it uses some of the decorations and props from Welles' stage production of the play) is cut by almost half an hour for its release, and the original Scottish accents replaced by the standard English soundtrack. Disillusioned, Welles goes into exile in Europe.

ITALIAN NEOREALISM

While film noir is America's greatest contribution to world cinema of the 1940s, a seemingly inconspicuous Italian film movement called **neorealism** is about to revolutionize the way people think about movies.

The origins of neorealism can be traced to **Lucino Visconti**'s (1906-76) **Obsession** (*Ossessione*, 1943), an adaptation of *The Postman Always Rings Twice* novel by **James M. Cain**. The movie, shot exclusively on location in the Italian countryside, tells a tragic story of sexual submission and murder. *Ossessione*'s preoccupation with the lives of ordinary people in their natural environment is a key element of neorealism.

Ossessione

Rome Open City

It isn't until Rossellini's **Rome Open City** (*Roma, città aperta*, 1945), the devastating Italian resistance movie, when the nearly-documentary feel of the action becomes a permanent addition to the neorealistic aesthetic.

Paisan (*Paisà*, 1946), Rossellini's next film, is constructed from five episodes which present a vast tapestry of Italian landscape in the later stages of war.

Again, the film is shot on location and deals with the lives of common soldiers and civilians trapped in tragic, often paradoxical circumstances. Some of the performers are nonprofessional actors hired to enhance the realism of the movie.

Rossellini's "war trilogy" is completed with **Germany, Year Zero** (*Germania, anno zero*, 1947), a movie which attempts to transplant the principles of neorealism onto German soil.

Paisà

Cesare Zavattini (1902-89), a Marxist screenwriter, becomes the key theoretician of neorealism. Rejecting commercial cinema, he calls for accurate representation of everyday life: people, things, and facts.

Zavattini

I SHALL TEACH PEOPLE TO APPRECIATE EVERY DETAIL OF EXISTENCE. NO MORE FANCY MONTAGE, AWAY WITH THE ANECDOTE! IDEALLY, A FILM SHOULD RECORD LIFE AS IT UNFOLDS BEFORE OUR VERY EYES.

VITTORIO, WHAT IS THAT NOISE OUTSIDE? I CAN HARDLY FOCUS...

IT'S THE CRY OF REALITY, CESARE. GO BACK TO WORK.

De Sica

Shoeshine (*Sciuscià*, 1946) is the first neorealist film scripted by Zavattini and directed by **Vittorio De Sica**. The two have been collaborating on movie projects since the 1930s. Their next film, **Bicycle Thieves** (*Lardi di biciclette*, 1948), becomes the most mature exponent of neorealism. A simple story of a bill poster who searches for his stolen bicycle turns into a moving, lyrical portrait of a father-and-son relationship and, on a larger scale, becomes a profound study of the roots of poverty and desperation in postwar Italy.

The key roles in *Bicycle Thieves* are played by amateur actors, and the action is presented in a linear, nearly real-time fashion.

Bicycle Thieves

Umberto D. (1952) is the last neorealist masterpiece created by Zavattini and De Sica. The film chronicles the downfall of an old government clerk who is unable to sustain his existence in a boarding house.

Umberto D.'s strategic use of sound advances the already impressive syntax of neorealist language.

Teaching an old dog new tricks: Carlo Battisti as Umberto D.

Lucino Visconti's **The Earth Trembles** (*La terra trema*, 1948) is a contemporary tale of a fishermen family from a Sicilian village.

Photographed by **G.R. Aldo** (*Umberto D.*) in long, astonishing takes, *La terra trema* confirms neorealism as an art form with a fully developed social agenda.

Other important, more commercially-oriented neorealist directors of the 1940s are **Giuseppe De Santis** (*Tragic Pursuit*/*Caccia tragica*, 1947; **Bitter Rice**/*Riso amaro*, 1949), **Alberto Lattuada** (*The Bandit*/*Il bandito*, 1946; **Without Pity**/*Senza pietà*, 1948), **Luigi Zampa** (*Living in Peace*/*Vievre in pace*, 1946) and **Alessandro Blasetti** (**A Day in a Lifetime**/*Un giorno nello via*, 1946).

Neorealist cinema represents only a small fraction of the Italian film production of the era. With a very few exceptions, neorealist films are financial failures domestically, and their depressing themes contribute to the premature decline of this sensitive genre. Luckily, the huge international impact of neorealism will greatly influence the next generations of filmmakers worldwide.

SCANDINAVIA

After a decade of artistic hibernation, Scandinavian cinema enjoys a great resurgence of talent in the 1940s.

Alf Sjöberg (1903-80) directs his allegorical *They Staked Their Lives* (*Med livet som insats*, 1940), a grim tale foreshadowing the upcoming Nazi invasion of Sweden. In *Scandal* (*Skandalen*, 1944), Sjöberg juxtaposes the conformist attitudes of the older generation with the inextinguishable spirit of youth. The film's screenplay is written by the then unknown theatre director assistant **Ingmar Bergman** (b.1918).

They Staked Their Lives

Carl-Theodor Dreyer returns to Danish cinema with *Day of Wrath* (*Vredens dag*, 1943), a 17th century story of witchcraft, love, and human solitude. The movie's starkly intense cinematography and shot composition are influenced by Flemish painting.

Bodil Ipsen, a veteran film actress, and **Lan Lauritzen Jr.** co-direct *Red Meadows* (*De Røde enge*, 1945), the first Danish postwar picture which deals with occupation in a realistic, documentary-influenced fashion.

Red Meadows

In *Foreign Harbor* (*Främmande hamn*, 1948), actor-director **Erik "Hampe" Faustman** touches upon the ideas of social consciousness and solidarity among seamen. The movie's political agenda and its visual aesthetic have its source in the Soviet cinema and Italian neorealism.

The Norwegian WWII drama *The Battle of Heavy Water* (*Kampen on tungtvannet*, **Titus Vibe-Müller** and **Jean Dreville**, 1948) sets new standards for movies based on authentic events.

Ingmar Bergman directs *Prison* (*Fängelse*, 1949), a contemporary drama with metaphysical themes. It is his first movie based on his own screenplay.

FRANCE

Children of Paradise

Marcel Carné and **Jacques Prévert** team up again to create two of the great French masterpieces of the 1940s—***The Devil's Envoy*** (*Les Visiteurs du soir*, 1943), an allegorical 15th Century tale of good versus evil, and ***Children of Paradise*** (*Les Enfants du paradis*, 1945). The latter is a poetic love story set against the backdrop of 19th century Parisian theatre.

Influenced by Renoir's *La Régle du jeu*, Prévert writes ***The Woman Who Dared*** (*Le Ciel est à nous*, 1944) for director **Jean Grémillon** (1902-59).

Jean Cocteau (1889-1963) writes and directs a surreal and symbolic version of ***The Beauty and the Beast*** (*La Belle et la Bête*, 1946). His ***Orphée*** is a post-apocalyptic, metaphorical adaptation of the Greek myth of Orpheus. In both films the leading man roles are performed by **Jean Marais** (b. 1912), who will become the next French superstar.

Jean Marais

Yves Montand in
Wages of Fear

Henri-Georges Clouzot's (1907-77) ***Jenny Lamour*** (*Quai des orfèvres*, 1947) is a tense thriller in the Hitchcockian tradition.

His masterpiece, ***Wages of Fear*** (*La Salarie de la peur*, 1953) takes place in a nondescript region in South America. A diverse group of losers undertakes the dangerous task of transporting a cargo of nitroglycerine to a remote oil refinery on fire. In Clouzot's skilled hands, the "only the strong survive" routine develops into a probing drama of human endurance and determination.

Clouzot's last great movie is the suspenseful psychological horror ***Diabolique*** (*Les Diaboliques*, 1955).

While René Clair's postwar films fail to live up to his earlier standards, **Jean Renoir** returns to his top form with ***The River*** (1951), shot on location in Bengal, India, ***Golden Coach*** (*Le Carosse d'or*, 1952), set in the 18th Century Peru, and ***French Cancan*** (1954), a film depicting the creation of Paris' most famous entertainment establishment, Moulin Rouge.

JAPAN

The majority of Japanese motion pictures produced during WWII contain strong nationalistic and militaristic themes. One of the better films in that category is **Akira Kurosawa**'s (b. 1910) directorial debut, ***The Saga of Judo*** (*Sanshiro Sugata*, 1943).

After the surrender, Kurosawa makes ***Drunken Angel*** (*Yoidore tenshi*, 1948), a bleak portrait of the postwar Japanese man. His socially-aware detective drama **Stray Dog** (*Nora-inu*, 1949) leaves little doubt about the complex problems of urban Japan.

Kurosawa

Women of the Night

Kenji Mizoguchi's ***Utamaro and His Five Women*** (*Utamaro o meguru go-nin no*, 1946) presents the colorful life of the famous 18th century Japanese painter.

Prostitution as a result of postwar poverty is the theme of two important movies made in 1948—Mizoguchi's ***Women of the Night*** (*Yoru no onna tachi*) and **Yasujiro Ozu**'s ***A Hen in the Wind*** (*Kaze no nako no mendori*).

After the postwar division of political powers in Europe into West (capitalist) and East (communist), America becomes increasingly paranoid about its own alleged communist infiltration.

To prevent "moral corruption" and protect the American Values in the motion picture industry, in 1947 the **House Committee on Un-American Activities** (known pejoratively as **HUAC**—House Un-American Committee) begins a series of investigations and congressional hearings of key film personalities. Ultimately, the persecuted have only two options:
– publicly confess to participating in communist activities or sympathizing with the socialist cause and receive full pardon
– refuse to cooperate and be banned from the profession

The famous **"Hollywood Ten"** stands up for what they believe in and refuses to name names and cooperate with Congress in what they believe is an unconstitutional and immoral procedure of eliciting confession and self-incrimination. The names of these honorable people are:  **Herbert Biberman**, **Alvah Bessie**, **Lester Cole**, **Edward Dmytryk**, **Ring Lardner Jr.**, **John Howard Lawson**, **Albert Maltz**, **Samuel Ornitz**, **Adrian Scott**, and **Dalton Trumbo**. All ten are sentenced to one year in prison and prevented from again working in motion pictures. Some of the condemned writers eventually manage to find employment under assumed names until, over a decade later, the blacklisting slowly dissipates.

Generally, careers of prominent writers and directors are shattered; some of the accused actors lose their lives as a result of stress (John Garfield), other simply cannot find work (Paul Muni), and others decide to leave the country (Joseph Losey, Jules Dassin). On the opposite end, the "friendly witnesses" who denounced their colleagues and close friends are rewarded with prominent positions in the industry and their careers flourish in the 1950s (e.g. Elia Kazan, Bud Schulberg).

In addition to witch-hunting and the increasing popularity of foreign films, another direct threat to American movie business is the advent of television. By 1952, it becomes quite clear that this new, ubiquitous medium is here to stay. The movie theatre attendance drops significantly, forcing major companies to develop new strategies for survival.

The main invention of the 1950s to revolutionize the way films are being shot is the **anamorphic lens**. The anamorphic lens on the camera squeezes an image onto a standard 35mm film stock. During projection, the image is stretched back to its original format with the help of an anamorphic lens of the projector. The process is called **CinemaScope**.

| ORIGINAL IMAGE | CAMERA'S ANAMORPHIC LENS | IMAGE SQUEEZED ONTO A 35mm STOCK | PROJECTOR'S ANAMORPHIC LENS | PROJECTED CINEMASCOPE IMAGE |

Standard screen aspect ratio (width to height) is **1.33** to **1**. CinemaScope offers **2.35** to **1**.

The chief advantage of the anamorphic process is its easy adaptability to the existing film equipment. The only component requiring replacement is the lens.

The first film shot in CinemaScope is ***The Robe*** (dir. Henry Koster, 1953), a costume drama starring a young British stage star **Richard Burton** (1925-85).

Other, more "gimmicky" cinematic inventions include **stereoscopic 3D** and **Cinerama**.

In the various versions of the 3D process spectators are required to wear special goggles which yield an illusion of depth. Generally, movies produced specifically for that format are pure entertainment: musicals (***Kiss Me Kate***, George Sidney, 1953), westerns (***Taza, Son of Cochise***, Douglas Sirk, 1954), horrors (***The House of Wax***, André de Toth, 1953), and science fiction (***Creature from the Black Lagoon***, Jack Arnold, 1954).

Horror star Vincent Price in 3D goggles

In Cinerama, a three-camera setup captures continuous action; the image is then displayed through a multiple-projector unit on a semicircular screen. The resulting picture is three times as wide as the traditional format. Technically, Cinerama is an advanced version of Polyvision—the process used by Abel Gance on ***Napoleon*** in 1927. Originally used for exotic documentary spectacles, Cinerama slowly makes its way into narrative cinema, culminating in 1962 with the extremely costly ***How the West Was Won*** and ***The Wonderful World of Brothers Grimm***. The process is abandoned shortly thereafter due to its financial impracticality.

The main competition of CinemaScope and Cinerama becomes the increasingly popular widescreen process which relies on a wide stock negative. A 70mm stock is developed by **Michael Todd** (1907-58) and used successfully in ***Oklahoma!*** (Fred Zinnemann, 1955) and ***South Pacific*** (Joshua Logan, 1958), among other films providing the sharpest image to date (ratio **2.2:1**).

M. Todd

Another important addition to the expanded film image is stereophonic sound recorded on a magnetic tape for greater mixing possibilities.

Other rival widescreen systems are **Panavision-70** and **Ultra Panavision**. The latter uses an anamorphic lens to squeeze a panoramic picture onto a 65mm negative which, in projection, produces an astounding format of **2.75:1**.

With the newly altered screen formats, the concept of mise-en-scène changes dramatically. Directors begin to utilize horizontal space the same way depth of field has been explored in the 1940s. Editing becomes secondary to shooting long, uninterrupted scenes. Each frame is now wide enough to simultaneously display a close-up, a medium shot, and a wide-angle.

Madeleine or Judy?
Kim Novak in a dual role in *Vertigo*

Hitchcock uses the **VistaVision** process (a competitor of CinemaScope) in such terrific thrillers as ***To Catch a Thief*** (1955), ***The Man Who Knew Too Much*** (1956, a remake of his own film from 1934), and ***Vertigo*** (1958). With its relentless spiral structure, *Vertigo* is a painful portrait of one man's obsession with his ideal woman whom he is doomed to lose twice.

Hitchcock's ***North by Northwest*** (1959) is a beautifully photographed adventure thriller culminating with a spectacular chase scene on top of Mount Rushmore.

Cary Grant

In ***A Star is Born*** (1954), George Cukor uses widescreen symbolically to emphasize its visual triumph over the restrictions of television.

James Mason and a friend
in *20,000 Leagues*

Nicholas Ray (1911-79) becomes a master of creating meaningful relationships between characters and their environments in such classics as ***Rebel Without a Cause*** (1955), ***The True Story of Jesse James*** (1957), and ***Party Girl*** (1958).

Anthony Mann reaches for epical themes to fill the sweeping widescreen frames of his ***The Last Frontier*** (1955) and ***El Cid*** (1961).

The versatile **Richard Fleischer** (b. 1916) provides high-octane entertainment in ***20,000 Leagues Under the Sea*** (1954), ***Bandido*** (1956), and ***The Vikings*** (1958).

The Western, a natural choice for widescreen format, enjoys its greatest popularity in the 1950s. The best pictures in that genre include **Anthony Mann**'s *The Man From Laramie* (1955), *The Tin Star* (1957), and *The Man of the West* (1958) and **Budd Boetticher**'s *Decision at Sundown* (1957), *Ride Lonesome* (1959), and *Comanche Station* (1960).

Randolph Scott
in
Decision at Sundown

One of the most beautifully composed westerns, **John Ford**'s *The Searchers* (1956), chronicles the 5-year odyssey of a man looking for his niece after she was abducted by the Comanches.

John Wayne

**Cooper in
High Noon**

Some of the best westerns of the 1950s are not always shot in widescreen; many focus on the psychology of characters rather than spectacular vistas.

Fred Zinnemann's superb *High Noon* (1952) pitches a strong and quiet sheriff (**Gary Cooper**) against an ethically corroded town.

Before turning to action-driven pictures (*The Magnificent Seven*, 1960), **John Sturges** (1911-92) directs such eloquent, character-driven westerns as *Gunfight at the O.K. Corral* (1957) and *The Last Train from Gun Hill* (1958).

Delmer Daves' (1904-77) *3:10 to Yuma* (1957) and *Cowboy* (1958) also fall under the category of psychological western.

Defying the usual racist attitude of most mainstream westerns, *Broken Arrow* (dir. Delmer Daves, 1950) and *Run of the Arrow* (dir. Samuel Fuller, 1957) take a more sympathetic view of the American Indians.

Nicholas Ray's unusual and often bizarre *Johnny Guitar* (1954) features one of the few, and definitely the most memorable, of the female leads (**Joan Crawford**) in the western genre.

> SHANE, COME BACK!
> COME BACK, SHANE!

Shane (dir. George Stevens, 1955), a tense and entertaining morality play, depicts an unlikely alliance between an errant gunslinger (**Alan Ladd**) and a cattle-raising family man (**Van Heflin**) who unite their efforts against a greedy neighbor.

The **musical** is another popular genre of the 1950s which benefits from the newly developed color and sound technologies.

The main studio responsible for some of the most entertaining and innovative song-and-dance movies is MGM, largely thanks to the producing genius of **Arthur Free** (1894-1973).

Freed promotes such directors as **Vincente Minnelli** (***The Pirate***, 1948, ***American in Paris***, 1951, ***Th Band Wagon***, 1953, ***Gigi***, 1958) and the **Stanley Donen Gene Kelly** team (***On the Town***, 1949, ***Singin' in the Rain***, 1952, ***It's Always Fair Weather***, 1955).

Astaire in
The Band Wagon

In *American in Paris*, Minnelli (1910-86) creates a unique visual aesthetic by integrating the abstract lighting and imaginative scenery with the brilliantly staged dance numbers.

Kelly in *American in Paris*

Singin' in the Rain, co-directed by Donen (b. 1924) and Kelly (1912-96), is an ingenious parody of the early day of cinema—specifically the MGM musical. In addition to producing the film, Arthur Freed provides lyrics to the playful **Nacio Herb Brown**'s score.

Judy Garland, the star of many musicals of the period, including *Summer Stock* and *A Star is Born*

The film noir tradition continues in the 1950s with **John Huston**'s *Asphalt Jungle* (1950), Nicholas Ray's *On Dangerous Ground* (1952), Samuel Fuller's *Pickup on South Street* (1953), and Robert Aldrich's *Kiss Me Deadly* (1955). The latter is an excellent adaptation of the book by a classic noir writer **Mickey Spillane**, whose famous protagonist, private eye Mike Hammer, is frequently portrayed in movies.

Sam Jaffe in *Asphalt Jungle*

Ralph Meeker as Mike Hammer in *Kiss Me Deadly*

In accordance with the paranoid spirit of the period, the individual screen villain is gradually replaced by collective evil. Communist threat becomes the focal point of such blatantly propagandistic pictures as *The Red Menace* (dir. R.C. Springsteen, 1949), *The Atomic City* (dir. Jerry Hopper, 1952), *A Bullet for Joey* (dir. Lewis Allen, 1955), and the quintessential Red Scare product—*My Son John* (dir. Leo McCarey, 1952).

Much more popular and artistically accomplished than the anticommunist films are **mafia** or **"the syndicate"** movies. Among the best are *The Enforcer* (dir. Bretaigne Windust, 1951), *The Big Heat* (dir. Fritz Lang, 1953), *The Big Combo* (dir. Joseph E. Lewis, 1955), *The Brothers Rico* (dir. Phil Karlson, 1957), and *Murder, Inc.* (dir. Stuart Rosenberg, 1960).

Glenn Ford in *The Big Heat*

Produced at the height of McCarthyism, **Elia Kazan**'s *On the Waterfront* (1954), one of the best films dealing with organized crime, is an open endorsement of informing as a civil duty.

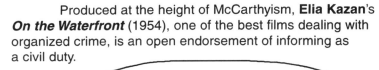

I WONDER WHAT MOTIVATES KAZAN TO STRUCTURE *ON THE WATERFRONT* AS A PAEAN TO SNITCHING...

Rod Steiger in *On the Waterfront*

The popular **heist films**, known as **capers**, prove that a minute presentation of the mechanisms of organized theft makes for great and suspenseful entertainment. The most impressive caper picture of the period is the French-produced **Rififi** (*Du Rififi chez les hommes*, 1955), directed by the HUAC witch-hunt victim **Jules Dassin** (denounced by, among other people, Elia Kazan).

Dassin in *Rififi*

Other notable examples of the heist genre are the excellent race track robbery film **The Killing** (dir. Stanley Kubrick, 1956), **Odds Against Tomorrow** (dir. Robert Wise, 1959), **Seven Thieves** (dir. Henry Hathaway, 1960), and **The League of Gentlemen** (dir. Basil Dearden, 1960).

With the Production Code tightening its grip on American-made movies, filmmakers are forced to find subtle, implicit ways to show sexuality and other "immoral" acts on screen. The results of these restrictions are often more graphic than the acts themselves.

Alfred Hitchcock becomes an undisputed master of sexual innuendos. His **Strangers on a Train** (1951) is full of indirect homosexual undertones which are concealed just enough to slip by the censors.

In **Rear Window** (1954), confined to a wheel chair James Stewart kills time by spying on his neighbors with a telephoto camera. In a subversive way, the film implies the voyeuristic nature of cinema itself.

SUBTLE!

Professionally impotent photographer (James Stewart) finds solace in pulling out his lens in *Rear Window*

Influenced both by the increasing popularity of the European film and the efficiency of television programs, American cinema of the 1950s begins to emphasize the director as the key individual responsible for the ultimate "look" of a movie.

The most emblematic picture to reflect the twilight of Hollywood glamour is **Sunset Boulevard** (1950), directed by the Austrian-born **Billy Wilder**. This cynical and relentlessly honest film deals with issues of success and power and the price one must pay for one's dreams to come true.

I'M READY FOR MY CLOSE-UP, **Mr. DeMILLE!**

Gloria Swanson in
Sunset Boulevard

In **Ace In the Hole** (also known as *The Big Carnival*, 1951), Wilder shatters the myth of free press. His triumphal adaptation of Agatha Christie's **Witness for the Prosecution** (1958) remains one of the best courtroom thrillers ever made. Wilder confirms his versatile talent with such comedies as **Sabrina** (1954), **Love in the Afternoon** (1957), and the gender-bending, fast-paced gangster parody, **Some Like It Hot** (1959). Always a shrewd commentator of the double standards of American life, Wilder analyzes the male-female dynamic with a humorous eye in **The Apartment** (1960).

Jack Lemmon:
he likes it hot

THE BEST DIRECTOR IS THE ONE YOU DON'T SEE.

Billy Wilder

Already famous for his theatre work in New York, **Elia Kazan** emerges as the dominant figure in the film drama genre with his excellent adaptation of **Tennessee Williams'** *Streetcar Named Desire* (1951)

IS THAT STREET-CAR NAMED DESIRE STILL GRINDING ALONG THE TRACKS AT THIS HOUR?

Vivien Leigh in *Streetcar*

John Steinbeck contributes a tight screenplay to Kazan's *Viva Zapata!* (1952), an emotional film based on the famous Mexican revolutionary's life.

Because of the unique acting talent and charisma of James Dean, *East of Eden* (1954), a loose adaptation of the Steinbeck novel, is a timeless story of youthful rebellion.

Baby Doll (1956) is yet another successful screen adaptation of Williams' work, in which Kazan questions spiritual morality of the South. In *A Face in the Crowd* (1957), Kazan tackles the roots of mass manipulation by the media, and, on a larger scale, exposes the totalitarian potential of a passive, pliable society.

Brando as Zapata

Robert Aldrich (1918-83) contributes to the drama genre the devastating *The Big Knife* (1955). Together with *It's a Lonely Place* (Nicholas Ray, 1950) and *The Bad and the Beautiful* (Vincente Minnelli, 1953), these films remain the most astute anti-Hollywood pictures of the decade.

With the sexually charged *The Moon is Blue* (1953), the Austrian-born **Otto Preminger** (1906-86) begins a streak of Production Code-defying pictures. *The Man with the Golden Arm* (1955) depicts a heroin addict (Frank Sinatra) who tries to find a fresh beginning. In *Anatomy of Murder* (1959), a terrific courtroom drama, Preminger deals with another 1950s taboo—rape; the film's cool, moody score is created by **Duke Ellington** himself. Preminger's thriller *Advise and Consent* (1962) becomes the first mainstream American movie to talk about homosexuality with maturity and understanding.

Otto Preminger

Otto Preminger should also be remembered for giving the first screen credit to a blacklisted writer, **Dalton Trumbo**, for *Exodus* (1960) and ending a decade of the HUAC repressions (some argue it was Kirk Douglas who had given Trumbo his first credit for *Spartacus*, also released the same year. Both Preminger and Douglas are equally audacious individuals and deserve to share the credit for breaking the blacklist).

Frank Sinatra in *The Man With the Golden Arm*

Preminger's lifelong collaborator is the preeminent graphic designer **Saul Bass**, whose opening credits and posters enhance many distinguished movies from the 1950s to 90s.

John Huston makes his mark on the 1950s with ***The Red Badge of Courage*** (1951), an anti-war picture whose semidocumentary style is significantly ahead of its time. This superb Civil War drama is drastically recut by MGM to eliminate all traces of moral ambiguity (the conflict in Korea has just begun).

Audie Murphy in
The Red Badge

Moulin Rouge

Huston's ***Moulin Rouge*** (1953) and ***Moby Dick*** (1956) are both exquisite adaptations of literary classics and feature beautiful color photography by **Oswald Morris**.

The modest, black and white ***Beat the Devil*** (1954) is Huston's self-reflexive parody of *The Maltese Falcon* and *Treasure of Sierra Madre*, and features a great ensemble cast including Humphrey Bogart, Peter Lorre, **Gina Lollobrigida**, and **Jennifer Jones**.

Other American directors to imprint their style on the drama genre of the period include **Stanley Kramer** (b. 1913) [***Defiant Ones***, 1958, ***Inherit the Wind***, 1960, and ***Judgement at Nuremberg***, 1961] and **Richard Brooks** (1912-92, ***The Blackboard Jungle***, 1954, ***The Cat on a Hot Tin Roof***, 1958, and ***Elmer Gantry***, 1961).

WHAT IS THE VICTORY OF A CAT ON A HOT TIN ROOF?

JUST STAYING ON IT, I GUESS. AS LONG AS SHE CAN.

Elizabeth Taylor and Paul Newman in *The Cat on a Hot Tin Roof*

Small independent film production finds its niche for success with such movies directed by **Delbert Mann** as *Marty* (1955), *The Bachelor Party* (1957), and *Middle of the Night* (1959). All three are produced by the **Hecht-Lancaster** company organized in 1947 by Harold Hecht and Burt Lancaster. The most prominent screenwriter of this cycle is **Paddy Chayefsky** (*Marty*, *The Bachelor Party*, *The Catered Affair*, *Middle of the Night*).

**Ernest Borgnine as Marty,
the butcher with a golden heart**

Sydney Lumet (b. 1924), a young TV director makes the impressive ***Twelve Angry Men*** (1957) for producers **Reginald Rose** (also the film's writer) and Henry Fonda (also the star). The realistic yet tightly organized composition of this intense courtroom movie is a result of the great working relationship between Lumet and his veteran cinematographer Boris Kaufman, and opens new narrative possibilities for cinema.

United Artists, a distribution company, becomes involved in releasing some of the most artistically accomplished independent productions of the period. Among them are the powerful anti-war drama ***Paths of Glory*** (Stanley Kubrick, 1957) and ***The Night of the Hunter*** (1955), the only directorial effort of **Charles Laughton** (1899-1962).

**Robert Mitchum in
*The Night of the Hunter***

Kirk Douglas in *Paths of Glory*

Aside from being a gifted director, Stanley Kramer produces several excellent movies for such filmmakers as Fred Zinnemann (*The Men*, 1950, *High Noon*, and *The Member of the Wedding*, 1953) and Laszlo Benedek (*Death of a Salesman*, 1952 and *The Wild One*, 1954).

WHAT ARE YOU REBELLING AGAINST?

WHAT'CHA GOT?

Brando in *The Wild One*

Along with the new trends in movies, film acting also undergoes a dramatic change in the 1950s. The mannered, heavily stylized enunciation of the previous decades is gradually replaced by a spontaneous, more naturalistic approach, as demonstrated by **Marlon Brando**, **James Dean**, **Paul Newman**, **Geraldine Page** and **Joanne Woodward**, to name a few. All of these accomplished actors receive their training at the **Actors Studio** in New York. One of the finest schools of the trade in the world, the Actors Studio embraces the acting techniques developed by **Konstantin Stanislavsky** (1863-1938), the famous Russian theatre actor and director who stressed emotional truth (motivation) and realism in performing arts. In New York, Stanislavsky's teachings are expounded upon by **Lee Strasberg**, **Cheryl Crawford**, and Elia Kazan and become known as **Method Acting**.

YOU'RE TEARING ME APART!

Method Acting personified:
James Dean in *Rebel Without a Cause*

Charles Chaplin (not a Method actor) completes his last great film, *Limelight* in 1952, only a few months before his political convictions force him to leave America permanently. The movie is a bitter and deeply personal account of the last days of a past-his-prime vaudeville clown. Two of Chaplin's colleagues from the glory days of silent burlesque make cameo appearances in the film: Buster Keaton and Edna Purviance.

Another exiled maverick, **Orson Welles**, directs his low-budget version of Shakespeare's *Othello* in 1953. Despite tremendous technical difficulties and an ongoing lack of completion funds, the film is a sheer triumph of cinematic ingenuity.

Welles returns to the U.S. in 1956, lured by Universal and **Charlton Heston** to direct and act in *Touch of Evil* (1958). This stunning black-and-white thriller set on the American-Mexican border is widely considered the last masterpiece of film noir. Unfortunately, its poor box office performance eliminates any possibility of a future for Welles in Hollywood. The man who helped to shape the modern American cinema will never be able to make an American film again.

Welles as Othello

Every artist has his muse: Rock Hudson becomes one for Sirk

The Danish-born **Douglas Sirk** (1900-87) carves an interesting niche for himself as the director of such melodramatic and artifice-rich hits as *All That Heaven Allows* (1955), *Written on the Wind* (1956), and *Imitation of Life* (1959), all featuring **Rock Hudson** (1925-85). However, his *A Time to Love, a Time to Die* (1958), based on the Erich Maria Remarque book, remains a strong and touching indictment of war.

The war film of the 1950s veers away from the heroic, nationalistic themes and becomes increasingly preoccupied with the impact of military conflicts on individual human life. Aside from the superb *Red Badge of Courage*, *Attack*, and *Paths of Glory*, some of the other psychologically complex films of the war genre are *The Steel Helmet* (dir. Samuel Fuller, 1950), *From Here to Eternity* (dir. Fred Zinnemann, 1953), and the British *The Bridge on the River Kwai* (dir. David Lean, 1957).

Montgomery Clift in *From Here to Eternity*

Along with the increasing sophistication of dramatic film, American comedy enjoys an influx of new talent and energy. Unquestionably the most dynamic comedic duo to grace movie screens of the 1950s is the **Dean Martin** (1917-96) – **Jerry Lewis** (b. 1924) team. Their success is based on the balance of Martin's slick, deadpan delivery and Lewis' zany and wacky goofiness. Among the most kinetic of their slapstick-driven films are *At War with the Army* (dir. Hal Walker, 1951), *Sailor Beware* (Walker, 1952), *Living It Up* (dir. Norman Taurog, 1954), and *Artists and Models* (dir. Frank Tashlin, 1955).

After the two split in 1956, Lewis continues working in comedy as a solo performer, frequently directing his own films (*The Bellboy*, 1960, *The Nutty Professor*, 1963).

Lewis in
The Nutty Professor

Judy Holliday (1922-65) establishes herself as a prima ballerina of American comedy with *Born Yesterday* (dir. George Cukor, 1950), *It Should Happen to You* (Cukor, 1954), and *The Bells are Ringing* (dir. Vincente Minnelli, 1960).

Another tragically short but brilliant career belongs to **Marylin Monroe** (1926-62), who uses her ebullient on-screen sexuality to great comedic advantage in *Gentlemen Prefer Blondes* (dir. Howard Hawks, 1953), *How to Marry a Millionaire* (dir. Jean Negulesco, 1953), *The Seven-Year Itch* (dir. Billy Wilder, 1955), and, of course, *Some Like It Hot*.

Marylin Monroe

Doris Day (b. 1924) develops her reluctant-virgin screen personality in a series of sex farces which pair her with some of the most glamorous men of the time: Rock Hudson (***Pillow Talk***, Michael Gordon, 1958; ***Lover Come Back***, Delbert Mann, 1961), Cary Grant (***That Touch of Mink***, Mann, 1962) and James Garner (***Move Over, Darling***, Michael Douglas, 1963).

Danny Kaye (1913-87) scores big hits with his merry ***The Court Jester*** (dir. Norman Panama, 1956) and jesting ***Merry Andrew*** (dir. Michael Kidd, 1958).

The Court Jester

Bob Hope (b. 1903), whose career is founded on a string of popular comedies he shot in 1940s with **Bing Crosby** (1903-77), continues his comedic success with solo performances in ***Son of Paleface*** (dir. Frank Tashlin, 1952) and ***Casanova's Big Night*** (dir. Norman Z. McLeod, 1954).

The pervasive fear of atomic holocaust and the increasing possibility of interplanetary travel are reflected in the newly refurbished **science-fiction** genre. The best of this group are ***The Day the Earth Stood Still*** (dir. Robert Wise, 1951), ***The Thing*** (dir. Christian Nyby, 1951), ***War of the Worlds*** (dir. Bryon Haskin, 1953), and ***Forbidden Planet*** (dir. Fred M. Wilcox, 1956).

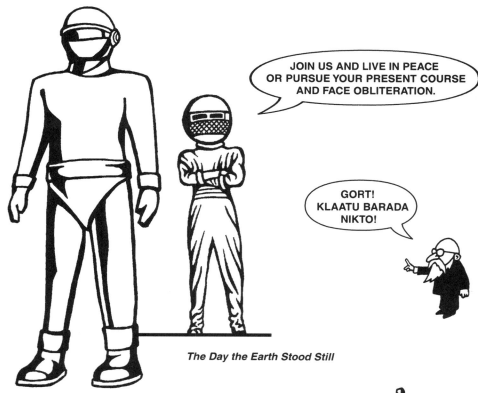

The Day the Earth Stood Still

Don Siegel's (1912-92) ***Invasion of the Body Snatchers*** (1956) suggests that the American society is being gradually populated by "pods" who superficially appear to be human but who are deprived of any feelings and emotions.

One of the most profound psychological sci-fi movies, ***On the Beach*** (dir. Stanley Kramer, 1959), depicts a grim vision of Earth after a nuclear attack.

In 1953, a charming independent low-budget film called ***Little Fugitive***, written and directed by **Ray Ashley**, **Morris Engel**, and **Ruth Orkin**, introduces viewers to a fresh, informal approach to narrative film. The spontaneity of a 7-year-old boy's adventures on Coney Island is enhanced by the use of nonprofessional actors, natural lighting, hand-held camera, and location shooting. *Little Fugitive* foreshadows the upcoming aesthetic of the French New Wave, especially its landmark films, *Breathless* and *400 Blows*.

FRANCE

René Clément (1913-96) directs *Forbidden Games* (*Jeux interdits*, 1952), a beautiful and moving story of a little orphaned girl who is left to the mercy of strangers in a French countryside during WWII. Clément's next film, *Gervaise* (1956), based on Zola's *L'Assommoir*, portrays the grim and hopeless world of the Parisian proletariat.

Aside from shamelessly showcasing the youthful beauty of **Alain Delon** (b. 1935), Clément's *Purple Noon* (*Plein solei*, 1959) is a remarkable suspense thriller and the closest imitation of Hitchcock ever afforded by French cinema.

René Clément

Excellent literary adaptations become a staple of French cinema of the 1950s. Some of the most impressive titles include Stendhal's *Red and Black* (*Le Rouge et le noir*, 1954), and Dostoyevsky's *The Gambler* (*Le Jouer*, 1958), both directed by **Claude Autant-Lara** (b. 1903) and written for the screen by **Jean Aurenche** and **Pierre Bost**.

The highly popular cloak-and-dagger subgenre of the costume film finds its great exponent in *Fanfan-la-tulipe* (dir. Christian-Jaque, 1952), starring the charming and irresistible **Gérard Philipe** (1922-59).

The Hole

Jacques Becker (1906-60), a former assistant to Jean Renoir, writes and directs *Golden Marie* (*Casque d'Or*, 1952), a turn-of-the century doomed love story set in Paris, whose composition is influenced by the sensual paintings of Auguste Renoir.

Becker's crafty gangster picture *Honor Among Thieves* (*Touchez pas au grisbi*, 1954) enhances the popularity of the genre, and influences Dassin's *Rififi*. *The Hole* (*Le Trou*, 1960), Becker's last film, chronicles a failed prison escape while exploring the theme of solidarity among strangers compelled by circumstance to act together and depend on mutual loyalty.

Stylistically, *The Hole* is a counterpoint to another prison masterpiece of French cinema, the 1956 movie by **Robert Bresson** (b. 1907), ***A Man Escaped*** (*Un Condamné à mort s'est echappé*). Like Bresson's earlier ***The Diary of a Country Priest*** (*Le Journal d'un curé de campagne*, 1950), the WWII prison film possesses a restrained, realistic style of narration which becomes the director's trademark.

For the hero of Bresson's powerful crime drama ***Pickpocket*** (1959), the habitual desire to steal becomes a way of defying the stale conformity of society.

A Man Escaped

In 1949, the German-born **Max Ophüls** (1902-57) returns to France, his adopted homeland, after completing a series of Hollywood pictures. ***La Ronde*** (1950), an episodic film of great visual beauty and liberal attitude, begins the cycle of Ophüls' artistic triumphs in costume melodrama. ***Earrings of Madame de...*** (*Madame de...*, 1953), a sparkling story of infidelity among the rich and powerful showcases Ophüls' unerring sense of composition and narrative rhythm. The same, only on a larger scale, can be said of the dazzling ***Lola Montès*** (1955), an expensive CinemaScope film which displays a decisively unique mise-en-scène.

Vittorio DeSica and DanielleDarrieux in *Madame de...*

Jean-Pierre Melville (1917-73), after an early collaboration with Jean Cocteau on ***Les Enfants terribles*** (1949), moves with great confidence into the realm of gangster film with two highly influential noir pictures: ***Bob le flambeur*** (1955) and ***Le Doulos*** (1962). The former's use of natural locations and low production values will contribute to the artistic program of the upcoming French **New Wave**.

Melville

THE FRENCH NEW WAVE

NOUVELLE VAGUE

In 1948, the French director **Alexandre Astruc** (b. 1923) creates the famous theory of *caméra-stylo* (camera-pen). Professing that true cinema should be like literature—subtle and rich in meaning, directors are to be considered authors (**"auteurs"** in French) of their films in the true literary sense of the word.

Three years later, influenced by Astruc's concepts, **André Bazin** (1918-58) cofounds *Cahiers du Cinéma*, a French film journal which assembles such young critics as Claude Chabrol, Jean-Luc Godard, and François Truffaut. Collectively known as *cinéphiles* (film lovers) the *Cahiers* group becomes famous for theoretical writings on world film—the first such undertaking in postwar film critique. Their ideology embraces two aspects of filmmaking:

1. **mise-en-scène** should be the basis for psychological and intellectual structure of a film (thus, the montage theory is rejected)
2. **the author theory**—each film should carry the individual signature of its director (auteur/author), both in the aesthetic and ideological contexts (thus the principles of impersonal studio production are rejected)

Before the end of the decade, most of the *Cahiers* critics decide to put their theories to the ultimate test—they begin to make movies of their own. *Cinéphiles* become *cinéastes*—filmmakers with an artistic agenda.

THE NEW WAVE IS BORN!!!

Preceded by a series of independent short *Nouvelle Vague* (New Wave) films, **Claude Chabrol** (b. 1930) directs what is perceived to be the first feature-length picture of the movement: *The Handsome Serge* (*Le Beau Serge*, 1958). It is here where Astruc's *caméra-stylo* principles become clearly visible for the first time—the story of a moral and spiritual rebirth of a drunkard is told in a highly personal and unconventional way which bears a distinct, individual style unlike that of mainstream cinema.

The Handsome Claude

Chabrol's success is sealed with *The Cousins* (*Les Cousins*), an originally constructed film depicting hedonistic attitudes of Parisian youth.

115

Alain Resnais' (b. 1922) narrative film debut, ***Hiroshima Mon Amour*** (1959), another seminal *Nouvelle Vague* film, is a structurally innovative meditation on death and love. The movie becomes the most celebrated picture among the *cinéastes* themselves, and enjoys a great commercial success worldwide.

I'LL FORGET YOU! I'M FORGETTING YOU ALREADY! LOOK HOW I'M FORGETTING YOU! LOOK AT ME!

Emmanuelle Riva
and Eiji Okada in
Hiroshima Mon Amour

HI-RO-SHI-MA.
HI-RO-SHI-MA.
THAT'S YOUR NAME.

The same year,
François Truffaut (1932-84)
directs his landmark
The 400 Blows
(*Les Quatre-cent coups*).
Partially a tribute to Vigo's
Zéro de conduite, this
sensitive film describes
a little odyssey of a young
delinquent searching for
his place in life.

Jean-Pierre Léaud
in *400 Blows*

The movie which embodies the rebellious principles of *Nouvelle Vague* best is **Jean-Luc Godard**'s (b. 1932) ***Breathless*** (*A Bout de souffle*), also completed in 1959. Based on Truffaut's idea, the movie is conceived as a parody of the American film noir and, at the same time, as a subversive tribute to the conventions of this genre. A young Parisian hoodlum (**Jean-Paul Belmondo**) with no respect for the authorities falls for an American student (**Jean Seberg**), who betrays him to the police. Godard molds this trivial plot into a deliberately chaotic sequence of events shot mostly with a hand-held camera and on location. The dialogues are deprived of their traditional explanatory function, the editing is "amateurish"—a conscious insult to the "daddy's cinema" of the older generation of filmmakers like Clément and Clouzot.

Belmondo and Seberg in *Breathless*

Godard trademark is the **jump-cut**, a sudden, self-conscious cut within a scene which causes the action to "jump" forward. The effect of a jump-cut is such that the sense of the action's continuity is broken, reality is distorted, and, what's more important for Godard, the editing traditions are upheaved.

French Comedy

In the macabre ***The Red Inn*** (*L'Auberge rouge,* Claude Autant-Lara, 1950), the famous French comedian **Fernandel** (1903-71) creates the most memorable role of his long career—a monk who involuntarily becomes a confessor to the murderous inn keepers.

Inspired by the best traditions of silent burlesque, the brilliant French entertainer **Jaques Tati** (1908-82) creates his blundering **Monsieur Hulot** screen persona. Mr. Hulot, a walking (or, rather, stumbling) anachronism, becomes entangled in the trappings of modern society in such comedic masterpieces as ***Mr. Hulot's Holiday*** (*Les Vacances de M. Hulot,* 1953), ***My Uncle*** (*Mon Oncle,* 1958), ***Playtime*** (1967), and ***Traffic*** (*Trafic,* 1971). In addition to performing the title character, Tati visually conceives his films in minute details and directs them with a clockmaker's precision.

Tati as Hulot in *Mon Oncle*

SCANDINAVIA 1950s

Alf Sjöberg successfully adapts for the screen August Strindberg's ***Miss Julie*** (*Fröken Julie*, 1951).

The cinema of Finland offers the beautifully stark ***The White Reindeer*** (*Valkoinen peura*, 1952), written, photographed and directed by **Erik Blomberg**. The film is an adaptation of the mythical Lapp story shot with an impeccable sense of composition on location in the Arctic Circle.

Carl-Theodor Dreyer directs ***The Word*** (*Ordet*, 1955), a restrained study of the power of faith. This austere film is an artistic testimony of the great Dane's enduring talent and integrity of vision.

Ingmar Bergman receives international recognition with ***The Seventh Seal*** (*Det sjunde inseglet*, 1956), an allegorical tale of the struggle between forces of life and death, set in Medieval Europe.

Wild Strawberries (*Smultronstället*, 1957) continues Bergman's metaphysical approach to cinema. A dying science professor engages in a memory game, eavesdropping on the ghosts from the past and remembering those still alive—every person that mattered in his long and rich life. In the role of the protagonist, Bergman casts his master and mentor, the legendary Swedish director **Victor Sjöström**.

In 1959, Bergman releases ***The Virgin Spring*** (*Jungfrükallan*), a poetic medieval ballad of one man's grief over his murdered daughter and his subsequent journey of violence and redemption.

Victor Sjöström
in *Wild Strawberries*

EASTERN EUROPE 1950s

THE SOVIET UNION

After Stalin's death in 1953 and the "thaw" of 1956, when the new Soviet leader **Nikita Khrushchev** officially criticized his predatory predecessor, the Russian cinema slowly begins to rise from the nearly twenty-year slump.

Sergei Yutkevich directs one of the first Russian color movies, ***Othello*** (1956), a strikingly designed version of Shakespeare's play.

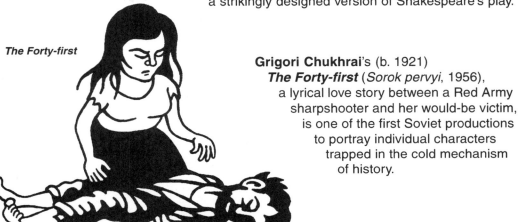

The Forty-first

Grigori Chukhrai's (b. 1921) ***The Forty-first*** (*Sorok pervyi*, 1956), a lyrical love story between a Red Army sharpshooter and her would-be victim, is one of the first Soviet productions to portray individual characters trapped in the cold mechanism of history.

In the moving anti-war drama ***Ballad of a Soldier*** (*Ballada o soldate*, 1959), Chukhrai focuses on an accidental war hero who, on a brief leave, travels back home to see his mother.

The exceptionally beautiful ***The Cranes are Flying*** (*Letiat zhuravli*, 1957), directed by **Mikhail Kalatozov** (1903-73), paints a very human portrait of a young soldier's fiancee waiting for her lover to come back from the front lines. This poetic movie becomes an instant classic and the first international triumph of postwar Soviet cinema.

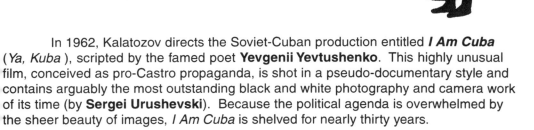

In 1962, Kalatozov directs the Soviet-Cuban production entitled ***I Am Cuba*** (*Ya, Kuba*), scripted by the famed poet **Yevgenii Yevtushenko**. This highly unusual film, conceived as pro-Castro propaganda, is shot in a pseudo-documentary style and contains arguably the most outstanding black and white photography and camera work of its time (by **Sergei Urushevski**). Because the political agenda is overwhelmed by the sheer beauty of images, *I Am Cuba* is shelved for nearly thirty years.

And Quiet Flows the Don

Two of the best literary adaptations of this period in Soviet cinema are based on the work of **Mikhail Sholokhov**: the epic *And Quiet Flows the Don* (*Tikhii Don*, Sergei Gerasimov, 1958) and *Fate of a Man* (*Sud'ba cheloveka*, Sergei Bondarchuk, 1959).

POLAND

The cinema of Poland, especially after the death of Stalin, enjoys a great resurgence of young talent coming out of the excellent **Lodz Film School**. Its recent graduates, **Andrzej Wajda** (b. 1926), **Jerzy Kawalerowicz** (b. 1922), and **Andrzej Munk** (1921-61), form the core of a new film movement commonly referred to as the **Polish School**.

Zbigniew Cybulski in
Ashes and Diamonds

Wajda's *A Generation* (*Pokolenie*, 1954) is a tragic story of the young freedom fighters in the Warsaw Resistance.

In *Canal* (*Kanal*, 1956), Wajda portrays the hopeless struggle of the Home Army soldiers in the last stage of the 1944 Warsaw uprising. The director's fine arts background helps to create the imagery of unforgettable beauty and strength. *Kanal* becomes the first major international success for Polish cinema.

Wajda's *Ashes and Diamonds* (*Popiol i diament*, 1958) presents the internal turmoil of a young nationalist soldier on a mission to assassinate a local communist leader. Perfectly composed and rich in allegory, the film becomes an instant classic with Polish audiences and gradually secures a permanent place as one of the great masterpieces of world cinema.

Jerzy Kawalerowicz's **A Night of Remembrance** (*Celuloza*, 1953) and **Under the Phrygian Star** (*Pod Gwiazda Frygijska*, 1954) create a diptych of the two decades of Poland's independence between the wars, set in a country environment.

After the engaging, dark and deliberately ambiguous psychological drama **Baltic Express** (*Pociag*, 1959) Kawalerowicz directs **Mother Joan of the Angels** (*Matka Joanna od aniolow*, 1961), an astonishing tale of a nun possessed by the Devil in a 17th century Polish convent. In the most expensive polish movie to date, **Pharaoh** (*Faraon*, 1965), based on the **Boleslaw Prus** novel, Kawalerowicz meticulously recreates the world of ancient Egypt and its political structure.

Pharaoh

Andrzej Munk completes merely three features before his untimely death in an auto accident, but they remain an enduring legacy to his artistic vision. His first feature, **Man on the Track** (*Czlowiek na torze*, 1956), analyzes individual attitudes of the Stalinist society. The satirical **Eroica** (1957) presents the traditional Polish myth of heroism at all cost in a less glorified light. **Bad Luck** (*Zezowate szczescie*, 1959) features the great Polish actor **Bogumil Kobiela** as a weasly opportunist capable of adapting to any political and economical circumstance. In Munk's last movie, **The Passenger** (*Pasazerka*, 1961), released unfinished two years after the director's death, an SS guard reminisces about one of her Jewish prisoners from Auschwitz. Even in this uncompleted version, *The Passenger* is a highly effective film about the nature of pain —those we receive and those we cause.

The Passenger

HUNGARY

Before the National Uprising of 1956, Hungarian film experiences a brief period of relative creative freedom. The most interesting films belong to **Zoltan Fábri** (1917-94) —**Fourteen Lives in Danger** (*Életjet*, 1954), **Merry-Go-Round** (*Körhinta*, 1955), and **Professor Hannibal** (*Hannibal, tanár úr*, 1956); **Károly Makk** (b. 1925)—**Liliomfi** (1954); **Felix Máriássy** (1919-76)—**Spring in Budapest** (*Budapesti tavász*, 1955) and **A Glass of Beer** (*Egy pikoló világos*, 1955).

Unfortunately, the surge of talent and optimism in all areas of the Hungarian life is brutally curtailed by the Soviet tanks, which roll into the streets of Budapest in November of 1956 to thwart the people's demand for true democracy.

Professor Hannibal

Akira Kurosawa enters the new decade with one of the most influential pictures ever made—**Rashomon** (1950). A samurai is killed in the woods; his wife, a captured bandit, and a woodcutter all witnessed the murder. Questioned by the authorities, all tell conflicting stories about the gruesome event. Even the victim's ghost, speaking through a medium, has his own version of the facts. Kurosawa weaves his film through the juxtaposition of viewpoints— each character's truth is relative and portrays him or her in the most favorable light.

Rashomon becomes a huge hit worldwide and paves the way for Japanese cinema's ensuing international success.

An avid fan of the European culture, Kurosawa adapts Dostoyevsky's **The Idiot** (*Hakuchi*, 1951) and, a few years later, Maxim Gorky's **Lower Depths** (*Donzoko*, 1957).

In the dark and gloomy **Ikiru** (*Living*, 1952), Kurosawa presents the triumph of one man's good will over the pettiness of society.

THE FARMERS ARE THE WINNERS. NOT US.

Seven Samurai (*Shichinin no samurai*, 1954), a jidai-geki of epic proportions, tells a story of vagabond samurai warriors for hire who take a job protecting poor villagers from the terror of local bandits. Kurosawa's technique ranges from a subtle, romantic approach in the first part of the film to the dynamic tour-de-force of the climactic battle in the rain.

Takashi Shimura in *Seven Samurai*

Another masterful jidai-geki from Kurosawa is **The Throne of Blood** (*Kumonosujo*, 1957), which transplants Shakespeare's *Macbeth* onto the soil of Medieval Japan. Magnificently directed, energetically edited and supported by a great cast led by **Toshiro Mifune** (1920-97), Kurosawa's favorite actor, *The Throne of Blood* rates as one of the best adaptations of Shakespeare on film.

Toshiro Mifune in *The Throne of Blood*

For **Kenji Mizoguchi**, the decade of the 1950s proves to be the most rewarding in terms of artistic accomplishments. The lives of prostitutes become the central theme of his *The Life of Oharu* (*Saikaku ichidai onna*, 1952) and *Street of Shame* (*Akasen chitai*, 1956). Both are shot with a great sense of humanism and compassion.

Ugetsu (*Ugetsu monogatari*, 1953) is a 12th century story of a pair of potters who abandon their families to pursue fame and fortune. Simultaneously realistic and fantastic, *Ugetsu* speaks out against materialistic ambitions of man and presents spiritual solace as the only meaningful reward in life.

Hailed as Mizoguchi's most outstanding picture, **Sansho the Bailiff** (*Sansho dayu*, 1954), contrasts issues of feudal injustice in 12th century Japan with beautiful, sumptuous imagery. Like most of the Mizoguchi films, *Sansho* is photographed by the brilliant cinematographer **Kazuo Miyagawa**. They pair up again for Mizoguchi's first color film, **New Tales of the Taira Clan** (*Shin Heike monogatari*, 1955), a multilayered 12th century historical tale.

 The Princess Yang (*Yokihi*, 1955) again showcases Mizoguchi's uncanny understanding of the dramatic function of color as a tool of emotional manipulation.

Sansho the Bailiff

Yasujiro Ozu's ***Tokyo Story*** (*Tokyo monogatari*, 1953) deals with the cyclical nature of human existence. The movie's visual economy and importance of detail are influenced by haiku—the Japanese seventeen syllable verse. Ozu's frequent use of low camera angles gives his movies the perspective of a detached observer sitting on the floor mat, silently witnessing the unhurried but steady flow of time. A similar aesthetic permeates Ozu's ***Floating Weeds*** (*Ukigusa*, 1959), a dramatic story of a Kabuki theater troupe, enhanced by the wonderful use of color. An undisputed master of composition, Ozu often utilizes **off-screen space** to draw attention to a particular action or narrative detail.

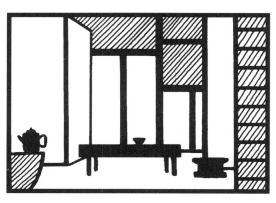

**Off-screen space at work
in *Tokyo Story***

YASUJIRO, WHAT HAPPENS
IN THIS SHOT?

ACTUALLY, THE ACTION
TAKES PLACE IN
THE OTHER ROOM.

**Setting-up the low angle:
Ozu at work**

Kon Ichikawa's poetic and deeply Buddhist *The Burmese Harp* (*Biruma no tategoto*, 1956) confronts an individual human being with the horrors of war.

Shoji Yasui in
The Burmese Harp

In Ichikawa's ***Conflagration*** (*Enjo*, 1958), based on **Yukio Mishima**'s novel, a young, misunderstood Buddhist monk sets fire to his beloved temple in a desperate attempt to bring purity to the corrupted world.

Enjo

Other notable Japanese films of the period include ***Gate of Hell*** (*Jigokumon*, 953) and ***The Snow Heron*** (*Shirasagi*, 1958) by **Teinosuke Kinugasa** and ***Twenty Four Eyes*** (*Nijushi-no hitomi*, 1954) by **Keisuke Kinoshita**.

The recent memory of the Hiroshima and Nagasaki holocaust echoes in the extremely popular disaster thriller ***Godzilla*** (*Gojira*, 1954), shot in a stark black-and-white by **Inoshiro Honda** (1911-93).

ITALY

Federico Fellini (1920-93) begins his film career as a screenwriter in the 1940s contributing to such classics as Rossellini's *Rome Open City* and *Paisan*, and Lattuada's *Without Pity*. In 1954, Fellini writes and directs ***La Strada***, a poetic yet relentlessly brutal story of Gelsomina (**Gulietta Masina**), a simpleminded country girl who is sold to the bestial Zampano (**Anthony Quinn**), a travelling circus strongman. Zampano's continuous abuse and lack of compassion toward Gelsomina gradually take toll on her health, but spiritually the girl remains an embodiment of purity and strength. Ultimately, her unconditional devotion awakens the human being in Zampano.

Anthony Quinn as Zampano
in *La Strada*

Fellini's next picture, ***The Swindle*** (*Il bidone*, 1955), a lyrical tale of two small-time crooks, is enshrouded in an atmosphere of loneliness and despair.

Human compassion is contrasted with ubiquitous egoism in ***The Nights of Cabiria*** (*Le notti di Cabiria*, 1957). As in *La Strada*, the central character of this devastating yet ultimately uplifting movie is portrayed by the charming Gulietta Masina (1920-94), Fellini's wife and muse.

While postwar Italian cinema is generally preoccupied with sociopolitical issues, Michelangelo Antonioni (b. 1912) focuses his attention on the more intimate subject of human psychology and behavior. In **The Girl Friends** (*Le amiche*, 1955), Antonioni analyzes relationships of bourgeois women from Turin, presenting their professional lives and emotional crises with subtle observation and a metaphorical use of scenery.

The tragic and unsentimental **The Cry** (*Il grido*, 1957) tells the story of a factory worker wondering across the barren landscape of the Po Valley with his daughter. Abandoned by his wife, unable to find personal happiness, the protagonist returns to the starting point of his journey only to take his own life.

Il grido

Antonioni's next film, **The Adventure** (*L'Avventura*, 1960), revolves around the fruitless search for a missing woman. The slow, contemplative action is reinforced by Antonioni's extraordinary mise-en-scène which places the protagonists against the unusually inhospitable Mediterranean island and Sycilian backdrops.

Monica Vitti in *The Eclipse*

The Night (*La notte*, 1961) and **The Eclipse** (*L'eclisse*, 1962) continue Antonioni's cycle of films about human alienation and loneliness in the modern, industrialized society. Rather than concentrate on a traditionally structured narrative, Antonioni chooses to tell us about his characters' feelings and emotions. Typical plot lines and dramatic denouements of the action are not the focus of this director's interest.

ANTONIONI'S FILMS SEEM TO BE COMPOSED OF INTERVALS IN THE MAIN NARRATIVE*.

* **Suggested by Umberto Eco**

GREAT BRITAIN

The 1950s bring to the British cinema a significant number of excellent comedies. **Ealing Studios** produces such hits directed by **Charles Crichton** (b. 1910) as ***The Lavender Hill Mob*** (1951) and ***The Titfield Thunderbolt*** (1953); **Alexander Mackendrick**'s (b. 1912) ***The Man in the White Suit*** (1951) and ***The Ladykillers*** (1955) solidify Alec Guinness' career as the most popular performer of his time.

The Lavender Hill Mob

The producer-director team of **John** (1913-85) and **Roy** (b. 1913) **Boulting** creates a series of memorable movies beginning with ***Brighton Rock*** (1947), which stars the very young **Richard Attenborrough** (b. 1923). Their best 1950s titles include ***The Magic Box*** (1951), ***Lucky Jim*** (1957), and ***I'm All Right, Jack*** (1959). The last one stars one of the greatest comedians of the screen, **Peter Sellers** (1925-80), who, with his multiple roles in ***The Mouse That Roared*** (dir. Jack Arnold, 1959), becomes the heir apparent to Alec Guinness.

Robert Donat as the British film pioneer William Friese in *The Magic Box*

Laurence Olivier returns to what he does best: Shakespeare; his ***Richard III*** (1955) is a brilliant spectacle shot in VistaVision.

By far the most unusual movie of the decade belongs to the veteran **Michael Powell**. His *Peeping Tom* (1959), written by **Leo Marks**, is a bizarre yet undeniably compelling allegory on the voyeuristic foundation of cinema. By day, the movie's protagonist Mark, played with an eerie conviction by **Carl Boehm** (Karl-Heinz Böhm), is a **focus puller** for a major film studio. In his spare time, he engages in production of amateur **snuff films**, in which the victims are forced to look at their own agony in a strategically placed mirror. In a disturbing way, Mark's scopophilia and murderous passions embody the essence of cinema—the cold, detached gaze of the camera records life with an unyielding, impersonal accuracy.

The shocking, self-condemning subject matter of *Peeping Tom* results in the end of Michael Powell's career as a filmmaker. Powell, who, along with **Emeric Pressburger**, was responsible for reinvigorating the British film industry after the lean war years (*Black Narcissus*, *The Red Shoes*) is practically banned from his profession and goes into exile.

**Carl Boehm as Mark
in *Peeping Tom***

THE BRITISH NEW WAVE

OR THE "KITCHEN SINK" CINEMA

Dissatisfied with the progressively commercial nature of the British film production, **Lindsay Anderson** (b. 1923) and the Czechoslovakia-born **Karel Reisz** (b. 1926) lay down theoretical foundations for the **Free Cinema** movement. Organizing a series of six film programs shown in London, Free Cinema devotes itself to supporting noncommercial movies which display a high degree of individuality.

In a broader sense, Free Cinema refers to a series of low-budget documentaries influenced by Italian neorealism, which focus on everyday life. By 1959, with the growing popularity of the French New Wave, Free Cinema turns to narrative film and becomes known as the **British New Wave**, or **"kitchen sink" cinema**, because of the working-class environment it portrays.

Tony Richardson (1928-91) adapts for the screen the rebellious hit play by **John Osborne**, *Look Back in Anger* (1959), in which he effectively presents dissatisfaction of the working class with the British establishment.

Room at the Top (dir. Jack Clayton, 1959), based on the novel by one of England's "angry young men," **John Braine**, presents the uncertainties of provincial youth in a fresh, dynamic manner.

Woodfall Films becomes the most influential studio of the New Wave movement. Founded by Tony Richardson and John Osborne (1924-94), it supports projects of ambitious young directors like Reisz, John Schlesinger, Lindsay Anderson, Sydney J. Furie, and Richardson himself.

**Laurence Harvey
in *Room at the Top***

Karel Reisz finds another "angry" literary source in **Alan Sillitoe**'s *Saturday Night and Sunday Morning.* Reisz's version of the book, shot in 1960 on a low budget with unknown actors on location in Northern England, becomes Woodfall's first film completed without a major studio backing.

In 1962, Sillitoe's other groundbreaking novel, ***The Loneliness of the Long Distance Runner***, provides foundation for the Tony Richardson movie of the same name. With its nervous, jittery editing and frequent flashbacks, *Loneliness* becomes one of the most celebrated examples of the "kitchen sink" cinema.

Tom Courtenay in *The Loneliness*

John Schlesinger (b. 1926) leaves his mark on the movement with *A Kind of Loving* (1962) and *Billy Liar* (1963). The latter stars *The Loneliness*'s **Tom Courtenay**.

The brutal, testosterone-driven existence of a minor league rugby player (**Richard Harris**) is presented by Lindsay Anderson in the intense *This Sporting Life* (1963).

SAY YOU HAVE SOME FEELING FOR ME.

Richard Harris as Frank Machin
in *This Sporting Life*

The Leather Boys (dir. S.J. Furie, 1963), considered the last important Woodfall film, focuses on a group of young rebels confined to a dead-end existence by the grim economic reality of England. The movie becomes notorious for its depiction of a homosexual relationship.

SPAIN AND LATIN AMERICA

In the wake of WW II, **Luis Buñuel** leaves his native Spain for New York. Here he begins to edit documentary war films for the Museum of Modern Art and also becomes

a Spanish language consultant for Hollywood studios. After a brief stint as a commercial director in Mexico in the late 1940s, Buñuel creates his first masterpiece, ***The Forgotten Ones*** (*Los olvidados*, 1950). Shot in an utterly realistic style and strongly reminiscent of the neorealist aesthetic, the movie presents problems of troubled Mexico City youth. Unable to rise above the surrounding poverty and filth, the forlorn children turn to violence and crime.

Los Olvidados

In 1952, Buñuel tackles the frequently filmed book *The Life and Strange Surprising Adventures of Robinson Crusoe of York, Mariner* by **Daniel Defoe**. His adaptation, however, puts a new twist on the familiar story of the shipwrecked nobleman—Buñuel's *Robinson Crusoe* mocks the foundations of "civilized" society by allowing the master-servant relationship between Crusoe and Viernes (Friday) to grow into a mature friendship.

Nazarín

Buñuel's *Nazarín* (1958) chronicles the spiritual journey of a Catholic priest who learns that good deeds can also be the roots of evil. Like most of this director's Mexican films, *Nazarín* is photographed with great sensitivity by **Gabriel Figueroa** (b. 1907).

Another important Mexican picture, **Roots** (*Raíces*, **Benito Alazraki**, 1954), is composed of four film novellas depicting lives of Mexican people with nearly ethnographic descriptiveness.

Death of a Cyclist

Juan Antonio Bardem's (b. 1922) *Death of a Cyclist* (*Muerte de un ciclista*, 1953), a tense psychological drama about moral attitudes in postwar **Spain**, becomes this country's first important film of the 1950s. In 1956, Bardem writes and directs *Main Street* (*Calle Mayor*), a sharp denouncement of the provincial Spanish mentality.

Argentinian cinema reaches its heyday with **Leopoldo Torre Nilsson**'s *The House of an Angel* (*La casa del angel*, 1957)—an expressive life story of a sexually frustrated upper class woman.

The Black Orpheus (*Orfeu negro*, Marcel Camus, 1958) is a beautiful **Brazilian** adaptation of the Greek myth set against the great carnival of Rio de Janeiro.

The Girl in Black (*To Koritsi me ta Mavra*, 1955), written and directed by **Michael Cacoyannis**, is the first important **Greek** movie whose fame stretches well beyond the country's boundaries.

In 1951, **Satyajit Ray** (1921-92), a former graphic designer and student of Rabindranath Tagore's, becomes an assistant to Jean Renoir on *The River*. A couple of years later, with his own money, Ray begins to shoot *The Song of the Road* (*Pather Panchali*, 1955), the most celebrated film of his "**Apu trilogy**," which focuses on a young Indian boy's journey into adulthood. The next two installments, *The Unvanquished* (*Aparajito*, 1957) and *The World of Apu* (*Apur sansar*, 1958) are slightly less cohesive in terms of theme and style, but, nonetheless, manage to paint a complex portrait of Indian society inseparably connected to its beautiful, if sometimes cruel, landscape.

The Apu trilogy: childhood, young adulthood, and maturity

Aaejay Kardar creates the first masterwork of the **Pakistani** cinema—*The Sun Raises Over Bengal* (*Jago hua savera*, 1958), which portrays a symbiotic relationship between man and nature.

USA 1960s

One of the first American directors to become involved in low-budget, highly personal film production is **John Cassavetes** (1929-89). A former television actor, Cassavetes directs his first movie, **Shadows**, for thirty thousand dollars with a 16mm camera. Shot in 1958 but re-edited and blown up to 35mm stock a year later for distribution, *Shadows* evolves as a series of spontaneous, non-scripted scenes portraying mulatto siblings as they attempt to assimilate into the hip scene of the New York bohemia. At once a study of interracial dynamics and a moving family drama, *Shadows* anticipates the maturity of cinematic themes in the 1960s.

Cassavetes continues his interest in observing people's behavior at its most vulnerable and intimate moments in **Faces** (1968) and **Husbands** (1970). Both movies are shot almost exclusively indoors, with an intrusive, documentary-style camera work, and rely heavily on the extreme close-up to convey maximum emotional intensity of the characters. In addition to writing and directing, Cassavetes does his own camera work and editing. He thus fully deserves to be named the premier American auteur.

I WANT TRUTH, TRUTH, AND NOTHING BUT THE TRUTH... BUT ONLY AS SEEN BY THE CHARACTERS IN MY FILMS, NOT ME.

John Cassavetes

After directing the multimillion Hollywood production of *Spartacus* (1959-60), **Stanley Kubrick** (b. 1928) focuses on less conventional themes such as male lust confronted with calculated innocence (*Lolita*, 1962) and the absurdity of nuclear tug-of-war between the world's great powers (*Dr. Strangelove; or, How I Learned to Stop Worrying and Love the Bomb*, 1964).

Dr. Strangelove

Always interested in the latest innovations of the cinema medium, Kubrick opts for Super Panavision stock and Cinerama projection to enhance the visual experience of his brilliant sci-fi epic *2001: Space Odyssey* (1968). Itself a product of sophisticated technology (**blue screen**, **travelling mattes**, **scale models**, **front projection**), the movie deals with the potentially disastrous effects of artificial intelligence on human life. Philosophically, however, *2001* becomes an astute, almost nonverbal essay on the ageless question of the origin and destination of our journey as a human kind.

2001: Space Odyssey

135

Alfred Hitchcock decides to open the fifth decade of his creativity with a relatively cheap black-and-white movie deprived of major stars. The result, **Psycho** (1960), is the most terrifying thriller of his entire oeuvre. Set in a remote, middle-of-nowhere motel, this stark story of a sexually repressed serial killer unfolds quietly, with a voyeuristic delight and keen sense of suspense.

OH, MOTHER...

Anthony Perkins in Psycho

In 1963, Hitchcock returns to big budget with **Birds**, an emotionally detached fantasy about a Northern California town attacked by killer seagulls. For its time technically outstanding, *Birds* becomes one of Hitchcock's biggest money-makers but it also marks the decline of his directing prowess.

WE'LL SHOW YOU WHOSE PROWESS IS DECLINING!!

BUT IT'S TRUE!! HITCH WILL NEVER DIRECT A GREAT FILM AGAIN!!

Among the younger directors possessing a unique style and perspective, **Sydney Lumet** (b. 1924) is one of the most prolific and eclectic ones. His *Long Day's Journey Into the Night* (1962) is a fine adaptation of **Eugene O'Neill**'s play; *The Pawnbroker* (1965)—an excellent movie based on the **Edward Lewis Wallant** book—features an unforgettable performance by **Rod Steiger** (b. 1925) in the role of a Spanish Harlem Jewish pawnshop owner haunted by his Auschwitz memories.

It is Lumet who gives **Sean Connery** (b. 1930) the first chance to flex his true acting muscle in *The Hill* (1965), a powerful military prison drama set in North Africa.

Arthur Penn (b. 1926), another energetic director with a television background, scores his first big hit with *The Miracle Worker* (1962). This rather traditionally shot story of a deaf and mute child's road to improvement is graced by the exquisite performances of **Anne Bancroft** (b. 1931) and **Patty Duke** (b. 1946).

Mickey One (1965), an offbeat film featuring **Warren Beatty** (b. 1937) as a celebrity stand-up comedian, indicates Penn's growing interest in anti-establishment subjects.

Bonnie and Clyde (1967) is co-produced by Beatty and directed by Penn with a gusto unprecedented in American cinema. It instantly acquires a cult status among the young audiences who see the rebellious bankrobbers as a metaphor for their growing dissatisfaction with America's involvement in Vietnam.

Warren Beatty and Faye Dunaway as Clyde Barrow and Bonnie Parker

Bonnie and Clyde, thematically a close relative of the 1950 noir classic **Gun Crazy** (dir. Joe Lewis), initiates a series of "outlaw" and "road" pictures of which **Butch Cassidy and the Sundance Kid** (dir. George Roy Hill, 1969) and **Easy Rider** (dir. Dennis Hopper, 1969) become the most popular ones.

Easy Rider, a low-budget independent movie with no recognizable stars, features a pair of social outcasts on a cross-country motorcycle trip. The free spirited outlook of the movie and its clearly defined counterculture attitude strike a chord with audiences worldwide.

The immediate result of *Easy Rider*'s success is, however, a change of Hollywood's perception of viable commodity—suddenly (and briefly), anti-establishment pictures become good business.

WHO'S THAT DUDE HUGGING MY CHOPS?

Prof. Flicker hitches a ride with Peter Fonda and Dennis Hopper in *Easy Rider*

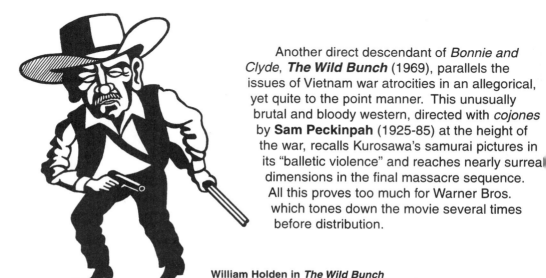

Another direct descendant of *Bonnie and Clyde*, **The Wild Bunch** (1969), parallels the issues of Vietnam war atrocities in an allegorical, yet quite to the point manner. This unusually brutal and bloody western, directed with *cojones* by **Sam Peckinpah** (1925-85) at the height of the war, recalls Kurosawa's samurai pictures in its "balletic violence" and reaches nearly surreal dimensions in the final massacre sequence. All this proves too much for Warner Bros. which tones down the movie several times before distribution.

William Holden in *The Wild Bunch*

From his memorable performance as Billy the Kid in *The Left-handed Gun* (dir. Arthur Penn, 1958), **Paul Newman**'s (b. 1925) most successful roles are antiheroes—people at odds with society and frequently misunderstood or even persecuted for their beliefs. An early archetype of an antihero can be found in *The Hustler* (dir. Robert Rossen, 1961), where Newman portrays a young, talented pool-shark who takes on an aging king of the pool halls (**Jackie Gleason**).

Martin Ritt's superb Texas drama, *Hud* (1963), presents Newman in the title role of a hardheaded, disrespectful son of a cattle farmer, who has a peculiar knack for abusing people. Newman's Hud is a poignant study of a character with no redeeming qualities and whose inherent evil attitude is beyond correction.

In addition to being one of the world's most popular stars, Paul Newman proves he is also a skilled, mature director. His feature film debut, *Rachel, Rachel* (1968), a small town story of a primary school teacher on the verge of spinsterhood, becomes the sleeper hit of the year. **Joanne Woodward** (b. 1930), Newman's real life wife, portrays the title character with a tremendous emotional range and vulnerability.

One of the most charming of the rebellious pictures of the late 1960s is the subversively religious *Cool Hand Luke* (dir. Stuart Rosenberg, 1967). Paul Newman plays a thinly disguised Christ figure confined to a Southern prison for disorderly conduct. His persistent defiance of the authorities and frequent escape attempts bring a spark of life and hope to the fellow inmates.

SOMETIMES NOTHING CAN BE A PRETTY COOL HAND.

Paul Newman as Luke

The antihero emblem is worn best by **Steve McQueen** (1930-80), a vigorous, tough actor whose performances in *Hell Is For Heroes* (dir. Don Siegel, 1962), *The Great Escape* (dir. John Sturges, 1963), *The Cincinnati Kid* (dir. Norman Jewison, 1965), and *Nevada Smith* (dir. Henry Hathaway, 1966) establish him as the new embodiment of "cool."

Newman and McQueen are also responsible for the decade's best detective pictures— *Harper* (dir. Jack Smight, 1966) and *Bullitt* (dir. Peter Yates, 1968), respectively. The latter becomes the first major Hollywood production to be shot entirely on location (San Francisco).

Steve McQueen in *Bullitt*

Another noteworthy throwback to the good days of noir is *Marlowe* (dir. Paul Bogart, 1969), in which **James Garner** (b. 1931) portrays the jaded Chandler detective with a great sense of self-deprecation.

John Frankenheimer (b. 1930), whose past TV experience is similar to Lumet's and Penn's, directs the highly controversial political thriller *The Manchurian Candidate* (1962) a year before the JFK assassination. Startled by similarities between the movie's plot and the conspiracy theories surrounding President's death, the producers decide to withdraw it from distribution.

In *Seven Days In May* (1964), Frankenheimer reflects upon the alarmingly influential position of the U.S. military in its political and economic involvement in the country's everyday life. Frankenheimer's Faustian medical thriller *Seconds* (1966) features Rock Hudson in the most complex role of his career—as the handsome reincarnation of an old banker who attempts to rejuvenate his body and spirit. The truly bizarre, distorted photography by **James Wong Howe** (*Body and Soul*, *Hud*) and the frequently disjointed editing contribute to the paranoid atmosphere of this brilliant film which foreshadows America's upcoming obsession with physical perfection.

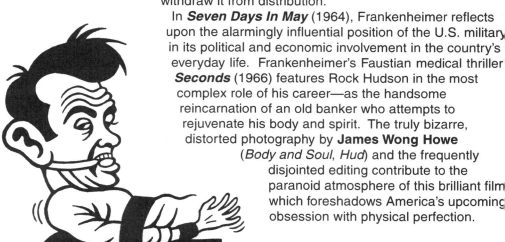

Rock Hudson in *Seconds*

Mike Nichols (b. 1931), a very successful stage director and a part of the sophisticated comedy team Nichols and May, chooses **Edward Albee**'s play *Who's Afraid of Virginia Wolf* for his film directing debut (1966). This largely static film showcases the brilliant talents of Richard Burton and Elizabeth Taylor as the ceaselessly feuding intellectual couple who find escape from reality in alcohol and elaborate, self-deluding mind games.

But it isn't until *The Graduate* (1967), when Nichols taps into the imagination of the masses. This inspired tragicomedy tells a simple story of the complicated love triangle between a recent college graduate (**Dustin Hoffman**),

an older woman (**Anne Bancroft**), and her daughter (**Katharine Ross**). Reinforced by the catchy if somewhat sentimental score by Simon and Garfunkel, *The Graduate* gives the younger generation a resonant voice of protest against their manipulative, calculating parents.

> MRS. ROBINSON, ARE YOU TRYING TO SEDUCE ME?

The most devastating of the "generation" pictures is **Sydney Pollack**'s *They Shoot Horses, Don't They?* (1969)—a tragic, slightly heavy-handed tale of maladjusted young people falling under the pressures of society (personified by the jury of a marathon dance contest).

> THERE'S GOTTA BE A BETTER WAY TO LOSE WEIGHT.

Jane Fonda and Michael Sarrazin in
They Shoot Horses, Don't They?

141

Billy Wilder's witty observations on the contemporary American values find a generous outlet in *One, Two, Three* (1961)—a corporate satire set in Berlin, and *The Fortune Cookie* (1966)—a scheming lawyer comedy. The former features **James Cagney** in his last role before retirement.

Arthur Miller supplies the screenplay for his then-wife Marylin Monroe's vehicle *The Misfits* (1961), directed by **John Huston**. This horse-wrangling drama co-stars Clark Gable in his last screen appearance before death of a heart attack and Montgomery Clift.

Huston's *The Night of The Iguana* (1964), based on the play by Tennessee Williams, delves into the chaotic life of a defrocked reverend, flawlessly portrayed by Richard Burton.

In the audacious but somewhat stereotypical *Reflection in a Golden Eye* (1967), Huston casts Marlon Brando as an army officer with overpowering homosexual desires, whose neglected wife, expertly played by Elizabeth Taylor, seeks comfort in another officer's arms. The timing couldn't be more precise—the film's overtly negative image of the internally decomposing military contributes to growing discontent with the Vietnam situation.

THERE'S NOTHING MORE FASCINATING – AND MORE FUN – THAN MAKING MOVIES. BESIDES, I THINK I'M FINALLY GETTING THE HANG OF IT.

John Huston

In the 1960s, focused more on literary than cinematic pursuits, **Elia Kazan** directs sporadically, though each time the results are outstanding. His *Splendor In the Grass* (1961), adapted from the **William Inge** play, describes psychological effects first sexual experiences have on young people.

Natalie Wood in
Splendor In the Grass

Kazan's next two pictures are based on his own writing: the semi-autobiographical ***America, America*** (1963) recalls the director's Turkish-Greek ancestry; ***The Arrangement*** (1969) paints a complex image of a middle-aged man evaluating his life. **Kirk Douglas** successfully creates one of his most textured performances.

Robert Aldrich continues his career of unpredictable choices with ***Whatever Happened to Baby Jane?*** (1962)—a very disturbing thriller in the noir tradition, featuring two once-glamorous screen divas—**Bette Davis** (1908-89) and **Joan Crawford** (1908-77).

Joan Crawford and Bette Davis in
Whatever Happened to Baby Jane?

Later in the decade, Aldrich scores his greatest financial hit with the relentlessly brutal anti-war movie, ***The Dirty Dozen*** (1967). Released in the heat of the Vietnam conflict, Aldrich's film takes a firm stand on the moral responsibility of military forces.

Richard Brooks directs **Burt Lancaster** (1913-94) in the most extroverted and flamboyant role of his career—the con-man turned revivalist preacher in ***Elmer Gantry*** (1962).

...AND WHEN I'M OLD AND GRAY AND BOOTLESS AND TOOTHLESS, I'LL GUM IT TILL I GO TO HEAVEN AND BOOZE GOES TO HELL!

Lancaster in *Elmer Gantry*

After the superior adventure western ***The Professionals*** (1966), also starring Lancaster, Brooks and screenwriter **Truman Capote** (1924-84) make the most devastating crime-and-punishment movie of the decade (if not the century). ***In Cold Blood*** (1969) is the chilling, true account of two murders—one committed by a couple of small time crooks, the other by the state in its execution of the killers.

Initiated with ***Dr. No*** (dir. Terrence Young, 1962), the **James Bond** series becomes the most profitable and longest running franchise in the history of cinema and a source of numerous less fortunate spin-offs.

The original five *Bonds*, all starring the progressively bored with the part Sean Connery, are produced by **Albert R. Broccoli** and **Harry Saltzman**, the financial backer of the "angry" Woodfall Films.

Inspector Clouseau becomes the comedic answer to James Bond in the **Blake Edwards**-directed series of ***Pink Panther*** movies, starring the chameleon-like **Peter Sellers**.

Before being effectively killed off by a string of disastrous pictures, the musical genre of the 1960s enjoys several highly creative seasons. **Robert Wise**'s and **Jerome Robbins**' dynamic *West Side Story* (1962) takes dancing out of the stale studio settings right into the city turf of New York streets (well, most of them are studio lots, too, but they make a good impression). This blood-and-guts update of *Romeo and Juliet* displays some of the most visceral and energetic dance numbers ever shown on screen.

Contagiously kinetic: Russ Tamblyn and the boys in *West Side Story*

In 1965, Wise returns with **The Sound of Music**, the true story of a musical family escaping the Nazi regime in Austria. The movie, starring the sensational **Julie Andrews**, becomes the highest grossing film to date in the history of cinema.

THE HILLS ARE LIVE WITH THE SOUND OF MUSIC...

Julie Andrews in
The Sound of Music

Other popular titles of the genre include **The Music Man** (dir. Morton da Casta, 1962), **My Fair Lady** (dir. George Cukor, 1964), and **Barbra Streisand**'s spectacular debut, **Funny Girl** (dir. William Wyler, 1968).

Sidney Poitier (b. 1927), virtually the only black actor cast in leading roles in Hollywood-made movies, scores two critical and commercial hits in 1967, ranking him the top male star at the box office (ahead of Paul Newman and Steve McQueen). The first one, *In the Heat of the Night* (dir. Norman Jewison), is a superb thriller in which Poitier plays an urbane Philadelphia detective sent to Mississippi to assist with an investigation being led by a racist cop (Rod Steiger).

Sidney Poitier in
In the heat of the Night

Poitier's second triumph of the year comes with the release of *Guess Who's Coming to Dinner* (dir. Stanley Kramer)—a family drama dealing with issues of cross-racial marriage. Spencer Tracy and Katharine Hepburn pair up for the last time as parents who gradually come to accept their daughter's black suitor (Poitier).

Cinema's most enduring couple: Spencer Tracy and Katherine Hepburn

It takes **Burt Lancaster** and the writer-director-producer team of **Frank** and **Eleanor Perry** three years to release their **John Cheever**-inspired movie, *The Swimmer* (1968). Delay results from the utterly non-commercial nature of Lancaster's character, who represents the emotional and spiritual disintegration of the upper-middle class America.

In 1968, after a noticeable change of pace in the thematic maturity of the mainstream American cinema, the long-lasting **Production Code Administration** is finally replaced by a new rating system implemented by the **Motion Picture Association of America** (**MPAA**):

G—all audiences
M—adults and mature youth
R—restricted to 18 and over
    except when in company of adults
X—18 and over

Before the X becomes a euphemism for pornography, several excellent films are awarded this rating because of their "uncomfortable" portrayal of the American reality of the day.

One of the first is ***Medium Cool***. The real-life riots during the 1968 Democratic National Convention in Chicago serve as a backdrop of *Medium Cool* (1969)—a disturbing movie about the impersonal but potentially manipulative nature of media coverage of political events. **Haskell Wexler** (b. 1926), the experienced Hollywood cinematographer (*Who's Afraid of Virginia Wolf*, *In the Heat of the Night*) directs the film with a fresh, uninhibited realism so uncommon in mainstream pictures; Wexler's frequent use of the ***cinéma-vérité*** (cinema-truth) technique, borrowed from documentary film, enhances the immediacy of the image flow and the utterly authentic feel of the movie.

Another highly innovative X-rated picture of the new American cinema is ***Midnight Cowboy*** (1969), directed by the recently transplanted to America **John Schlesinger**. The film focuses on the relationship between a male prostitute (**Jon Voight**) and a consumptive bum (Dustin Hoffman) as they try to survive the dehumanizing chaos of 1960s New York. It is Schlesinger's uncommonly honest approach to the subject of sex and his unflattering cross-section of American society that result in *Midnight Cowboy*'s dreaded X-rating.

Jon Voight and Dustin Hoffman
in *Midnight Cowboy*

The perennial vagabond of Cinema, **Orson Welles**, manages to put together enough international funds to make two films of exquisite style and substance. In the French-produced version of Franz Kafka's *The Trial* (1962), Welles creates a haunting vision of a metropolis governed by the paranoid laws of technocrats. **Anthony Perkins**, fresh from his demented role in *Psycho*, is cast as Joseph K., *The Trial*'s passive protagonist whose fate is manipulated by the nebulous forces of bureaucracy.

Elements from several plays by Shakespeare form the plot of ***Chimes at Midnight*** (also known as ***Falstaff***, 1966), Welles' triumphal return to his beloved author. The movie's outstanding black and white photography, elaborate crane shots, and toned-down editing contribute to the nostalgic mood of this story of decomposing friendship and war.

A GOODLY PORTLY MAN I'FAITH, AND A CORPULENT...

Sadly, *Chimes at Midnight* is to be Welles' last completed theatrical work. Unable to find producers in the U.S., he continues to scramble for money around the world. He appears in TV commercials, talk shows, and numerous movies of varied quality, working intermittently on several of his own projects, none of which is ever brought to a fully realized form.

Welles as Falstaff

Ray Harryhausen (b. 1920), the master of stop-motion animation technique, contributes his talent to two of the decade's most visually stimulating sci-fi pictures— ***Jason and the Argonauts*** (1963) and ***One Million Years, B.C.*** (1966), both directed by **Don Chaffey**.

The most intriguing sci-fi of the period is the futuristic ***Planet of the Apes*** (dir. Franklin Schaffner, 1968), in which **Charlton Heston**'s spacecraft crashes onto a planet populated by a highly organized, fascist society of primates.

WHERE'S YOUR 12-GAUGE NOW, RIFLE-BOY?

GET YOUR HANDS OFF ME, YOU DIRTY APE!

Heston and his captor in *Planet of the Apes*

Jean-Luc Godard works diligently on becoming the most "incorrigible" of the *Nouvelle Vague* directors. His next films after *Breathless*, **The Little Soldier** (*Le Petit soldat*, 1960), **A Woman is a Woman** (*Une Femme est une femme*, 1961), and **The Soldiers** (*Les Carabinieres*, 1963) by design revolt against cinematic conventions. None of these films, however, contains as much disdain for mainstream cinema values as **Contempt** (*Le Mépris*, 1963)—Godard's first international megaproduction starring **Brigitte Bardot**, **Michel Piccoli**, and **Jack Palance**, with a cameo appearance by **Fritz Lang**, and photographed in widescreen by **Raoul Coutard** (b. 1924).

The brilliantly conceived **Alphaville** (1965) is Godard's first venture into the science-fiction genre, but his approach to the computerized future looks more like an homage to film noir than a slick, high-tech vision. Surprisingly, *Alphaville* displays a strong, nearly traditional (for Godard) narrative format and rather restrained editing.

Eddie Constantine in *Alphaville*

As if to reassure his rebellious nature, Godard's next projects progressively slip into the abyss of self-reflexive cinema. **Pierrot le fou** (1965) is a gangster drama with only the traces of a plot and an abundance of accidental events. In **Masculin/feminin** (1965), Godard abandons virtually all narrative conventions and structures his film as a series of random *cinéma-vérité* interviews with the young French "consumer" generation. Godard's progressively anti-capitalist attitude and markedly Marxist ideology become prominent in **La Chinoise** (1967) and **Weekend** (1967)—his ultimate denouncement of Western civilization as an industrialized form of cannibalism.

MONSIEUR GODARD, DOES A MOVIE HAVE TO HAVE A BEGINNING, A MIDDLE, AND AN END?

WELL, YES, BUT NOT NECESSARILY IN THAT ORDER.

François Truffaut carries the *Nouvelle Vague* torch with **Shoot the Piano Player** (*Tirez sur le pianiste*, 1960), a tribute to American noir. The film's disjointed structure has more in common with Godard's ideology than with **Down There** (dir. David Goodis)—the American B-movie which inspires *Piano Player's* plot.

Jules and Jim (1962), a romantic ménage-à-trois set against the turbulent first decades of the century, marks Truffaut's departure from the program of the New Wave. The film, photographed by his frequent collaborator Raoul Coutard, recalls the French cinematic tradition of poetic realism and is decisively more conservative in its editing and camera work than the director's earlier films.

Like Godard, Truffaut tries his hand at sci-fi; his adaptation of **Ray Bradbury**'s **Fahrenheit 451** (1966) is an intellectual non-action adventure.

Oskar Werner in *Fahrenheit 451*

Truffaut's fascination with Hitchcock results not only in a book-sized interview with the British-American master, but also in the choice of his new movie—**The Bride Wore Black** (*Marié était en noir*, 1967), a well crafted thriller starring the exquisite **Jeanne Moreau** (b. 1928).

Stolen Kisses (*Baisers volés*, 1968) brings back the hero of *400 Blows*, Antoine Doinel (Jean-Pierre Léaud), who now experiences the emotional tribulations of young adulthood.

Jeanne Moreau in *The Bride Wore Black*

"Nature or nurture" is the focus of the fascinating **The Wild Child** (*L'Enfant sauvage*, 1969), in which Truffaut reflects upon the age-old question of what makes man a free human being.

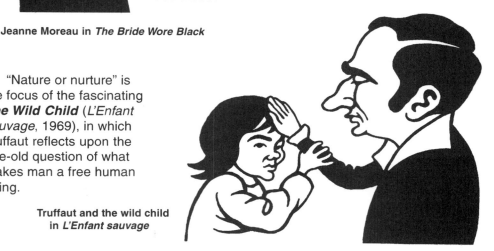

Truffaut and the wild child in *L'Enfant sauvage*

Alain Resnais is responsible for the most enigmatic yet strangely compelling French movie of the decade—***Last Year at Marienbad*** *L'Anneé derniére à Marienbad*, 1961). Eluding all classifications, the film recreates fluidity of thought and memory through the abstract juxtaposition of characters in a geometrically composed environment.

Resnais' next film, ***Muriel*** (*Muriel, ou le temps d'un retour*, 1963), is an elaborate study of a woman and her stepson; each of them confronts demons from the past. On a political level, *Muriel* is one of the most eloquent pictures to question the morality of French involvement in the Algerian war.

In the even more politically committed ***The War is Over*** (*La Guerre est fini*, 1966), Resnais presents a middle-aged Spanish revolutionary whose visit to Paris results in a sudden re-evaluation of his strategies, both as an activist and a human being.

Resnais

Similar to Godard and Truffaut, Resnais is lured by the sci-fi mystique and directs the deeply individualistic and philosophical ***I Love You, I Love You*** (*Je t'aime, je t'aime*, 1968). Influenced by **Chris Marker**'s ***La Jetée*** (1962), a futuristic short composed entirely of still images, Resnais opts for poetic language and a non-traditional, thought-provoking structure which supports well the movie's theme of entrapment in time.

Sidetracked by several purely commercial projects, **Claude Chabrol** makes his *Nouvelle Vague* comeback with ***The Does*** (*Les Biches*, 1968), an audacious lesbian story, and ***The Unfaithful Wife*** (*La Femme infidele*, 1968), an insightful analysis of adultery and its consequences.

The Butcher (*Le Boucher*, 1969), Chabrol's masterful thriller set in a quiet provincial town, chronicles the relationship between a local school teacher and a charming meat shop worker with a penchant for slaying young women. The restrained, precise direction and sustained suspense of *The Butcher* are a direct result of Chabrol's infatuation with Hitchcock. Like every true *cinéaste*, Chabrol elevates Hitch to the Pantheon of cinema gods.

Stéphane Audran in *Le Boucher*

Cléo from Five to Seven (*Cléo de cinq à sept*, 1962), shot by **Agnès Varda** (b. 1928), is an intriguing portrait of a young woman awaiting a verdict of a cancer examination; the movie is one of the best examples of real-time narrative filmmaking, where the on-screen action takes exactly the same amount of time to unravel as it would in real life.

Louis Malle's best film of the 60s, **The Fire Within** (*Le Feu follet*, 1963), describes the downward spiral of a jaded young alcoholic unable to find peace with the world he detests.

The Fire Within

Claude Lelouch (b. 1937) directs the visually innovative romance **A Man and A Woman** (*Un Homme et une femme*, 1966) which features one of the most memorable uses of a popular song in film—*The Girl from Ipanema*.

The theme of psychosis and ensuing madness is prevalent in **Alain Jessua**'s (b. 1932) engaging **Life Upside Down** (*La Vie à l'envers*, 1964) and **The Killing Game** (*Jeu de massacre*, 1967).

On the lighter side of the French cinematic spectrum, **Phillipe de Broca** (b. 1933) directs Jean-Paul Belmondo in the highly popular James Bond spoof **That Man From Rio** (*L'Homme de Rio*, 1964) and creates the brilliant anti-war satire **The King of Hearts** (*Le Roi de coeur*, 1966).

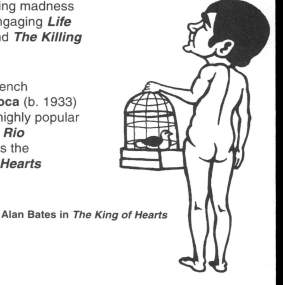

Alan Bates in *The King of Hearts*

Pierre Etaix (b. 1928), a former collaborator of Jaques Tati and actor for Bresson, scores a major European success with **The Suitor** (*Le Soupirant*, 1962) and **Yoyo** (1965)—both shot in the Max Linder/Buster Keaton tradition of comedy.

Pierre Etaix in *Yoyo*

Claire's Knee

Between 1962 and 1972, **Eric Rohmer** (b. 1920) completes a series of six films which comprise his "Contes moraux" ("Moral Tales")— a prolonged dissertation on how human nature is riddled by the conflicting forces of sexual desire and emotional passiveness. The first two installments of the cycle are short films; the remaining four—feature-length. Their respective titles are: **My Night at Maud's** (*Ma nuit chez Maud*, 1967), **The Collector** (*La Collectioneusse*, 1968), **Claire's Knee** (*Le Genou de Claire*, 1969), and **Chloe in the Afternoon** (*L'Amour, l'aprés midi*, 1972).

Jaques Demy's (1931-90) melodramatic **Lola** (1961) recalls in its visual splendor the work of Max Ophüls. In his next two films, Demy pays a tribute to the American musical genre. **The Umbrellas of Cherbourg** (*Les Parapluies de Cherbourg*, 1964) is an inventive, elegantly decorated film with no spoken dialogue—every word is sung. The dance numbers in Demy's **The Young Women of Rochefort** (*Les Demoiselles de Rochefort*, 1966) are choreographed by **Gene Kelly**, whose appearance in the film marks one of his last dancing performances on screen.

Luis Buñuel is finally permitted to direct a movie in his native Spain, which is still governed by the fascist regime of General Franco. Buñuel's choice of material, **Viridiana** (1961), is a perceptive and extremely well executed parody of people who misinterpret Christian values.

Partially because of Spain's outrage over *Viridiana*'s "blasphemous" message, Buñuel returns to Mexico, where he directs **The Exterminating Angel** (*El ángel exterminador*, 1962), a relentless attack on his new favorite subject: the bourgeoisie.

Almost as great a vagabond as Orson Welles, Buñuel arrives in France to direct **Diary of a Chambermaid** (*Le Journal d'une femme de chambre*, 1964), a political statement against fascism, set in the pre-WWII Paris. Often brutal and perverse, the film carefully examines the atmosphere of moral decay which lies at the core of Nazism.

Buñuel's **Belle de Jour** (1967), also produced in France, is a study of sexual obsession full of symbolic, surreal subplots which blur reality and runaway imagination of the protagonist—a beautiful bourgeois housewife who becomes a prostitute to satisfy her peculiar erotic fantasies.

Catherine Deneuve as *Belle de Jour*

153

GREAT BRITAIN 1960s

After the short but prolific period of the British New Wave movement (roughly 1959-63), the core members steer their attention away from gritty working class themes.

Karel Reisz's ***Morgan—A Suitable Case For Treatment*** (1966), a detailed study of a young man's mental decomposition, is generally considered the last gasp of the social realism genre. The "kitchen-sink" film—a bold, black and white picture with industrial settings and blue collar heroes— is gradually replaced by mainstream color productions such as ***Alfie*** (dir. Lewis Gilbert, 1966), a portrait of a small-time crook set in swinging London.

Albert Finney and Joan Greenwood in *Tom Jones*

Tony Richardson focuses on period film; his ***Tom Jones*** (1963) is not, however, a typical costume adventure. Scripted by **John Osborne**, this witty 18th century story of a rambunctious, lusty young fellow owes as much to slapstick as it does to *Nouvelle Vague*.

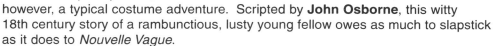

In 1968, Richardson returns to historical setting with the entertaining ***The Charge of the Light Brigade***.

The Innocents (1961), a magnificent adaptation of the **Henry James** novel, ***The Turn of the Screw***, is shot by **Jack Clayton,** who uses a shifting point of view to a great dramatic effect. His next film, ***The Pumpkin Eater*** (1964), written by **Harold Pinter**, also presents a highly individual approach to the art of filmmaking.

The Innocents

154

Before moving to the U.S., **John Schlesinger** directs a couple of sophisticated and enormously popular films: *Darling* (1965) examines the sexual and professional attitudes of a young, attractive woman on a slash-and-burn quest for personal fulfillment; *Far From the Maddening Crowd* (1967) is a visually and textually brilliant adaptation of the **Thomas Hardy** novel. Both films star Schlesinger's muse, the versatile **Julie Christie** (b. 1940).

Julie Christie in *Darling*

The only truly subversive post-New Wave film belongs to **Lindsay Anderson**—his *If...* (1969) is a pronouncedly anti-establishment picture in the tradition of Jean Vigo's *Zéro de conduite* (1933).

**Malcolm McDowell
in *If...***

A blacklisted American director **Joseph Losey** (1909-84), in close collaboration with Harold Pinter, creates exquisite psychological portrayals of the British upper middle-class in *The Servant* (1963) and *Accident* (1967).

MY ONLY AMBITION IS TO SERVE YOU, YOU KNOW THAT, DON'T YOU?

Dirk Bogarde in *The Servant*

155

Another American enjoying a successful directing career in England is **Richard Lester** (b. 1932), who becomes an instant celebrity with ***A Hard Day's Night*** (1964) and ***Help!*** (1965)—two outrageously funny and visually stimulating films featuring **The Beatles**. Lester's skillful use of virtually every cinematic technique ever invented and his uncanny eye for humorous detail rank him as one of the most influential filmmakers of his generation and, as some argue, the inventor of the music video format.

After the superb sex farce ***The Knack*** (1965), Lester directs ***How I Won the War*** (1967), which combines slapstick humor with incisive, thought-provoking observations on military incompetence. Both films feature the agile and charismatic **Michael Crawford** (b. 1942).

Petulia (1968) is one of Lester's infrequent stabs at serious drama; the film's loose narrative style effectively reflects the mental degradation of the protagonists.

John Lennon in *How I Won the War*

Bryan Forbes's (b. 1926) ***Whisperers*** (1966) is a restrained but emotionally charged drama of old age.

Edith Evans in *Whisperers*

Among the more traditional British directors of the period, veteran **Basil Dearden** (1911-71) remains the most consistent in delivering such popular films as ***The League of Gentlemen*** (1960), ***The Mind Benders*** (1963), and ***Karthoum*** (1966).

Dearden's lesser known drama, ***The Victim*** (1961), starring Dirk Bogarde, deals with the tremendous pressure which the conservative British society exerts upon homosexuals.

In the group of the conservative filmmakers, **David Lean** is undoubtedly the most widely popular and respected. His finest films of the decade include *Lawrence of Arabia* (1962) and *Doctor Zhivago* (1965), an adaptation of the **Boris Pasternak** novel.

Stretching the widescreen frame: Peter O'Toole as Lawrence

LEAN'S 70mm SUPER PANAVISION ADVENTURE *LAWRENCE OF ARABIA* RANKS AS THE BEST EPIC FILM EVER MADE AND DISPLAYS THE MOST EFFECTIVE USE OF A WIDESCREEN FRAME TO DATE.

Peter Brook (b. 1925), the famed British theater director, turns **William Golding**'s *The Lord of the Flies*, into a successful movie of the same name (1962).

The politically radical television documentalist **Peter Watkins** (b. 1935) makes his narrative debut with *Privilege* (1967), a fantasy about totalitarian regime in Britain.

Two very exciting British directors who will come to prominence in the upcoming decade make impressive debuts in the late 1960s. The first is **Nicholas Roeg** (b. 1928), a renowned cinematographer (*Fahrenheit 451*, *Petulia*, second unit photography on *Laurence of Arabia*) who co-directs with **Donald Cammell** the disturbing pseudo-documentary *Performance* (1968), featuring **Mick Jagger**.

The second is **Ken Russell** (b. 1927), a former BBC-TV director whose visually brilliant adaptation of **D.H. Lawrence**'s *Women in Love* (1969) garners vast critical acclaim despite rising a few moral eyebrows.

SCANDINAVIA 1960s

In 1963, Sweden restructures the relationship between the state and the private film industry. As a result, enormous distribution taxes are replaced by a much lower fee paid directly to the newly created **Svenska Filminstitutet** (The Swedish Film Institute). Other Scandinavian countries soon adopt a similar model of financing their cinema industry.

In terms of the artistic quality of his movies, **Ingmar Bergman** still remains an unequalled master of the Scandinavian cinema. Early in the decade, Bergman creates the so called "vertical" trilogy—three films unified by the theme of modern man's relationship to god. Not overtly religious, ***Through a Glass Darkly*** (*Såsom i en spegel*, 1961), ***Winter Light*** (*Nattvardsästerna*, 1963), and ***The Silence*** (*Tystnaden*, 1963) function as philosophical probes into the lives of people who find themselves on the brink of spiritual and mental collapse.

Bergman's ***Persona*** (1966) is a visually complex study of the fluid nature of human personality and our ability to assume traits and habits of other people—sometimes consciously, other times out of perversion, and frequently without even realizing it. By opening the movie with an arranged breakdown of the projector and,

Bibi Andersson and Liv Ullmann in *Persona*

later, by superimposing the face of one of the protagonists onto the other, Bergman suggests the fusion of reality with fiction—the illusion of life substitutes for true existence.

Persona is photographed by the outstanding **Sven Nykvist** (b. 1922), Bergman's steady collaborator since *The Virgin Spring*.

In ***Shame*** (*Skammen*, 1968), Bergman explores human behavior under the cruel circumstances of war, when the protagonists' moral and spiritual values are put to the ultimate test.

Bo Widerberg (b. 1930), a former writer and film critic, makes the first Swedish New Wave picture, ***Raven's End*** (*Kvarteret Korpen*, 1963), whose loose structure and spontaneous, episodic narration are borrowed directly from Godard.

Thommy Berggren in *Raven's End*

The Finnish-born **Jörn Donner** (b. 1933), critic, writer, and filmmaker, creates his "horizontal" trilogy— **A Sunday in September** (*En söndag i september*, 1963), **To Love** (*Attälska*, 1964), and **Adventure Starts Here** (*Här börjär äventyret*, 1965). Those films address relationships between individuals of a concrete social environment as opposed to Bergman's "vertical" polemic with God.

Harriet Andersson in *Adventure Starts Here*

In the sensuously photographed **Elvira Madigan** (1969), Widerberg steers away from the avant-garde treatment of contemporary themes. This period drama tells a lyrical, true story of a pair of tragic lovers in the late 19th century, who break away from society to enjoy brief moments of idyllic happiness.

Widerberg's **The Adalen Riots** (*Ådalen 31*, 1968) focuses on the 1931 massacre of striking factory workers in a small Northern town while also paralleling the social situation in contemporary Sweden.

The cinematography of **Finland** reaches its finest hour with **The Diary of Newlyweds** (*Työmieken päivakirja*, 1967) directed by **Risto Jarva** (1934-77). Composed of three parts, the movie revolves around a young married couple of mixed social backgrounds, whose everyday problems expose larger, cross-generational issues.

Frustrations and insecurities of the **Danish** middle-class are exposed in the groundbreaking **Weekend** (1962), directed in the New Wave mode by **Palle Kjaerulff-Schmidt** (b. 1931).

The most notorious picture of the Swedish cinema is undoubtedly the Godard-influenced **I Am Curious— Yellow** (*Jag är nyfiken–gul*, 1967), directed by **Vilgot Sjöman** (b. 1924) with a great sense of humor and irreverence for his country's traditions. Shot in a self-reflexive, movie-about-making-a-movie fashion, *I Am Curious* attempts to eradicate all boundaries between reality and fiction.

Vilgot Sjöman

THE CZECH NEW WAVE

The greatest period of Czech cinema happens in the 1960s and coincides with the liberal socio-political reforms of Party leader **Alexander Dubcek**. His **Prague Spring** campaign attempts to limit Soviet influence in Czechoslovakia.

The famous state-run film school **FAMU**—Film Faculty of the Academy of Performing Arts—is responsible for educating the country's most innovative and prolific directors.

The early 1960s offer several important WWII stories of which *I Survived Certain Death* (*Prezil jsem svou smrt*, Vojtech Jasny, 1960) and *Transport From Paradise* (*Transport z raje*, Zbynek Brynych, 1963) are the most eloquent and expertly handled.

Klos   **Kadár**

The prolific director team of **Ján Kadár** (1918-79) and **Elmar Klos** (1910-93) enters the decade with another unforgettable WWII survival picture, *Death Is Called Engelchen* (*Smrt si riká Engelchen*, 1963).

In 1965 the dynamic duo creates what is considered the key Czech New Wave film, *The Shop on Main Street* (*Obchod na korze*), a profoundly moving WWII story which re-evaluates attitudes of the Czech society toward the Jewish pogrom by the Nazis.

The most famous FAMU graduate, **Milos Forman** (b. 1932), directs his first feature, *Black Peter* (*Cerny Petr*, 1963) in the *cinéma-vérité* style, which fits perfectly with the lighthearted story of generational miscommunications.

Forman's next two projects, *Loves of a Blonde* (*Lásky jedné plavovlasky*, 1965) and *Firemen's Ball* (*Hori, má panenko*, 1967) betray strong influences of the British New Wave in their careful observation of the blue collar environment, but still manage to create a fresh and unique blend of satire and seriousness.

Firemen's Ball

The *cinéma-vérité* aesthetic also permeates the work of **Vera Chytilová** (b. 1929), the most accomplished female director of the era, whose ***Another Way of Life*** (*O necem jiném*, 1963) and ***Daisies*** (*Sedmikrásky*, 1966) portray young city women attempting to understand their place in contemporary society. The bold visual treatment and satirical tone of *Daisies* suggests a rather subversive and destructive answer to the question of female role in urban civilization.

Daisies

Chytilová's ***The Fruit of Paradise*** (*Ovoce rajskych stromu jime*, 1969), reaches surreal proportions in its depiction of male dominance over the world.

Josef Kilián (*Postava k podpírání*, 1963), written and directed by **Pavel Jurácek** and **Jan Schmidt**, is inspired by the writings of Franz Kafka and stylistically affected by German Expressionism.

Another influential Czech New Wave director, **Jaromil Jires** (b. 1935) scans the strata of society in his structurally remarkable ***The First Cry*** (*Krik*, 1963). Jires's brutal ***The Joke*** (*Zert*, 1967), based on a book by **Milan Kundera**, probes the nightmarish reality of the Stalinist years.

The **Bohumil Hrabal** story, ***Closely Watched Trains*** (*Ostre sledované vlaky*), becomes the basis for the outstanding debut film by **Jiri Menzel** (b. 1938). Set during the German occupation, the movie (released 1966) tells the bittersweet story of a young railway guard's first erotic adventures and his accidental involvement in the Resistance movement.

Closely Watched Trains

After a great black comedy, **Capricious Summer** (*Rozmarné léto*, 1967) and a successful musical parody, **Crime in the Nightclub** (*Zlocin v santánu*, 1968), Menzel adapts another Hrabal story, **Larks on a String** (*Skrivánci na niti*, 1969), which is banned for nearly twenty years for its allegorical critique of socialsim.

Menzel in *Capricious Summer*

The Czech New Wave finds its spiritual and moral spokesmen in two FAMU graduates: **Evald Schorm** (1931-81) and **Jan Nemec** (b. 1936).

Schorm's somber **Everyday Courage** (*Kazdy den odvahu*, 1964) presents a young communist activist whose conscience begins to collide with his ideals.

In **Return of the Prodigal Son** (*Návrat straceného syna*, 1966), Schorm portrays a dramatic conflict between a strongly opinionned man and the repressive society which tries to suppress his independent spirit.

Jan Nemec

Nemec's first picture, the harrowing **Diamonds of the Night** (*Démanty noci,* 1964) recounts two Jewish boys' escape from Nazi persecution.

The Party and the Guests (*O slavnosti a hostech*, 1966) is a scathing, allegorical satire on the internal politics of the Communist Party; the film's uncompromising depiction of party members' psychological abusiveness and corruptive practices results in an immediate ban of the film. It is ultimately released in 1968 during the Prague Spring.

Evald Schorm as the guest who refused to be happy in *The Party*

All My Good Countrymen (*Vsichni dobri rodáci*, 1968), written and directed by **Vojtech Jasny** (b. 1925), is universally considered the foremost example of technical ingenuity and thematic audaciousness of the Czech New Wave. Combining traditional poetic realism with dynamic editing and bold camera movement, Jasny recalls the difficul and morally ambiguous period of establishing communist rule in postwar Czechoslovakia

Other notable films of the period include **Deserters and Nomads** (*Zbehovia a pútníci*, Juraj Jakubisko, 1968), and **The Cremator** (*Spalovac mtrvol*, Juraj Herz, 1968).

Tragically, barely over a decade after the bloody suppression of the Hungarian revolution, in August of 1968, tanks of the Warsaw Pact roll into Prague to put an end to one of the most vital and spontaneous outbursts of social reforms and creative forces in postwar Europe.

The state-run cinema industry is split up into several autonomous units of production; each group has its chief director, who supervises the work of his junior colleagues. This model of organization permits Polish cinema to maintain a relative creative freedom. However, since the premature death of Andrzej Munk and the end of the Polish School period (roughly 1956-63), the quality of production rarely reaches its previous standards.

Andrzej Wajda directs the historical epic **Ashes** (*Popioly*, 1965), based on the classic novel by **Stefan Zeromski**. The accidental death of **Zbigniew Cybulski** (1927-57), Poland's most beloved actor, compels Wajda to re-evaluate his emotional approach to cinema in **Everything For Sale** (*Wszystko na sprzedaz*, 1969), which remains one of the most moving exponents of self-reflexive film.

Knife in the Water

Two of the younger generation's best directors, **Roman Polanski** (b. 1933) and **Jerzy Skolimowski** (b. 1938), create their best work outside Poland.

Polanski's remarkable debut feature, **Knife in the Water** (*Noz w wodzie*, 1962), is the director's only Polish film; his next three are produced in England.

The eerie **Repulsion** (1965) chronicles a mental breakdown of a beautiful woman (Catherine Deneuve); **Cul-de-Sac** (1966), a brilliant film noir satire, depicts a strange married couple living on an inhospitable, deserted island. All is turned upside down by the sudden arrival of murderous gangsters on the lam. Polanski's last British film, **The Fearless Vampire Killers** (1967) is a moody parody of horror film.

The outstanding supernatural thriller, **Rosemary's Baby** (1968), becomes his first American production. *Knife In the Water*'s composer **Krzysztof Komeda** provides a haunting score.

Mia Farrow as Rosemary

Jerzy Skolimowski, who co-wrote *Knife in the Water* with Polanski while still at the Lodz Film School, creates his first mature film, **Walkover** (*Walkower*) in 1965. But it is **The Barrier** (*Bariera*, 1966) which seals Skolimowski's status as the most innovative director of his generation.

His last Polish film, **Hands Up!** (*Rece do gory!*, 1967), an imaginative critique of the socialist society, is immediately shelved by the authorities. Skolimowski decides to emigrate.

The Barrier

The most unusual Polish movie of the decade is **The Saragossa Manuscript** (*Rekopis znaleziony w Saragossie*, Wojciech Jerzy Has, 1964), a costume adventure film whose multiple narratives create a complex, deeply textured tale of mystery and romance.

HUNGARY

Around 1962, the stronghold of the **Janos Kádár** leadership begins to slowly subside.

András Kovács

The outburst of artistic activity in the Hungarian cinema can be observed first in the work of **András Kovács** (b. 1925) and **Miklós Jancsó** (b. 1921).
Kovács' **Difficult People** (*Nehéz emberek*, 1964) and **Walls** (*Falak*, 1968) depict the complicated reality of Hungary under the socialist rule. **Cold Days** (*Hideg napok*, 1966), a WWII movie, audaciously confronts Hungary's fascist past and includes the infamous 1942 Novi Sad massacre of Serbs and Jews.

Jancsó first important film, the WWII drama **My Way Home** (*Igy jöttem*, 1964), presents a young Hungarian army deserter on an eventful journey home which proves morally and spiritually disheartening.
Jancsó's **The Round-Up** (*Szegénylegények*, 1965), a historical drama of great pictorial beauty, is based on real-life events from the bloody period of the 1848 revolution. Another historical film, the widescreen masterpiece **Red and White** (*Csillagosok, katonák*, 1967), presents the early days of the power struggle in the postrevolutionary Russia. Both films, exquisitely photographed by **Tamás Somló** (b. 1929), are characterized by long tracking shots and carefully choreographed blocking—the trademark Jancsó techniques.

The Confrontation (*Fényes szelek*, 1969), Jancsó's portrait of the 1947 student unrest, overtly parallels the dramatic 1968 events. Shot in color, the movie displays outstanding composition and orchestration of movement.

Other noteworthy directors who started their careers in the 1960s include **István Szabó** (***Father***/*Apa*, 1966), **István Gaál** (***Baptism***/*Keresztelö*, 1967), **Ferenc Kósa** (***Ten Thousand Suns***/*Tízezer nap*, 1965), and the VGIK-educated **Márta Mészáros** (***The Girl***/*Eltávozott nap*, 1968).

YUGOSLAVIA

The greatest director of the so-called **Novi Film** (New Film) movement, the Yugoslavian New Wave, is **Dusan Makavejev** (b. 1932). His ***Man is Not a Bird*** (*Covek nije tica*, 1966) and ***An Affair of the Heart, or the Tragedy of a Switchboard Operator*** (*Ljubavini slucaj ili tragedija sluzbenice PTT*, 1967) are brilliant satires with an avant-garde streak.

An Affair of the Heart

Kaja, I'll Kill You (*Kaja, ubit cu te*, Vartoslav Mimica, 1967) receives attention for its highly experimental technique and its dissection of Fascism.

Among other interesting films of the period are ***Three*** (*Tri*, 1965) and ***I Even Met Happy Gypsies*** (*Skupljaci perja*, 1967) by **Aleksander Petrovic** (b. 1929) and ***Awakening of the Rats*** (*Budjenje pacova*, 1967) and ***When I'm Dead and Pale*** (*Kad budem mrtav i beo*, 1968) by **Zivoin Pavlovic** (b. 1933).

ROMANIA

Romanian film industry may not be as dynamic as its other Eastern European counterparts, but it nevertheless manages to produce several significant works in the 1960s.

The first major movie to break into the international scene is ***The Forest of the Hanged*** (*Padurea spinzuralitor*, Livin Ciulei, 1965).

Lucian Pintilie

Romania finds its first true auteur in **Lucian Pintilie** (b. 1933), whose ***Sunday at Six*** (*Duminica la ora 6*, 1965) is a story about Resistance shot in a style reminiscent of Alain Resnais' *Hiroshima, mon amour*. In the satirical ***Reconstruction*** (*Reconstituirea*, 1969), Pintilie confronts Romania's national vices with a blend of scathing humor and sobering seriousness.

BULGARIA

Binka Zhelazkova

Rangel Vulchanov's (b. 1928) poignant Cold War drama **Sun and Shadows** (*Slantseto i syankata*, 1962) is one of the first Bulgarian movies to reach international acclaim.

Bulgaria's first woman director, **Binka Zhelazkova** (b. 1923) is one of the most mature and innovative filmmakers of the period. Her **When We Were Young** (*A biiahme mladi*, 1961) is a poetic WWII love story; **The Attached Balloon** (*Privarzaniat balon*, 1966) is an allegorical tale about the inability to escape one's fate.

> ACTUALLY, MY FILM FEATURES A RUNAWAY DIRIGIBLE BALLOON...

Another important movie of the so-called Bulgarian "poetic realism" is **Vulo Radev**'s (b. 1923) **The Peach Thief** (*Kradetsat na praskovi*, 1964), a WWI romance.

The Stalinist-era drama, **Sidetrack** (*Otklonenie*, Grisha Ostrovski and Todor Stoianov, 1967) and the historical epic **Iconostasis** (dir. Todor Dinov and Hristo Hristov, 1969) are among the finest Eastern European movies of the decade.

166

Despite their heavily totalitarian attitude, **Khrushchev** and, later, **Brezhnev** grant Russian artists greater creative freedom than the Stalinist regime. After the outstanding achievements of the second half of the 1950s, the Soviet cinema of the 1960s reaches new heights of excellence.

The Armenian-born, VGIK-trained **Sergei Parajanov** (1924-90) directs his first masterwork, the Carpathian folk tale **Shadows of Forgotten Ancestors** (*Teni zabytykh predkov*, 1964) with a entirely unique cinematic style; it incorporates sweeping 360° camera movements, dramatic changes of focus, and mise-en-scène based on traditional folk tableaux art. The rich color schemes which permeate each frame of the movie play a dramatic part in creating the mystical atmosphere of *Shadows*; this mood is similarly enhanced by the soundtrack, which ranges from religious chants to folk and electronic music.

In **The Color of Pomegranates** (*Sayat Nova*, 1969), Parajanov creates a beautifully stylized biography of the Armenian 18th century poet Sayat Nova. The movie is structured as a series of loosely connected vignettes, each presented in lavish colors and rich symbolic detail which enhance the myth surrounding the poet rather than describe his life realistically.

The Color of Pomegranates

Parajanov's extraordinary imagination doesn't fare well with the authorities—he is gradually removed from active filmmaking, and, in 1974, imprisoned on trumped-up charges.

Andrei Tarkovsky (1932-86), the son of a great Russian poet Arseni Tarkovsky, directs his first independent feature, *Ivan's Childhood* (*Ivanovo detstvo*) in 1962. This stark portrait of a young boy during WWII is praised by Western critics for its evocative, nearly surreal atmosphere.

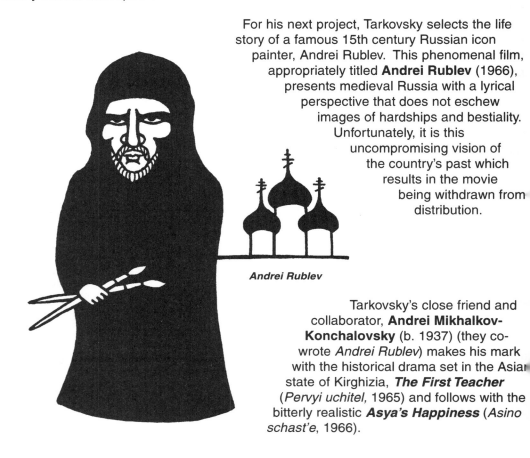

For his next project, Tarkovsky selects the life story of a famous 15th century Russian icon painter, Andrei Rublev. This phenomenal film, appropriately titled **Andrei Rublev** (1966), presents medieval Russia with a lyrical perspective that does not eschew images of hardships and bestiality. Unfortunately, it is this uncompromising vision of the country's past which results in the movie being withdrawn from distribution.

Andrei Rublev

Tarkovsky's close friend and collaborator, **Andrei Mikhalkov-Konchalovsky** (b. 1937) (they co-wrote *Andrei Rublev*) makes his mark with the historical drama set in the Asian state of Kirghizia, **The First Teacher** (*Pervyi uchitel,* 1965) and follows with the bitterly realistic **Asya's Happiness** (*Asino schast'e*, 1966).

Mikhail Romm, Tarkovsky's teacher at VGIK, directs **Nine Days in a Year** (*Deviat' dnei odnogo goda*, 1962); **Mikhail Kalatozov** and **Sergei Urushevski** create **The Letter That Wasn't Sent** (*Neotpravlennoe pismo*, 1960)—both films meet with official criticism due to their "objectionable" depiction of contemporary Soviet society.

Another Romm student, **Vassili Shukshin** (1929-74), follows the auteur path with **There Was a Lad** (*Zhivet takoi paren*, 1964) and **Your Son and Brother** (*Vash syn i brat*, 1966). These insightful portrayals of the Russian rural life are based on a series of Shukshin's own short stories.

Classical literary themes are most interestingly presented by **Sergei Bondarchuk** (1920-94) in the monumental **War and Peace** (*Voina i mir*, 1964-67), with Bondarchuk himself assuming the leading part of Pierre. **Grigori Koznitzev** (1905-73) directs **Hamlet** (*Gamlet*, 1964) and **King Lear** (*Korol' Lir*, 1969).

ITALY

After the twilight of neorealism, Italian cinema becomes increasingly identified with the work of **Federico Fellini**. In the 1960s, the Maestro creates some of the most fascinating films ever to grace the silver screen.

In **La dolce vita** (1960), Fellini offers a rather pathetic vision of the jaded, hedonistic life of Rome's international bohemians. The wonderfully hypnotic mood of the film is accomplished by elevating seemingly normal, realistic events to nearly fantastic proportions—Fellini's most admirable gift as a filmmaker.

A perfect combination of the real, the surreal, and the bizarre forms the essence of Fellini's **Eight and a Half** (*Otto e mezzo,* 1963), a poetic meditation on the process of artistic creation.

Marcello Mastroianni in *Eight and a Half*

Gulietta Masina creates another memorable character as the neglected upper class housewife who descends into a fantasy world in Fellini's **Juliet of the Spirits** (*Gulietta degli spiriti*, 1965).

Fellini Satiricon (1969) is a lavishly produced ancient Roman epic whose extravagant design and multitude of colorful characters underscore the theme of hedonistic decadence.

The remarkable **Nino Rota** (1911-79) enhances all of Fellini's films with beautiful, multilayered musical scores.

Marco Bellocchio's (b. 1939) allegorical **Fist in the Pocket** (*I pugni in tasca*, 1965) is as much impressive as it is disturbing in its portrayal of a maladjusted, angry epileptic young man whose family consists mostly of physically and mentally handicapped individuals.

In **China is Near** (*La Cina é vicina*, 1967), Bellocchio continues his mockery of Italian society, this time taking on the political arena.

Fist in the Pocket

Michelangelo Antonioni enjoys tremendous critical success with his first color film, *Red Desert* (*Il deserto rosso*, 1964), which continues the director's preoccupation with the dehumanizing effects of industrialization. The movie probes the unhappy existence of a factory engineer's wife, who meanders through the unfriendly, foreign landscape of chemical waste in search of her own fulfillment. Antonioni utilizes extremely shallow depth of field (opposite of Welles' deep focus) to accentuate the protagonist's alienation and unrealistic, cold color schemes to manipulate the emotional intensity of individual scenes.

In *Blow-Up* (1966), Antonioni's most popular masterpiece, the convoluted story of an accidental witness to murder is enlarged to a parable of human helplessness in finding objective reality.

David Hemmings in *Blow-Up*

Francesco Rosi (b. 1922) directs the Sicilian folk hero story *Salvatore Guliano* (1962) and follows it with *Hands Over City* (*Le mani sulla città,* 1963), a socially conscious drama revolving around real-estate scams in contemporary Italy.

Pier Paolo Pasolini (1922-75) creates his first work of importance, *The Gospel According to St. Matthew* (*Il Vangelo secondo Matteo*, 1964), using non-professional cast and an informal, pseudo-documentary style of narration.

His *Theorem* (*Teorema*, 1968) and *Pigsty* (*Porcile*, 1969) attack the hypocrisy of the Catholic church and religiousness with a vicious, unrestrained anger.

The Gospel According to St. Matthew

170

The deeply political work of **Gillo Pontecorvo** (b. 1919) reaches its pinnacle with the utmost realistic **The Battle of Algiers** (*La battaglia di Algieri*, 1966), which chronicles the struggle of indigenous Algerians to overcome the French rule. Pontecorvo's **Burn!** (*Queimada!*, 1969) features **Marlon Brando** as a British agent stirring up political unrest on a Portuguese Third World island.

The neorealist veteran **Lucino Visconti** directs his last blue-collar picture, **Rocco and His Brothers** (*Rocco e i suoi fratelli*) in 1960. His **The Leopard** (*Il Gattopardo*, 1962) is a 19th century costume drama set in Sicily during the island's struggle to preserve its independence from Italy. In an unusual but highly effective casting maneuver, Visconti offers the title role of a dignified Sicilian aristocrat to **Burt Lancaster**.

Another former co-founder of neorealism, **Vittorio De Sica**, gives **Sophia Loren** (b. 1934) her first chance to shine as a serious dramatic actress in **Two Women** (*La ciociara*, 1961), a tragic, heartbreaking story of mother and daughter trapped in the maddening reality of WWII. The movie is scripted by Zavattini after a novel by Alberto Moravia.

Sophia Loren and Eleonora Brown in *Two Women*

De Sica's future films carry a significantly less disturbing load—**Marriage Italian Style** (*Matrimoni all'Italiana*, 1964) is an enormously popular comedy starring Sophia Loren and Marcello Mastroianni. In the outrageously funny **After the Fox** (*Caccia alla volpe*, 1966), co-produced with the U.S., De Sica satirizes the Italian film industry by casting **Peter Sellers** in the role of a con-man posing as an intellectual film director.

Among other phenomenally successful Italian films of the era are the spaghetti westerns of **Sergio Leone** (1921-89):
A Fistful of Dollars (1964), **For a Few Dollars More** (1965), and **The Good, the Bad, and the Ugly** (1966), all starring **Clint Eastwood** (b. 1930).

DESPITE ITS PICTORIAL QUALITIES, **A FISTFUL OF DOLLARS** REMAINS AN INFERIOR REPLICA OF THE ORIGINAL AKIRA KUROSAWA WIDESCREEN MASTERPIECE **YOJIMBO**.

Leone's greatest stylistic achievement is **Once Upon a Time in the West** (*C'era una volta il West*, 1969), an epic western with a John Ford touch, carrying the Eastwood-initiated tradition of The Man With No Name.

The inventive composer **Ennio Morricone** (b. 1923) contributes unique, moody soundtracks to all of Leone's movies.

Charles Bronson spots a target in *Once Upon a Time In the West*

Franco Zeffirelli's (b. 1923) **Romeo and Juliet** (*Romeo e Giulietta*, 1968) remains one of the most faithful adaptations of Shakespeare to date.

GREECE

The American outcast **Jules Dassin**, who settles down in Greece, directs his future wife **Melina Mercouri** in **Never on Sunday** (1960), a satirical contemporary comedy.
The most acclaimed film shot in Greece in the 1960s is the international production of **Michael Cacoyannis'** **Zorba the Greek** (1964), based on the novel by **Nikos Kazantzakis**, and features a visceral performance by **Anthony Quinn** in the title role of a simple man with an unquenchable zest for life and a knack for epicurean philosophy.

Akira Kurosawa continues his extremely popular streak of jidai-geki films with *The Hidden Fortress* (*Kakushi toride no san-akunin*, 1958), *Yojimbo* (1960), *Sanjuro* (*Tsubaki sanjuro*, 1962), and *Redbeard* (*Akahige*, 1965). Rigorously formal and magnificently composed, these supremely entertaining pictures stand out as prime examples of widescreen cinema.

Toshiro Mifune handles a foe in *Redbeard*

In 1963, Kurosawa directs the contemporary crime story, *High and Low* (*Tengoku to jigoku*). Planning to kidnap an industrialist millionaire's son, the perpetrators mistakenly abduct the chauffeur's child. The extremely high ransom causes a moral dilemma for the industrialist played by **Toshiro Mifune**: should he risk personal ruin at the cost of saving his low-level employee's son? The ensuing drama involves a painstaking police crackdown on the criminals, which gives Kurosawa an opportunity to penetrate all strata of the economically unbalanced Japanese society. Shot in widescreen format, the black-and-white *High and Low* proves that a socially committed drama and an intense crime story not only may coexist in film but may also unite into a masterpiece of magnificent complexity.

Mifune in *High and Low*

Visual restraint and sparse, ascetic editing mark **Yasujiro Ozu**'s last cycle of his meditation on life and perishing traditional values in contemporary Japan: *Late Autumn* (*Akibiyori*, 1960), *The End of Summer* (*Kohayagawa-ke no aki*, 1961), and *An Autumn Afternoon* (*Samma no aji*, 1962).

The frequently adapted story of 19th century family revenge, **An Actor's Revenge** (*Yukiniojo hengei*), finds its greatest screen representation in **Kon Ichikawa's** sumptuously photographed 1963 film of the same title.

Masaki Kobayashi pitches individual independence against the despotic feudal society in the grim **Hara Kiri** (*Seppuku*, 1962) and **Rebellion** (*Joi-uchi*, 1967).

Between these two films, Kobayashi creates in **Kwaidan** (1964) a richly woven anthology of ghost stories shot in breathtaking color and widescreen format.

Akira Ishihama in *Hara Kiri*

The Japanese cinema reaches its own brand of New Wave with **Hiroshi Teshigahara's** (b. 1927) **Woman in the Dunes** (*Suna no onna*, 1964), a starkly beautiful, existential parable.

Woman in the Dunes

Susumu Hani's (b. 1928) innovative **The Inferno of First Love** (*Hatsukoi jigoku-hen*, 1968) follows the love story of a contemporary teenage couple to its sad conclusion.

Masashiro Shinoda (b. 1931) rises to prominence as the New Wave director of *Assassination* (*Ansatsu*, 1964), a study of violent feudal politics, and the brilliantly conceived tragic romance, *Double Suicide* (*Shinju ten no amijima*, 1969), whose action unravels according to the principles of the traditional Bunraku puppet theatre.

Double Suicide

Shohei Imamura (b. 1926), a former Ozu collaborator, remains one of the most consistent of the Japanese New Wave directors. The *cinéma-vérité* style permeates Imamura's *Intentions of Murder* (*Akai satsui*, 1964), a bold treatment of the demoralizing effects of rape. His *The Insect Woman* (*Nippon konchuki*, 1964) parallels prostitution with modern Japan's rapid rise to economic prominence. The grotesque, visually arresting *The Pornographers* (*Jinruigaku nyumon*, 1966) is another of Imamura's scathing contemporary allegories which presents a respectful middle-class family man engaged in the production of pornography.

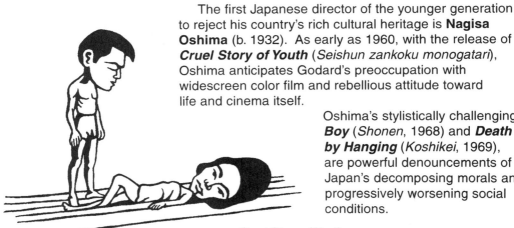

The first Japanese director of the younger generation to reject his country's rich cultural heritage is **Nagisa Oshima** (b. 1932). As early as 1960, with the release of *Cruel Story of Youth* (*Seishun zankoku monogatari*), Oshima anticipates Godard's preoccupation with widescreen color film and rebellious attitude toward life and cinema itself.

Oshima's stylistically challenging *Boy* (*Shonen*, 1968) and *Death by Hanging* (*Koshikei*, 1969), are powerful denouncements of Japan's decomposing morals and progressively worsening social conditions.

Cruel Story of Youth

SOUTH AMERICA 1960s

ARGENTINA

The end of the increasingly dictatorial **Peron** era in Argentinian politics (1955) marks a new beginning for the country's aching cinema industry. One of the first directors of international importance is **Leopoldo Torre Nillson** (1924-78) whose *The Fall* (*La caída*, 1959) and *The Hand in the Trap* (*La mano en la trampa*, 1961) deal with the mendacity of the bourgeois environment.

Fernando Birri (b. 1925), a famed Argentinian documentalist, directs his neorealistic *Flooded Out* (*Los inundados*, 1962), which becomes the thematic foundation for many films of the fledgling *nuevo cine* (new cinema) movement.

One of the pioneers of the European-influenced *nuevo cine* is **Manuel Antín** (b. 1926) who directs the **Julio Cortázar**-scripted *The Odd Number (La cifra impar*, 1961) and *Circe* (1962). Other acclaimed pictures of the movement are *Shunko* (1960) and *Little Gardel* (*Alias Gardelito*, 1961), both by **Lautaro Marúa**, and *Chronicle of a Boy Alone* (*Crónica de un nino solo*, Leonardo Favio, 1965).

The highly political group of the Argentinian **Cine Liberación** movement of the late 1960s creates the avant-garde three-part docudrama, *The Hour of the Furnaces* (*La hora de los hornos*, Fernando Solanas and Octavio Getino, 1968), and influences such films as *Invasion* (*Invasión*, Hugo Santiago, 1968) and *The Road Toward Death of the Old Reales* (*El camino hacia la muerte del Viejo Reales*, Gerardo Vallejo, 1969), which display a revolutionary agenda.

The Hour of the Furnaces

CUBA

A country with a strong Soviet-influenced documentary tradition, Cuba of the 1960s produces several politically-infused narratives. Among them, the most acclaimed is *Lucia* (dir. Humberto Solás, 1968), a monumental three-part epic devoted to various facets of Cuban's colorful political history in the 1890s, 1930s, and 1960s.

Lucia

Other artistically accomplished Cuban films of the late 1960s are the contemporary bourgeois critique, *Memories of Underdevelopment* (*Memorias del subdesarollo*, Tomás Guitiérrez Alea, 1968) and *The First Charge of the Machete* (*La primera carga al machete*, Manuel Octavio Gómez, 1969), a chronicle of the 1868 war for Cuban independence from Spain.

BRAZIL

The socially conscious *cinema novo* (new cinema) of Brazil draws its inspiration from the Marxist foundations of the neorealists and absorbs certain stylistic elements of the *Nouvelle Vague*. The first internationally recognized entry of that movement is *Pagador de Promessas* (dir. Anselmo Duarte, 1962).

The prominent *cinema novo* figure, **Glauber Rocha** (1939-81), directs the revolutionary story of a peasant rebellion, **Black God, White Devil** (*Deus e o diablo na terra do sol*, 1964). Other notable films with similar themes include **Barren Lives** (*Vidas secas*, Nelson Pereira dos Santos, 1963) and **The Guns** (*Os fuzis*, Ruy Guerra, 1964).

Rocha's **Land in Anguish** (*Terra en transe*, 1967) shifts its focus to the political conscience of the urban-intellectual environment.

Black God, White Devil

BOLIVIA

The single most influential picture to emerge out of this small Andean country is **Blood of the Condor** (*Yawar mallku*, Jorge Sanjinés, 1969), a neorealist treatment of the native Indians' plight for survival in the face of Peace Corps-sponsored sterilization.

Blood of the Condor

USA 1970s

The antiestablishment attitudes of American cinema of the late 1960s spill over into the new decade. The **Johnson/Nixon** administration continues to keep American troops in Vietnam, but the war now has very little public support. The high-profile assassinations of Robert Kennedy and Dr. Martin Luther King, Jr. increase the nation's mistrust of the government.

The sentiments of the younger generation of Americans are represented best in **Arthur Penn**'s counterculture satire, ***Alice's Restaurant*** (1969), which portrays the once-idealistic antiwar movement as disillusioned, cynical people with no clear plans for the future. The film is based on a song by **Arlo Guthrie**, a popular Woodstock-era folk singer-songwriter, who also portrays one of the central characters in the movie.

Penn continues his rebellious, uncompromising analysis of American history with one of the first revisionist westerns—***Little Big Man*** (1970). This epic film stars the magnificent **Dustin Hoffman** as a 121-years old frontiersman recalling his involvement in most of the famous and infamous episodes of the Old West.

Another outstanding anti-western which presents the drama of Native Americans with an honest and sympathetic approach is ***Soldier Blue*** (dir. Ralph Nelson, 1972). Its climactic massacre of the Indians by a Calvary unit, based on the historical Sand Creek event, remains unparalleled in its directness and devastating brutality.

Given the Native American takeover of Alcatraz Island (1970) in a symbolic gesture of recapturing their lost heritage and the Wounded Knee protest (1973), both of which resulted in a forceful government intervention, *Little Big Man* and *Soldier Blue* should be regarded as extremely valid (and rare) examples of Hollywood's involvement in a rightful political cause. However, one must remember that the late 1960s-early 1970s era is an unprecedented period of strong creative personalities, and Hollywood's initial support of directors like Penn or Robert Altman was only possible because of the viable commodity their uncompromising attitude represented. As soon as their thought-provoking movies ceased to rake in the bucks, Hollywood shifted its attention to another 1970s phenomenon—the blockbuster picture.

Robert Altman's (b. 1925) *M*A*S*H* (1970), a Korean War farce with obvious references to Vietnam, breaks the creative grounds on several levels. It is the first major American film to incorporate an ensemble cast as opposed to one or two central characters. Its structure deliberately lacks a main plot line and revolves around a series of loose episodes shot with voyeuristic delight. Altman also develops a new approach to sound editing, shifting the audio-focus from one plane of action to another within a single shot (**subjective sound**).

Donald Sutherland and Elliott Gould in *M*A*S*H*

Altman's next films confirm his unique talent for turning American iconography upside down. The unusual western ***McCabe and Mrs. Miller*** (1971) is a satire on the nature of independent entrepreneurship and corporate imperialism set in snow-covered, rain-soaked Washington State. The movie features the quintessential Penn antihero, **Warren Beatty** (*The Mickey One*, *Bonnie and Clyde*), as the shrewd but unfortunate businessman McCabe.

In ***The Long Goodbye*** (1973), Altman puts a new spin on Raymond Chandler's detective Philip Marlowe, played here with an easygoing, exaggeratedly detached manner by **Elliott Gould** (b. 1938). Along with Penn's exquisite ***Night Moves*** (1975), *The Long Goodbye* represents the best of the revisionist film noir—a complex, nearly paranoid crime scheme strongly rooted in the contemporary Watergate reality of betrayal.

Altman's most socially committed work of the period is ***Nashville*** (1975), an informal, episodic epic on America's preoccupation with fame and success, both of the pop-cultural and the political nature, and the country's astonishing refusal to re-examine its own recent past.

PERHAPS NOT SO COINCIDENTALLY, *NASHVILLE* IS RELEASED IN TIME FOR AMERICA'S 200th BIRTHDAY.

One of the most intense pictures to evaluate class-differences in the contemporary America is **Bob Rafelson**'s *Five Easy Pieces* (1970), an allegorical portrayal of a dysfunctional family.

Joe (dir. John G. Avildsen, 1970) paints a distressing image of the descent of young people into drugs and the even more disturbing reaction of the older generation.

In early 1970s cinema, the most straightforward rebellion of an individual against the establishment is *The Vanishing Point* (dir. Richard Sarafian, 1971), a suicidal car-driving *Easy Rider* spin-off.

Peter Bogdanovich (b. 1939), the author of the serial killer cult classic, *Targets* (1968), creates his first masterwork, the black-and-white *The Last Picture Show* (1971), a moving and universal portrayal of teenagers from a small Texan town of the 1950s.

**Timothy Bottoms and Cloris Leachman
in *The Last Picture Show***

The mainstream *Paper Moon* (1973), Bogdanovich' next film, stands out as a true artistic accomplishment of Hollywood. The film teams up the real-life father and daughter duo of **Ryan** and **Tatum O'Neal** as Depression-era partners in the fine art of survival.

Ironically, the most acute analysis of the American psyche of the era can be found in the work of a Czech filmmaker. **Milos Forman**'s first American film, *Taking Off* (1971), is a satirical New Wave look at middle-class parents who attempt to emulate their children's experimentation with sex, drugs, and rock'n'roll.

Forman's next film, *One Flew Over the Cuckoo's Nest*, (1975) an adaptation of the Merry Prankster **Ken Kesey**'s novel, becomes an instant classic of cinema. Constructed as a beautiful metaphor for freedom, the movie deals with an unruly patient's incessant desire to break out of the confining walls of a mental institution.

In 1979, Forman successfully adapts for the screen the hit Broadway musical, *Hair*, which presents the hippie peace movement of the Vietnam era with honest exuberance.

Doing what comes naturally: Jack Nicholson in *Cuckoo's Nest*

The first outstanding Broadway musical adaptation of the decade, though, belongs to **Bob Fosse** (1927-87), whose human, gritty *Cabaret* (1972) describes the seedy world of entertainment in Germany at the gate of fascism.

Liza Minnelli and Joel Grey on stage in *Cabaret*

LIFE IS A CABARET, OL' CHUM, SO COME TO THE CA-BA-RET!

In 1974, Fosse directs a brilliant biography of the doomed stand-up comedian Lenny Bruce, *Lenny*, which allows the versatile Dustin Hoffman to reach new artistic heights.

All That Jazz (1979) is Fosse's semi-autobiographical account of the unbelievably prolific life of a Broadway entertainer, choreographer, and film director, portrayed with subdued emotion and great charm by **Roy Scheider** (b. 1935). *All That Jazz*'s multilayered structure, its heavy reliance on flashbacks and flashforwards, the use of surreal elements bleeding increasingly into reality, and the rhythmic heartbeat of the score, rank Fosse's film as one of the key artistic triumphs of American cinema.

*#&!%$$‡**!!

Dustin gets dirty in *Lenny*

After the outrageous, life-affirming *Harold and Maude* (1971), **Hal Ashby** (1929-88) creates his first important picture dealing with the contemporary American conscience— *The Last Detail* (1973), a not-so bright episode from the life of Navy sailors.

But it is not until his *Coming Home* (1978), when Ashby's perceptiveness and unmitigated honesty reach their finest hour. This superbly acted film (**Jane Fonda**, **Jon Voight**, **Bruce Dern**) is the first and arguably best mainstream Hollywood production to face the consequences of the Vietnam War on individual participants and their families.

Bruce Dern in
Coming Home

Adapted from the **Jerzy Kosinski** novel, Ashby's *Being There* (1979), a poetic satire on the adoration of innocence in life and politics, features **Peter Sellers** in his last screen appearance—a great exit for one of cinema's most talented performers.

During the actual years of military conflict between Vietnam and the U.S., only one Hollywood film is produced on the subject—the propagandistic John Wayne vehicle *The Green Berets* (dir. J. Wayne, 1968). It is not until several years after the fall of Hanoi and the withdrawal of U.S. troops from Vietnam that the first realistic pictures about the war and its aftermath begin to emerge.

The first Vietnam combat picture, the little seen *Go Tell the Spartans* (dir. Ted Post, 1978), presents a grim, unglamorous vision of U.S. military outfit's road to failure in the early stages of the conflict. As the doomed platoon's leader, **Burt Lancaster** creates here one of the strongest performances from the later stages of his long career.

The immensely popular *The Deer Hunter* (dir. Michael Cimino, 1979) contrasts the lives of a group of friends before and after their traumatic participation in the war. As with *Coming Home*, *The Deer Hunter* deals more with the process of the emotional healing of veterans than the actual combat.

Christopher Walken in
The Deer Hunter

Karel Reisz, of British New Wave fame, directs the great allegorical picture, *Who'll Stop the Rain* (1978), based on the **Robert Stone** bestseller *Dog Soldiers*. Structured as a modern-day western, the movie vividly examines the post-Vietnam period of disenchantment and anguish, and persistently questions the government's integrity.

Shortly after the Watergate scandal, Hollywood releases a series of excellent conspiracy thrillers which further undermine the already shabby credibility of the country's political leadership. The best of the lot are two films by **Alan J. Pakula** (b. 1928): *Parallax View* (1974) and *All the President's Men* (1975); both are structural descendants of the newspaper genre of the 1930s.

The former casts Warren Beatty as a reporter trailing the crime syndicate responsible for a series of political assassinations. The latter chronicles the famous Woodward/Bernstein investigation into the abuses of power in the Nixon administration.

SOMETHING IS ROTTEN IN THE STATE OF D.C.

**Robert Redford as Bob Woodward
in *All the President's Men***

Pakula is also responsible for one of the decade's best detective thrillers, *Klute* (1971)—a dark, creepy exploration of society's seedy underbelly.

Incest, corruption, and murder rise to the surface of the world of politics and high finance in **Roman Polanski**'s extraordinary *Chinatown* (1974), a stylish, 1930s thriller superbly written by **Robert Towne**. By casting **John Huston** as the omnipotent patriarch of evil, "bad girl" **Faye Dunaway** as his daughter, and the irreverent **Jack Nicholson** as the weathered gumshoe, Polanski skillfully manages to rehash traditional film noir themes, reinvent the antiestablishment rebellion, and top it all off with a dose of sarcasm and general disillusionment so pervasive in contemporary America. As a result, *Chinatown* manages to transcend the very components of popular mythology that create its glossy surface and offers the ultimate exposition of the American Dream's rotten core.

Faye Dunaway
in *Chinatown*

The outstanding, moody photography of the picture is that of **John A. Alonzo** (b. 1934), whose work also includes *Harold and Maude* and *The Vanishing Point*.

Since the smash success of *Bullitt*, the detective genre enjoys a steady flow of films which present a more questionable image of the strong arm of the law.

In the morally ambiguous ***Dirty Harry*** (dir. Don Siegel, 1971), a police detective, played with maximum emotional restraint by **Clint Eastwood**, deals his own brand of justice: his weapon speaks more often than his character. The title of the movie's sequel, ***Magnum Force*** (dir. Ted Post, 1973), needs no further explanation. Harry Callahan's (Eastwood) crime-fighting methods are not far removed from the psychosis of the villains he disposes of with frightening efficiency.

DO YOU FEEL LUCKY, PUNK? WELL, DO YOU?

RELAX, CLINT. THEY'RE JUST READERS.

Urban crime is portrayed to a much greater effect in **William Friedkin**'s (b. 1939) *The French Connection* (1971), a highly kinetic police drama set in the violent streets of New York City. Aside from his expert handling of the action's pace, Friedkin resorts to several visual techniques to enhance the movie's tension. One of them is **rack focusing** (or **selective focusing**), which permits the director to isolate particular aspects of the action through shifting the planes of focus within a single shot. This technique allows for establishing a cause-and-effect relationship between two or more elements in a scene.

Gene Hackman in *The French Connection*

The rack-focus effect can be achieved best with a **telephoto lens**—a lens with a long **focal length**, which yields less depth of field than a wide-angle lens.

LENS EFFECTS

WIDE-ANGLE	TELEPHOTO	FISH-EYE

- all distance planes in focus (great depth of field)
- wider range of view

- everything but the point of focus remains blurred
- perspective of distance planes is flattened (low depth of field)
- narrow range of view

- extreme sphere distortion of picture

When used in proper narrative context, lens effects may create or enhance the desired psychological impact of a scene.

The **zooming effect**—a quick close-up or pullback achieved by a dramatic change of the focal length on a **zoom lens**, is the most frequently abused technique in the cinema of the 1970s. Many low-budget filmmakers use the slow zooming effect to substitute for the dolly-in or out effect, which requires more equipment.

One of the few sequels to equal the original, ***The French Connection II*** (dir. John Frankenheimer, 1975), transports its protagonist, again played with detailed perfection by **Gene Hackman** (b. 1931), to Europe where he investigates a heroin-smuggling ring.

Other absorbing detective pictures of the decade are ***Serpico*** (dir. Sydney Lumet, 1973) and ***Cruising*** (dir. William Friedkin, 1980). Both films feature the quintessential star of the period—**Al Pacino** (b. 1940), as an undercover NY police office obsessed with his investigation: police corruption and gay serial killings, respectively.

Sydney Lumet continues to make strong, socially committed pictures which deal with various aspects of American urban life— ***Dog Day Afternoon*** (1975) and ***Network*** (1976 are both black comedies based in New York. Scripted by *Marty*'s Paddy Chayefsky, *Network* carries the torch lit by *Ace in the Hole* and *A Face in the Crowd*; its uncompromising, no-holds-barred attack on profit-driven mentality and absolute lack of scruples of the syndicated television ranks the film as one of cinema's most potent and entertaining allegories on the perverted, out of control entertainment imperialism.

Victory for the underdog:
Al Pacino in *Dog Day Afternoon*

HE LOOKS LIKE HE'S MAD AS HELL AND HE'S NOT GONNA TAKE IT ANY MORE...

Peter Finch loses it in *Network*

After his critical and financial success with *The French Connection*, Friedkin elevates the horror genre to a new level of disgust with ***The Exorcist*** (1973), one of the first blockbusters of the 1970s.

Other inherently New York director is **Paul Mazursky** (b. 1930), whose unsentimental, often humorous psychological portrayals of different facets of urban existence find their greatest representation in *Harry and Tonto* (1974), *Next Stop, Greenwich Village* (1976), and *Unmarried Woman* (1978). The latter is a perceptive study of human relationships and takes an optimistic look at divorce as the only option for saving one's sanity.

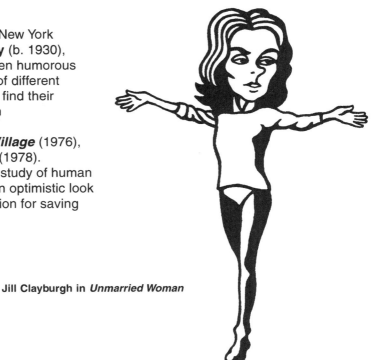

Jill Clayburgh in *Unmarried Woman*

The most poetic and nostalgic look at America's past is provided by two films of the writer-director **Terrence Malick** (b. 1945). His *Badlands* (1973) takes an ironic approach to the youthful rebellion of the 1950s, while *Days of Heaven* (1978) chronicles the pioneer struggle in the Old West. Both films incorporate voice-over narration by teenage protagonists and contrast lavish open-air vistas with themes of violence.

Another ironic commentator on American history, the veteran **Sam Peckinpah**, continues to subvert popular mythology with such anti-westerns as *The Ballad of Cable Hogue* (1970) and *Pat Garrett and Billy the Kid* (1973). His solid contemporary crime dramas, *The Getaway* (1972) and *Bring Me the Head of Alfredo Garcia* (1974), resort to absurd amounts of violence to underscore the darker, psychotic aspects of America's reality.

GOTTA RAISE ME SOME HELL!

Sam Peckinpah

Early in the decade, a new breed of young, creative talent enters the motion picture arena—the first generation of American filmmakers to receive formal education in cinema at one of the country's recently created film schools (**UCLA**, **NYU**, **USC**).

Among the most influential individuals in that group are **Francis Ford Coppola** (b. 1940), **Martin Scorsese** (b. 1942), **George Lucas** (b. 1944), and **Steven Spielberg** (b. 1946).

After an early apprenticeship with the B-movie king **Roger Corman** (b. 1926), the UCLA-trained Coppola directs the low-budget *The Rain People* (1969), an intriguing, offbeat road movie with a strong feminist theme. Already an established Hollywood screenwriter (*Patton*), with a few mainstream directorial credits, Coppola begins to work on the **Mario Puzo**-written Italian-American Mafia epic, *The Godfather* (1972). Directed with the sure hand of a seasoned pro, the film displays a rigorous, formal composition punctuated by outbursts of dynamic montage in the superbly staged scenes of physical violence.

Coppola's tremendous success with the movie (it becomes, briefly, the top grossing film of all time) continues with the equally brilliant sequel, *The Godfather, Part* (1974), which incorporates an innovative use of parallel narration. Besides the obvious historical merits of the *Godfather* saga, both masterpieces explore the psyche of an individual trapped between the ethics of business and personal morality.

Coppola's engrossing *The Conversation* (1974) is a detailed study of a bugging expert's (Gene Hackman) descent into paranoia. The movie's outstanding manipulation of sound parallels the complexity of image manipulation in Antonioni's *Blow-Up* (1966).

**Marlon Brando
as the Godfather**

In 1939, the young, pre-*Kane* Orson Welles began the intensive preproduction work on what was to be his first movie—an adaptation of Joseph Conrad's **Heart of Darkness**. Realizing the puzzling, ahead-of-its-time complexity of Welles' vision, the studio (RKO) pulled the plug on the project.

In 1976, Francis Coppola embarks on a three-year odyssey to bring Conrad's novel to the screen. This time, however, the screenplay, written by another film school graduate, **John Millius** (b. 1944), shifts the original setting of the story from Africa to war-torn Vietnam. The result, appropriately titled **Apocalypse Now** (1979), is an operatic, breathtaking masterpiece with unmitigated violence reaching nearly abstract proportions. Many Vietnam veterans will testify that no other picture on the subject has ever before or since been able to approximate so well the horrors of that war and convey the utter physical and emotional chaos of its participants.

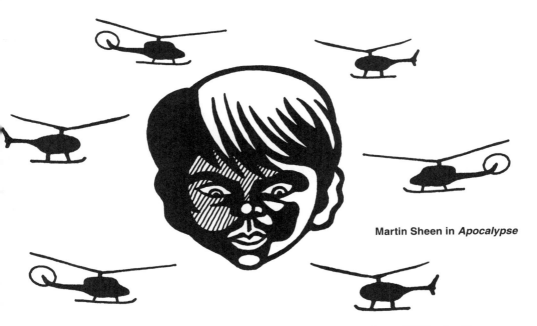

Martin Sheen in *Apocalypse*

Partial credit for *Apocalypse*'s artistry is due to the genius of **Vittorio Storaro** (b. 1940), the famed Italian stylist of light who photographed such visually enticing pictures as *The Conformist* and *The Last Tango in Paris*.

MY MOVIE IS NOT ABOUT VIETNAM. IT *IS* VIETNAM.

Francis Coppola

Martin Scorsese, a graduate of the NYU film school, begins his directing career with the ultra low-budget *Who's That Knocking On My Door* (1969), a fine debut in the *Nouvelle Vague* tradition, with noticeable influence from Cassavetes. After a stint at the Roger Corman "stables", where he directs the outlandish exploitation flick, *Boxcar Bertha* (1972), Scorsese makes his first mature film, *Mean Streets* (1973). Like most of his movies, *Mean Streets* is rooted in the violent, blue-collar environment of Brooklyn and features Italian-American protagonists torn between a life of crime and Catholic guilt. Aside from some expressive camera movements, the movie's key innovation is the soundtrack of rock tunes spilling out of car radios and jukeboxes in almost every scene, juxtaposed with traditional Italian feast music pumping into the night from the loudspeakers of the San Gennaro celebration.

In an atypical move, Scorsese places the action of his next picture, *Alice Doesn't Live Here Anymore* (1974) in the Southwest. It is a story of a hard-working, blue-collar single mother (**Ellen Burstyn**) who attempts to take control over her troubled life.

I'VE GOT SOME BAD IDEAS IN MY HEAD.

Robert de Niro
in *Taxi Driver*

For his next project, Scorsese reaches for the super screenplay by **Paul Schrader** (b. 1946) called *Taxi Driver* (1976). Like *Mean Streets*, the movie presents the darker side of New York's night life, delving deep into the world of child prostitution, psychopaths, drug abuse, and violent crime. The remarkable **Robert de Niro** (b. 1943) is cast as Travis, an insomniac Vietnam veteran unable (or unwilling) to adjust to the surrounding world of scum. Travis' mission in life becomes the rescue of an adolescent hooker (**Jodie Foster**) kept on the streets by her abusive, dope-smoking pimp (**Harvey Keitel**).

On the technical level, *Taxi Driver* displays extremely well-planned, fluid camera work which probes the seedy, evil environment with an eerie intimacy. The moody, lamenting soundtrack is supplied by the great **Bernard Hermann** (*Citizen Kane*, *Psycho Fahrenheit 451*), who dies shortly after the film's completion.

Paul Schrader, himself a graduate of UCLA, directs several interesting movies including *Blue Collar* (1978), an auto industry caper about assembly-line workers attempting to rob the very labor union that is supposed to improve their lives.

Schrader's intense *Hardcore* (1979) studies the porno film industry in LA.

In 1968, freshly out of USC, **George Lucas** is invited by Francis Coppola to shoot documentary footage on the making of *The Rain People*. Three years later, Lucas directs a full-length version of his sci-fi student film, ***THX 1138***, which offers a vision of a bleak, paranoid, totalitarian future.

In the slick ***American Graffiti*** (1973), his first major studio production, Lucas outlines the car-cruising culture of listless small town teenagers. Similarly to *Mean Streets*, but on a less dialectical level, Lucas' film contains a loud soundtrack of 1950s rock'n'roll songs.

Eastern and Western mythology, the inventiveness of samurai and western films, and the choreography of WWII Air Force movies are represented in Lucas' futuristic comic book, ***Star Wars*** (1977), the first installment in an interplanetary trilogy of struggle between good and evil forces.

For the first time since Kubrick's *2001* (1968), moviemaking technology is pushed to new limits. The sensational *Star Wars* special effects are created at **Industrial Light and Magic** (ILM), a state-of-the-art Lucas postproduction facility. For the first time in film history, the visual effects department headed by **Dennis Murren** utilizes computer-coordinated camera movement to produce the seamless fusion of scale models, blue-screen photography, front and rear projection, and numerous other techniques.

The execution of such meticulous and vast undertaking as *Star Wars* would not have been possible without careful preproduction work including **concept art design** and **storyboarding**—a frame-by-frame diagramming of the entire film on paper.

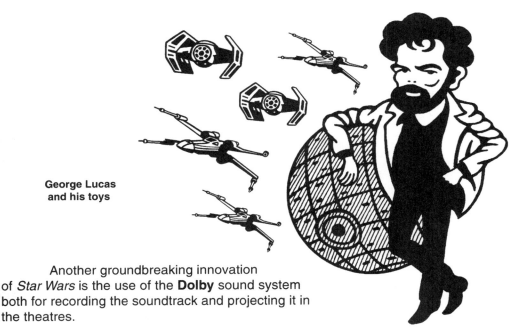

George Lucas and his toys

Another groundbreaking innovation of *Star Wars* is the use of the **Dolby** sound system both for recording the soundtrack and projecting it in the theatres.

Star Wars and its Lucas-produced sequels, ***The Empire Strikes Back*** (dir. Irvin Kershner, 1980) and ***The Return of the Jedi*** (dir. Richard Marquand, 1983) become a worldwide phenomenon, breaking all previous box-office records and initiating a marketing frenzy of related merchandise.

Steven Spielberg, who after film school worked in television, makes his theatrical debut with the intense **Sugarland Express** (1974), a fugitive thriller. His next project, **Jaws** (1975), the superb horror movie about a killer shark terrorizing a Pacific Coast resort, establishes a new standard for popular cinema. It also makes Spielberg the new king of the box office and reinforces Hollywood's belief that an expensively produced, highly publicized film will automatically turn into a blockbuster.

In **Close Encounters of the Third Kind** (1977), Spielberg creates a spectacular, sophisticated vision of an alien arrival on Earth. The movie's special effects team, headed by *2001's* **Douglas Trumbull**, creates some of the most breathtaking visuals ever to grace the screen.

I'VE NEVER BEEN THROUGH PSYCHOANALYSIS. I SOLVE MY PROBLEMS WITH THE PICTURES I MAKE.

HEY, WHO'S GOT MY MASHED POTATOES?!

Steven Spielberg on the set of *Close Encounters*

In the sensitive part of the scientist who coordinates communication with the aliens, Spielberg casts none other than the French director **François Truffaut**.

The 1970s abounds in interesting sci-fi movies. **Silent Running** (dir. Douglas Trumbull, 1971) and **Star Trek** (dir. Robert Wise, 1979) implement some highly innovative visual effects; **The Andromeda Strain** (dir. R. Wise, 1970), **Soylent Green** (dir. Richard Fleischer, 1973), **Zardoz** (dir. John Boorman, 1974), **Rollerball** (dir. Norman Jewison, 1975), and **Capricorn One** (dir. Peter Hyams, 1978) offer intriguing, thought-provoking plots.

The anti-corporate sci-fi thriller, **The China Syndrome** (dir. James Bridges, 1979), loses its "fi" affix after the real-life Three Mile Island nuclear power-plant crisis mirrors the movie's plot line.

Another popular genre to enjoy a revival in the 1970s is comedy. Radically different stylings are displayed by two of the most entertaining comedians of the period, **Mel Brooks** (b. 1927) and **Woody Allen** (b. 1935).

Brooks' breakthrough film, ***The Producers*** (1968), set in the zany world of Broadway musicals, takes an unusual and yet successful approach to the subject of Nazism. After the outrageous Western farce, ***Blazing Saddles*** (1973), Brooks directs his masterpiece, ***The Young Frankenstein*** (1974), a brilliantly conceived comedic homage to the classic horror genre. Shot in moody black and white, the movie makes terrific use of the original *Frankenstein* movie sets.

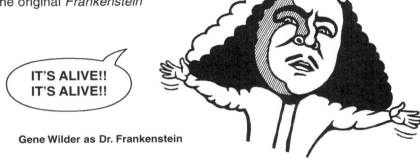

IT'S ALIVE!!
IT'S ALIVE!!

Gene Wilder as Dr. Frankenstein

Silent Movie (1976) must be regarded as Brooks' most audacious effort: the entire film contains no dialogue, except for a single word spoken by a mime (**Marcel Marceau**). The movie's humor relies mostly on slapstick in the Keystone tradition; the most popular stars of the period are featured in cameo appearances, including Paul Newman, Brut Reynolds, and Liza Minnelli.

Dom de Luise, Marty Feldman, and Mel Brooks in *Silent Movie*

In the uproarious ***High Anxiety*** (1977), Brooks pays a somewhat irreverent tribute to the cinema of Alfred Hitchcock, spoofing the most memorable scenes from the Master's famous films.

Woody Allen, a former comedy writer and stand-up performer, makes his writing-directing-starring debut with **Take the Money and Run** (1969), a fast-paced farce about a highly unsuccessful crook. Allen's **Bananas** (1971), **Everything You Always Wanted to Know About Sex But Were Afraid to Ask** (1973), and the wacky sci-fi satire **Sleeper** (1973) rely heavily on outlandish props, sight-gags, and well-timed verbal humor with frequent references to classic films. Allen's comedic persona, like that of Chaplin's, Keaton's, or Lloyd's, remains consistent from one picture to another, and could be characterized best (but not simply) as a neurotic, insecure, sexually repressed, cynical, self-deprecating, and obsessively introspective man on a doomed quest to belong to something or somebody.

> I DON'T WANT TO ACHIEVE IMMORTALITY THROUGH MY WORK. I WANT TO ACHIEVE IT THROUGH NOT DYING.

Woody Allen

Allen's first sign of filmmaking maturity comes with **Love and Death** (1975), a spoof on both Tolstoy's *War and Peace* and the cerebral cinema of Bergman. **Annie Hall** (1977) is a complex, inspired satire of New York's intellectual life, starring the inimitable **Diane Keaton** (b. 1946), Allen's most enduring collaborator.

In his first serious film, **Interiors** (1977), Allen imitates the introspective, pensive quality of Bergman's work, only to return to his neurotic Jewish shtick in the black-and-white **Manhattan** (1979), a stylish comedy about male mid-life crisis.

With his progressively sophisticated film technique and complete creative control over writing, directing, and performing, Woody Allen remains the most impressive and consistent auteur of contemporary American cinema.

Diane Keaton as Annie Hall

It should be noted that Allen's critical success as a filmmaker, which begins with *Annie Hall*, is influenced by the beautiful cinematography of **Gordon Willis**, who rose to fame with his spectacular work on the *Godfather* films and will continue to collaborate with Allen well into the next decade.

The work of another American independent auteur, **John Cassavetes**, continues in the vein he established in *Faces* and *Husbands*. In ***Minnie and Moskovitz*** (1971), Cassavetes studies his favorite subject—people's inability to communicate their emotions. A similar theme permeates the brilliant ***A Woman Under the Influence*** (1974), which presents the outstanding **Gena Rowlands** (b. 1930) as a deeply disturbed lower middle-class housewife unwilling to mold her existence according to society's norms.

**Under the influence:
Gena Rowlands**

With ***The Killing of a Chinese Bookie*** (1976), Cassavetes deviates from his traditional territory and enters the violent world of gambling, prostitution, and organized crime. Far from a typical gangster film, the movie is a poignant character study of desperation.

The intimate atmosphere of Cassavetes' work is reinforced by his frequent casting of family and friends in leading and supporting roles and by financing his movies with his own money, even when that means taking acting jobs in inferior films or mortgaging his house. No other domestic filmmaker can claim such tremendous courage and dedication to his craft, and this may be the very reason why Cassavetes' films, as inaccessible to mainstream audience as they are, remain singularly the most perceptive portrayals of human nature in American cinema of that period.

1970-74 The violent and sexually charged black exploitation (**blaxploitation**) films put a definite end to such screen taboos as portrayal of mixed-race relations and create a plethora of entertaining, empowered black characters who know how to take care of business—brothas and sistas kickin' Da Man's ass and livin' to brag 'bout it.

Richard Roundtree voices his dissatisfaction with *Shaft* being labeled as a blaxploitation picture

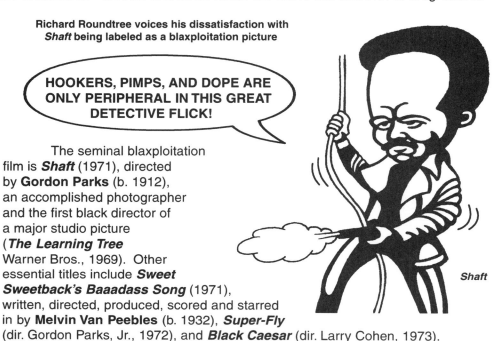

HOOKERS, PIMPS, AND DOPE ARE ONLY PERIPHERAL IN THIS GREAT DETECTIVE FLICK!

The seminal blaxploitation film is ***Shaft*** (1971), directed by **Gordon Parks** (b. 1912), an accomplished photographer and the first black director of a major studio picture (***The Learning Tree*** Warner Bros., 1969). Other essential titles include ***Sweet Sweetback's Baaadass Song*** (1971), written, directed, produced, scored and starred in by **Melvin Van Peebles** (b. 1932), ***Super-Fly*** (dir. Gordon Parks, Jr., 1972), and ***Black Caesar*** (dir. Larry Cohen, 1973).

Shaft

Bruce Lee

The first and only Asian-American actress to have had a career in Hollywood as a leading lady is **Anna May Wong** (1907-61). However, due to the interracial taboos of the period, she is not permitted to kiss her on-screen leading men.

It is not until 1973, that martial arts virtuoso **Bruce Lee** (1940-73) becomes the first Asian male performer to be cast as the protagonist in a Hollywood picture, ***Enter the Dragon*** (Warner Bros.). Tragically, Lee dies before his terrific groundbreaking action film reaches the screen.

Both Anna May Wong and Bruce Lee are of Chinese descent.

The most popular interpretation of
the American Dream myth in its purest form
is presented in **Rocky** (dir. John G. Avildsen, 1976),
a story of an underdog boxer (**Sylvester Stallone**)
rising from a Philadelphia slum to the stardom of
a World Championship fight.

I DON'T THINK I'M VERY COOL AS
A PERSON. I'M JUST BETTER THAN
ANYONE ELSE AT ACTING COOL.

Saturday Night Fever
(dir. John Badham, 1977),
an interesting social study
of the younger generation of
the 1970s, features the
legendary performance of
John Travolta (b. 1954)
as a working-class man with
a disco attitude and a white
polyester suit.

In an intriguing twist of Hollywood fate, Sylvester Stallone will direct
John Travolta in the *Rocky*-structured sequel to *Saturday Night Fever*, **Staying Alive**
(1983)—a sweaty celebration of the male body and the spandex-clad, blow-dried hair
culture of the early 1980s.

Most of the New British Cinema directors who relocate to Hollywood after their domestic success continue to produce solid, entertaining films which may not be as ambitious as their early work, but remain well above the general commercial standards of American film.

John Schlesinger's intense drama **Sunday, Bloody Sunday** (1971) cleverly utilizes the issue of bisexuality to explore universal themes of love, pride, and loneliness.

In the freaky **The Day of the Locust** (1975), set in 1930s' Hollywood, Schlesinger chronicles the breakdown of society; his next film, **The Marathon Man** (1976), is arguably the most intelligent action thriller of the decade.

WAS THAT A PIG I HEARD SQUEAL IN THE WOODS FOR MERCY?

The British-born **John Boorman** (b. 1933) builds a successful career on several thrillers made in the U.S. His Darwinian **Hell in the Pacific** (1969) and **Deliverance** (1972) are very insightful parables about the self-destructive nature of man.

Burt Reynolds tenses in *Deliverance*

Peter Yates (b. 1929) of *Bullitt* fame enjoys huge critical success with **Breaking Away** (1979), a moving, human story of hard-pedaling Indiana teenagers scoring big on and off the bicycle racetrack.

GREAT BRITAIN 1970s

On the domestic front, British directors remain much more adventurous than their expatriate colleagues.

Kes

The incisive, introspective work of **Ken Loach** (b. 1936), especially **Kes** (1969), **Family Life** (1972), and **Black Jack** (1979) proves highly influential on other non-commercial filmmakers focused on realistic, down-to-earth themes.

Peter Medak emerges as an absorbing visual stylist with such films as *A Day In the Death of Joe Egg* (1970) and *The Ruling Class* (1972).

Joseph Losey's ongoing collaboration with Harold Pinter results in the restrained, enjoyable romantic period drama, *The Go-Between* (1971).

A more experimental approach to cinema can be found in the work of **Ken Russell**, whose engaging technique relies on wrapping lofty ideas in flamboyant decor. His most interesting films, *The Music Lovers* (1970), a Tchaikovsky story, *Mahler* (1974), and *Lisztomania* (1975) address psychological aspects of musical creativity; *Tommy* (1975) is an adaptation of one of the greatest contemporary rock operas— The Who's *Tommy*.

Russell's designed-to-shock *The Devils* (1971), about a possessed medieval nun, displays a great deal of beautifully crafted sequences.

Vanessa Redgrave: possessed

Russell's chief experimental rival, **Nicholas Roeg**, achieves his first filmmaking triumph with *Walkabout* (1971), an amazingly composed feature which contrasts Western culture with the Aboriginal environment of the Australian outback. The film will prove immensely influential in shaping the blooming Australian cinema.

Roeg's outstanding psychological horror, *Don't Look Now* (1972), and the unusual, provocative science-fiction picture, *The Man Who Fell to Earth* (1975), starring the original Space Oddity **David Bowie**, remain classics of their respective genres.

Walkabout

A new generation of British filmmakers who receive hands-on training in television advertising produces two astonishing talents—**Alan Parker** (b. 1944) and **Ridley Scott** (b. 1939).

Parker's *Bugsy Malone* (1976), a parody of gangster film, incorporates a singing all-child cast. In the moody, claustrophobic *Midnight Express* (1978), scripted by the young writer **Oliver Stone**, Parker recreates the frightening real-life experiences of a young American heroin smuggler in a Turkish prison. The movie is a testimony to the strength of the human spirit and to perseverance of moral values under seemingly hopeless circumstances.

With his first feature, the impressive adaptation of **Joseph Conrad**'s Napoleonic story, *The Duelists* (1977), Ridley Scott establishes himself as a master of sustained tension and breathtaking composition. In his next project, *Alien* (1979), a masterpiece of the sci-fi horror genre, Scott explores the darkest, most primal regions of interplanetary adventure. Swiss artist **H.R. Giger** provides spectacular design for the movie's organic environments and the slimy, gut-ripping space creature.

In the following decade, both Parker and Scott relocate to Hollywood and provide a badly needed supply of fresh air.

Sigourney Weaver in *Alien*

Richard Lester devotes his talents to such swashbuckling extravaganzas as *The Three Musketeers* saga (1973, 1974, 1989), and the *Superman* sequels (II, 1980; III, 1983), all of which display contagious energy and great sense of humor.

Lester also successfully ventures into the suspense thriller genre with his edge-of-your-seat *Juggernaut* (1972) and offers an interesting take on the Robin Hood myth in *Robin and Marian* (1976).

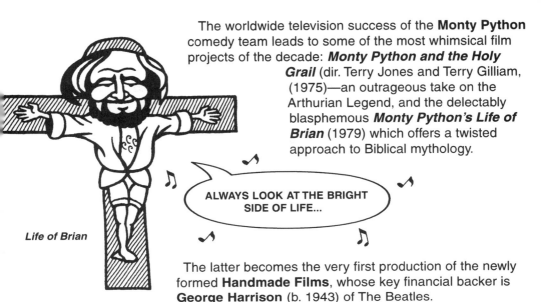

The worldwide television success of the **Monty Python** comedy team leads to some of the most whimsical film projects of the decade: *Monty Python and the Holy Grail* (dir. Terry Jones and Terry Gilliam, (1975)—an outrageous take on the Arthurian Legend, and the delectably blasphemous *Monty Python's Life of Brian* (1979) which offers a twisted approach to Biblical mythology.

ALWAYS LOOK AT THE BRIGHT SIDE OF LIFE...

Life of Brian

The latter becomes the very first production of the newly formed **Handmade Films**, whose key financial backer is **George Harrison** (b. 1943) of The Beatles.

In 1977, **Terry Gilliam** (the only American in Monty Python) directs a Pythonesque medieval dragon comedy-adventure *Jabberwocky*, based on the writings of **Lewis Carroll**.

After settling in Britain permanently, **Stanley Kubrick** continues to pursue his idiosyncratic vision. His first picture of the decade is *A Clockwork Orange* (1971), a loose adaptation of the brilliant **Anthony Burgess** novel. Supported by ingenious art design, this futuristic movie presents a believable, utterly disturbing image of rampant anarchy which comes as a direct result of a totalitarian regime. To sustain the edgy atmosphere of the film, Kubrick resorts to hand-held camera shots, fish-eye lens distortion, and nearly balletic choreography of violence.

I'M SINGIN' IN THE RAIN...

A Clockwork Orange

In *Barry Lyndon* (1975), the 19th century epic story of the rise and fall of an aspiring socialite, Kubrick and his director of photography, **John Alcott**, apply **fast stock** film to capture **natural light** in the interior shots without having to resort to **artificial lighting** techniques. The movie also makes a terrific us of a specially designed telephoto lens to produce some of the most spectacular shots in history. The widescreen format of *Barry Lyndon* is suited perfectly for such visual manipulation, and Kubrick's ingenious use of depth of field ranks him among such masters of perspective as Antonioni and Jancsó.

Kubrick's engaging *The Shining* (1980), a flattened version of the **Stephen King** classic horror novel, downplays the domestic violence theme for the sake of sheer visual extravaganza fortified by the over-the-top bravura of **Jack Nicholson**'s performance.

The bad boy of the British cinema, **Lindsay Anderson**, follows the anti-establishment path of *If...* with *O, Lucky Man!* (1973), a sarcastic social satire about a coffee salesman (the irreplaceable **Malcolm McDowell**) who is persecuted by the government. The film's disjointed, nonlinear structure and the continuous blending of reality and fantasy make Anderson's movie a fitting tribute to the cinema of Godard.

The veteran master of British cinema, **David Lean**, makes only one film during the entire decade, the beautifully photographed (by **Freddie Young**) *Ryan's Daughter* (1970), a coming-of-age story of an Irish woman set in the historically turbulent year of 1916.

Also noteworthy is the first feature by **Alan Bridges** (b. 1927), *The Hireling* (1973), a social class-division drama.

Superman (dir. Richard Donner, 1978), the British-made superproduction about the quintessential American superhero, displays dazzling visual effects and the most expensive cameo in history of cinema—**Marlon Brando**'s total of $18.5 million for a mere 10 minutes of screen time (the sum includes his nominal fee of $3.5 million plus a percentage of the film's earnings). This otherwise indecent information serves as an indication of the upcoming increase in star salary, which in the 1980s and 1990s reaches outlandish sums of money and ultimately results in a dramatic increase in the average studio production budget. As a result, mainstream cinema progressively moves away from intelligent entertainment and enters the arena of appealing to the lowest-common-denominator for quick financial profit. In short, big-budget B-movies replace the A-category.

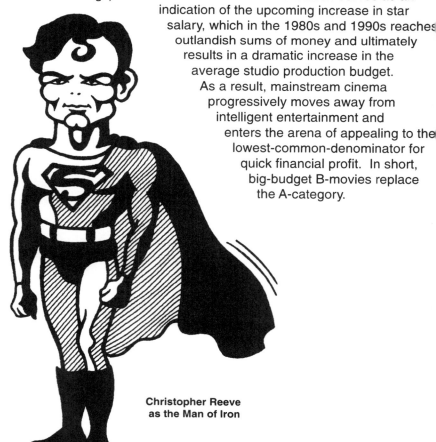

**Christopher Reeve
as the Man of Iron**

AUSTRALIA 1970s

Despite a colorful film legacy which reaches as far back as 1896, the Australian film industry produces few pictures of international importance. In the late 1960s, the Liberal Government becomes increasingly supportive of the Arts. The **Australian Film Development Corporation** (**AFDC**) receives solid commitment from the Federal Parliament to assist in film and television production.

AFDC's first accomplishment is the **Bruce Beresford**-directed *The Adventures of Barry McKenzie* (1972), a technically proficient sex comedy.

Another government-subsidized institution to shape the new Australian cinema is the **Experimental Film and Television Fund** (EFTF), which supports short format alternative filmmaking and promotes first-time directors. The EFTF-produced *Stork* (dir. **Tim Burstall**, 1971) becomes the most popular Australian production of that period. Burstall's next film, the sex farce *Alvin Purple* (1973) also enjoys great commercial success. His *Petersen* (1974) tells the story of an ambitious working class man trying to escape suburbia only to find alienation in the big city.

The replacement of the Liberal Government with the Labor Party leadership in the early 1970s leads to further federal support for the Arts.

The direct beneficiary of this situation is the newly formed **Australian Film and Television School** (AFTS), whose first director is the famous Polish film historian, critic, and the former president of the Lodz Film School, **Jerzy Toeplitz**. As early as 1974, the AFTS student **John Papadopoulos** receives great critical acclaim for his *Matchless*, a story of three people afflicted by illnesses who coexist in a mutually-respectful environment.

Other noted AFTS graduates to embark on successful directing careers include **Philip Noyce** (b. 1950, *Newsfront*, 1978), and **Gillian Armstrong** (b. 1950). Armstrong's *My Brilliant Career* (1979), based on a book by Australian woman writer **Miles Franklin**, takes a feminist look at a young woman's struggle to overcome the country's patriarchal mentality.

Judy Davis in *My Brilliant Career*

The most outstanding figure in the Australian cinema is undoubtedly **Peter Weir** (b. 1944). After the anarchic horror *The Cars that Ate Paris* (1974), Weir directs his first masterwork, *The Picnic at Hanging Rock* (1975). This stylish, dreamy movie tells a mysterious story of three college girls who disappear with their mistress during a summer excursion into the country's spectacular volcanic region.

Weir's atmospheric *The Last Wave* (1977), a supernatural tale rooted deeply in the Aboriginal mythology, magically manages to bridge the past with the present while offering a disturbing vision of the future. The movie marks one of the first involvements of an American studio (UA) in production of an Australian picture.

Richard Chamberlain
in *The Last Wave*

The subdued, nearly claustrophobic ambience of the gritty, 16mm format of *The Plumber* (1979) conveys perfectly the movie's theme: a confrontation of the rational, academic perception of human existence with the raw, primal force of life. In *The Plumber*, just like in *The Picnic*, Weir succeeds in creating an almost unbearable atmosphere of implicit peril without resorting to on-screen explosions of violence.

Bruce Beresford (b. 1940) continues to amuse domestic audiences with *Don's Party* (1976) and *The Getting of Wisdom* (1977) before breaking into international attention with *Breaker' Morant* (1980)—a historical account of a court-martial case during the turn-of-the-century Boer War in South Africa. Beresford's presentation of the Commonwealth involvement in the conflict with Dutch settlers echoes with the recent memory of Vietnam.

Bryan Brown in *Breaker Morant*

After *Devil's Playground* (1976), **Fred Schepisi** (b. 1939) attacks bigotry and racism in *The Chant of Jimmy Blacksmith* (1978)—an eloquent statement for the rights of Australia's native minority, the Aborigines, who are forced to abandon their heritage by the white ruling class. ☞

BAAA!

One of the best pictures to focus on the outback sheep sheering environment is *Sunday Too Far Away* (dir. Ken Hannam, 1975), the first Australian film to enjoy European success.

Peter Cummins in
Sunday Too Far Away

The Lost Weekend (dir. Colin Eggleston, 1978) is a simple but extremely nerve-wracking horror which chronicles a brief and uneven struggle between nature and a city couple.

Produced with just $350,000, the insanely entertaining futuristic vengeance road movie *Mad Max* (dir. George Miller, 1979) holds the world record of budget-to-revenue ratio (approximately 1: 290) and instantly becomes Australia's most sought-after export. It also introduces the World to the special talents of **Mel Gibson** (b. 1956).

CANADA

The government-subsidized Canadian film industry, under the auspices of the **National Film Board** (NFB), enjoys a rich documentary heritage, particularly the outstanding WWII production. It also sponsors some of the world's best animators and experimental filmmakers such as the extremely influential **Norman McLaren** (1914-87). One of the few NFB-produced narrative films of substantial artistic quality is ***Nobody Waved Goodbye*** (dir. Don Owen, 1964).

The **Canadian Film Development Corporation** (CFDC), established in 1967, begins to promote narrative film production, while the Canadian government offers tax shelters for domestic and international producers. The Canadian film industry enters its most prolific period.

After directing the violent but irresistibly alluring Australian picture ***Outback*** (1971), **Ted Kotcheff** scores major international success for Canada with ***The Apprenticeship of Duddy Kravitz*** (1974), a coming of age story about a Jewish-Canadian man, set in the late 1940s, which is also a terrific study of runaway greed.

Richard Dreyfuss as Duddy Kravitz

Other notable Canadian English-language films include ***Act of the Heart*** (dir. Paul Almond, 1970) and ***Outrageous!*** (dir. Richard Benner, 1977).

Among the more interesting French-Canadian (Quebecois) films are ***Wounded Love*** (*L'Armour blessé*, Jean-Pierre Lefebre, 1975), ***My Uncle Antoine*** (*Mon oncle Antoine*, Claude Jutra, 1971) and ***Kamouraska*** (C. Jutra, 1973), ***My Childhood in Montreal*** (*Mon enfance à Montréal*, Jean Chabot, 1972), and ***Réjeanne Padovani*** (dir. Denys Arcand, 1972).

Geneviéve Bujold
in *Act of the Heart*

The only Canadian director to achieve cult following and, ultimately, international success with his domestic work is **David Cronenberg** (b. 1943), whose frequently surreal horror and science-fiction films (***Rabid***, 1977; ***The Brood***, 1979; ***Scanners***, 1980) combine undeniable visual artistry with thickly woven existential themes.

Some of the best known Canadian-born filmmakers who achieve fame while working outside their country are **Norman Jewison**, **Sidney J. Furie**, and **Arthur Hiller**.

NEW GERMAN CINEMA

DAS DEUE KINO

The origins of the **New German Cinema** (**das neue Kino**) emerge as early as 1962, when a group of young West German filmmakers frustrated by the stale imagination of their older colleagues and the low quality of the domestic film production, compose the famous **Oberhausen Manifesto** during the short film festival at Oberhausen.

**THE REVOLUTIONARY
OBERHAUSEN MANIFESTO
IN A NUTSHELL**

- The Old German cinema is dead
- Give the younger generation a
  chance to direct New Wave films
- The New German Cinema shall
  be free of any commercial restraints

The Manifesto paves the way for establishing the **Kuratorium junger deutscher Film** (Board of Curators of the Young German Cinema, 1965) which provides interest-free loans to aspiring directors.

One of the Oberhausen revolutionaries, **Alexander Kluge** (b. 1932) debuts with *Yesterday Girl* (*Abschied von Gestern*, 1966) and scores tremendous international success. The movie tells the painful story of a young East German woman of Jewish heritage wandering through the Federal Republic. Shot in a decisively New Wave style, Kluge's film utilizes episodic narration, juggles realistic and fantastic perspectives, and incorporates documentary footage.

Kluge's wonderfully paradoxical *Occasional Work of a Female Slave* (*Gelegenheitsarbeit einer Sklavin*, 1973) remains one of the most ideologically ambiguous films ever made. To support her family, the movie's protagonist runs an abortion clinic; after her operation is dismantled by the police, the woman becomes an ardent political activist, only to find herself peddling frankfurters which she wraps in her own political pamphlets outside her husband's factory.

**Alexandra Kluge in her
brother's *Occasional Work***

207

The difficult early work of the French-born **Jean-Marie Straub** (b. 1933), frequently based on the writings of **Heinrich Böll**, offers a disturbing vision of German past (***Machorka-Muff***, 1962, and ***Not Reconciled***/*Nicht versöhnt*, 1965).

Dedicated Marxists, Straub and his wife, **Danièle Huillet**, co-direct numerous movies which are inaccessible to wide audiences: ***The Chronicle of Anna Magdalena Bach*** (*Chronik der Anna Magdalena Bach*, 1968), a story about J. S. Bach told from his wife's viewpoint, and ***Moses and Aaron*** (*Moses und Aron*, 1974), an adaptation of Arnold Schoenberg's opera, remain true examples of non-commercial, deeply individualistic cinema defying nearly all established conventions.

Volker Schlöndorff (b. 1939), a former assistant to Melville, Resnais, and Malle, co-directs with **Margarethe von Trotta** the scathing critique of the West German mentality in ***The Lost Honor of Katharina Blum*** (*Die verlorene Ehre der Katharina Blum*, 1975), another adaptation of Heinrich Böll's prose. The movie's tragic plot concerns an innocent woman whose accidental love affair with an alleged army deserter results in a media campaign portraying her as a whore and a terrorist.

The critically acclaimed ***The Tin Drum*** (*Die Blechtrommel*, 1979), Schlöndorff's solo effort, is a colorful adaptation of the **Günter Grass** novel, and depicts a young German-Polish boy who rebels against the cruel adult world by refusing to grow. It is the boy's three-foot perspective which enables us to witness some of history's most atrocious events, including the Nazi invasion of Poland.

David Bennent as Oskar
in *The Tin Drum*

After a series of documentaries and short narratives, **Werner Herzog** (b. 1942) directs his breakthrough ***Even Dwarfs Started Small*** (*Auch Zwerge haben klein angefangen*, 1970), a doomed prison revolt story with an all-dwarf cast, set on a desolate volcanic island.

Right from the onset of his career, Herzog makes it clear that he regards cinema as an extension of the county-fair amusement and not the academic tradition.

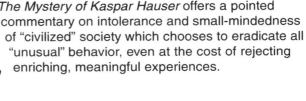

In ***Aguirre, the Wrath of God*** (*Aguirre, Der Zorn Gottes*, 1972), Herzog stages another intriguing rebellion. This time a mad Spanish conquistador (**Klaus Kinski**) secedes Pizarro to establish his own kingdom in the tropical forest of Peru.

Frequently explored in the German arts is the subject of Kaspar Hauser, a 19th century man-child foundling who is also the focus of Herzog's deeply humanistic and philosophical ***The Mystery of Kaspar Hauser*** (*Jeder für sich und Gott gegen alle*, 1974). Kaspar has been imprisoned in a dark cell all his life and doesn't know how to speak or relate to other people; he has no memories. In order to convey

Klaus Kinski in *Aguirre*

Kaspar's first sensory observations after his introduction to the "real" world, Herzog resorts to unusual camera angles, unique lighting configurations, and celebrates the natural beauty of the rural landscape with strikingly composed shots.

Ultimately, perhaps as a polemic with Truffaut's *The Wild Child*, *The Mystery of Kaspar Hauser* offers a pointed commentary on intolerance and small-mindedness of "civilized" society which chooses to eradicate all "unusual" behavior, even at the cost of rejecting enriching, meaningful experiences.

In a peculiar and yet highly appropriate maneuver, Herzog casts in the part of Kasper a former schizophrenic, **Bruno S.**, who also stars in his next project, ***Stroszek*** (1977). This eccentric movie chronicles the misadventures of an odd trio of Berliners—two social misfits and a hooker who run off to Wisconsin to evade the violent wrath of her pimps.

Herzog's humorous ballad of displaced identity quickly turns into an ironic, very disturbing study of contemporary American reality, complete with a mobile home experience, an oversized turkey, and an amusement park zoo. It would be futile to search for a more perceptive look at the Land of the Free even among the American films of the era.

Stroszek

In 1976, Herzog directs the moody ***Heart of Glass*** (*Herz aus Glas*)—
a mysterious, fantastic story about a well-kept secret of a glass factory, set in the timeless
landscape of deep forest and volcanic terrain. To sustain the poetic, elusive atmosphere
of the film, Herzog hypnotizes his cast during the filming. Avoiding easily perceptible
meaning, *Heart of Glass* is dismissed by many as pretentious and gimmicky, but in fact
the movie comes close to capturing the enigmas surrounding artistic creation.

The internationally produced **Nosferatu the Vampire** (*Nosferatu —Phantom der
Nacht*, 1978) is Herzog's audacious attempt to redo the 1922 Murnau masterpiece.

In his adaptation of **Georg Büchner**'s **Woyzeck** (1979), Herzog continues to
explore his favorite subject: the tragedy of an individual who dares to defy the norms of
society. Both films feature the unique Klaus Kinski (1926-91) in the title role of outcasts.

The most prolific and internationally recognized of the New German Cinema
directors is **Rainer Werner Fassbinder** (1946-82). A great admirer of the artificial,
glossy magnificence of the Douglas Sirk movies, Fassbinder sets out to transplant some
of the soapy American melodrama onto German soil. However, he does it with a gritty,
realistic touch that becomes his trademark.

Why ***Does herr R. Run Amok*** (*Warum läuft Herr R. amok?*, 1969) is an example
of the early, wild Fassbinder work characterized by the strong antisocial, psychopathic,
and suicidal traits that mark most of his loveless protagonists. Similar mentalities
permeates ***The Merchant of Four Seasons*** (*Der Händler der vier Jahreszeiten*, 1971),
Fassbinder's first success with domestic audiences.

In **Ali: Fear Eats the Soul**
(*Angst essen Seele auf*, 1973),
thematically close to Sirk's *All That
Heaven Allows*, the unlikely romance
between an older German widow
and a handsome Moroccan
gastarbeiter (immigrant worker)
serves as a catalyst for Fassbinder's
exposition of the xenophobic
attitudes of the German society.

Another outcast story,
Fox and His Friends
(*Faustrecht der Freiheit*, 1975),
presents a young gay man
whose sudden lottery win and
proletarian status make him a
perfect target for the exploits of
the bored Munich homosexual
upper-class. Openly gay,
Fassbinder assumes the title
role in his movie with great
sensibility and conviction.

Fassbinder in *Fox*

Both ***Mother Küster's Trip to Heaven*** (*Mutter Küsters Fahrt zum Himmel*, 1975) and ***Fear of Fear*** (*Angst vor der Angst*, 1975) depict the emotional traumas of German housewives and continue Fassbinder's denouncement of modern urban civilization.

In 1978, Fassbinder makes the ironic, complex ***Despair*** (*Die Reie ins Licht*), an adaptation of **Vladimir Nabokov**'s novel that is scripted by the British playwright **Tom Stoppard**. The movie's hero, Hermann Hermann, suffers from identity crisis which compels him to assassinate the man he believes to be his double.

> THE SPLIT PERSON.
> A MAN WHO STANDS BESIDE HIMSELF.
> I'M THINKING OF WRITING A BOOK
> ABOUT SUCH PERSON...
> MAYBE TWO BOOKS.

*Dirk Bogarde in *Despair**

The ***Marriage of Maria Braun*** (*Die Ehe der Maria Braun*, 1979) marks Fassbinder's return to high melodrama, this time set in the disjointed reality of postwar Germany.

Wim Wenders' (b. 1945) first feature, ***The Goalie's Anxiety at the Penalty Kick*** (*Die angst des Tormanns beim Elfmeter*, 1971), is a psychological study of mental degradation shot in the murder mystery convention.

After the wonderfully feminist ***The Scarlet Letter*** (*Der Scharlachrote Buchstabe*, 1972), Wenders directs the first of his "road movies"—***Alice in the Cities*** (*Alice in den Städen*, 1974), about an unlikely alliance between a disillusioned photojournalist and a young girl on a quest to find her grandmother. Wenders' next picture, ***Wrong Move*** (*Falsche Bewegung*, 1974), is an inherently German tale of wasted existence.

Alice in the Cities

Kings of the Road (*Im Lauf der Zeit*, 1976) continues Wenders' obsession with the unfulfilled desire for belonging. Two men travel across Germany—not much happens, very little is said, but after almost three hours are over, one has a comforting feeling of having been cuddled in the arms of a master.

Wenders makes brilliant use of off-screen space, travelling shots, and long takes, which create and sustain the film's meditative mood. The essence of *Kings of the Road* lies not in the story line, or lack of a plot, but in the ingeniously composed imagery, which serves as a metaphor for Americanization of the German landscape (and the subconscious), and laments the loss of personal identity in the modern world.

Rüdiger Vogler and Hanns
Zischler are Kings of the Road

The American Friend (*Der Amerikanische Freund*, 1977), Wenders' first international coproduction, is an allegorical thriller with familiar overtones: the exploitation of European culture by the expanding American imperialism.

Peter Handke, the writer of Wenders' *Goalie* and *Wrong Movement*, directs the Wenders-produced (and heavily influenced) **The Left-Handed Woman** (*Die Linkshändige Frau*, 1977), one of the best films about women realized by a man. The painterly cinematography of this movie is created by **Robby Müller**, the photographer of *Kings of the Road*.

Among other exceptional German directors of this prolific era are **Hans Jürgen Syberberg** (b. 1935, **Hitler: A Film From Germany**/*Hitler: Ein Film aus Deutschland*, 1977) and **Reinhard Hauf** (b. 1939, **Knife in the Head**/*Messer im Kopf*, 1978).

Titles not to be neglected include **Jane is Jane Forever** (*Jane bleibt Jane*, 1977) and **Flaming Hearts** (*Flamende Herzen*, 1978), both by Walter Bockmayer and Rolf Bührmann, as well as **Lina Braake** (dir. Bernhard Sinkel, 1975), an important statement about the deplorable situation of Germany's elderly citizens.

Far From Home (*In der Fremde*, Sohrab Shadid Saless, 1975) and **Shirin's Wedding** (*Shirins Hochzeit*, Helma Sanders, 1975) are the most prominent films in the *Gastarbeiter* genre.

FRANCE 1970s

With the *Nouvelle Vague* running out its course, French cinema of the 1970s enters a prolific period of introspective, individualistic films which, for the most part, stay away from heavy structural experimentation yet continue to astonish viewers with thematic inventiveness.

According to some sources, the last truly New Wave picture is **The Mother and the Whore** (*La Maman et la putain*, Jean Eustache, 1973)—a painfully long, self-absorbed work whose aggressive dialectic appears to be pointed against everything.

In 1973, François Truffaut, by now a veteran of the industry, directs **Day For Night** (*La Nuit américaine*), the ultimate film-within-a-film experience whose title derives from a cinematic technique permitting the shooting of night scenes in daylight. The movie is Truffaut's tribute to his beloved Hollywood masters (Hitchcock, Ford, Hawks) and the inherently French tradition of lyrical, personal cinema.

In his next movie, the masterfully executed **The Story of Adèle H.** (*L'Histoire d'Adèle H.*, 1975), Truffaut paints a moving portrait of Victor Hugo's daughter, Adèle (**Isabelle Adjani**)—a perpetual wanderer locked within her own impassioned world.

The Last Metro (*Le Derniere métro*, 1980) becomes Truffaut's only overtly political film. It addresses the clash of moralities in a small Parisian theater during the Nazi occupation.

Adèle H.

Gérard Depardieu in *My Uncle in America*

Another veteran of the New Wave, **Alain Resnais** achieves critical acclaim with his beautifully stylized, traditionally shot **Stavisky** (1974), a story of the great financial scandal in the French government of 1934.

In the more subdued **My Uncle in America** (*Mon oncle d'Amérique*, 1980), Resnais engages in an incisive philosophical debate on the influence of success on human relationships. Structured with mathematical precision, the film develops three parallel narratives which deal with career, love, and illness respectively. The action is intermittently punctuated with scientific commentary by **Dr. Henri Laborit**, the famous behaviorist.

Claude Chabrol continues to work with strange murder schemes in *The Break-Up* (*La Rupture*, 1970), *Blood Wedding* (*Les Noces Rouges*, 1973), and *Violette* (*Violette Nozière*, 1978). In addition to their Hitchcock-influenced entertainment value, Chabrol's films offer mature, psychologically complex portrayals of women, most frequently played by the exquisite **Stéphane Audran**, the director's wife.

One of the key feminist directors of the era, **Agnes Varda**, directs *One Sings, the Other Doesn't* (*L'Une chante, l'autre pas*, 1977), a complex study of friendship between two dramatically different women.

Louis Malle returns to top form with *Murmur of the Heart* (*Le Souffle au coeur*, 1971), a sensitive and humorous take on the issue of incest in a middle-class family, set against the turbulent backdrop of the mid 1950s (war in Indochina, unrest in Algeria).

In another historically rooted film, *Lacombe Lucien* (1974), Malle deals with the uneasy issue of Vichy France. The story concerns a young French peasant boy who collaborates with the Gestapo and must face the question of whether to denounce his object of love—a Jewish girl.

Lacombe Lucien

Malle's subsequent films are produced outside of France: *Pretty Baby* (1978) is a sensuous Louisiana love story between a photographer and a 12-year old prostitute; *Atlantic City* (1980), financed by Canada, depicts small-time schemers in the seedy gambling environment of New Jersey's famous resort.

Yves Montand in
The Confession

The highly political cinema of the Greek-born **Constantine Costa-Gavras** (b. 1933) begins with *Z* (1969), a superb analysis of a military dictatorship's strategies in subduing democratic opposition, based on an infamous episode from the recent Greek history.

Costa-Gavras' subsequent *The Confession* (*L'Aveu*, 1970) recalls postwar Stalinist purges in Czechoslovakia; *State of Siege* (*L'Etat de siège*, 1973) criticizes American involvement in South American politics. The latter is written by **Franco Solinas**, the author of *The Battle of Algiers* screenplay.

Jaques Rivette's most enjoyable picture of the period is ***Celine and Julie Go Bathing*** (*Céline at Julie vont en bateau*, 1974), a curious mixture of fantasy and reality shot on 16mm film.

After the sumptuously photographed ***The Marquise of O*** (*La Marquise d'O*, 1976), **Eric Rohmer** directs ***Perceval*** (*Perceval le Gallois*, 1978)—a 12th century tale whose visual style recalls medieval painting.

Bertrand Blier (b. 1939), a former assistant to Truffaut, develops his carefree, radiant style of eccentric comedy with ***Going Places*** (*Les Valseuses*, 1974) and ***Get Out Your Handkerchiefs*** (*Préparez vos mouchoirs*, 1977), starring the irresistibly charming duo of **Patrick Dewaere** and **Gérard Depardieu**.

Cold Cuts (*Buffet froid*, 1979), a wonderfully odd, surreal comedy, reunites Blier with his father, the famous French actor **Bernard Blier** and Depardieu.

Patrick Dewaere in *Handkerchiefs*

The thematically versatile cinema of **Bertrand Tavernier** (b. 1941) bridges the traditions of *Nouvelle Vague* with the more conservative poetic realism. His best films of the decade include ***The Clockmaker*** (*L'Horloger de Saint Paul*, 1974)—a story of finding understanding between a father and son, disguised as a murder mystery, and ***The Judge and The Assassin*** (*Le Juge at l'assassin*, 1976), which chronicles another mutually dependent relationship, this time between a judge and a murderer.

In the futuristic ***Deathwatch*** (*Le Mort en direct*, 1979), starring **Harvey Keitel**, Tavernier suggests that observing deaths captured on film will soon take the place of pornography.

Philipe Noiret in *The Clockmaker*

The Swiss-born **Alain Tanner** (b. 1929) becomes internationally recognized for his ***Jonah Who Will Be 25 in the Year 2000*** (*Jonah qui aura 25 ans en l'an 2000*,1976) an ensemble film which ponders issues of social responsibility, political activism, and family.

Another Swiss director, **Claude Goretta**, makes a beautiful, lyrical film about lost love, ***The Lacemaker*** (*La Dentellière*, 1977).

André Téchiné (b. 1943), another former *Cahiers du cinéma* critic, comes to prominence with ***Souvenirs d'en France*** (1975), ***Barocco*** (1976), and ***Les Soeurs Brontë*** (1978). The last two films benefit from the outstanding cinematography of **Bruno Nuytten**.

Also notable is the early work of **Claude Miller** (b. 1942), ***A Better Way of Walking*** (*La Meilleur façon de marcher*, 1975), and ***Tell Him That I Love Him*** (*Ditez-lui que je l'aime*, 1977).

Madame Rosa (*La Vie devant soi*, Moshe Mizrahi, 1977) is the touching story of a retired Jewish prostitute whose home becomes an informal shelter to children of all races and religions.

Simone Signoret as Madame Rosa

216

The sensitive, realistic, and independent films of **Maurice Pialat** (b. 1925) equal Cassavetes in their unglamorous depiction of human existence. His best titles include ***The Mouth Agape*** (*La Gueule ouverte*, 1974), ***Passe ton bac d'abord*** (1979), and ***Loulou*** (1980).

Jean-Pierre Melville continues his cool modernist interpretation of the American gangster genre in ***Le Samouraï*** (1967) and ***The Red Circle*** (*Le Cercle rouge*, 1970), both starring the mysterious **Alain Delon**.

The Polish-born **Walerian Borowczyk** (b. 1923), a former collaborator of Chris Marker and a world-class animator, carries his uniquely personal vision into such live-action features as ***Goto, Island of Love*** (*Goto, L'île d'amour*, 1968), ***Immoral Tales*** (*Contes immoraux*, 1974), and the Polish-made ***The Story of Sin*** (*Dzieje Grzechu*, 1975), an adaptation of the controversial novel by **Stefan Zeromski**. All of these films deal with various aspects of provocative sexuality—empowerment, obsession, perversion—and present a somewhat jaded image of humanity.

Roman Polanski, now living in France, the place of his birth, makes his disturbing masterpiece about a Polish immigrant in Paris, ***The Tenant*** (*Le Locataire*, 1976). This meticulous study in psychosis and schizophrenia is based on a book by the surreal illustrator **Roland Topor**.

The British/French-produced ***Tess*** (1979), Polanski's competent version of the Thomas Hardy novel, presents the tragic love story of a socially ambitious young woman who is played with great intuition by the young **Nastassja Kinski**.

Polanski in
The Tenant

IF YOU CUT OFF MY HEAD,
WHAT WILL IT SAY:
ME AND MY HEAD,
OR ME AND MY BODY?
WHAT RIGHT HAS MY HEAD
TO CALL ITSELF ME?

The extremely popular films of **Claude Sautet** (b. 1924)— *__Max and the Junkmen__* (*Max et les ferrailleurs*, 1971), *__Cesar and Rosalie__* (*César et Rosalie*, 1972), and *__A Simple Story__* (*Une Histoire simple*, 1978)—present the everyday routine of middle-class people with a human, humorous approach.

France's most successful movie to date, both domestically and internationally, becomes *__La Cage aux folles__* (dir. Edouard Molinaro, 1978), a hysterical comedy about a gay couple.

Michel Serrault in *La Cage aux folles*

Arguably, the most popular French movie star of the period is the comedian **Louis De Funès** (1908-83), whose *__Fantomas__* and *__Gendarme__* series of the 1960s made him a favorite of European audiences. His films of the 70s include *__La Folie des grandeurs__* (1971), *__The Adventures of Rabbi Jacob__* (*Les Adventures de Rabbi Jacob*, 1973), and *__A Wing or a Thigh__* (*L'Aile ou la cuisse*, 1976).

Louis De Funès

Federico Fellini's first theatrical film of the decade is *Fellini Roma* (1972), a colorful, semidocumentary account of the Italian capital's past, based on the director's memories and permeated with his irreverent, surreal sense of humor.

**Fashion show for the clergy
in *Fellini Roma***

With his next film, ***Amarcord*** (1974), Fellini delves into another aspect of his own past—his childhood in the seaport town of Rimini. In the director's magical hands, the movie assumes the proportions of a complex, funny, and nostalgic allegory of Italian life under the Mussolini regime.

After the sumptuously shot ***Casanova*** (1976), Fellini produces his most direct though still metaphorical, movie on Italian history and politics—***Orchestra Rehearsal*** (*Prova d'orchestra*, 1979).

Michelangelo Antonioni's only theatrical release in the 1970s is the masterful existentialist thriller, ***The Passenger*** (*Professione: Reporter*, 1975). Trapped in the overwhelming heat of the African summer, the protagonist (**Jack Nicholson**) assumes the identity of a dead stranger only to find himself locked into the man's violent and morally questionable past. Antonioni's disimpassioned camera clings to the hero like a sweaty shirt, frequently following the action in precise, long, uninterrupted takes. Such technique, supported by the sparse, insignificant dialogue, underlines the despair at failing to find one's place and purpose in life.

After an intriguing adaptation of **Thomas Mann**'s ***Death in Venice*** (*Morte a Venezia*, 1971), **Lucino Visconti** directs ***Ludwig*** (1973), a unique look at the mad king of 19th century Bavaria.

Conversation Piece (*Gruppo di famiglia in un interno*, 1974) reunites Visconti with Burt Lancaster, and ***The Innocent*** (*L'innocente*, 1976), a nostalgic look at *fin-de-siècle* Italy, becomes the great filmmaker's last film, released posthumously in 1979.

Lucino Visconti

219

With his Marxist ideology spelled out in **Before the Revolution** (*Prima della revoluzione*, 1964), **Bernardo Bertolucci** (b. 1940) paints a richly textured portrait of the socio-political decadence of Fascist Italy in **The Conformist** (*Il conformista*, 1970), based on Alberto Moravia's book. The mood of virtually every scene in the film is enhanced by the striking color photography of Vittorio Storaro, who will serve as cinematographer for all of Bertolucci's subsequent films until the mid 1990s.

The Conformist

Bertolucci's **The Last Tango in Paris** (*Ultimo Tango a Parigi*, 1972) is an eloquent study of human sexuality at its most primal, base form deprived of intellectualization and even feelings.

IF DESIRED, *LAST TANGO* COULD ALSO BE INTERPRETED IN FAR-FETCHING MARXIST TERMS AS AN ANALYSIS OF EXPLOITATION AND INTERDEPENDENCE BETWEEN AMERICA (MARLON BRANDO) AND EUROPE (MARIA SCHNEIDER).

SHUT UP, PROFESSOR!

In **1900** (*Novecento*, 1976), Bertolucci weaves an elaborate saga about two families at the onset of the century—one is wealthy, the other poor. The movie examines the interconnectedness of sex and politics in the great flow of history.

The neorealist tradition thrives in the work of **Ermano Olmi** (b. 1931), most prominently in his outstanding portrayal of the late 19th century peasant life, **The Tree of Wooden Clogs** (*L'albero degli zoccoli*, 1978).

Francesco Rosi continues his socially committed work with ***Christ Stopped at Eboli*** (*Christo si è fermato a Eboli*, 1979), presenting a moving, realistic picture of peasant poverty in the Southern region of Mussolini's Italy.

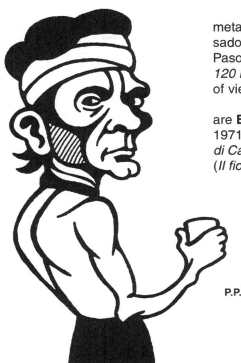

For **Pier Paolo Pasolini**, sex is a direct metaphor for politics, especially the perverse sado-masochism of Fascism and Nazism. Pasolini's ***Salò*** (1975), influenced by **De Sade**'s *120 Days of Sodom*, displays exactly that point of view.

Other films of Pasolini's "literary" period are **Boccaccio**'s ***Decameron*** (*Il Decameron*, 1971), **Chaucer**'s ***Cantenbury Tales*** (*I racconti di Cantenbury*, 1972), and ***The Arabian Nights*** (*Il fiore delle mille e una notte*, 1974).

P.P.P. in *Decameron*

Ettore Scola (b. 1931) becomes internationally recognized for his respectful parody of De Sica's *Miracle in Milan*, ***Dirty, Mean, and Nasty*** (*Brutti, sporchi, e cattivi*, 1976), a gritty look at urban poverty.

Stashing the money in a safe place:
Dirty, Mean, and Nasty

In ***A Special Day*** (*Una giornata particolare*, 1977), Scola brings together the talents of **Sophia Loren** and **Marcello Mastroianni** to create one of the most beautiful, restrained statements against Fascism to grace the Italian screen.

Liliana Cavani (b. 1937), one of Italy's more notorious filmmakers, directs *The Night Porter* (*Il portiere di notte*, 1974) which, like Pasolini's *Salò*, examines Fascism from the sadomasochistic perspective, emphasizing the devastating psychological effects of concentration camp experiences on survivors.

In *Beyond Good and Evil* (*Al di là del bene e del male*, 1977), Cavani focuses on the sexual experimentation of the aged Friedrich Nietzsche and presents his lover, the insatiable Lou Salomé, as the truly liberated, uninhibited person Nietzsche could only aspire to be.

Another woman director of international reputation, **Lina Wertmüller** (b. 1928), a former assistant to Fellini, joins Cavani in the process of reexamining Italy's Fascist past in *Love and Anarchy* (*Film d'amore e d'anarchia*, 1973) and in the controversial masterwork *Seven Beauties* (*Pasqualino Settebellezze*, 1975), a compellingly repulsive study of a Nazi concentration camp survivor.

Wertmüller's seemingly simple story of male-female power struggle, *Swept Away* (*Travolti da un insolito destino nell azzurro mare d'agosto*, 1974), traps together a rich, spoiled society woman and a sexist Communist seaman on a secluded island. The director shrewdly avoids a feminist approach to the subject of dominance as well as stays away from stereotyping her characters, allowing the story to assume a rarely seen hint of objectivity in dealing with intersexual relations.

Seven Beauties

Paolo and **Vittorio Taviani** direct *Padre Padrone* (1977), a multilayered tale of a Sardinian shepherd's rise to academic prominence, based on the real-life story of the famous linguist **Gavino Ledda**. Shifting between documentary and fiction narratives, the movie transcends the usual superficiality of political pictures by presenting an ideologically convincing image of social reality in the Italian provinces.

In 1970, two Scandinavian films simultaneously take a sympathetic look at the troubled, maladjusted younger generation remaining at odds with the established order of society—the Danish *Regarding Lone* (*Ang. Lone*, Franz Ernst) and the Swedish *A Swedish Love Story* (*En kärlekshistoria*, Roy Andersson).

Jan Troell (b. 1931) undertakes the monumental task of adapting the series of **Vilhelm Moberg** novels addressing the 19th century migration of impoverished Swedish families to the United States. The result is *The Emigrants* (*Utvandrarna*, 1970), one of the last examples of great epic cinema; this outstanding film enjoys a well-deserved worldwide popularity.

Liv Ulmann in *Emigrants*

Ingmar Bergman creates *Cries and Whispers* (*Visknigar och rop*, 1972), a stark, meditative portrait of human solitude in the face of death. The action takes place at the end of the 19th century; two well-to-do sisters (**Ingrid Thulin** and **Liv Ullmann**) arrive at their family estate to be with their terminally ill sister (**Harriet Andersson**) in the last days of her life. While the two women, driven apart by marriage and egoism, are unable to emotionally connect with their dying sibling, her caring, selfless maid (**Kari Sylvan**) tends to her every need and offers pure, boundless love. At once cruel and heartwarming, *Cries and Whispers* unveils a complicated landscape of human suffering, sorrow, and compassion brought to life by the magnificent acting of Bergman's favorite actors and supported by the sensitive photography of Sven Nykvist.

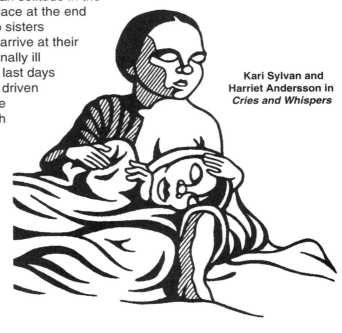

Kari Sylvan and Harriet Andersson in *Cries and Whispers*

Bergman's next project, *Scenes from a Marriage* (*Scener ur ett aktenskap*, 1974), originally shot for television, lives up to its title—the movie chronicles a decomposing marriage and follows the couple's ongoing relationship after they each remarry.

Partially due to tax difficulties, Bergman's subsequent films are produced outside of Sweden. *The Magic Flute* (1975) is an imaginative, playful account of the stage production of Mozart's opera.

The disturbing **Serpent's Egg** (1977) explores the loss of personal privacy and the increasing paranoia of prewar German society.

In the restrained **Autumn Sonata** (*Herbstsonate*, 1978), Bergman offers **Ingrid Bergman** her last screen role—a demanding concert pianist entangled in a difficult relationship with her daughter (Liv Ullmann).

After **The Life of the Marionettes** (1980), another insightful look into a trouble-ridden relationship, Bergman sets out to direct what he considers to be his last film and a fitting testament to the art of moviemaking. **Fanny and Alexander** (*Fanny och Alexander*, 1982) becomes Bergman's most widely seen and appreciated film, undoubtedly because of its straightforward and accessible theme—a semiautobiographical account of the director's childhood populated with intriguing, sometimes charmingly eccentric characters and just enough magic and sadness to call it a classic Bergman masterpiece.

**INGMAR BERGMAN'S COMMANDMENTS
FOR FILMMAKERS**

- **THOU SHALT BE ENTERTAINING AT ALL TIMES**
- **THOU SHALT OBEY THY ARTISTIC CONSCIENCE AT ALL TIMES**
- **THOU SHALT MAKE EACH FILM AS IF IT WERE THY LAST**

TO SHOOT A FILM IS TO ORGANIZE A COMPLETE UNIVERSE.

Ingmar Bergman

One of the best Swedish films to take on the issues of alienation and social responsibility is **Christopher's House** (*Kristoffers hus*, 1979), directed by **Lars Lennart Forsberg** (b. 1933) and co-written by **Vilgot Sjöman** of *I Am Curious* fame.

Initiated in 1968 with **Pippi** (dir. Olle Hellbom), the immensely popular series of films featuring the effervescent supergirl Pippi Longstocking finds its way into the hearts and imagination of children worldwide. The series is based on the writings of **Astrid Lindgren**, Sweden's foremost author of children's books.

Pippi

One of the most intriguing cinematic works to emerge out of **Norway** in the 1970s is **Wives** (*Hustruer*, 1975), directed with a charming, New Wave touch by the feminist filmmaker, **Anja Breien** (b. 1940). Inspired by Cassavetes' *Husbands*, *Wives* develops from improvised scenes focusing on three married middle-class women who decide to shake off the shackles of their mundane domestic existence.

The debut feature of **Vibeke Løkkeberg** (b. 1945), a former model and actress, is another prime example of Norwegian film from this era; **The Revelation** (*Åpenbaringen*, 1978) depicts a frustrated fifty-year-old woman who is driven to suicide by her husband's unfaithfulness and insensitivities.

Marie Takvam in *Revelation*

Another important achievement of Norwegian cinema is **Rallarblod** (dir. Erik Solbakken, 1979), an epic proletarian story of railroad workers, based on the prose of **Kristofer Updal**.

The cinema of **Finland** produces its greatest picture of the decade, **The Earth is a Sinful Song** (*Maa on syntinen laulu*, 1973). Directed by **Rauni Mollberg** (b. 1929), this beautiful, nearly ethnographic ballad of a remote Lapland village, based on the teenage novel by **Timo K. Mukki**, juxtaposes human morality with the threatening brutality of nature.

Another absorbing Finnish film dealing with the relationship between man and his environment is **Risto Jarva**'s (1934-77) **The Year of the Hare** (*Jäniksen vuosi*, 1977), in which an advertising agent finds himself stranded in and gradually seduced by the wilderness of Northern Finland only to become imprisoned by the shortsighted bureaucracy of civilization.

Antti Litja in *The Year of the Hare*

SPAIN 1970s

Shortly after the 1973 assassination of Franco's successor, Admiral Luis Carrero Blanco, Spain's dictatorial regime loosens its grip, allowing for the gradual resurrection of the arts.

One of the first great films to emerge from this period is **The Spirit of the Beehive** (*El spíritu de la colmena*, Victor Erice, 1973)— a lyrical, contemplative picture of haunting beauty and stark, uncompromising imagery. The elliptical narrative of the movie, permeated with allegorical references to Spain's fascist past, depicts two little sisters who, after watching James Whale's *Frankenstein*, explore their newly discovered power of imagination.

The Spirit of the Beehive

Carlos Saura's (b. 1932) **The Hunt** (*La caza*, 1965), one of the greatest films of the previous decade, was a cruel allegory of the Fascist oppression of the Civil War rebels. The autobiographical **Cousin Angelica** (*La prima Angélica*, 1974) becomes Saura's best work of the 1970s; this nostalgic movie presents an older man's recollections about his romance interwoven with the political tapestry of the early Franco regime.

In **Raise Ravens** (*Cría cuervos*, 1975), Saura once more delves into his ghost-ridden past, this time witnessing the reality of Fascist Spain through the eyes of a perplexed nine-year old girl (**Ana Torrent**). As usual, the movie is full of references to the present-day political situation in Saura's country.

Toward the end of the decade, Saura's movies begin to attract large international audiences, especially **Mama Turns 100** (*Mama cumple 100 años*, 1979) and **Hurry, Hurry!** (*Deprisa, deprisa*, 1980).

After the enactment of the democratic constitution in 1978, **Juan Antonio Bardem** makes the engaging thriller about political murder, ***Seven Days in January*** (*Siete dias de enero*, 1978), whose semi-documentary style recalls *The Battle of Algiers*.

Other important directors of the New Spanish cinema are **Jaime de Armiñan** (b. 1927) and **Jose Luis Borau** (b. 1929).

De Armiñan's ***The Love of Captain Brando*** (*El amor del capitán Brando*, 1974) brings to mind *The Spirit of the Beehive* in its tale of an adolescent country boy who develops an imaginary father/authority figure. In the post-Franco ***The Nest*** (*El nido*, 1980), de Armiñan deals with an older man's affection for a teenage girl in a lyrical and sensitive manner.

Borau's contribution to the politically allusive cinema is ***Poachers*** (*Furtivos*, 1975); his later ***La Sabina*** (1979) depicts an Andalusian myth of a woman who inspires love but also brings destruction to the world made by men.

Borau in *Poachers*

Luis Garcia Berlanga (b. 1921), one of the pioneers of the postwar Spanish cinema (***A Miracle Every Thursday***/*Los jueves, milagro*, 1957), emerges in the 1970s as the director of the extremely popular political satire, ***The National Shotgun*** (*La escopeta nacional*, 1977).

When discussing the political cinema of the period, one must not neglect **Ricardo Franco**'s (b. 1935) devastating ***Pascual Duarte*** (1975).

Among other essential films of the decade are ***Torment*** (*Tormento*, Pedro Olea, 1974), ***Family Portrait*** (*Retrato de familia*, Antonio Gimenez Rico, 1976), ***The Long Vacations of '36*** (*Las largas vacacciones del 36*, Jaime Caino, 1976), ***Black Brood*** (*Camada negra*, Manuel Gutierrez Aragon, 1977), ***The Truth About the Savolta Case*** (*La veridad sobre el caso Savolta*, Antonio Drove, 1978), and ***The Cuenca Crime*** (*El crimen de Cuenca*, Pilar Miro, 1979).

Although technically a French/Italian production, the action of **Louis Buñuel**'s *Tristaña* (1970) takes place in the historic Spanish city of Toledo. In a typically perverse, satirical manner, Buñuel presents the bizarre relationship between an old man (Fernando Rey) and his beautiful ward (Catherine Deneuve). Their continual tests of each other's emotional limits parallel the country's socio-political landscape.

The French-produced
The Discreet Charm of the Bourgeoisie
(*Le Charme discret de la bourgeoisie*,
1973) recalls Buñuel's earlier
The Exterminating Angel as well as
L'Age d'Or in a highly humorous but
relentlessly scornful attack on the
hypocritical upper middle-class.

Fernando Rey in
The Discreet Charm of the Bourgeoisie

The Phantom of Liberty (*Le Fantôme de la liberté*, 1974), Buñuel's episodic, dreamy narrative, combines seemingly disjointed political, social, and artistic vignettes to create a surreal commentary on the trappings of societal conventions.

In his last film, ***That Obscure Object of Desire*** (*Cet obscur object du desir*, 1977), Buñuel subverts the concept of objective reality by having two distinctly different actresses portray the conflicting facets of one woman's personality—her alluring, innocent sweetness (**Carole Bouquet**) and her fierce sexual power (**Angela Molina**). The director suggests that it is that irresistible dichotomy of woman's nature, however imagined it may be, which drives men to the edge of physical and mental collapse.

CINEMA IS A MAGNIFICENT
AND PERILOUS WEAPON
WHEN WIELDED BY
A FREE SPIRIT.

Louis Buñuel

POLAND

In December 1970, two years after the Warsaw Pact thwarted the Prague Spring revolt, Polish shipyard workers of Szczecin and Gdansk suffer a similar fate when military troops put a bloody end to their demands for better wages and living conditions. Poland enters a period of increasing tension between its citizens and the socialist government.

Nearly a decade after the end of the "Polish School" cinema, **Andrzej Wajda** enters his second important period of intense creativity with *Landscape After Battle* (*Krajobraz po bitwie*, 1970) and *The Birch Wood* (*Brzezina*, 1970). Wajda's *Wedding* (*Wesele*, 1972), an evocative adaptation of the classic allegorical drama by **Stanislaw Wyspianski**, presents a colorful cross-section of the late 19th century Polish society as it mirrors present-day Polish sentiments.

In the spectacular *The Promised Land* (*Ziemia Obiecana*, 1976), based on the novel by **Wladyslaw Reymont**, Wajda presents the development of textile industry in the Russian-occupied territory of Poland in the 1860s. Out of the three protagonists, a Pole, a German, and a Jew, it is the third who appears most sympathetic during the film's concluding denouncement of uncontrolled capitalism.

But it isn't until 1977 when Wajda reaches for an openly political theme. His *Man of Marble* (*Czlowiek z marmuru*) becomes the most influential film in Polish history. With a structure similar to *Citizen Kane*, Wajda's movie concerns a young, uncompromising TV reporter (**Krystyna Janda**) who is researching the truth about Poland's Stalinist past. After her investigation inevitably brings up politically and morally questionable facts, she must face the immediate problem of contemporary censorship.

Jerzy Radziwillowicz in *Man of Marble*

Without Anesthesia (*Bez znieczulenia*, 1978), scripted by **Agnieszka Holland**, continues Wajda's critique of the morally reprehensible practices of the Polish media, which remains unaccountable for its frequently irresponsible actions.

After Wajda, the most influential Polish director of the decade is **Krzysztof Zanussi** (b. 1939). Since his background is in physics, Zanussi's approach to cinema tends to be more analytical and restrained than Wajda's; films like ***The Structure of Crystals*** (*Struktura Krysztalu*, 1969) and ***Family Life*** (*Zycie Rodzinne*, 1971) focus on the individual predicaments of Polish people against the backdrop of their immediate environment.

In the philosophical ***Illumination*** (*Iluminacja*, 1973), Zanussi contrasts the intellectual and the biological models of human existence and reaches the disturbing conclusion that people do not amount to much more than a sack of unbalanced chemicals.

Zanussi's subsequent films, ***Quarterly Balance*** (*Bilans Kwartalny*, 1975) and ***Camouflage*** (*Barwy Ochronne*, 1977) again deal with small groups of individuals whose problems reflect the larger issues of the increasingly difficult political and economical situation in Poland of the 1970s.

Spiral (*Spirala*, 1978), another deeply philosophical picture of Zanussi's, is a story of a terminally ill man who chooses to end his life while on a mountaineering trip. Zanussi transforms death into a catalyst for life—the man is found alive by a rescue team. He acquires a new perspective on his illness which takes into account those who care for him and who will have to deal with his loss.

In mid 1970s, the term **"cinema of moral anxiety"** becomes a popular phrase to describe all Polish films concerned with the country's progressively worsening state of affairs.

Among the first films to fall into this category are **Krzysztof Kieslowski's** (1944-96) ***Personnel*** (*Personel*, 1975), in which the backstage life of a large theatre becomes a microcosm of society, and ***The Camera Buff*** (*Amator*, 1979), a tale of an amateur filmmaker whose hobby becomes a tool of political manipulation.

Morally anxious: Jerzy Stuhr in *The Camera Buff*

The strongest denouncements of the demoralizing corruption of authority appear in such allegorical films as *Top Dog* (*Wodzirej*, Feliks Falk, 1978), *Transfiguration Hospital* (*Szpital Przemienienia*, Edward Zebrowski, 1979), and **Provincial Actors** (*Aktorzy Prowincjonalni*, Agnieszka Holland, 1980).

Tadeusz Huk in *Provincial Actors*

One of the more unconventional Polish films of the decade, **The Cruise** (*Rejs*, Marek Piwowski, 1970), is a brilliant satire on the mentality of a socialist society.

After his depressing allegory of contemporary Polish existence, **The Move** (*Przeprowadzka*, 1972), which remains shelved until the mid 1980s, **Jerzy Gruza** dramatically shifts his attention with **Alice** (1978), a Polish/French production of the Lewis Carroll book, shot as an entertaining romantic musical with a gloomy twist.

CZECHOSLOVAKIA

While the socioeconomic situation of Czechoslovakia nearly mirrors that of neighboring Poland, the Czechoslovak film industry is still severely shaken after the Soviet invasion of 1968.

Vera Chytilová, the Czech New Wave pioneer, is forbidden to direct until 1975, when the easing government grip on the arts permits her to make **The Apple Game** (*Hra o jablko*)—a controversial farce about male-female dynamics set against a background of deplorable health care system.

Jiri Menzel in *The Apple Game*

Chytilová's next two films, **Prefab Story** (*Panelstory*, 1978) and **Calamity** (*Kalamita*, 1979), confirm the director's uncompromising artistic vision and dissident commitment.

231

Similar fate befalls **Jirí Menzel**, who also returns to directing in 1975, after a six-year hiatus. His truly notable film of the decade is the stylized tribute to the Czech film industry titled ***Those Wonderful Movie Cranks*** (*Bájecní muzi s klikou*, 1978).

After the surreal, baroque horror-fantasy, ***Valérie and Her Week of Wonders*** (*Valérie a tyden divu*, 1969), **Jaromil Jires** (b. 1935) directs ***And Give My Love to the Swallows*** (*A pozdravují vlastovky*, 1971), a beautifully filmed tragic story based on the diaries of a young Czech Resistance sympathizer executed by the Nazis during WWII.

And Give My Love to the Swallows

Frantisek Vlácil (b. 1924), the famed veteran of Czech film, whose past work includes the great Bohemian epic, ***Markéta Lazarová*** (1967) returns to prominence with ***Smoke on the Potato Fields*** (*Dym bramborové nate*, 1976) and ***Shadows of a Hot Summer Day*** (*Stíny horkého léta*, 1977).

Other notable personalities in Czech cinema of this period include **Juraj Herz** (b. 1934, ***The Cremator***/*Spalovac mrtvol*, 1968; ***Morigana***, 1972; and ***A Day for My Love***/*Den pro mou lásku*, 1977) and **Oldrich Lipsky** (b. 1924, ***Dinner For Adele***/*Adéla jeste nevecerela*, 1978, and ***Long Live Ghosts***/*Atzijí duchové!*, 1979).

The Slovak director **Dusan Hanak**, whose work is mostly shelved or shown only abroad, enjoys critical praise for ***399*** (1969) and ***Rose-Tinted Dreams*** (*Ruzové sny*, 1976), a sensual, poetic love story between a gypsy woman and a Slovak man.

Rose-Tinted Dreams

THE SOVIET UNION

The classic, existential science-fiction novel by the Polish author **Stanislaw Lem**, *Solaris*, becomes the source of **Andrei Tarkovsky**'s contemplative movie by the same name (1971); many critics consider it a philosophical polemic with Kubrick's *2001*.

In 1974, Tarkovsky directs the introspective, poetic **Mirror** (*Zerkalo*), an autobiographical account of his childhood presented in a stylized, elliptical manner which will become Tarkovsky's trademark.

His next project, **Stalker** (1979), unveils a gloomy, apocalyptic vision of the not-too-distant future, where people are confined to prison-like compounds and all intellectual activities are prohibited. Stalkers are the outlaw outsiders who know the way to a secret Chamber in "The Zone," where people's dreams and wishes come true. The movie chronicles one such illegal excursion, with a mysterious Stalker guiding two men, a scientist and a writer, through the desolate Zone to fulfill their thirst for self-knowledge. Without being preachy, *Stalker* strips human existence to its very essence, discarding the burden of analytical thought in favor of human contact and the elusive beauty of life.

Aleksandr Kaidanovsky in *Stalker*

Andrei Michalkov-Konchalovsky's greatest achievement of the decade is the two-part epic, *Siberiad* (*Sibiriada*, 1979)—a magnificent chronicle of three generations of Siberian families caught in the dramatic flow of Soviet history. Konchalovsky's uncanny skill in combining utterly realistic action with poetic imagery, nostalgic interludes, and surreal visions make *Siberiad* one of the most rewarding experiences of world cinema.

Vassili Shukshin continues his auteur path with *Shop Crumbs* (*Pechki-lavochki*, 1972) and *The Red Snowball Tree* (*Kalina krasnaya*, 1973), which deal with the contemporary provincial Soviet life in a straightforward, human way. Besides writing and directing both movies, Shukshin convincingly plays the leads.

Vassili Shukshin in *Shop Crumbs*

The Moldavian filmmaker **Emil Lotianu** (b. 1936) creates two great lyrical Gypsy pictures, *The Leutary* (*Leutary*, 1971) and *Gypsies Take Off for the Sky* (*Tabor uhodit v nebo*, 1976).

Otar Ioselani's (b. 1934) *There Lived a Singing blackbird* (*Zhil pevichy drozd*, 1970) and *Pastorale* (1976) offer an unembellished portrayal of the Soviet reality in the director's native republic of Georgia. Problems with distribution ensue.

The republic of Azerbaijan produces such memorable films as *My Seven Sons* (dir. Tofik Tagi-Zade, 1970), *The Price of Happiness* (dir. Gasan Seidbejili, 1976), and *The Interrogation* (dir. Rasim Odzagov, 1979), among many, many others.

The Ukraine-born, VGIK-trained **Larissa Shepitko** (1939-79), creates her last film, *The Ascent* (*Voskhozhenie*, 1977), which subverts the Soviet myth of indomitable Russian heroism in WWII.

Shepitko is also responsible for directing one of the very first movies in the republic of Kirghizia, *Heat*, in 1963.

Larissa Shepitko

BULGARIA

The restructuring of the Bulgarian film industry in the early 1970s paves the way for a new wave of creative talent.

One of the first beneficiaries of this change, **The Goat Horn** (*Koziyat rog*, Metodi Andonov, 1972), a historical tragedy from the Turkish oppression period, becomes a great critical and financial success.

The technically innovative, surreal **The Last Summer** (*Posledno lyato*, 1974) by **Hristo Hristov**, the co-author of the famous *Iconostasis*, deals with a dam development project threatening peasant life-style.

Hristo Hristov on the set of *The Last Summer*

Eduard Zahariev's (b. 1938) **Hare Census** (*Prebroyavane na divite zaytsi*, 1973) remains the most accurate satire on the modern Bulgarian bureaucratic mentality. In another absurdist film, **Villa Zone** (*Vilna zona*, 1975), Zahariev probes the contemporary issue of peasant migration to the cities. His **Manly Times** (*Muzhki vremena*, 1977) tells of a love story between a peasant girl and her *haiduk* abductor.

The veteran of the industry **Binka Zheliazkova** directs **The Last Word** (*Poslednata duma*, 1973), a patriotic WWII story of six women condemned to death for their participation in the Resistance movement. Zheliazkova's subsequent **The Swimming Pool** (*Basseynat*, 1977) delves into Bulgaria's Stalinist past.

The Unknown Soldier's Patent Leather Shoes (*Lachenite obouvki na neznainiya voin*, Rangel Vulchanov, 1979), set in a rural milieu between the wars, displays some of the most lyrical images of childhood ever to appear on film.

ROMANIA

The poetic, strikingly beautiful romantic diptych **The Stone Wedding** (*Nunta de piatra*, 1971) announces the emergence of two outstanding talents: **Mircea Veroiu**'s (b. 1941) and **Dan Pita**'s (b. 1938), the picture's co-directors.

Pita's **Philip the Kind** (*Filip cel bun*, 1974) displays deep concern for issues of morality. His turn-of-the-century **Summer Tale** (*Tanase scatiu*, 1977) benefits from beautiful cinematography and meticulous mise-en-scène.

Mircea Daneliuc (b. 1943) breathes fresh air into the Romanian cinema with **The Race** (*Cursa*, 1975), an entertaining road movie, and **Special Issue** (*Editie speciala*, 1978), a taut thriller set against the politically repressive backdrop of prewar Romania.

HUNGARY

In the second decade after the tragic events of 1956, Hungary becomes the most economically stable country of the Warsaw Pact. Hungarian cinema continues to produce some of the most stimulating movies ever to emerge out of the Eastern Block.

Miklós Jancsó's best movie of the period is undoubtedly **Red Psalm** (*Még kér a nép*, 1972), the 19th century epic of a failed agrarian revolt, composed of breathtaking visuals and complex choreography within each long take.

Similarly, Jancsó's allegorical **Elektreia** (*Szerelmem, Elektra*, 1974) is structured around only twelve long shots—all full of elaborate camera movement and incredibly precise mise-en-scène.

Elektreia

In a typically symbolic, visually irresistible fashion, Jancsó's two-part epic **Hungarian Rhapsody** and **Allegro Barbaro** (1979) recreate the first half of the nation's 20th century history.

Some of the most visually astonishing Hungarian movies belong to the renowned painter and designer **Zoltan Huszárik** (1931-81). His melancholic, nonlinear **Sindbad** (*Szindbád*, 1971) ponders the organic nature of time and love while **Csontváry** (1980) contemplates the essence of artistic creativity.

István Gaál's outstanding *The Falcons* (*Magasiskola*, 1970) is a metaphorical study of the Hungarian Fascist past. In *Dead Landscape* (*Holt vidék*, 1971), Gaál conducts an analysis of human loneliness and the devastating effects of alienation.

Ferenc Kósa, of *Ten Thousand Suns* fame, returns to top form with *Beyond Time* (*Ninc idö*, 1972), a political prison allegory set in the 1920s, and *Snowfall* (*Hószakadás*, 1974), a moving portrait of the aftermath of WWII from the perspective of a young soldier and his grandmother on an arduous quest to find his missing parents.

The keenest observer of the contemporary Hungarian reality, especially the ever uncertain situation of women and children, is the VGIK-educated **Márta Mészáros** (b. 1931). Her *Adoption* (*Örökbefogadás*, 1975) and *Nine Months* (*Kilenc hónap*, 1976) possess a nearly clinical objectivity in presenting such issues as unfulfilled dreams of motherhood and single-parent predicaments, respectively.

Mészáros' restrained, unsentimental style also permeates *Just Like At Home* (*Olyan, mint otthon*, 1978), a movie about the spiritual union of a lonely middle-aged man and a little girl.

Márta Mészáros

In 1979, **István Szabó** creates his masterpiece of intimate cinema, *Confidence* (*Bizalom*), co-written with **Erika Szántó**, and beautifully photographed by **Lajos Kolotai** (*Just Like At Home, Angi Vera*). This muted, carefully orchestrated film follows the increasingly complicated relationship between a man and a woman who pretend to be married in order to evade the Nazi persecution in the 1944 Budapest.

Confidence

Imre Gyöngyössy (1930-94), a former screenwriter for Gaál, Kósa, and Jan Kadár, develops his own unique directing style with *Legend About the Death and Resurrection of Two Young Men* (*Meztelen vagy*, 1971) and *Sons of Fire* (*Szarvassá vált fiúk*, 1974). Both deal with society's smallmindedness manifesting itself in unmotivated cruelty and violence. In the former film, Gyöngyössy provides viewers with some very dramatic montage sequences designed to disrupt the linear continuity of the narrative.

YUGOSLAVIA

Yugoslavia enjoys a relative economic prosperity, partially due to its close proximity to Western Europe. However, the early 1970s bring unrest to Tito's domestic politics; the government begins to suppress "undesirable elements" in both the political and cultural environments. *Novi film* is one of the first victims.

WR

One of the last working *Novi film* directors, **Dusan Makavejev** enters the 1970s with the vivid, surreal ***WR—The Mysteries of the Organism*** (*WR —Misterije organizma*, 1971), which combines documentary and fiction narratives in a fearless fashion. The movie's parallel between sexual power struggle and totalitarian politics does not gain the approval of Yugoslav censors. Makavejev chooses exile.

DEATH TO MALE FASCISM! FREEDOM FOR FEMALE PEOPLE!

The next period of fresh, imaginative cinema falls in the late 1970s, when a group of young Yugoslavian filmmakers educated at the Czech FAMU returns home and takes movie industry by storm. They are collectively known as the "**Prague Group**" or the "**Czech School**."

The most internationally recognized film of the group is **Lordan Zafranovic**'s (b. 1944) ***Occupation in Twenty-Six Scenes*** (*Okupacija u 26 slika*, 1978)—a poetic, if frequently brutal, look at the country's horrific WWII experiences, set in the beautiful Adriatic seaport of Dubrovnik.

In the elegant satire, ***The Scent of Wild Flowers*** (*Miris pljskog cveca*, 1978), **Srdan Karanovic** (b. 1945) presents a media frenzy surrounding a renowned elderly actor's private life.

Some of the most popular early films of the "Prague Group" belong to **Goran Paskaljevic** (b. 1947), especially ***The Beach Guard in Winter*** (*Cuvar plaze u zimskom periodu*, 1976) and ***The Dog Who Liked Trains*** (*Pas koji je voleo vozove*, 1978).

The "Prague Group" will reach its climax in the following decade.

GREECE 1970s

Theo Angelopoulos (b. 1936) establishes himself as a prominent director with *Reconstruction* (*Anaparastassi*, 1970), a picture with a structure similar to Lucian Pintilie's film of the same name. Angelopoulos' movie, however, deals with the issue of emigrant workers—a Greek *gastarbeiter* is killed by his wife and her lover upon his return from Germany.

Angelopoulos' **The Traveling Players** (*O Thiassoss*, 1975), a Brechtian epic covering the 1939-52 period of Greek history, displays intricate mise-en-scène and camera movement appropriate to the aesthetic of the traveling theater performance.

Theo
Angelopoulos

Nikos Panayotopoulos' (b. 1941) internationally renowned surreal satire *The Idlers of the Fertile Valley* (1978), presents the gradual decomposition of bourgeois mentality.

In the dramatic **Happy Day** (1976), **Pantelis Voulgaris** (b. 1940) creates a poetic political allegory with an isolated concentration camp society composed of exiled dissidents, their guards, and occasional visitors.

Happy Day

One of the most lyrical films of the decade is **Nikos Koundouros'** *1922* (1978), which depicts the horrors and agony of Greek prisoners of the Asia Minor Disaster.

Classical Greek tragedy finds its apt screen representation in **Michael Cacoyannis'** (b. 1922) masterful *Iphigenia* (1977), an adaptation of the Euripides play.

INDIA 1970s

The decade of the 1970s bears witness to the tremendous boom in the Indian film industry. With mass media still a rarity in this country of nearly a billion people, cinema remains the single most accessible form of entertainment. The overwhelming number of film productions (approximately 700 a year!), mostly of little artistic merit, makes India the World Champion of cinematic output.

One of the few masters of Indian film whose work transcends international boundaries is **Satyajit Ray**, the author of the famous *Apu* trilogy. In the 1970s, Ray focuses on socio-political themes including the unemployment of educated youth (***The Adversary**/Pratidwandi*, 1971), business practices (***The Middle Man**/Jana aranya*, 1979) and detachment from political reality (***The Chess Players**/Shatranj ke khilari*, 1977).

As a direct response to the garish popular cinema, India's more ambitious filmmakers develop the so-called **Parallel Cinema**. One of its most stalwart exponents is **Ritwik Ghatak** (1925-76), whose autobiographical ***Reason, Debate and a Tale*** (*Jukti takko aur gappo*, 1974) concerns the troubled conscience of an alcoholic Marxist intellectual caught in the midst of agrarian tensions in Eastern India.

Samila Patil in
In Search of Famine

The success of the milestone ***Mr. Shome*** (*Bhuvan Shome*, 1969), a light contemporary satire in the *Nouvelle Vague* mode, makes its director, **Mrinal Sen** (b. 1923), a preeminent figure of the Parallel Cinema.

Sen culminates the 1970s with ***In Search of Famine*** (*Aakaler sandhaney*, 1980) a socially conscious drama of the exploitation of the poor.

The most popular director of the group is **Shyam Benegal** (b. 1924), whose work is also directed toward the class inequalities and economic exploitation within Indian society. Benegal's first film, **The Seedling** (*Ankur*, 1974), sets a stylistic standard for the new generation of "parallel" filmmakers. Among Benegal's most interesting films is **The Churning** (*Manthan*, 1976), financed by milk farmers' donations from the Gujarat State; the movie deals with the hierarchical confrontations and caste clashes in the regional dairy industry.

The Churning

Other directors of importance include **Mani Kaul** (**A Day's Bread**/*Uskiroti*, 1970), **Kumar Shahani** (**Maya Darpan**, 1972), **Girish Karnad** (**The Forest**/*Kaadu*, 1973), **Girish Kasaravalli** (**The Ritual**/*Ghatashraddha*, 1977), **G. Aravindan** (**Golden Sita**/*Kanchana Sita*), and, of course, many others.

JAPAN 1970s

Due to the government ban on censorship (!) between 1966 and 1972, Japanese cinema allows itself to lower its standards of excellence and focuses on the highly profitable production of potboilers and actioneers, quite frequently pornographic, such as the *yakuza-eiga* genre of Mafia/gangster pictures which emphasizes brutality and sadism.

Somewhat lost in that time of absent aesthetic, **Akira Kurosawa** directs **Dodesukaden** (1970), his first film in color. Virtually plotless, but utterly absorbing, the movie depicts episodes from the extremely impoverished Tokyo slums. Severely depressed after *Dodesukaden*'s commercial failure and fearing the collapse of his creative powers, Kurosawa attempts suicide— a morally understandable decision for a *bushido* worshiper.

Dodesukaden

241

His miraculous survival forever changes Kurosawa's approach to life and art. No longer shunning publicity, the famous director begins to participate in lucrative TV commercials and grants multiple interviews. In 1975, Kurosawa returns to cinema with *Dersu Uzala*, a Soviet-Japanese production which chronicles a friendship between a Siberian hunter and a Russian land surveyor. Shot in spectacular widescreen format, with brilliant use of color, *Dersu Uzala* enjoys a well deserved critical success and international popularity.

Another veteran of Japanese cinema, Kon Ichikawa, creates **The Wanderers** (*Matatabi*, 1973)—a beautiful, if traditionally shot, 19th century sword epic.

Yoshishige Yoshida (b. 1933), one of the more political Japanese New Wave filmmakers, directs the anarchic **Eros Plus Massacre** (*Eros purasu gyakusatsu*, 1970) and the equally controversial **Martial Law** (*Kaigenrei*, 1973), an informal biography of Kita Ikki, the right-wing rebel of the 1930s.

Nagisa Oshima shocks viewers and enamors critics with **In the Realm of Senses** (*Ai no corrida*, 1976), an atmospheric *amour fou* story with pornographic interludes, artistic sensibility, and a feminist slash.

Eiko Matsuda in *In the Realm of Senses*

Shohei Imamura, who spends most of the decade in the documentary field, returns to narrative film with **Vengeance Is Mine** (*Fukushu suru wa are ni ari*, 1979), which follows the bloody path of a mass murderer with distressing detachment and realism.

Other noteworthy films of the period include **The Family** (dir. Yoji Imada, 1970), **Tsugaru Folksong** (dir. Koichi Saito, 1973), and **The Assassination of Ryoma** (dir. Kazuo Kuroki, 1974). Yes, there are more, many more.

SOUTH AMERICA 1970s

It can be stated without much exaggeration that virtually all Latin American countries of the 1970s experience similar political situations: right-wing governments suppress their leftist opposition, usually with the use of military and police forces. Cultural activity suffers from varying degrees of censorship, and film production is reduced to the lowest-common denominator; light, run-of-the-mill sex comedies and violent, macho-adventure pictures dominate South American cinema.

The **Argentinian** *nuevo cine* approaches its final days. The last important picture of that period is **Rebellion in Patagonia** (*La Patagonia rebelde*, **Héctor Olivera**, 1974), a historical picture dealing with the bloody suppression of a farm workers' revolt in the 1920s.

The films of **Raúl de la Torre** (b. 1938) possess unusual for Latin America complexity and sensibility in portraying female characters . Some of his titles from the 1970s include **Story of a Lady** (*Crónica de una señora*, 1971) and **Alone** (*Sola*, 1976).

The situation in **Brazil** is nearly identical: *cinema novo* ceases its existence with the increasing pressure of the military junta.

Ironically, the most popular film of the 1970s, both domestically and internationally, becomes **Xica da Silva** (1976), a movie directed by *cinema novo* pioneer, **Carlos Diegues** (b. 1940, **Ganga Zamba**, 1963). *Xica da Silva* tells the true story of a former slave woman's rise to political prominence in 18th century colonial Brazil.

POLITICS AND FASHION MIX.

Zezé Motta as Xica

Diegues' eye-opening, cross-country adventure **Bye Bye Brasil** (1980) enjoys similar success.

Another extremely popular Brazilian picture of the period is the contemporary social farce, **Dona Flor and Her Two Husbands** (*Dona Flor e seus dois maridos*, Bruno Barretto, 1976).

The cinema of **Cuba** enjoys a period of increasingly sophisticated works, most notably by such directors as **Tomás Gutiérrez Alea** (b. 1928, **The Last Supper**/*La última cena*, 1977), **Sara Gómez** (1943-75, **One Way of Another**/*De cierta manera*, 1974), and **Manuel Octavo Gómez** (**A Woman, a Man, a City**/*Una mujer, un hombre, una ciudad*, 1978).

The military coup of 1971 forces most of **Bolivia**'s opposition into exile. **Antonio Equino**, who, as a member of the Grupo Ukamau film unit, collaborated on the famous *Ywar mallku* in 1969, directs **Chuquiago** (1977), Bolivia's most popular film to date. The movie is a thorough study of the social dynamics in the country's capital, La Paz.

In **Chile**, the 1970 election of the Marxist Allende government results in a wave of such politically-oriented movies as **No One Said a Thing** (*Nadie dijo nada*, Raúl Ruiz, 1971), **Praying is No Longer Enough** (*Ya no basta con rezar*, Aldo Francia, 1971), and **The Promised Land** (*La tierra prometida*, Miguel Littín, 1973).

In 1973, regarding Salvador Allende as a pro-Cuban communist, the CIA backs the General Augusto Pinochet coup to overthrow his socialist government. Chile enters its darkest hour of civil rights repressions.

Among the many directors forced into exile, **Raúl Ruiz** (b. 1941) becomes most internationally recognized for such wonderfully enigmatic films as **Hypothesis of a Stolen Painting** (*L'Hypothèse d'un tableau volé*, 1978), which attempts to penetrate the mystery of a painting's surface.

The Promised Land

Mexico's newly established film school, **Centro Universitario de Estudios Cinematográficos** (**CUEC**) is responsible for producing some of the most interesting directors of the decade.

Alexandro Jodorovsky's violent **El Topo** (1970), the messianic, intellectual parable hidden beneath the veil of a Western parody, acquires a deserved worldwide cult following.

Jaime Humberto Hermosillo creates a series of intelligent, anti-patriarchal portrayals of women in **The Passion According to Berenice** (*La pasión según Berenice*, 1975) and **My Dearest Maria** (*María de mi corazón*, 1979), among other titles. The latter is based on a story by **Gabriel García Márquez** and concerns a good witch who runs a magic show for children.

The Passion According to Berenice

With the echo of the Vietnam loss still in the air, America enters the 1980s in the shadow of new foreign-policy crises: the Soviet invasion of Afghanistan and the rise of Khomeini to power in Iran. The Democratic Carter administration suffers its last blow from the unfortunate hostage situation in the U.S. embassy in Teheran.

In the 1980 election, America joyfully chooses the former governor of California, the Republican **Ronald Reagan** (b. 1911), as its 40th President.

Reagan's biography is particularly intriguing in the context of cinema history. As a Hollywood B-list actor, he fails to become a bona-fide star. During WWII, Reagan focuses his attention on keeping up the patriotic morale of the film industry; he becomes active in the Screen Actors Guild and, in 1947, is elected its president. The five-year period of Reagan's rule (1947-52) is marked by extremely conservative policies, including the mandatory loyalty oath for the SAG members to insure their anticommunist attitude. During the infamous HUAC hearings, Reagan becomes an FBI informer (code name: T-10) and is one of the first actors to name names of colleagues suspected of "un-American" activities.

This man becomes President of the United States in 1981. Hollywood, of course, follows the leader. The popular American cinema of the 1980s gears itself toward the aggressive, macho-adventure movies which mirror Reagan's foreign policies.

THE SELF-CONFESSED ERROL FLYNN OF THE B's, RONALD REAGAN DUKES IT OUT IN *SECRET SERVICE OF THE AIR* (1939)

After the mildly revisionist Vietnam veteran adventure **Rambo: First Blood** (dir. Ted Kotcheff, 1982), **Sylvester Stallone** returns to Vietnam in **Rambo: First Blood Part 2** (dir. George P. Cosmatos, 1985) to single-handedly rescue the American POWs and, in the process, show the Vietnamese who's really the boss (in the third installment the series, Rambo triumphs in Afghanistan). The tremendous appeal of these films proves that the American moviegoers (mostly males aged 16-30) crave psychopathic, testosterone driven entertainment as much as they support testosterone-driven politics.

The last scene of Stallone's **Rocky IV** (1986) sums up the essence of the Reagan era: after demolishing a Russian fighter on his home Soviet turf, Rocky wraps himself in the American flag and utters a wild howl of dominance. The echo of that fatef roar carries well into the next decade.

Coiffured to kill, Sylvester Stallone threatens the enemy with his naked blade in *Rambo II*

The example of the Stallone phenomenon is critical to understanding what went wrong in mainstream American cinema in the 1980s. The sheer difference of quality between the humane, intelligent first two *Rocky* pictures (1976 and 1978) and the brutal, narcissistic macho feast of No. III and IV, epitomize the shift in the American psyche, so skillfully exploited by the Reagan-Bush administration. Celluloid heroes boost the deflated ego of the nation and help to foster unprecedented military spending by the Republican government. The most outlandish White House initiative of the period, the Star Wars Program, aimed at the U.S. military colonization of space, derives its popular name from America's favorite movie.

WHAT WAS THAT THING LENIN SAID ABOUT CINEMA?

To understand the political backdrop of the era is to understand why such overtly propagandistic, pro-male American pictures as the *Rambo* and *Rocky* series, as well as the similar vehicles of **Clint Eastwood** (*Heartbreak Ridge*, 1986) and **Chuck Norris** (*Missing in Action*, 1984) not only see the light of day but also go on to dominate domestic and overseas markets.

Another curious phenomenon of the star-driven Hollywood of the 1980s is the rise of the Austrian-born **Arnold Schwarzenegger** (b. 1947), the most celebrated epitome of the American Dream. His breakthrough mythical sword epic, ***Conan the Barbarian*** (1982), is not only directed by John Millius of *Apocalypse* fame but also written by Oliver Stone. The severely limited range of Schwarzenegger's acting doesn't stand in the way of elevating his Mr. Olympia bulk into superstar status with such overblown machismo trips as ***Commando*** (dir. Mark L. Lester, 1985) and ***Red Heat*** (dir. Walter Hill, 1988). The mass audiences of the 1980s continue to prove that they are in it for the ride and not for the high flying ideology or thespian bravura of the previous decade.

Among other emblematic blockbusters of the 1980s are ***Top Gun*** (dir. Tony Scott, 1986), ***Lethal Weapon*** (dir. Richard Donner, 1987), and ***Die Hard*** (dir. John McTiernan, 1988), whose respective titles form a rather telling pattern.

The situation of the American film industry, however, is not completely despicable. In a quick succession, three movies with similar topics raise the level of American cinema's conscience: *The Year of Living Dangerously* (dir. Peter Weir, 1982) and *Under Fire* (dir. Roger Spottiswoode, 1985) present Western journalists exposing the political regimes of 1960s Indonesia and Somoza's Nicaragua, respectively. Costa-Gavras' harrowing *Missing* (1982) deals with an American man searching for his son lost in the political chaos of Pinochet's Chile.

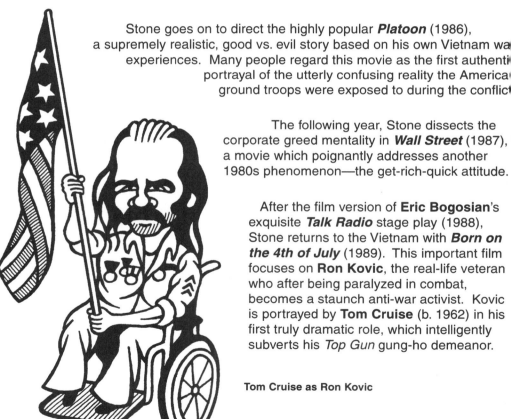

Nick Nolte in
Under Fire

The similarly structured *Salvador* (1986), directed by **Oliver Stone** (b. 1941), takes a deeply critical look at the US-backed military regime of this South American country. Made with the help of British backers, *Salvador* finally manages to break the spell of the "winning attitude" promoted by studio productions.

Stone goes on to direct the highly popular *Platoon* (1986), a supremely realistic, good vs. evil story based on his own Vietnam war experiences. Many people regard this movie as the first authentic portrayal of the utterly confusing reality the American ground troops were exposed to during the conflict.

The following year, Stone dissects the corporate greed mentality in *Wall Street* (1987), a movie which poignantly addresses another 1980s phenomenon—the get-rich-quick attitude.

After the film version of **Eric Bogosian**'s exquisite *Talk Radio* stage play (1988), Stone returns to the Vietnam with *Born on the 4th of July* (1989). This important film focuses on **Ron Kovic**, the real-life veteran who after being paralyzed in combat, becomes a staunch anti-war activist. Kovic is portrayed by **Tom Cruise** (b. 1962) in his first truly dramatic role, which intelligently subverts his *Top Gun* gung-ho demeanor.

Tom Cruise as Ron Kovic

After the success of *Platoon*, the Vietnam War becomes the topic of the hour. Many projects which have been postponed for years suddenly find financial backing. The notable **Stanley Kubrick**'s *Full Metal Jacket* (1987) dissects the Vietnam myth to its very core by parodying the madness of the military machine.

Francis Coppola enters the 1980s with two intense teen-angst dramas: *The Outsiders* (1982) and *Rumble Fish* (1983), both based on **Susan E. Hinton**'s books and both relying on **Matt Dillon**'s youthful charisma. The latter film displays the outstanding black-and-white cinematography of **Steve Burum** and contains engaging visual gimmickry which borders on the surreal. **Stewart Copeland**, the drummer for The Police, provides a haunting, innovative musical score.

> **THERE'S AN OCEAN OUT THERE THAT I GOTTA SWIM.**

Matt Dillon in *Rumble Fish*

Other intriguing stylistic adventures of Coppola's include the self-indulgent *One from the Heart* (1982), a deliberately artificial romance-musical with a glossy neon look and no substance, *The Cotton Club* (1984), an engaging noirish look at Jazz-age Harlem, and the charming fable *Peggy Sue Got Married* (1985).

One of the best movies of the decade, in terms of artistic merit, is **Martin Scorsese**'s *Raging Bull* (1980), a story of redemption in the world of boxing. Based upon **Jake La Motta**'s autobiography, the film focuses on the obsessive, macho fighter's internal rage which spills out of the ring and ruins his personal life. Influenced by Visconti's *Rocco and His Brothers* (1962), Scorsese utilizes a black-and-white aesthetic to recreate America's postwar reality (or, rather, *neo*reality) and encourages his cast to engage in tour-de-force performances: **Robert de Niro** triumphs as the vicious, paranoid La Motta, whose frequent mood swings correspond to his fluctuating weight.

> **...SO GIMME A STAGE WHERE THIS BULL HERE CAN RAGE, AND THOUGH I CAN FIGHT I'D MUCH RATHER HEAR MYSELF RECITE.**

De Niro as La Motta

In the outstanding *King of Comedy* (1983), Scorsese analyses America's obsession with the Warholian "15 minutes of fame." The movie pairs de Niro (as the freaky fan) with the comedy legend **Jerry Lewis**, who displays excellent dramatic skill as the stalked talk show host.

In his most visually audacious movie to date, the satirical *After Hours* (1985), Scorsese presents the symbolic one-night odyssey through a man's subconscious fears, embodied by Manhattan's nocturnal universe.

Scorsese's lifelong fascination with Catholic mythology results in the adaptation of the controversial **Nikos Kazantzakis** novel, ***The Last Temptation of Christ*** (1988). The movie takes a human look at what might have happened if Jesus had chosen the path of an ordinary man, and effectively presents the ultimate agony of isolation which marks His true destiny.

Willem Dafoe as J.C.

Robert Redford's competent directing debut, ***Ordinary People*** (1980), is particularly impressive in the handling of his actors, specifically **Timothy Hutton** and **Mary Tyler Moore**. The movie's portrayal of the gradual decomposition of a seemingly perfect WASP family ranks among the best in recent history.

Another distinguished family drama, **James L. Brooks**' ***Terms of Endearment*** (1983), takes an unsentimental look at coping with terminal illness and trying to maintain troubled relationships.

In ***Broadcast News*** (1987), Brooks undermines the credibility of network TV news reporting which emphasizes its anchors' good looks and slick news-packaging over substance and insight.

The *Broadcast News* star, **Albert Brooks**, writes and directs the topical ***Lost in America*** (1985)—a relentless attack on the values and dreams of the yuppie generation.

Milos Forman directs his sumptuous ***Amadeus*** (1984), which presents the artistic rivalry between Antonio Salieri (**F. Murray Abraham**) and the youthful, hip Wolfgang Amadeus Mozart (**Tom Hulce**).

Tom Hulce as W.A.M.

The tragic life story of Frances Farmer, the screen actress of the 1930s and 40s, is sensitively presented in *Frances* (dir. Graeme Clifford, 1982); **Jessica Lange** creates an unforgettable performance as the doomed star whose career is affected by mental illness.

Another movie which strongly condemns the entertainment world is **Bob Fosse**'s last film, *Star 80* (1983). The ill-fated Dorothy Stratten (**Mariel Hemingway**), a former Playboy model, is slain by her unstable husband (**Eric Roberts**) when she is on the verge of becoming a movie star. Sven Nykvist's glossy photography accentuates the emptiness behind showbiz' glamorous facade.

River's Edge (dir. Tim Hunter, 1986) and *Stand by Me* (dir. Rob Reiner, 1986) examine interpersonal relationships among teenagers. The former takes a provocative, psychopathic approach, while the latter is sentimental and nostalgic. Both succeed.

Warren Beatty's *Reds* (1981), one of a few worthwhile Hollywood historical epics of the era, focuses on the Soviet Revolution of 1917 as seen through the eyes of the American journalist John Reed (Beatty). One of the greatest strengths of *Reds* is Vittorio Storaro's atmospheric photography.

Bernardo Bertolucci, also supported by Storaro's gift for magnificent color and composition, creates another spectacular epic—*The Last Emperor* (1987), which depicts the life of Pu Yi (**John Lone**), China's last monarch before the dawn of Communism.

John Lone as The Last Emperor

251

The Argentinian director **Hector Babenco**'s outstanding drama, ***Kiss of the Spider Woman*** (1985), based on the Argentinian novel by **Manuel Puig**, chronicles a growing friendship between two inmates in an unspecified South American prison. Molina (**William Hurt**) is a homosexual sentenced for child molestation; Valentin (**Raul Julia**) is a persecuted revolutionary. The movie's multiple layers resonate as the prisoners indulge in film-related fantasies and confront diametrically opposing attitudes toward life in society.

Kiss of the Spider Woman

At the first glance, **Philip Kaufman**'s ***The Right Stuff*** (1983) may seem like just another example of the period's patriotic fanfare, but, actually, this movie probes the 1960s US space program with enough cynicism and satirical overtones to be criticizing the government's hidden agenda—militarization of space and exploitation of the astronauts' celebrity status for political gain.

Offering a satirical look at contemporary America in ***Something Wild*** (1986), **Jonathan Demme** weaves a colorful, explosive tapestry of relationships between a yuppie, a punker, and a low-life looser.

The neglected issue of rape is carefully examined in **Jonathan Kaplan**'s intense courtroom drama, ***The Accused*** (1987). With an unwavering honesty the movie presents the devastating results of rape for the victim as well as outlines the broader sociological context which encourages such deplorable behavior.

Jodie Foster in *The Accused*

Brian De Palma (b. 1940), who in the 1970s directed a series of intriguing, gory horror extravaganzas (e.g., *Carrie*, 1976, *Fury*, 1978), enters mainstream cinema with *Blow Out* (1981), a tribute to both Antonioni's *Blow-Up* and Coppola's *Conversation*. De Palma's **Body Double** (1984) plays off the Hitchcock iconography of *Rear Window* and *Vertigo*, and goes on to prove that his particular talent for filmmaking relies mostly on imitating established masters.

In his most successful picture to date, **The Untouchables** (1987), De Palma skillfully recreates the mood of gangster genre, spicing it up with a contrived tribute to the "Odessa Steps" sequence of Eisenstein's *Potemkin*.

Another classic American cinematic form to enjoy revival in the 1980s is film noir, now assuming the appropriate term **neonoir**.

Lindsay Crouse in
House of Games

Undeniably, the most unique neonoir pictures of the period are **Angel Heart** (dir. Alan Parker, 1987), a seedy, moody, and devilishly entertaining detective story set in New Orleans, and **House of Games** (1987), an intense study of trust in the con artists world.

The latter is written and directed by the renowned playwright **David Mamet** (b. 1947, *American Buffalo*, *Glengarry Glen Ross*), who subverts one of the key elements of noir—the male protagonist is replaced by a strong, intelligent, if somewhat naive woman (**Lindsay Crouse**), whose life becomes slightly complicated after meeting her *homme fatal* (**Joe Mantegna**).

Other entertaining neonoirs include **Body Heat** (dir. Lawrence Kasdan, 1981), **Manhunter** (Michael Mann, 1986), **The Big Easy** (dir. Jim McBride, 1987), **Someone to Watch Over Me** (dir. Ridley Scott, 1987), and **No Way Out** (dir. Roger Donaldson, 1987), based on *The Big Clock* (dir. John Farrow, 1947), a noir classic.

Peter Weir's masterful **Witness** (1985) ranks among the best crime dramas since *Chinatown* (1974). The movie makes great use of the contrast between the peace-loving, minimalistic Pennsylvania Amish society and the bloodthirsty, power-driven modern world of corruption.

**Eddie Murphy in *Trading Places*
(dir. John Landis, 1983), a comedic
retort to racism in America.**

The popular TV comedy show Saturday Night Live breeds some of the
brightest stars of screen comedy in the 1980s: **Eddie Murphy** (b. 1961, *Beverly Hills
Cop*, *Trading Places*, *Coming to America*), **Bill Murray** (*Stripes*, *Caddyshack*), **Chevy
Chase** (b. 1943, *National Lampoon's Vacation*, *Fletch*), **Dan Aykroyd** and **John Belushi**
(*The Blues Brothers*, John Landis, 1980), and the most consistent of the group, **Steve
Martin** (b. 1945), whose comedy combines slapstick with unique verbal wit and
outrageous handling of props. Martin's best work includes the exceptional film noir
parody ***Dead Men Don't Wear Plaid*** (1982), the horror spoof ***The Man With Two Brains***
(1983), both directed by **Carl Reiner** (b. 1922), and the updated version of *Cyrano de
Bergerac*, ***Roxanne*** (dir. Fred Schepisi, 1987).

The Blues Brothers: on a mission from God

Other excellent comedies of the era which deal with the younger generation of
Americans are ***Fast Times at Ridgemont High*** (dir. Amy Heckerling, 1982), and two
John Hughes' movies: ***The Breakfast Club*** (1985) and ***Ferris Bueller's Day Off*** (1986).

The nonsensical and devastatingly funny ***Airplane!*** (dirs. Jim Abrahams, David
Zucker, and Jerry Zucker, 1980) and its equally entertaining sequel ***Airplane II***, are the
quintessential titles from the parody subgenre and offer a yummy multiple-course feast
for any cinema lover.

Three enormously popular gender-bending comedies increase America's tolerance for alternative life-styles: **Blake Edwards**' sophisticated musical *Victor, Victoria* (1982), which has Julie Andrews portraying a male cabaret singer; **Sidney Pollack**'s *Tootsie* (1982), in which out of work Dustin Hoffman finds acting jobs as a woman; and Carl Reiner's hysterical *All of Me* (1984), a sex farce that combines male (Steve Martin) and female (**Lily Tomlin**) personalities in a man's body (Martin's).

PRETTY HAIRY KNUCKLES FOR A CHICK.

All of Me

Rob Reiner (b. 1945), Carl's son, directs the outrageous mockumentary (mock documentary) of a fictitious rock band *This Is Spinal Tap* (1984). The eventual real-life tour of the band suggests that many heavy-metal fans take the joke seriously. The genius behind the Spinal Tap operation is writer/actor **Christopher Guest** (b. 1948)

Another clever satire of the music industry mentality is presented in *Tapeheads* (dir. Bill Fishman, 1989), which showcases the talents of the very young **Tim Robbins** and **John Cusack**.

When it comes to visual artistry and offbeat, intelligent satire, nothing surpasses **Terry Gilliam**'s richly textured *Brazil* (1984). In this Monty-Pythonesque take on George Orwell's *1984*, Gilliam creates a surreal, frightening environment of a technocratic authoritarian regime gone wild.

The American producer of *Brazil*, MCA-Universal, finds the movie's uncompromisingly grim conclusion too disturbing for domestic audiences. In an irresponsibly stupid censorship decision, which itself mirrors the reality of *Brazil*, Universal excises some of the more "questionable" footage from the movie's ending. The European version remains intact and, therefore, superior.

Brazil

Gilliam's subsequent Age of Reason fantasy, *The Adventures of Baron Munchausen* (1989) dazzles with its rococo splendor and vivid imagination.

Charles Crichton's *A Fish Called Wanda* (1988) combines two traditions of British comedy—the restrained perversity of Crichton's own classics (e.g., *The Lavender Hill Mob*) and the wacky, in your face satire of Monty Python.

The 1980s is also a fruitful decade for the sci-fi genre. The most impressive picture in that group is arguably **Blade Runner** (dir. Ridley Scott, 1982), which combines elements of futurism with a noir aesthetic, supported by the remarkable special effects of the Douglas Trumbull team and the unforgettable score by the Greek composer **Vangelis**.

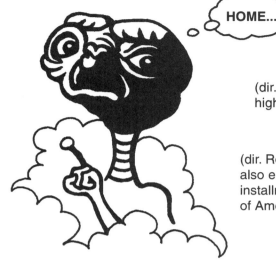

The children's sci-fi fable, **E.T.** (dir. Steven Spielberg, 1983), becomes the highest grossing motion picture to date.

The **Back to the Future** series (dir. Robert Zemeckis, 1985, 1989, 1990) also enjoys tremendous popularity; its third installment contains the most disturbing vision of America since *It's a Wonderful Life* (1946).

The first truly groundbreaking science fiction movie of the 1980s is **TRON** (1982), written and directed by a computer wizard by the name of **Steven Lisberger**. This visually breathtaking movie successfully combines live action with three-dimensional computer generated imagery (**3D CGI**), creating a one-of-a-kind expressionistic aesthetic. Two key art designers for *TRON* are the brilliant illustrator and concept artist **Syd Mead** (*Blade Runner*) and the French master of fantasy comic books, **Jean "Moebius" Giraud**. Stylistically way ahead of its time, *TRON* is not commercially successful and its profound influence on the future of 3D movie graphics technology seems all but forgotten.

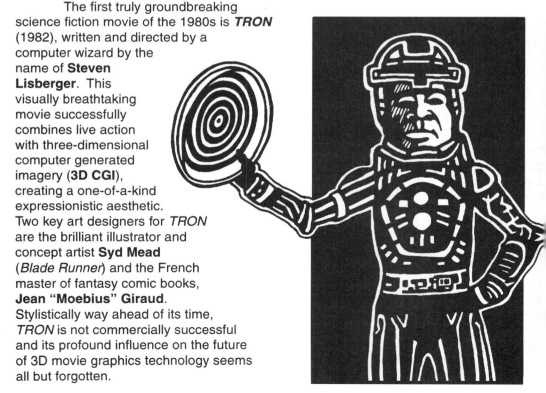

TRON

The best of the adventure genre lot is indisputably ***The Raiders of the Lost Ark*** (dir. Steven Spielberg, 1981) and its progressively less inspired sequels, ***Indiana Jones and the Temple of Doom*** (1984) and ***Indiana Jones and the Last Crusade*** (1989).

The Princess Bride (dir. Rob Reiner, 1987) and ***The Willow*** (dir. Ron Howard, 1988) and offer some high-class entertainment of the fantasy kind.

The Spielberg-produced ***The Young Sherlock Holmes*** (dir. Barry Levinson, 1985), a smart, imaginative adventure yarn, incorporates the first-ever computer-generated 3D character with live action. This spectacular effect is created at ILM's computer animation division called **Pixar**.

Man and his whip: Harrison Ford as Indy

Another groundbreaking picture from the animated corner is the astonishing film noir pastiche, ***Who Framed Roger Rabbit*** (dir. Robert Zemeckis, 1988), which seamlessly integrates human actors with cartoon characters.

A former Disney animator, **Tim Burton** (b. 1960), emerges as the most stylistically innovative comedy/fantasy director with ***Pee-wee's Big Adventure*** (1985) and ***Beetlejuice*** (1988), before scoring worldwide success with the moody ***Batman*** (1989).

Michael Keaton as the Caped Crusader

INDEPENDENT AMERICAN FILM

The truly essential cinematic legacy of the modern American cinema belongs to movies produced outside the studio system— the independent, mostly low-budget films which rely on strong, unconventional story lines and innovative technique. Some independent films do receive studio backing, mostly in postproduction and distribution phases; few are actually produced by studios but retain an independent spirit.

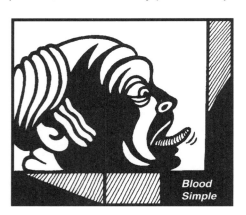

Blood Simple

The filmmaking team of the **Coen Brothers**, **Joel** (b. 1954, director) and **Ethan** (b. 1957, producer) reigns over the offbeat approach to traditional Hollywood genre movies. Their independent debut feature, **Blood Simple** (1984), is an inspired homage to film noir, full of surprising turns of fate and multiple betrayals, all treated with a fresh cinematic style that celebrates elusive details and stresses life's ambiguities.

Coen's ebullient **Raising Arizona** (1987) encloses the stylistic elements of a road movie within the framework of a romantic comedy. Again, the visual treatment of the material abounds with uniquely crafted irony, as the wild storyline offers many unpredictable, outlandishly humorous events.

The undisputed king of camp, **John Waters**, left his indelible mark on trash cinema of the 1970s with **Pink Flamingos** (1972), which challenged viewers' tolerance for bad taste.

In the 1980s, Waters returns with yet another sensory challenge—the olfactory adventure of **Polyester** (1981). In the justifiably forgotten 1960s tradition of Smell-O-Vision and the electric-stimulus cinema of William Castle, both of which interacted directly with the audience through devices hidden under the theatre seats, Waters introduces *Polyester* in Odorama. A scratch-and-sniff card is given to the spectators who are instructed to scrape off numbers as the corresponding visual clues appear on the screen. The resulting scents are often downright revolting.

Gimmickry aside, Waters' subsequent odorless **Hairspray** (1988), a masterpiece of camp cinema, provides a valid social commentary on the mentality of 1960s America, which to a certain degree is still very much alive. Particularly astute, despite its clear comedic overtones, is the high-hairdo teenagers' fight for racial integration against the traditionally coiffured older generation.

The glamor of drag: Divine in *Hairspray*

One of the first independent films to attract critical attention and an immediate cult following is *Eraserhead* (1977), directed by **David Lynch** (b. 1956), an abstractionist painter and photographer, who receives his film training at the **American Film Institute**.

Sponsored by AFI, *Eraserhead* displays an unprecedented contempt for the traditional Hollywood storytelling mold; shot in grainy black and white, the movie utilizes surrealist imagery and jarring, industrial sounds to create a post-apocalyptic marriage horror. This nightmare comes complete with disturbingly delusional in-laws, a repulsive spouse, and a skinless chimera offspring that won't quit crying. But that, of course, is just the surface.

I AM NOT AN ANIMAL!

Lynch's *The Elephant Man* (1980), also a black-and-white picture, shot by the accomplished British cinematographer **Freddie Francis**, is an allegorical study of human alienation set in the Victorian England. Despite its traditional methods of narration, *The Elephant Man* remains one of the most unusual movies to ever receive worldwide release. It is produced by Mel Brooks' Brooksfilm.

John Hurt as the Elephant Man

The Norman Rockwell, apple-pie America receives a long overdue stab in the back with the release of Lynch's *Blue Velvet* (1986). No other film in history of domestic cinema was able to do what this outstanding movie does so well: expose the perversity and sickness of small-town America hiding behind the white picket-fence.

IRRESISTIBLY PUZZLING...

Rigorously subversive, *Blue Velvet* becomes Lynch's greatest hit—the evil-behind-the-surface theme strikes a very familiar chord with viewers around the globe.

She wore blue velvet: Isabella Rossellini

While Lynch devotes his time to charting the landscape of the American subconsciousness, the Coens joyfully manipulate cinematic conventions, and Waters weaves his synthetic tapestries, the cinema of **Jim Jarmush** (b. 1953) offers quite a different experience.

His ultra low-budget independent feature, ***Stranger Than Paradise*** (1984) turns its financial restraints into a great stylistic advantage. This minimalistic film is brilliantly composed of a series of long, unedited takes, each of which tells a relevant anecdote. The scenes are separated by short blackouts—theatrical device which punctuates the action like a heartbeat. The plot of *Stranger Than Paradise* is as simple as its structure: a newly arrived Hungarian emigrant (**Eszter Balint**), her low-life American cousin (**John Lurie**), and his best buddy (**Richard Edson**) embark on a series of accidental, mostly troublesome adventures while traveling from New York to Florida, with a convenient layover in Cleveland, Ohio. What matters to Jarmush is not adherence to mainstream narration's formulas, but small, isolated, mundane experiences his characters share. Ozu and Antonioni couldn't have agreed more.

On the lam: Tom Waits, John Lurie and Roberto Benigni in *Down By Law*

Jarmush follows with the equally mesmerizing ***Down By Law*** (1986), also a gritty black-and-white picture, photographed by the Wim Wenders collaborator, Robby Müller. This time, the odyssey of three convicts who escape a Louisiana prison provides a satirical look at the "other" reality of America—the world of perpetual vagrants who are so used to being marginalized by society that they lack the will to pull themselves out of their pathetic existence.

If *Stranger Than Paradise* portrays America the way Americans imagine Eastern Europe, *Down By Law*'s vision of the country's underbelly recalls the neorealistic tradition of De Sica.

Both films are beautifully scored by **John Lurie**, who also plays one of the three charismatic losers in the latter film. The other two characters are portrayed by the Italian funnyman **Roberto Benini** and the brilliant musician **Tom Waits**, who also supplies *Down By Law* with a couple of stylishly disheveled songs.

The most celebrated recent graduate of the NYU Film School is undeniably **Spike Lee** (b. 1956). His first feature, the NYU-produced *She's Gotta Have It* (1986), becomes another milestone of American independent cinema. This energetic movie presents a young liberated African-American woman on a quest for self-discovery. Her rejection of sexual promiscuity (her favorite pastime) symbolizes a growing self-awareness and refusal to allow anybody to exploit her because of her sex, color, or moral values.

In the studio-backed but still independent *Do the Right Thing* (1989), Lee engages in an extended polemic about racial interrelations. The story takes place on one block of an all-black New York neighborhood where all the businesses are owned by Koreans or Italians.

As the heat of the summer day intensifies, tensions between members of different races inevitably erupt into reciprocated violence. Closing the movie with contradicting viewpoints by Dr. Martin Luther King, Jr. and Malcolm X, Lee suggests that regardless of one's beliefs, a dialogue about racial inequalities in America is absolutely necessary.

HOLLYWOOD'S IDEA IS TO KEEP THE FILM INDUSTRY CONFINED, LET A SMALL GROUP OF PEOPLE HAVE THE CONTROL AND MAKE ALL THE MONEY. THIS IS WHY ONE OF MY GOALS HAS BEEN THE DEMYSTIFICATION OF FILM. I'M SAYING DON'T FALL FOR THAT JUNK LIKE, *YOU GOTTA BE STRUCK BY LIGHTNING TO BE A FILMMAKER**.

*From *Five for Five:* The Films of Spike Lee

Spike Lee

After writing screenplays for a series of B-grade horror movies (e.g., *Piranha*, 1978, *The Howling*, 1980), **John Sayles** (b. 1950) turns to directing his own films, most of which contain strong sociopolitical statements against bigotry, racism, and economic imbalance. Sayles' most intriguing work of the 1980s include the allegorical *The Brother From Another Planet* (1984), which presents a black space fugitive trapped in present-day Harlem, and *Matewan* (1987), a coal miners tale set in 1920, focusing on the capitalist exploitation of the working class.

The early work of **Wayne Wang** (b. 1949), the Hong Kong-born American filmmaker, probes issues of racial stereotyping as well as sexual relations within minority communities. His best titles of the 1980s include *Chan Is Missing* (1982), *Dim Sum: a little bit of heart* (1984), and *Eat a Bowl of Tea* (1989).

The Chicano experience is outlined best in *Zoot Suit* (1981), the film version of the stage musical written and directed by **Luiz Valdez** and scored by his brother **Daniel**. Derived from the flamboyant outfit preferred by the stylish Mexican-Americans of the 1940s, the title symbolizes the essence of Chicano survival in urban America.

Edward James Olmos in a zoot suit

Luis Malle's enjoys another American success with his brilliantly simple *My Dinner With André* (1981), a thrilling one-evening encounter between the New York-based playwright/actor **Wallace Shawn** and **André Gregory**, a renowned theater director. Shawn's deadpan appreciation for life's smaller pleasures bounces off Gregory's lofty, but sincere, ideals about the meaning of human existence. *My Dinner With André* is a plea for honest communication between people in the unfriendly chaos of the modern world.

ISN'T IT A LITTLE UPSETTING TO COME TO A CONCLUSION THAT THERE IS NO WAY TO WAKE PEOPLE UP ANYMORE EXCEPT TO GET THEM INVOLVED IN SOME STRANGE CHRISTENING IN POLAND?

Wallace Shawn in
My Dinner with André

With his breakthrough *Drugstore Cowboy* (1989), **Gus Van Sant** (b. 1952) establishes himself as the preeminent visual stylist of the independent American cinema. The movie's episodic structure, supported by exaggerated color and poetic imagery, compliments the unsettling adventures of a wild pack of heroin addicts.

The German-born **Barbet Schroeder**, a former assistant to Jean-Pierre Melville, comes into his own with the magnificently moody *Barfly* (1987), an autobiographical tale of the gutter written by cult author **Charles Bukowski**.

TO ALL MY FRIEEENDS!

Mickey Rourke in *Barfly*

Another German transplant, **Percy Aldon** (b. 1935), scores his greatest hit to date with the ultra-hip *Bagdad Cafe* (1986), a charming, poetic story of personal discovery set in a steamy Mojave desert diner.

The ultimate success of independent American cinema comes in 1989, when the modestly budgeted *sex, lies, and videotape*, written and directed by **Steven Soderbergh** (b. 1963) receives the coveted Palm d'Or at the Cannes Film Festival and goes on to enjoy tremendous popularity around the world. The movie focuses on interpersonal relationships with an honest, direct manner. Soderbergh's minimalistic direction proves to be a brilliant decision: his well-defined characters dominate the screen, leaving no room for flashy camera work or montage. The result is a rare atmosphere of true intimacy—*sex, lies, and videotape* becomes an intense lesson in what it takes to rediscover one's feelings and heal the wounds of love.

Andie McDowell in *sex, lies, and videotape*

The neo-feminist *Ms. 45* (1981) exemplifies best the iconic, grotesquely violent cinema of **Abel Ferarra** (b. 1952), the low-budget king of New York.

It takes four years to release **John McNaughton**'s independently produced ***Henry: Portrait of a Serial Killer*** (1986, released 1990)—the most chilling mass murder story since *Cold Blood* (1969) and *Vengeance Is Mine* (1979). Simple and restrained, *Henry* is a work of great originality which shuns the genre's typical stylistic flamboyancy and analyzes with precise detachment the environment that breeds evil.

The British-born **Alex Cox** (1954) creates the brilliant social satire ***Repo Man*** (1983), which becomes world's first and only punk sci-fi thriller. Cox's off-kilter ensemble piece, ***Straight to Hell*** (1986) is world's only punk Western, and a very enjoyable one at that.

In the solidly acted, British-made ***Sid and Nancy*** (1985), Cox chronicles the turbulent relationship between Sex Pistols' Sid Vicious (**Gary Oldman**) and his junky girlfriend Nancy Spungen (**Chloe Webb**).

Gary Oldman as Sid Vicious

After directing a series of outlandish B-movies (*Death Race 2000*, 1975), **Paul Bartel** (b. 1938) establishes himself as an irreverent social satirist with *Eating Raoul* (1981), a witty farce about a middle-class couple whose dreams of opening a restaurant are temporarily sidetracked by another profitable venue.

Paul Bartel prepares to tenderize his dinner in *Eating Raoul*

Always following the beat of his own little drummer girl, **Woody Allen** creates some of his most diverse work in the 1980s. *Midsummer Night's Sex Comedy* (1982) is an enchanting, lighthearted farce reminiscent of Shakespeare's *A Midsummer Night's Dream* as well as Bergman's *Smiles of Summer Night* (1955).

In the ingenious *Zelig* (1983), Allen chronicles the fictitious life story of one Leonard Zelig, by all accounts an ordinary Jewish man whose chameleon nature allows him to participate in all major events of the 20th century. Once again, Gordon Willis and his crew come through to deliver astonishing cinematographic effects.

Woody Allen and Mia Farrow
in *Hannah and Her Sisters*

The gangster genre receives a hysterical treatment in Allen's *Broadway Danny Rose* (1984); his nostalgic, self-reflexive *Purple Rose of Cairo* (1985) blends the grim reality of the Depression with the escapist Hollywood mythology.

After the great success of *Hannah and Her Sisters* (1986), a probing look into love, marriage, and adultery, Allen explores similar themes in the more complex *Crimes and Misdemeanors* (1989). The latter offers a bitterly cynical suggestion that trust is an overrated and potentially harmful feeling.

Martin Landau ponders his crimes and misdemeanors

GREAT BRITAIN 1980s-present

Since the coming of **Margaret Thatcher** to power in 1979, the Conservative British government strengthens its central power by limiting local government influence, shows off its military muscle by recapturing the Falkland Islands from Argentina, and becomes increasingly inflexible in its dialogue with Northern Ireland. Thatcher's anti-inflation measures bring positive results at tremendous expenses: taxes nearly double, prices go up, and unemployment rises at an alarming rate.

Domestic film production experiences the lowest output in decades; many cinemas close, and the industry, in order to survive, offers its services to international markets.

London's **Channel 4 Television** becomes largely responsible for rejuvenating British cinema in the 1980s. As an alternative to the BBC, Channel 4 commissions independent filmmakers with a strong, uncompromising attitude who are marginalized by the mainstream industry; many of their most interesting made-for-TV movies enjoy theatrical release. Some of the directors sponsored by Channel 4, such as Mike Leigh, Stephen Frears, and Peter Greenaway, go on to become major players in the international cinema of the 1990s.

The early films of **Mike Leigh** (b. 1943), *Meantime* (1983) and *High Hopes*, (1988) are human, satirical portrayals of Thatcher's lower-middle-class England; both offer a poignant analysis of the social problems which characterize their socioeconomic environments. Leigh's *Life Is Sweet* (1990) continues to examine the dynamics of a low-income family with a style that borders on caricature, but somehow remains deeply human.

Noted for developing his movies through intense period of improvised rehearsals with his performers, Leigh's unique style shines in *Naked* (1993). This dark comedy about the self-destructive nature of urban society is punctuated by the Apocalyptic interludes of its repulsive, yet strangely compelling protagonist, played to perfection by **David Thewlis**.

YOU SEE, WHAT I'M SAYING, BASICALLY, IS YOU CAN'T MAKE AN OMELETTE WITHOUT CRACKIN' A FEW EGGS, AND HUMANITY IS JUST A CRACKED EGG. AND THE OMELETTE STINKS.

D. Thewlis as Johnny offers his take on life in *Naked*

266

Director **Stephen Frears** (b. 1931), a onetime assistant to Karel Reisz and Lindsay Anderson, and his screenwriter **Hanif Kureshi** (b. 1954) emerge as the most internationally popular filmmaking team of the Channel 4 group. Their breakthrough collaboration, *My Beautiful Laundrette* (1985), is an energetic tale about Pakistani entrepreneurs who find their opportunity for success in a rundown South London laundromat. Frears skillful handling of this explosive material ranges from naturalistic to downright surreal, when the rebuilt facility comes alive in full neon glory.

Sammy and Rosie Get Laid (1987), the next product of the Frears-Kureshi team, cuts deep into the troubled, multicultural, inner-city London, while retaining a strong focus on interpersonal relationships.

Between these two films, Frears directs the equally engaging *Prick Up Your Ears* (1987), which chronicles the turbulent and ultimately tragic relationship between Joe Orton (Gary Oldman), a young and successful British playwright, and his lover, Kenneth Halliwell (**Alfred Molina**), a frustrated actor.

Joe whispers the unspeakable truth into Kenneth's reluctant ear in *Prick Up Your Ears*

In the late 1980s, Frears departs for America, where he continues making interesting mainstream films, most notably the superior neonoir *The Grifters* (1990), based on a Jim Thompson book.

Hanif Kureshi comes into his own as the writer-director of *London Kills Me* (1991), a very insightful and bittersweet look at the dead-end generation of young Englishmen.

Peter Greenaway (b. 1942) emerges as the new art-house guru with *The Draughtsman Contract* (1983), an enigmatic mocking of the 17th century British aristocracy. The highly stylized mise-en-scène, full of puzzling innuendos and unresolved mysteries, becomes the director's trademark.

Greenaway's most popular film to date becomes *The Cook, the Thief, His Wife, and Her Lover* (1989)—a witty, allegorical, and nearly theatrically staged social farce with a cannibalistic twist.

Among Greenaway's less accessible work, most of which is sponsored in part by Channel 4, *A Zed and Two Noughts* (1985), *Drowning by Numbers* (1988), and *Prospero's Books* (1991), a take on Shakespeare's *The Tempest*, offer unique and savagely humorous commentaries on human nature. Greenaway's truly intriguing structural solutions have more in common with collage art than traditional narrative.

A Zed

Drowning by Numbers

Another director whose early career is jump-started by Channel 4 is **Mike Newell** (b. 1943). His *Dance With the Strangers* (1985) presents a tacky club owner (**Miranda Richardson**) whose compulsive promiscuity is just one facet of her completely clueless, out-of-control existence. Newell's *The Good Father* (1986) follows a man's (**Anthony Hopkins**) obsession with his estranged wife and child.

In contrast, *Enchanted April* (1991) is a rather sweet portrait of four women from different backgrounds vacationing in Italy, while *Four Weddings and a Funeral* (1994) charms viewers with its harmless, witty romantic tale of persistence in love and solidifies Newell's success in America.

The Irish-born **Neil Jordan** (b. 1950), a novelist turned filmmaker, directs his first feature, *Angel* (1982), in Ireland for Channel 4. His subsequent British productions, *The Company of Wolves* (1984), a revised Little Red Riding Hood fantasy, and *Mona Lisa* (1985), display well-paced action and elegant visual style. The latter is an intense thriller with a complex, skillfully developed plot and a cynical, disillusioned protagonist (**Bob Hoskins**).

Forrest Whitaker and Stephen Rea in *The Crying Game*

Jordan's greatest critical and popular success comes with the independently produced, politically charged sex thriller, *The Crying Game* (1992). Its narrative structure displays the most effective shift of dramatic tension since Hitchcock's *Psycho* (1960). But audiences will remember this brilliant film for a quite different, rather dangling reason.

Nigel Terry as Caravaggio

Another film to enjoy partial Channel 4 backing is **Derek Jarman**'s (1942-94) *Caravaggio* (1986), a sexually charged portrait of Italy's most visceral early baroque painter. Himself a fine artist and art director (*The Devils*, 1970), Jarman evokes the meditative mood of the period utilizing simple, nearly barren sets and a chiaroscuro lighting technique reminiscent of Caravaggio's own work.

Among Jarman's most memorable pictures are an eccentric version of Shakespeare's *The Tempest* (1979), a homoerotic take on Marlowe's *Edward II* (1991), and the minimalistic yet highly engaging *Wittgenstein* (1993).

If there is one person whose influence on the contemporary mainstream British cinema can be called paramount, it is **David Puttnam** (b. 1941). Film producer and impresario with a keen eye for talent and quality, Puttnam enters the international arena with two films directed by Alan Parker, *Bugsy Malone* (1976) and *Midnight Express* (1978). His newly formed **Enigma** company hires Ridley Scott to direct *The Duellists* (1977) and goes on to produce Britain's most internationally celebrated movie of the period, *Chariots of Fire* (dir. Hugh Hudson, 1981).

Among other notable Puttnam-produced films are **Local Hero** (dir. Bill Forsyth, 1982), a charming satire on the perils of industrialism, set in Scotland; **Cal** (dir. Pat O'Connor, 1984), a dramatic story of a young Irishman trapped in the middle of the political tug-of-war in Northern Ireland; and the magnificent **The Killing Fields** (dir. Roland Joffé, 1984), which brings worldwide attention to the atrocities of the Khmer Rouge regime in 1970s Cambodia.

Haing S. Ngor in
The Killing Fields

In the late 1980s, Puttnam accepts an offer to head Columbia Pictures, one of the largest Hollywood studios.

THE AMERICANS WILL LOVE MY LIBERAL ATTITUDE AND SLIGHT SUBURBAN SENTIMENTALITY!

In 1989, Puttnam is fired from Columbia for his liberal attitude.

LIKE THEY SAY: LIBERAL ATTITUDE DON'T PAY.

Before departing for the US to shoot **Birdy** (1984), a moving study of a Vietnam veteran's trauma, **Alan Parker** directs the outstanding musical **Pink Floyd—The Wall** (1982), which combines symbolic, surreal live action with equally surreal animation, both arranged to fit the moody score by Pink Floyd.

In 1991, Parker returns to the subject of music with **The Commitments**, a highly energetic story of an all-white soul band in Dublin, Ireland.

After directing the American-produced ***Altered States*** (1981), an existential horror fantasy with a surreal twist, **Ken Russell** continues to make provoking, visually flamboyant films such as ***Gothic*** (1987) and the ***Lair of the White Worm*** (1988). The first presents the sexually charged events of one long night at Lord Byron's Swiss retreat, during which the host and his guests, including Mary Shelley, engage in hair-rising mind games and carnal adventures. The second offers a satirical take on the horror genre, while dissecting the British class structure.

> **I AM GOING TO KICK YOUR CROTCH INTO AWARENESS NOW!**

grand-père terrible
Ken Russell in action

After the anarchic punk musical, ***The Great Rock'n'Roll Swindle*** (1979), **Julien Temple** (b. 1953) returns to international attention with ***Absolute Beginners*** (1986), an elegantly stylized teenage fable full of exuberant energy and music.

Sally Potter (b. 1947), one of the most accomplished and talented of feminist directors, creates her debut feature, ***The Gold Diggers*** (1983), with an all-female crew. The movie challenges the established stereotypes of women in traditional cinema.

More recently, Potter's ***Orlando*** (1992), a truly international production based on **Virginia Woolf**'s book, becomes a crossover success for avant-garde cinema. One of the key issues of this beautiful film is exploration of gender identity.

Tilda Swinton in *Orlando*

The all-but-forgotten theme of the Arthurian legend is successfully revived by **John Boorman** in *Excalibur* (1981), a richly textured movie noted for its outstanding art design and beautiful costumes.

In the mature, exquisitely crafted *Hope and Glory* (1987), Boorman reflects upon children's experiences during the London Blitz.

Excalibur

The politically conscious cinema of **Ken Loach** offers the restrained but emotionally powerful *Hidden Agenda* (1990), a film about the abuses of Government Security Forces in Northern Ireland, with a strong performance by **Frances McDormand** as a civil rights activist investigating her husband's murder.

Michael Radford's (b. 1946) first narrative film, *Another Time, Another Place* (1983), sponsored in part by Channel 4, is a moody WWII tragedy involving Italian POWs interned in the barren landscape of Scotland in 1944.

His harrowing *1984*, released in 1984, captures the mood of Orwell's totalitarian nightmare with eerie accuracy.

More recently, Radford scores a major international success with *The Postman* (*Il Postino*, 1994), a charming tale of friendship between the exiled Chilean poet Pablo Neruda (Philippe Noiret) and his gentle postman, played by the late Italian actor **Massimo Troisi** (1953-94), who also contributes to the movie's exquisite screenplay.

John Hurt in *1984*

Two great British epic films deserve special attention: **Richard Attenborrough**'s *Ghandi* (1982), for its humanistic aspirations, and **David Lean**'s last movie, *A Passage to India* (1985) for spectacular pictorial beauty reminiscent of his masterpiece, *Lawrence of Arabia* (1962).

Ben Kingsley as Ghandi

Among other films created by British directors of the older generation, the two most absorbing pictures are the magnificently acted *Educating Rita* (dir. Lewis Gilbert, 1983) and *The Dresser* (dir. Peter Yates, 1984). The latter teams up two bad boys of the "angry" years, Albert Finney and Tom Courtenay.

In 1989, a young Belfast-born actor-director by the name of **Kenneth Branagh** (b. 1960) shoots to instant fame with his exciting adaptation of Shakespeare's *Henry V*. With his radiant *Much Ado About Nothing* (1993) and the lavish 70mm *Hamlet* (1996), Branagh should be credited for making the Bard's work accessible to mass audiences around the world without compromising the integrity of the original texts. However, unlike Lawrence Olivier and Orson Welles, who fearlessly experimented with visual form, Branagh's approach to Shakespeare is marked by a far less original style—a conscious choice for someone striving for mass popularity.

HOW WEARY, STALE, FLAT, AND UNPROFITABLE SEEM TO ME ALL THE USES OF THIS WORLD!

MR. BRANAGH, SIR! A WORD FROM HER MAJESTY: YOUR PETITION FOR PREMATURE KNIGHTHOOD HAS BEEN REJECTED AGAIN, SIR!

AY, THERE'S THE RUB!

Kenneth Branagh in dress rehearsal for *Hamlet*

Ian McKellen (b. 1939) adapts for the screen and performs the title character of Shakespeare's *Richard III* (1995); the action is set in a fascist England of the 1930s and offers astute comments on political affairs in the real world.

A TANK! A TANK!
MY KINGDOM FOR A TANK!

Ian McKellen as Richard III

On the opposite end of the British cinematic spectrum lies the dynamic, off-center talent of **Danny Boyle** (b. 1956), a former theatre and TV director. His first feature, the eccentric urban thriller *Shallow Grave* (1994), vibrates with fresh, unrestricted energy—its symmetrical visual composition, jolting editing rhythms, and unexpected camera angles are the most original phenomenon in British cinema since Richard Lester's *A Hard Day's Night* (1964).

Boyle's follow-up, *Trainspotting* (1995), the strangely upbeat junkie farce, is said to be Scotland's greatest contribution to the rest of the world since Sean Connery. Be it as it may, *Trainspotting* is a piece of pure, unadulterated cinema, full of splashy visuals and outlandish, disarmingly vulgar humor.

New talent emerges:
Ewan McGregor in *Trainspotting*

The sophisticated, elegant movies of the Merchant-Ivory team become a staple of the English heritage film. The American-born director **James Ivory** (b. 1928), the Indian-born producer **Ismail Merchant** (b. 1936), and the German of Polish descent writer **Ruth Prawer-Jhabvala** (b. 1927) create memorable, if somewhat sentimental pictures like *A Room With a View* (1985), *Maurice* (1987), *Howard's End* (1991), and *The Remains of the Day* (1993).

IRELAND

The Dublin-born **Jim Sheridan** (b. 1949) emerges as the quintessential Irish director with *My Left Foot* (1989), a colorful biography of **Christy Brown (Daniel Day Lewis)**, the accomplished paraplegic writer and painter. Sheridan's *The Field* (1990), a pastoral view of pre-modern Ireland, benefits from a strong performance by Richard Harris who plays an ambitious farmer attempting to purchase the field he has been cultivating for years. In his overtly political *In the Name of the Father* (1993), Sheridan retells the true story of two young Irishmen who fall prey to the biased, vicious British antiterrorism practices.

WELL, JUST POINT ME IN THE RIGHT DIRECTION AND I'LL TAKE IT FROM THERE.

My Left Foot

The absurdity of violence between the Catholics and the Protestants in Belfast receives a thoughtful, carefully orchestrated treatment in Sheridan's *The Boxer* (1997). No other movie in recent memory was capable of such eloquence and forcefulness in presenting the results of the Irish conflict on innocent civilians and, specifically, the children. *The Boxer* pleads to both sides for an immediate, mature and, above all, peaceful solution to this atrocious political unrest.

Less internationally famous Irish directors include **Bob Quinn** (b. 1939), whose *Budawanny* (1987) and *The Bishop's Story* (1994) deal with the issue of celibacy in Catholic church, and **Pat Murphy** (b. 1951), whose two films, *Maeve* (1981) and *Anne Devlin* (1984), are solid examples of independent cinema which questions the male-dominated social-structure of Ireland, past and present.

AUSTRALIA 1980-present

In his last Australian picture, the antiwar *Gallipoli* (1981), **Peter Weir** masterfull[y] recreates the disastrous South Turkey campaign of 1916, which was instigated by Churchill and resulted in nearly 35,000 casualties of mostly Australian and New Zealand troops.

Working intermittently between the U.S. and Australia, **Fred Schepisi** scores his greates[t] success with *A Cry In the Dark* (Australian title *Evil Angels*, 1988), a real-life story of a grisly infanticide case which shook Australia in 1980.

THE DOG DID IT, MATE.

DINGO.

Meryl Streep masters yet another accent in *A Cry In the Dark*

George Miller's (b. 1945) blockbuster sequel to *Mad Max*, *The Road Warrior* (aka *Mad Max II*, 1981), successfully transplants the Western aesthetic of John Ford int[o] the Australian wasteland. He substitutes futuristic punk freaks and high-powered muscl[e] cars for Indians and horses. **Mel Gibson** (b. 1956) recreates his lone John Waynesque hero who reluctantly sides with the good guys.

The less appreciated ***Mad Max Beyond Thunderdome*** (1985) is the most artistically accomplished of the Mad Max trilogy.

ONE DAY I'M GONNA TRADE THIS FOR A SPEAR AND A KILT.

BUT THE HAIR EXTENSIONS SHOULD STAY.

Suspended between takes on *Mad Max Beyond Thunderdome*, Mel Gibson plans his future career

The greatest international success for Australian commercial cinema becomes ***Crocodile Dundee*** (dir. Peter Faiman, 1986), an energetic, machismo-spoofing comedy whose action shifts effortlessly between the beautiful Outback and the pretentious wilderness of Manhattan.

Gillian Armstrong enjoys a second wave of popularity with the ***Last Days of Chez Nous*** (1991). She follows this well crafted domestic drama of betrayal with the sugary adaptation of **Louisa May Alcott**'s ***The Little Women*** (1993).

Philip Noyce's socially conscious ***Heatwave*** (1982) investigates real estate manipulation in Sydney, while his taut, noirish thriller ***Dead Calm*** (1989) is clearly influenced by the American aesthetic of the genre, yet retains a certain amount of moodiness typical of Australian cinema.

Nicole Kidman and Sam Neil take five on the set of *Dead Calm*

WHAT'S ON YOUR HORIZON, NICOLE?

TOM CRUISE. WHAT'S ON YOURS?

T-REX.

Noyce's recent Hollywood movies (*Patriot Games*, 1992, *Clear and Present Danger*, 1994, *The Saint*, 1997) are as successful as they are undistinguished.

Carl Schultz (b. 1939), the Hungarian-born director of Australia's great children's picture, ***Blue Fin*** (1978), scores a minor international hit with the uplifting ***Travelling North*** (1987), a retirement-age romance set on the Queensland coast.

A sex, drugs, and rock'n'roll attitude permeates ***Dogs In Space*** (dir. Richard Lowenstein, 1987), a perceptive, funny, and quick-paced look at the 1970s.

One must not forget the **Yahoo Serious** (b. 1954) contribution to cinema Down Under: ***Young Einstein*** (1988) and ***Reckless Kelly*** (1993) are both comedies full of slapstick and parody. The latter updates the myth of Australia's famous folk hero, Ned Kelly, who was also the subject of the world's first ever feature film, ***The Story of the Kelly Gang*** (dir. Charles Tait, Australia, 1906).

The intelligent, low-key cinema of **John Duigan** (b. 1949) includes such interesting movies as the unsentimental right of passage tale *The Year My Voice Broke* (1987), and its equally enjoyable sequel, *Flirting* (1989), an interracial love story about a couple of teenagers from neighboring boarding schools in the 1960s. Both star the engaging young actor **Noah Taylor**.

Noah Taylor in
The Year My Voice Broke

The Dutch-born **Paul Cox** (b. 1940), a former photographer, comes to international attention with *Man of Flowers* (1983), which studies an intense love triangle between a model, her crooked, coke-snorting artist boyfriend, and her mature, sophisticated admirer.

In *Cactus* (1986), Cox chronicles a blooming relationship between a French woman (Isabelle Huppert) who is losing her eyesight and a blind man (**Robert Menzies**) a connoisseur of prickly plants. Both pictures tremendously benefit from the iridescent photography of **Yuri Sokol**.

Bliss (dir. Ray Lawrence, 1985) presents a memorable story of an advertising executive who realizes after a heart attack that his domestic life may not be as pure as he once believed.

Bliss

After the popular but not exactly highbrow **The Puberty Blues** (1981), **Bruce Beresford** relocates to America, where his career oscillates between misfires and well crafted work, most notably **Tender Mercies** (1982) and **Driving Miss Daisy** (1989). The magnificent Canadian/ Australian production of Beresford's **Black Robe** (1991) depicts a Catholic priest travelling through the 17th century Quebec on a mission to convert Indians.

Sandrine Holt in *Black Robe*

The New Zealand-born **Jane Campion** (b. 1955), a graduate of the Australian Film and Television School, announces her unique talent with the debut feature, **Sweetie** (1989), an offbeat, charming satire on human relationships. Her subsequent, originally made for TV, **An Angel At My Table** (1990), is a beautifully conceived, turbulent biography of the writer **Janet Frame** (**Kerry Fox**). Constructed as a triptych, the movie follows Frame's life from her early childhood through the wrongful internment in a psychiatric institution and culminates with her rise to literary fame in Britain.

The Piano

Campion's stark **The Piano** (1993), almost unanimously hailed as a masterpiece, tells the dramatic Victorian story of a mute Scottswoman with a child who discovers passion in the misty landscape of coastal New Zealand. To a handful of sceptics, *The Piano* appears heavy-handed in its symbolism and pretentious stylization.

The verdict on Campion's **The Portrait of a Lady** (1996), however, is unanimously less optimistic; the skeptics become the majority.

Jocelyn Moorhead establishes herself as a director of considerable skill with *Proof* (1991), a story of a blind man who takes photographs of his surroundings in an attempt to confirm his idea of reality.

Paul J. Hogan, Moorhead's husband, comes to international attention with his satirical suburban fairy tale about an overweight young woman in search for happiness, *Muriel's Wedding* (1994).

One of the greatest worldwide success stories of Australian cinema is *Strictly Ballroom* (1992), an upbeat paean to originality set in the weird and wonderful world of ballroom dancing. **Baz Luhrmann** (b. 1962), the movie's director, reaches for the brass ring in America with an ambitious version of Shakespeare's *Romeo and Juliet* (1996), that visually resembles a prolonged music video.

The eccentric road happenings of three crossdressing divas constitute the plot of the tremendously enjoyable comedy, *The Adventures of Priscilla, Queen of the Desert* (1994), written and directed by **Stephan Elliott** (b. 1964).

Terence Stamp in
The Adventures of Priscilla

The true story of David Helfgott, whose brilliant piano skills are affected by the emotional instability brought on by his demanding father, is the subject of Australia's most recent success, *Shine* (dir. Scott Hicks, 1996).

Geoffrey Rush as David in *Shine*

The cinema of New Zealand, the strikingly beautiful South Pacific country, enjoys several international hits, mostly produced with government subsidies.

Before embarking on a commercial career in Hollywood, **Geoff Murphy** (b. 1938) directs the visually arresting *Goodbye Pork Pie* (1980), a road movie with three young protagonists getting in trouble with the law. Murphy's *Utu* (1983) is an outstanding film about the 19th century Maori revolt against the British imperialists.

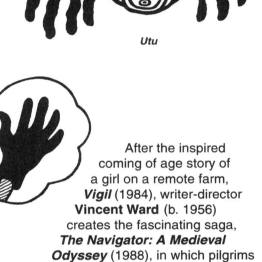

Utu

Roger Donaldson (b. 1945), also working in Hollywood in the last decade, creates his downbeat *Smash Palace* (1981), a portrait of a disturbed car-wrecking business owner who doesn't cope well with his wife's departure.

After the inspired coming of age story of a girl on a remote farm, *Vigil* (1984), writer-director **Vincent Ward** (b. 1956) creates the fascinating saga, *The Navigator: A Medieval Odyssey* (1988), in which pilgrims from the Black Plague travel through a tunnel of time to seek cure in the modern world.

The Navigator

One of the most talented directors to emerge out of New Zealand in recent years is definitely **Peter Jackson** (b. 1961), a former cult author of low-budget horrors (*Bad Taste*, 1987) and perverse puppet macabre (*Meet the Feebles*, 1989). His breathtaking *Heavenly Creatures* (1994) is based on a true story of two schoolgirls whose bond of love, brought on by shared fantasies, manifests itself through psychotic violence. Dazzling with its dreamy photography and sweeping camera work, *Heavenly Creatures* is an instant classic.

The issue of domestic abuse of women finds its outspoken masterpiece in *Once Were Warriors* (1994), directed with a strong hand by **Lee Tamahori** (b. 1950), a former graphic artist. This disturbingly realistic tale of a Maori mother of two and her beer drinking, skull-crushing beast of a husband becomes New Zealand's most successful movie to date.

CANADA 1980s-present

With the limited worldwide appeal of its mainstream production, the true strength of contemporary Canadian cinema lies in smaller independent work which challenges traditional modes of filmmaking.

The French-Canadian director **Denys Arcand** (b. 1941) reaches international success with his ambitious *The Decline of the American Empire* (*Le Déclin de l'empire Américain,* 1986), a witty, conversation-driven film about the nature of love, sex, and politics.

Arcand's *Jesus of Montreal* (*Jésus de Montréal*, 1989) offers an ironic, highly perceptive look at contemporary morality—an actor portraying Jesus in a theatrical production begins to share his character's experiences.

Lothaire Bluteau in *Jesus of Montreal*

Patricia Rozema (b. 1958) directs the offbeat romance, *I've Heard the Mermaid Singing* (1987), which is set in the world of art.

Bruce McDonald's (b. 1959) quirky road movie, *Highway 61* (1991) becomes an instant cult classic. Its richly textured narrative involves a male hairstylist (**Don McKellar**, also the film's writer) and a female rocker (**Valerie Buhagiar**) who travel to New Orleans with a coffin and the Devil (**Earl Pastko**) in hot pursuit. The film easily transcends the usual limitations of the genre.

Highway 61

Night Zoo (*Un Zoo de la nuit, 1987),* an oddly paced urban thriller directed by **Jean-Claude Lauzon**, touchingly portrays reconciliation between a convicted drug pusher and his aging father.

Lauzon's inspired tragicomedy, ***Léolo*** (1992), presents the extraordinary adventures of a 12-year old boy who develops a keen sense of imagination to cope with the wacky reality of his impoverished Montreal family in the 1960s.

The segmented, contemplative format of ***Thirty-Two Short Films About Glenn Gould*** (dir. François Girard, 1993) fits perfectly with the eccentric nature of the famous piano virtuoso who left music at the age of 32. The short, impressionistic vignettes illustrating parts of Gould's life are supported by his original recordings of selections from Bach, Beethoven, and others.

Colm Feore as Glenn Gould

Atom Egoyan (b. 1960), a Canadian director of Armenian heritage, establishes himself as a filmmaker with an original style that eludes easy classification.

In ***Speaking Parts*** (1989), Egoyan creates an allegory of failed interpersonal communication: unable to form emotionally fulfilling relationships, his characters begin to connect through the medium of video.

THE DIFFERENCE BETWEEN HOLLYWOOD AND MY WORK IS THIS: IN MAINSTREAM FILMS YOU'RE ENCOURAGED TO FORGET THAT YOU'RE WATCHING A MOVIE, WHEREAS IN MY FILMS, YOU'RE ALWAYS ENCOURAGED TO REMEMBER THAT YOU'RE WATCHING A COLLECTION OF DESIGNED IMAGES.

Atom Egoyan

Egoyan's **The Adjuster** (1991) depicts an insurance loss agent who becomes entangled in the sexual games of his clients. Full of absorbing visuals and intelligent turns of action, the movie delicately compares voyeurism with cinema.

In his psychological thriller **Exotica** (1994), Egoyan slowly develops a slick, erotic tale into an elaborately crafted exploration of interpersonal relationships between emotionally crippled people. Egoyan brings the suspense to a boiling point by masterfully withholding critical information until the last reel, and then denuding the true motivations of his protagonists in an unexpected but highly gratifying conclusion.

Exotica

The Sweet Hereafter (1997) becomes the first picture which Egoyan adapts from a literary source (the **Russell Banks** novel). The tragic story of a small-town school bus accident is told in a poetic, melancholic manner yet manages to probe deeply into the issues of parental responsibility for the fate of our children. The enormous critical success of this beautiful picture solidifies Egoyan's transition into an internationally renowned filmmaker.

❃❃❃

FRANCE 1980-present

With the advent of the Socialist government in 1981, French cinema enjoys increasing support from the state; when most of the indigenous European cinemas suffer financial setbacks and bow to the dominance of Hollywood, France establishes a solid output of commercial and independent films that continue to gain worldwide popularity.

In 1986, the newly formed **FEMIS** (Institute for the Training and Teaching of Audio-visual Profession), incorporates and replaces the famous French film school **IDHEC** (Institute des Hautes Etudes Cinémathographiques).

Maurice Pialat, whose work had been relatively low-key in the previous decade, establishes himself as the preeminent director of social consciousness with **To Our Loves** (*A nous amours*, 1983). In the film, a teenage girl from a disintegrating family searches for love but settles for easy sex.

Police (1985), Pialat's documentary-like drama revolving around a ring of Tunisian drug dealers, becomes one of the most popular films in France. Starring Gérard Depardieu and **Sophie Marceau**, this intense picture is deprived of a musical score until the end credits, which feature a haunting piece by **Henryk Mikolaj Gorecki**, the sublime Polish composer.

Depardieu reunites with Pialat in **Under Satan's Sun** (*Sous le solei du Satan*, 1987), a disturbing tale of a country priest who comes to believe in Satan's overwhelming power over the world.

Under Satan's Sun

Pialat's **Van Gogh** (1991) focuses on the last months of the tormented Dutch painter's life and presents him in a realistic, unromanticized manner.

The darkly satirical, absurdist cinema of **Bertrand Blier** enjoys two notable hits in the 1980s: **Evening Dress** (*Tenue de soirée*, 1986), an outrageous attack on bourgeois values, and **Too Beautiful For You** (*Trop belle pour toi!*, 1989), a sex farce about a successful car dealer who diverts his attention from his stunning wife to his homely secretary. Naturally, both films star the ubiquitous Depardieu.

Even though his career as a filmmaker began in the 1960s, **Claude Berri** (b. 1934) reaches truly international fame in the 1980s with his nostalgic French heritage films, **Jean de Florette** and **Manon des Sources** (both 1986) and moves on to high-profile literary adaptations such as **Uranus** (1990) and **Germinal** (1993), both starring the iconic Depardieu. The latter epic, based on **Emile Zola**'s socially committed book about the 1870s coal miner strikes, becomes one of the most expensive French productions to date.

Berri is also a noted producer of such films as *Tess* (1979), *The Lover* (1991), and *Queen Margot* (1994).

Manon des Sources

Bernard Tavenier continues to direct strong, visually arresting movies such as *Clean Slate* (*Coup de Torchon*, 1981), based upon a **Jim Thompson** book *POP. 1280*, a brilliant thriller in the film noir tradition set in West Africa of 1938, and *Sunday In the Country* (*Un Dimanche a la Campagne*, 1984), an enchanting chronicle of a meeting between an elderly painter and his family. The former features the astonishing camera work of the **Steadicam**, a body brace with an articulated arm which supports the camera and allows the operator to move with nearly total freedom in any type of terrain while maintaining a smooth, perfectly balanced image.

Philippe Noiret and Isabelle Huppert in *Clean Slate*

Other interesting work by Tavenier include *Round Midnight* (*Autour de minuit*, 1986), a tribute to Jazz greats, and *Daddy Nostalgie* (1990), a subtle family drama abou a relationship between a screenwriter (**Jane Birkin**) and her frail father (Dirk Bogarde).

In *Vagabond* (*Sans toit ni loi*, 1985), Agnès Varda presents a bleak, tragic story of a young drifter in the French countryside. Told in flashbacks, the movie is a terrific example of detached, dispassionate cinema recording life's brutal reality with a nearly clinical accuracy and allowing the audience to draw its own conclusions.

Sandrine Bonnaire as the vagabond

The female perspective on family and human emotions is represented best by **Diane Kurys** (b. 1948) in such naturalistic, autobiographical movies as the nostalgic *Entre Nous* (*Coup de foudre*, 1983), about the friendship between two women who leave their spouses to live and work together, and *C'est la vie* (*La Baule-les-pins*, 1990), which deals with the final stage of Kurys' parents' marriage, as seen through their two daughters' eyes.

Diane Kurys speaks out:

LABELING ME AS A WOMAN DIRECTOR IS NEGATIVE, DANGEROUS, AND REDUCTIVE.

Jean-Jaques Annaud (b. 1943), an IDHEC graduate, receives enormous critical acclaim for his debut feature, ***Black and White in Color*** (*La Victoire en chantant*, 1976), a colonial West Africa satire set at the outbreak of WWI. The most internationally successful mainstream director of his generation, Annaud goes on to create such memorable spectacles as the primitive man epic, ***Quest For Fire*** (1981), co-produced with Canada, and ***The Name of the Rose*** (1986), the US-produced adaptation of the **Umberto Eco** book. The former movie contains special language created by **Anthony Burgess**, the author of *A Clockwork Orange*.

Quest For Fire

Recently, Annaud scores another colonial hit with his heavily erotic adaptation of **Marguerite Duras'** ***The Lover*** (*L'Amant*, 1992), about a 15-year old French girl's obsession with a wealthy Chinese suitor. Herself a notable screenwriter (*Hiroshima, mon amour*) and feminist filmmaker (*Woman of the Ganges*, 1974), Duras strongly disapproves of Annaud's treatment of her autobiographical novel.

Patrice Leconte (b. 1947), a former comic book artist, emerges as a mature filmmaker with the eerie psychological thriller of sexual obsession, ***Monsieur Hire*** (1989), based on a novel by **Georges Simenon**. His equally stylish romantic tale, ***The Hairdresser's Husband*** (*Le Mari de la Coiffeuse*, 1990), presents a charming but obsessive relationship between a middle-aged man (**Jean Rochefort**) and a hairdresser (**Anna Galiena**).

Michel Blanc in
Monsieur Hire

In his recent lavish costume extravaganza, ***Ridicule*** (1996), Leconte abandons his delicate, human approach to cinema for the sake of spectacle and detached witticism.

André Techiné creates the intensely emotional ***Ma saison préferée*** (1993), a family drama structured in four parts corresponding to year's seasons.

Catherine Deneuve
and Daniel Auteuil in
Ma saison préferée

In ***Wild Reeds*** (*Les Roseaux sauvages*, 1993), Techiné explores themes of sex and politics among provincial schoolboys of the early 1960s. His delicate portrayal of homosexuality ranks among the finest in recent memory.

Un Coeur en hiver (1993), a romance set in the world of classical music, becomes **Claude Sautet**'s greatest hit in the 1990s.

Jaques Rivette's masterful ***La Belle noiseuse*** (1991), based on a short story by Balzac, is an unconventionally structured meditation on two passionate obsessions: love and artistic creation.

Another interesting director of the period is **Coline Serreau** (b. 1947), a former actress and a trapeze artist, who manages to thrill domestic audiences with her poignant topical social satire, ***Three Men and a Cradle*** (*Trois hommes et un couffin*, 1985), which is remade in Hollywood as *Three Men and a Baby*. She also creates a terrific comedic portrait of bourgeois life in ***La Crise*** (1992).

On the lighter side, the famous French comic, **Pierre Richard** (b. 1934), the charmingly goofy star of ***The Tall Blond Man with One Red Shoe*** (1972), scores tremendous hits in the 1980s with ***The Goat*** (*Le Chèvre*, 1981) and ***The Fugitives*** (1986). Later remade by Hollywood into dull, humorless flops, *Pure Luck* and *Three Fugitives*, respectively, unsuccessfully substitute the curiously unappealing Martin Short for Richard's unique screen personality.

Pierre Richard

Cinéma du look

The advent of video, MTV, and television commercials, which invade Western European consciousness in the early 1980s, finds its inevitable reflection in cinema. *Cinéma du look* is a newly coined phrase which applies to French films that consciously emphasize slick, gimmicky filmmaking over substance. In the age when the language of advertising supplies instant idioms for youth culture, form becomes a goal unto itself.

The generation of French filmmakers preoccupied with style for its own sake includes Jean-Jacques Beineix, Luc Besson, and Leos Carax.

With his breakthrough *Diva* (1981), a suspense thriller which connects a black prima donna to the criminal underworld of Paris, **Jean-Jacques Beineix** (b. 1946) establishes himself as a new master of flamboyant mise-en-scène, exaggerated color, and surreal visuals mixed with gritty, realistic violence.

Beineix' hot romance *Betty Blue* (*37°2 le matin*, 1985) tells a story of an exuberant waitress who falls for a sexy literary genius masquerading as a handyman. Again, Beineix uses his uncomplicated plot line as a frame for magnificent visuals, and effortlessly sustains a compelling, sensual mood throughout the film.

Betty Blue

Beineix' other curious exercises in style include *Moon In the Gutter* (*La Lune dans le caniveau*, 1983), whose openly artificial design bears resemblance to Coppola's *One From the Heart* (1982), an obvious precursor to *cinéma du look*. He also directs *IP5* (1992), a road movie remembered for the very last performance by **Yves Montand**.

Hailing from TV advertising and music videos, **Luc Besson** (b. 1959) makes his impressive debut with *The Last Combat* (*Le Dernier combat*, 1982), a black-and-white, nearly silent futuristic tribute to the samurai genre. Besson's ultra-slick, neo-baroque *Subway* (1985), is a big budget production involving major stars (**Christopher Lambert**, Isabelle Adjani), whose eccentric action takes place in the Parisian Metro.

Besson's picture-perfect *Big Blue* (1988), produced by the US, exemplifies what the French critics dismiss as postcard aesthetic: a virtually plotless film with startling underwater photography and imaginative treatment of dream sequences, which ultimately fails to convey a single emotion.

A junkie-turned-government assassin is the neo-feminist hero of Besson's explosive **Nikita** (*La Femme Nikita*, 1990), which betrays stylistic influences of Hong Kong's **cinema of heroic bloodshed** in its rush of pure adrenaline. Again, the trivial plot line becomes nearly superfluous in the barrage of spectacularly staged sequences of combat that leave the stupefied viewer begging for more.

The Professional

The US-production of Besson's **The Professional** (*Léon*, 1994), follows the stylistic pattern of *Nikita*, but adds a few dramatic twists to its fantastic display of cinematic fireworks: a hitman (**Jean Reno**) befriends a little girl (**Nathalie Portman**) who witnessed the brutal murder of her parents and gradually initiates her into the art of handling shiny guns. As a bonus, Gary Oldman creates one of the most psychotic villains of the decade.

In 1997, Besson directs the international mega-production of **The Fifth Element**—a truly breathtaking sci-fi adventure of intergalactic proportions, which displays art design by **Jean "Moebius" Giraud** and haute couture by **Jean-Paul Gautier**. The stylistic offspring of *Blade Runner* and *Diva*, *The Fifth Element* is the greatest triumph of *cinéma du look* to date.

The third most successful exponent of the new French stylists is **Leos Carax** (b. 1960), whose arresting, off-center visual style is spelled out in **Boy Meets Girl** (1984) a low-budget, black-and-white romance whose main asset is the presentation of sublime, nocturnal Paris. Carax' subsequent **The Night Is Young** (*Mauvais sang*, 1986) is a high-profile variation of his first movie, with some borrowings from Godard: primary color schemes and **Juliette Binoche**, who is made-up to resemble Anna Karina, Godard's frequent star.

Les Amants du Pont Neuf

The big-budget **Les Amants du Pont Neuf** (1991) becomes a post-modern variation on the *amour fou* theme, with Binoche and **Denis Lavant**, Carax alter ego, portraying maladjusted street people who find shelter on the oldest bridge in Paris, which is under renovation. The wafer-thin narrative unleashes the director's imagination with a baroque panache of beautifully composed visuals, and rigorous, constantly flowing camera work.

The freshest, most mature, and visually imaginative work of the new generation of French filmmakers belongs to the writing/directing team of **Jean-Pierre Jeunet** and **Marc Caro**. Their debut feature, *Delicatessen* (1990), is a surreal, post-apocalyptic tale of a vegetarian revolt against a meat-loving butcher. From the amazing detail of the art design and precise staging of each frame, to the ingenious sound effects and offbeat editing, *Delicatessen* offers a multilayered feast for the eye and mind in the tradition of Hieronymus Bosch.

THIS IS A JOB FOR THE AUSTRALIAN.

Dominique Pinon
in *Delicatessen*

Jeunet's and Caro's follow-up, the grim, futuristic *City of Lost Children* (*La Cité des les enfants perdus*, 1995) pays equally close attention to visual stylization, while its convoluted plot yields more pleasure with each viewing. Again, the outstanding photography of **Darius Khondji** sustains the dark atmosphere of impending doom, while **Angelo Badalamenti**, the frequent collaborator of David Lynch,' provides a fittingly dreamy score.

One of the most unusual French movies of late is *Baxter* (dir. Jerome Boivin, 1991), which satirizes life from the perspective of a talking dog.

THE BAREFOOT WOMAN I PASSED ON THE STREET THE OTHER DAY, SHE TOUCHED MY HEAD. THAT REMINDED ME OF CERTAIN...CERTAIN DESIRES.

Of the very recent French films of note, *La Haine* (1995), written and directed by **Mathieu Kassovitz**, receives the most domestic and international attention. This harrowing account of the violent clashes between the impoverished multicultural urban community and the police benefits from the realistic, almost documentary-style presentation and dynamic performances of the three young protagonists.

While no longer a trend-setting force in world cinema, Italy of the recent decade and a half boasts a solid output of internationally popular films, by either already established directors as Bertolucci, the Tavianis, and Fellini, or a new generation of comics —Roberto Benigni, Maurizio Nichetti, and Nanni Moretti.

Unquestionably the most commercially viable name in Italian Cinema today is **Bernardo Bertolucci**. After his smash hit, *The Last Emperor* (1987), Bertolucci directs the austere version of **Paul Bowles'** *The Sheltering Sky* (1990), and the straightforward *Little Buddha* (1993), which transplants an American family into the unfamiliar setting of Eastern culture. Bertolucci's latest effort, **Stealing Beauty** (1996), deals with the lost innocence of a young girl vacationing in Italy.

While not as provocative and groundbreaking as his early work, all of Bertolucci's recent movies provide viewers with unforgettable visual experiences; especially impressive are his impeccable sense of widescreen composition, his emotional use of color, which is enhanced by Vittorio Storaro's magic feel for light, and feature astonishing soundtracks by the Japanese composer, rock musician, and occasional actor **Ryiuichi Sakamoto** (b. 1952).

In 1981, **Paolo** and **Vittorio Taviani** direct *The Night of Shooting Stars* (*La Notte di San Lorenzo*), a compelling, introspective portrait of the last stages of WWII in Italy. Blending pastoral lyricism with unmitigated brutality, the film provides one of the most astute commentaries on the Fascist and Nazi atrocities perpetrated on civilian population.

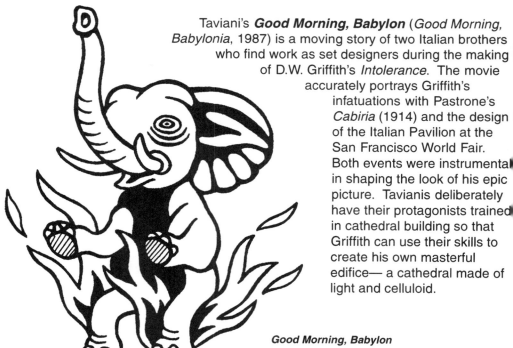

Taviani's **Good Morning, Babylon** (*Good Morning, Babylonia*, 1987) is a moving story of two Italian brothers who find work as set designers during the making of D.W. Griffith's *Intolerance*. The movie accurately portrays Griffith's infatuations with Pastrone's *Cabiria* (1914) and the design of the Italian Pavilion at the San Francisco World Fair. Both events were instrumental in shaping the look of his epic picture. Tavianis deliberately have their protagonists trained in cathedral building so that Griffith can use their skills to create his own masterful edifice— a cathedral made of light and celluloid.

Good Morning, Babylon

Interestingly, other notable work of Italian cinema of recent years also deals with various aspects of film medium itself.

Federico Fellini's ***And the Ship Sails On*** (*E la nave va*, 1983) becomes a loving, self-reflexive tribute to the art of cinema. The movie presents a microcosm of European society at the verge of WWI—a cruise ship carries its passengers to the open sea where ashes of a famous diva are to be scattered to the winds. The movie opens with a sepia-toned sequence reminiscent of the Lumière documentaries, then shifts its tone to progressively accentuate the artifice of moviemaking by relying on overtly stylized sets, including a synthetic sun setting into a sea of plastic, and, ultimately, reveals the famous Cinecittà studio, where the movie is being made.

Fellini's ***Ginger and Fred*** (1986), also deals with the nature of spectacle and constantly makes nostalgic references to the history of cinema, while satirizing the influence of television on contemporary culture.

OUR DREAMS ARE OUR REAL LIFE.

Federico Fellini

Another excellent movie preoccupied with the legacy of cinema and the inability of its protagonists to adjust to the modern reality shaped by television is **Maurizio Nichetti**'s (b. 1948) ***The Icicle Thief*** (*Lardi di saponette*, 1989). At once a tribute to neorealism (*The Bicycle Thief* in particular) and a spoof on the contemporary predicaments of commercial cinema, the movie seamlessly blends reality with fantasy in the tradition of Buster Keaton's *Sherlock Jr.* (1924).

In the clever erotic comedy ***Volere Volare*** (1991), co-directed with **Guido Manuli**, Nichetti transforms himself into an animated cartoon character at the whimsy of a demented sex industry professional.

WHO SAYS ONLY REAL MEN CAN MAKE LOVE TO A WOMAN?

**Maurizio Nichetti
in *Volere Volare***

One of the most nostalgic depictions of movie magic can be found in **Giuseppe Tornatore**'s *Cinema Paradiso* (1989), which depicts a film director's childhood memories of his friendship with a small-town movie projectionist.

Tornatore's **Pure Formality** (*Una Pura formalita*, 1994) is astonishing in its effective use of virtually one location—a run-down provincial police station which hosts the spectacular stand-off between two great screen personalities of our time, Gérard Depardieu and Roman Polanski. A famous writer (Depardieu) is being interrogated by a callous police chief (Polanski), who suspects him of crimes reaching far beyond local jurisdiction.

For a movie relying exclusively on two performers and the brilliance of its director, who squeezes the claustrophobic set for every possible camera angle without being gimmicky, *Pure Formality* remains peerless.

One of the most intriguing cinematic experiments of the period is **Ettore Scola**'s *Le Bal* (1983), a French-Italian-Algerian production, which tells the history of Europe from 1936 to 1983 through meticulously recreated dance numbers without relying on spoken word.

Marco Bellocchio's notoriously erotic *The Devil in the Flesh* (*Il diavolo in corpo*, 1986) is regarded in some circles as the most eloquent picture on post-terrorism Italy.

In his beautifully shot adaptation of Gabriel García Márquez's *Chronicle of a Death Foretold* (*Cronaca di una morte annunciata*, 1987), **Francesco Rosi** studies the traditional norms of masculinity and female innocence in picturesque 1950s Colombia.

After a series of highly topical films in the 1980s, **Lina Wertmüller** scores international success with the socially conscious *Ciao Professore* (1993), a story of a big town school-teacher who reluctantly decides to make a difference in his boisterous provincial pupils' lives.

Roberto Benigni (b. 1952), the extremely popular television and stage comic with a surreal twist, makes his first significant mark with ***Non ci resta che piangere*** (1984), a strange look at Tuscany's 15th century past, made in full collaboration with **Massimo Troisi**.

Benigni's wild parody of the Mafia, ***Johnny Stecchino*** (1991), becomes one of the most successful films at the Italian box office, including American pictures.

The Monster (1996), his recent outrageous comedy of mistaken identity, combines slapstick with situation comedy and verbal humor, and makes a fantastic use of Benigni's quirky screen personality—a cross between the innocently awkward Woody Allen and the accident-prone Pierre Richard, whom the actor also resembles physically.

Roberto Benigni explains himself:

IN REALITY, I'M THE PRODUCT OF A DISPUTE BETWEEN GOD AND THE ITALIAN COMMUNIST PARTY.

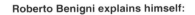

Another writer-director of the new generation of Italian comics is **Nanni Moretti** (b. 1953), whose open-ended, informally structured work wins him the title of a contemporary auteur. His humorous and astutely perceptive ***Dear Diary*** (*Caro Diario*, 1993) becomes the most popular title among his many films which deal with the paradoxes of modern existence.

Moretti in *Dear Diary*

As the director with a penchant for exploring life's oddities, **Marco Ferreri** succeeds with ***I Love You*** (1986), a satire about a man's obsessive attachment to a found key-ring that features a little doll's head saying: "I love you!"

In ***The Flesh*** (*La Carne*, 1991), Ferreri relentlessly satirizes the male fantasy of possessing the perfect woman.

SPAIN 1980-present

The abolishment of censorship, which comes with the euphoric outburst of civil liberties after the death of Franco in 1975, finds its most pronounced reflection in cinema. Spanish films of the late 1970s and early 1980s are notorious for their infatuation with nudity, which becomes the easiest, most direct form of recapturing the long-suppressed artistic sensuality.

However, the newly established Conservative Party government fails to provide support for cinema industry, in terms of both subsidies and control over the abundance of imported, mostly American films. In order to ensure commercial viability of their work without compromising quality, Spanish filmmakers reach for the classics of domestic literature.

A former student of Carlos Saura at **IIEC** (Instituto de Investigaciones y Experiencias Cinematográficas, est. 1946), **Mario Camús** (b. 1935) becomes internationally famous for his literary adaptations, most notably of **Camilo José Cela**'s *The Beehive* (*La colmena*, 1982) and **Miguel Delibes**' *The Holy Innocents* (*Los santos inocentes*, 1984). The latter is a devastatingly bleak portrait of Spanish rural life in the feudal 1960s, realized in emotionally intense flashbacks.

Francisco Rabal in *The Holy Innocents*

Carlos Saura and his collaborator, the actor and choreographer **Antonio Gades** (b. 1936), create the enormously popular flamenco trilogy of **Blood Wedding** (*Bodas de sangre*, 1981), **Carmen** (1983), and **Love, the Magician** (*El amor brujo*, 1985).

Blood Wedding

More recently, Saura directs the big budget Amazonian epic, **El Dorado** (1988), and recreates the period of the Franco regime in the musical, **Ay, Carmela!** (1990), one of the most inventive films of the Spanish heritage genre.

296

In **On the Line** (*Río Abajo*, 1984) and **Dear Nanny** (*Tata mía*, 1986), **José Luis Borau** denounces the deceptive allure of nationalism and its effects on Spanish society.

Pilar Miró (b. 1940), Spain's first woman director in television, begins her feature film career with highly controversial films about sexuality and politics, **La petición** (1976) and **El Crimen de Cuenca** (1979), respectively. Her recent work includes the noir thriller **Prince of Shadows** (*Beltenebros*, 1991), co-written with Mario Camús, and **The Bird of Happiness** (*El pájaro de la felicidad*, 1993), an existentialist drama concerned with social change in contemporary Spain.

Patriarchal family as a microcosm of Spanish society is represented best by **Manuel Gutiérrez Aragón** (b. 1942) in such dramas as **Demons in the Garden** (*Demonios en el jardín*, 1982) and **Half of Heaven** (*La Mitad del cielo*, 1986).

Matriarchy time:
Half of Heaven

The most poetic director of contemporary Spanish cinema, **Victor Erice**, creates **The South** (*El sur*, 1983), a meditative, chiaroscuro film about a young girl who attempts to comprehend her father's suicide.

Erice's contemplative **The Quince Tree Sun** (*El sol del membrillo*, 1992) is one of the most extraordinary movies dealing with the process of artistic creation.

The Quince Tree Sun

Other notable directors of recent years are **José Luis Garci** (**To Begin Again**/ *Volver a empezar*, 1982), **Augustin Villaronga** (**In a Glass Cage**/*Tras el cristal*, 1986), **José Juan Bigas Luna** (**Jamon, Jamon**, 1992), and **Fernando Trueba** (**Belle Epoque**, 1992).

No other Spanish director since Buñuel receives as much international attention as **Pedro Almodóvar** (b. 1949), whose big break comes with the cult classic, ***Pepi, Luci, Bom and Other Girls in the Crowd*** (*Pepi, Luci, Bom y otras chicas del montón*, 1980), a satirical look at the post-Franco generation of hedonistic youth.

Pedro announces his artistic agenda:

> I BELIEVE I'M ONE OF THE LEAST MACHISTA MEN IN THE WORLD AND ONE OF THE MOST AUTHENTICALLY FEMINIST.

In a rapid succession, Almodóvar releases ***Labyrinth of Passion*** (*Labierinto de pasiones*, 1982), ***What Have I Done to Deserve This*** (*¿Que he hecho para merecer esto?*, 1984), ***Matador*** (1986), ***The Law of Desire*** (*La ley del deseo*, 1987), ***Tie Me Up! Tie Me Down!*** (*¡Atame!*, 1989), ***High Heels*** (*Tacones lejanos*, 1991), and ***Kika*** (1993).

In such melodramatic and irreverent films, Almodóvar crystallizes his unique cinematic style which spoofs genre filmmaking—romance, thrillers, and horrors, glorifies a garish pop-art aesthetic, celebrates kitsch, and thrives on incessant pop-cultural references spiced with campy gay sensibility. His influences can be traced to the films of Douglas Sirk and R.W. Fassbinder, as well as Coppola's excessive exercise in form, *One from the Heart*, the tacky, synthetic movie which continues to inspire filmmakers everywhere but in the U.S.

Julieta Serrano in Almodóvar's greatest hit to date,
Women On the Verge of a Nervous Breakdown
(*Mujeres al borde de un ataque de nervios, 1988*)

Thematically, Almodóvar's films invariably deal with issues of sexual dominance, runaway desires, and destructive passions (his own production company is called Deseo —Passion), and ostensibly shun political themes, while continuing to provoke, disturb, and, above all, stretch the boundaries of cinema.

GERMANY 1980-present

The most successful export of German cinema, **Wolfgang Petersen**'s **The Boat** (*Das Boot*, 1981), concerns a crew of a Nazi U-boat in the midst of WWII. After directing one of the most expensive German films ever, **The Neverending Story** (*Die unendliche Geschichte*, 1984), a children's fable, Petersen relocates to Hollywood, where he continues to make such top-grossing hits as **In the Line of Fire** (1993), with Clint Eastwood, and **Air Force One** (1997), starring Harrison Ford.

**Jürgen Prochnow
in *Das Boot***

Edgar Reitz (b. 1932), one of the creators of the Oberhausen Manifesto and a frequent collaborator of Alexander Kluge, creates his enormously popular **Heimat** (1984), a soul-searching epic on German history from 1919 to 1982. Originally shot as a television series, the movie is released in theatres as a marathon 924-minute event. The title, *Heimat*, refers to a German film genre, *Heimatfilme*, which originated in the Weimar Republic in 1920s and emphasized folk traditions and simple human values over complexities of the modern world.

A year before scoring huge international success with **Bagdad Café** (1987), **Percy Adlon** (b. 1935) directs the equally off-beat **Sugarbaby** (*Zuckerbaby*), also starring **Marianne Sägebrecht** as an overweight woman who becomes obsessed with a young subway train operator. Stylistically akin to French *cinéma du look*, especially in its bright neon color schemes, *Sugarbaby* is an unpretentious, witty romantic comedy with a charming twist.

The untimely death of **R.W. Fassbinder** in 1982 of drug overdose becomes a symbolic end to the New German Cinema. Two main factors contribute to the gradual decline of this prolific period: the cuts in government funding for the arts, imposed by Chancellor **Helmut Kohl**, and the increasing power of television to devour many creative talents. Never quite popular with domestic audience, only a few of the German auteurs manage to continue their work with the help of international backing.

The lesser known New German Cinema director, **Werner Schroeter** (b. 1945), whose frequently campy cinema is, like Fassbinder's, always concerned with the outside (eg. ***The Death of Maria Malibran***/*Der Tod der Maria Malibran*, 1972), attracts the attention of the critics with ***Palermo oder Wolfsberg*** (1980), a perceptive social drama.

In 1980, Fassbinder creates his omnibus adaptation of **Alfred Döblin**'s novel, ***Berlin Alexanderplatz***, a made-for-television series which deals with *Lumpenploretariat* of the 1920s Berlin, reflecting the tensions, fears, and decay of German society at the brink of Nazism. Many consider this monumental work to be Fassbinder's finest contribution to filmmaking.

In ***Lola*** (1981) and ***Veronika Voss*** (1982), Fassbinder continues his postwar Germany trilogy which began with *The Marriage of Maria Braun* (1979).

In his last film, ***Querelle*** (1982), based on **Jean Genet**'s homoerotic novel, *Querelle de Brest*, Fassbinder tells a story of a sailor in a seedy French seaport who stumbles into the world of unfamiliar, yet strangely alluring passions. Deliberately artificial in its set design and intensely provocative, *Querelle* may not be everyone's cup of java, but still remains one of the most daring cinematic experiments of its time.

Brad Davis in *Querelle*

Klaus Kinski as Fitzcarraldo

In his last important narrative film, **Werner Herzog** returns to the Amazon rain forest with ***Fitzcarraldo*** (1982), a tale of an obsessive 19th century Irish rubber baron, who embarks on an arduous journey to construct an opera house in the heart of Peruvian jungle.

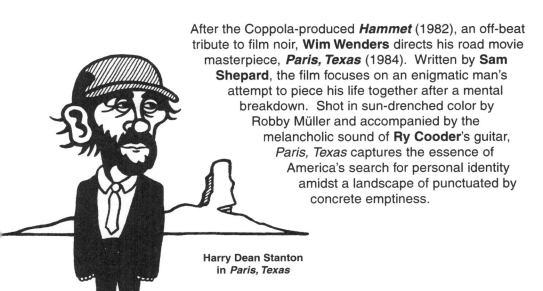

After the Coppola-produced **Hammet** (1982), an off-beat tribute to film noir, **Wim Wenders** directs his road movie masterpiece, **Paris, Texas** (1984). Written by **Sam Shepard**, the film focuses on an enigmatic man's attempt to piece his life together after a mental breakdown. Shot in sun-drenched color by Robby Müller and accompanied by the melancholic sound of **Ry Cooder**'s guitar, *Paris, Texas* captures the essence of America's search for personal identity amidst a landscape of punctuated by concrete emptiness.

Harry Dean Stanton
in *Paris, Texas*

Next, Wenders turns his attention to Germany with **Wings of Desire** (*Der Himmel über Berlin*, 1987), an unusual, poetic film portraying a pair of angels who try to soothe the souls of Berliners; when one angel decides to shed his wings after falling in love with a trapeze artist, he must face his irreversible decision of becoming mortal. This beautifully photographed story develops into a compassionate meditation on the state of humanity on the verge of historical changes in Europe.

Bruno Ganz in
Wings of Desire

Wenders' sequel to *Wings of Desire*, **Far Away, So Close** (*In weiter Ferne, so nah!*, 1993), is shot after the fall of the Berlin Wall and attempts to weave similar existential questions with political commentary while in the format of a thriller. The effect, if sporadically fascinating, is mostly forced and overly sentimental.

While remaining in the shadow of its male counterpart, the feminist cinema of Germany offers some work that deserves to be recognized beyond local boundaries.

Margarethe von Trotta's ***The German Sisters*** (*Die bleierne Zeit*, 1981) portrays two sisters from an affluent background who develop strikingly different viewpoints on life and politics.

In the somewhat conventionally shot ***Rosa Luxemburg*** (1986), Trotta presents the turbulent life of the famous Polish-born German communist.

Barbara Sukova as Rosa

Germany, Pale Mother

Helma Sanders-Brahms's ***Germany, Pale Mother*** (*Dutschland, bleiche Mutter*, 1980), whose symbolic title is derived from a 1933 poem by Bertolt Brecht, explores the relationship between a single mother and her little baby girl, as they trek through war-torn German landscape pretending to be in a fairy-tale fantasy.

Another interesting director is **Monika Treut** (b. 1954), who concentrates strictly on lesbian themes which, like ***Virgin Machine*** (*Jugenfrauenmashine*, 1988), defy norms of traditional morality and offer some refreshingly inventive stylization.

Some of the independent ***Berlin underground*** directors of importance include **Frank Ripploh**, whose gay cult classic ***Taxi to the Loo*** (*Taxi zum Klo*, 1981) is an unflinching portrait of a horny homosexual schoolteacher, **Lothar Lambert** (***Damned City***/*Verdemmte Stadt*, 1981), and **Rosa von Praunheim** (***City of Lost Souls***/*Stadt der verlorenen Seelen*, 1983).

With the retirement of Ingmar Bergman from filmmaking in 1982 and the diminished interest in politics and sexual exploration which fueled Swedish cinema in the past, creative confusion permeates the industry.

Lasse Hallström (b. 1946) shoots to instant international fame with *My Life as a Dog* (1965), a charming portrayal of a 12-year old boy coping with life's tribulations on a Swedish country farm.

After a couple of films based on Astrid Lindgren's classics of children literature (e.g., *The Children of Bullerby Village*/*Alla Vi Barn Bullerby*, 1986), Hallström departs for the US, where he directs another endearing, if slightly less effective, study of young, small-town people, *What's Eating Gilbert Grape* (1993), which benefits from strong performances of **Leonardo di Caprio** and **Johnny Depp**.

The Dutch-born **Bille August** (b. 1948), who received his training at the Danish Film School, relocates to Sweden, where he creates the successful *Pelle the Conqueror* (*Pelle Erobreren*, 1987), a turn-of-the-century epic of a young Swedish boy learning the fine art of survival in a Danish countryside.

Max von Sydow and Pelle Hvenegaard in *Pelle the Conqueror*

Subsequently, August directs the superbly detailed *Best Intentions* (*Den Goda Viljan*, 1992), a semi-autobiographical story written by Ingmar Bergman which deals with the early stages of his parents' marriage.

Other notable directors of contemporary Swedish cinema include **Hans Alfredson** (***The Simple-Minded Professor****/Den enfalidige mördaren*, 1982), **Christer Dahl** (***At Last!****/Antiligen!*, 1985), **Kjell Grede** (***Hip, Hip Hurrah!***, 1987), **Agneta Elers-Jarleman** (***Beyond Sorrow, Beyond Pain****/Smärtgränen*, 1983), and **Susan Osten** (***The Mozart Brothers****/Bröderna Mozart*, 1986).

Among the recent successful Swedish films which find their way to international recognition are ***House of Angels*** (dir. Colin Nutley, 1992) and ***Slingshot*** (dir. Ake Sandgren).

FINLAND

The cinema of Finland boasts two major new talents in the form of the **Kaurismaki** brothers, **Aki** (b. 1957) and **Mika** (b. 1955), whose early team work combines the stylistic influence of *Nouvelle Vague* with a touch of Finnish melancholy punctuated by unexpected euphoria or death (e.g. ***The Worthless****/Avvottomat*, 1982). Their own production company's name, Villealfa, is a homage to Godard's *Alphaville.*

Now directing independently, the Kaurismakis continue to support one another in their parallel careers. Their work reflects the duality of the modern Finnish soul, trapped between the influence of Western pop-culture and the indigenous mystique of Northeastern Europe.

Leningrad Cowboys Go America

Aki establishes himself as the more artistically inclined auteur with such restrained, pensive films with a sociopathic twist as ***Ariel*** (1988) and ***The Match Factory Girl*** (*Tulitikkutchtaan tytto*, 1989). But he feels equally comfortable with the energetic comedy of misplaced dreams of stardom, ***Leningrad Cowboys Go America*** (1989), which combines the Jarmusch tradition of a bizarre road adventure with the exuberance of *The Blues Brothers*.

Similarly to his brother, Mika produces his films with the sponsorship of international financing; his films (e.g. ***Rosso***, 1985, ***Helsinki-Napoli—All Night Long***, 1987), however, are not as widely recognized as Aki's.

The most "Americanized" of the Finnish directors, **Lenny Harlin** (b. 1959), becomes famous for such glossy Hollywood blockbusters as ***Die Hard II*** (1990), starring Bruce Willis, and ***Cliffhanger*** (1993), which, for better or for worse, defrosts Sylvester Stallone's career; both are testosterone-fueled action films with a lot of snow and fire. Harlin's disastrous, estrogen-driven **Gena Davis** pirate vehicle, ***CutThroat Island*** (1995) might have benefited from a blizzard or two.

Two exciting adventure films *Orion's Belt* (*Orions belte*, Ola Solum, 1985) and *Pathfinder* (*Veiviseren*, 1987), are the most visible achievements of the otherwise dormant Norwegian cinema. The latter, directed with gusto by **Nils Gaup** (b. 1955), based on a 12th century Lapp legend, tells of a young boy's quest to avenge his parents who were murdered by wild tribesmen. Photographed in carefully composed widescreen, *Pathfinder's* magical evocation of man living in harmony with nature recalls the best traditions of Scandinavian film.

Mikkel Gaup in *Pathfinder*

In the field of art cinema, **Oddvar Einarson** enjoys critical acclaim for *X* (1986), a lowly paced study of a relationship between an Oslo photographer and a homeless girl.

CELAND

The budding Icelandic film industry enjoys its first independently produced uccess with **Land and Sons** (*Land og synir*, August Gundmundsen, 1979), an incisive ocial drama.

Today, the most exciting director of Iceland is **Fridrik** Thor Fridriksson (b. 1954), a highly regarded documentary filmmaker, whose dramatic feature film, **Children of Nature** (*Börn náttúrunnar*, 1991), becomes a critical success and an art-house hit.

Fridriksson's recent **Cold Fever** (1996), produced internationally, is a mysterious, poetic, and frequently humorous road movie in the Jarmusch tradition, which depicts a Japanese executive played by *Mystery Train's* **Masatoshi Nagase**) on a mystical mission to the heart of frozen celand.

Cold Fever

The delinquent **Remote Control** 1992), written and directed by **Óskar Jónasson**, is an intelligent, offbeat satire of Reykjavik's younger generation.

DENMARK

The Danish government support of children-oriented movies, which comes into effect in 1982, results in a quick succession of engaging pictures, including **Nils Malmros**' (b. 1944) *The Tree of Knowledge* (*Kundskabens Troe*, 1983) and Bille August's *Twist and Shout* (*Tro, håb og koerlighed*, 1984).

Lars von Trier

The adult-oriented cinema of Denmark finds its new master in **Lars von Trier** (b. 1956), a graduate of **Den Danske Filmskole** (Danish Film School). His first feature-length movie, *The Element of Crime* (*Forbrydelsens element*, 1984), is an avant-garde exercise in style whose aesthetic derives from German Expressionism and the intellectual cinema of Andrei Tarkovsky; the movie's plot remains deliberately obscured by an abundance absurd and surreal symbolism.

After directing the **Carl-Theodor Dreyer** script of *Medea* (1987) for Danish television, von Trier makes the little seen *Epidemic* (1987) and, finally, his moody formalistic masterpiece, *Zentropa* (*Europa*, 1991). A stylistic amalgam of film noir, Hitchcock, and post-modern cinema, Zentropa contains some of the most complex visuals to appear on the contemporary screen. Von Trier's refusal to bow to the restrain of traditional narration leaves plenty of room for open interpretation of the movie's plot, which follows an American sleeping-car attendant on a German train in 1945.

Zentropa

The harrowing, surreal TV series, **The Kingdom** (*Riget*, 1994), confirms von Trier's complete control over creating a sustained, compelling atmosphere, while his recent **Breaking the Waves** (1996), explores new aesthetic grounds with its intimate depiction of a young woman's unswerving love for her paralyzed husband. The movie's unbelievable emotional intensity is enhanced by the mostly **hand-held** camera work and the grainy, realistic color photography of **Robby Müller**, the famed collaborator of Wenders and Jarmusch.

Another notable, more traditional Danish film, **Babette's Feast** (dir. Gabriel Axel, 1987), is a bacchanalian 19th century tale based on **Isak Dinesen**'s book.

THE NETHERLANDS

By far the most accomplished director to emerge out of the modest cinema of the Netherlands is **Paul Verhoeven** (b. 1938). His eclectic early career features the erotic middle-class satire **Turkish Delight** (*Turks Fruit*, 1973), the war drama **Soldier of Orange** (*Soldaat van oranje*, 1979), both of which star **Rutger Hauer** (b. 1944), and the black comedy of confused reality and fantasy, **The Fourth Man** (*De Vierde Man*, 1983).

Soldier of Orange

Upon his arrival in Hollywood, Verhoeven quickly establishes himself as a visually inventive director of such sci-fi adventures as **Robocop** (1987), **Total Recall** (1990), and **Starship Troopers** (1997), which fare extremely well at the box office. He is also responsible for the obnoxiously provocative soft-core thriller **Basic Instinct** (1992), a blatant Hitchcock rip-off, and the unfortunate **Showgirls** (1996).

The subject of Jewish persecution by the Nazis is eloquently presented in **Bittersweet** (dir. Kees van Olstrum, 1985).

George Sulzier (b. 1932), a former documentarian, directs his outstanding road thriller, **The Vanishing** (*Spoorloos*, 1987), one of Holland's greatest international triumphs.

The Lift (dir. Dick Maas, 1983) offers a light, enjoyable entertainment in the horror genre.

BELGIUM

Despite being marginalized threefold as woman, Belgian, and Jewish filmmaker, **Chantal Akerman** (b. 1950) displays tremendous resilience in practicing her craft, which ranges from feminist avant-garde (***Jeanne Dielman 23 Quai du Commerce 1080 Bruxelles***, 1975), to moody, stylized melodrama (***All Night Long***/*Toute une nuit*, 1983), and post-modern musical (***Golden Eighties***, 1986).

Jeanne Dielman becomes famous for utilizing a minimalist narration to challenge the established conventions of cinema by persistently focusing on the unspectacular but significant details of woman's daily routine. Akerman treats her static, Ozu-like mise-en-scène as a method of political commentary on the sexual repression and exploitation of women.

KITCHEN AS PRISON: AKERMAN'S FEMINIST MODERNISM COMPELS THE VIEWER TO OBSERVE SPACES NEGLECTED BY MAINSTREAM CINEMA AND REEVALUATE THEIR MEANINGS.

Jeanne Dielman

On the very opposite end of the political and conceptual spectrum of cinema, the bold trio of Belgian first-time filmmakers, **Rémy Belvaux**, **André Bonzel**, and **Benoît Poelvoorde**, directs the irreverent pseudo-documentary on a serial killer, ***Man Bites Dog*** (*C'est arrivé près de chez vous*, 1992).

Repulsive in its graphic presentation of violence yet brilliantly mocking the voyeuristic process of moviemaking, the film raises very important questions about cinema's appeal—how far should images be manipulated and exploited to remain appropriate for public presentation, and where do filmmakers cease to be mere recorders of action and become active participants.

Man Bites Dog

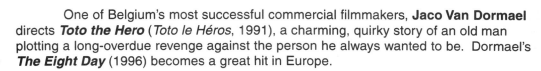

One of Belgium's most successful commercial filmmakers, **Jaco Van Dormael** directs ***Toto the Hero*** (*Toto le Héros*, 1991), a charming, quirky story of an old man plotting a long-overdue revenge against the person he always wanted to be. Dormael's ***The Eight Day*** (1996) becomes a great hit in Europe.

AUSTRIA

The austere, apocalyptic cinema of **Michael Haneke** (b. 1942, *Benny's Video*, 1992, *Funny Games*, 1997) focuses on the dehumanizing effects of modern civilization which, incapable of providing us with spiritual comfort, gradually replaces our self-preservation mechanism with auto-destructiveness. In the emotionally devastating *The Seventh Continent* (*Der Siebte Kontinent*, 1989), Haneke allows his camera to reflect upon details of an upper-middle-class family's existence, relying on close-ups of commercial products and appliances, and chronicling the simple, repetitive chores which methodically drive his protagonists to insanity.

Michael Haneke

MY FILMS ARE POLITICAL STATEMENTS AGAINST THE AMERICAN "TAKING-BY-SURPRISE-BEFORE-ONE-CAN-THINK" CINEMA AND ITS DISEMPOWERMENT OF THE SPECTATOR. I WANT THE SPECTATOR TO THINK.

TURKEY

The key figure in modern Turkish cinema is unquestionably **Yilmaz Güney** (1937-84), a former movie star of the 1960s, who turns to writing and directing movies preoccupied with social injustice and critique of the right-wing military government (e.g. *Hope*/*Umet*, 1970). Continually harassed by the state for his politically oriented work, Güney is eventually imprisoned on fabricated charges. *Yol* (1982), Güney's greatest work, is actually shot by one of his colleagues, **Serif Gören**, who is supplied a detailed **shooting script** while the director is still in jail. Güney manages to edit the film himself in France, following his successful escape from prison.

The epic plot of *Yol* concerns the fate of five prisoners on a furlough who trek across Turkey to visit their families or settle old disputes. Blending realism of action with poetic flashbacks, the movie exposes the rigid patriarchal traditions which prevail throughout the land and result in violence, domestic abuse, and, ultimately, a torn nation.

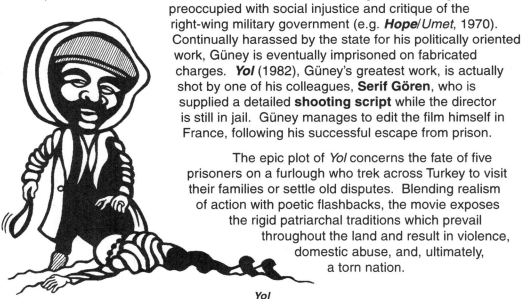

Yol

GREECE

Theo Angelopoulos remains the single most important Greek filmmaker of the 1980s with his melancholic "trilogy of silence": *Voyage to Cythera* (*Taxidi sta Kithiria*, 1984), *The Beekeeper* (*O melissokomos*, 1986), featuring a subtle performance by Marcello Mastroianni, and *Landscape in the Mist* (*Topio stin omihli*, 1988). All three pictures are united by metaphysical journeys and personal displacement and rely on long takes, minimal dialogue, and symbolic imagery.

EASTERN EUROPE 1980s-present

The first Eastern European nation to organize independent trade unions, collectively known as **Solidarność** (Solidarity), Poland of 1980-81 experiences freedom of speech unprecedented for a communist country which allows both the working class and the intellectuals to voice their anger over the deplorable socio-economic state of the nation.

Entering the fourth decade of his artistic creativity as Poland's most respected filmmaker, **Andrzej Wajda** unites with his *Man of Marble* screenwriter **Aleksander Scibor-Rylski**, to create ***Man of Iron*** (1981)—an impressive historical record of Solidarity's rise to power disguised as narrative film.

Lech Walesa, the future president of Poland, appears as himself in *Man of Iron*

The increasing demands for replacing the Soviet-controlled Polish Union Worker Party with a freely elected democratic government result in the imposition of martial law by the Moscow-backed **Gen. Wojciech Jaruzelski** in December of 1981, only a few months after the release of *Man of Iron.*

Unable to create overtly political work, Wajda reaches for the subject of post-French Revolution power struggle in ***Danton*** (1982) to create an allegory about state oppression of civil liberties.

After the intense romance between a Jewish POW and a German woman, ***A Love in Germany*** (*Eine Liebe in Deutschland*, 1983), Wajda continues his examination of WWII themes in ***Korczak*** (1990), a true account of the last days of Warsaw's beloved Dr. Janusz Korczak (real name Henryk Goldszmit), a renowned Jewish author and educator who sacrificed his life protecting Jewish orphans during the Holocaust. The movie, shot in evocative black-and-white by Robby Müller, is a noteworthy precursor to Spielberg's *Schindler's List* (1993).

Andrzej Wajda ponders the limited appeal of Eastern European cinema:

IN A COMMUNIST COUNTRY EVERYTHING CONSTITUTES A MYSTERY. FILMS CREATED IN EASTERN BLOC COUNTRIES SPOKE TO THEIR AUDIENCES, WHICH KNEW MUCH MORE ABOUT THE SUBJECT THAN ANY OTHER AUDIENCE. SUCH WAS THE FOUNDATION OF OUR COMMUNICATION.

One of the quickest responses to the suppression of civil liberties by General Jaruzelski comes with the allegorical *Moonlighting* (1982), by Polish emigré **Jerzy Skolimowski**. **Jeremy Irons** stars as a scheming Polish building contractor in London who is unable to return home after the imposition of martial law.

Agnieszka Holland completes her insightful, harrowing study of the contemporary Polish reality, *A Woman Alone* (*Kobieta samotna*, 1981) shortly before martial law forces her to relocate to Paris. For a West German producer, Holland directs *Angry Harvest* (*Bittere Ernte*, 1985), a tragic story of a Jewish woman hiding from the Nazis in a German farmer's cellar.

Holland's greatest international triumph comes with *Europa, Europa* (1990), an epic film which chronicles the extraordinary and true experiences of a young Jewish boy during the horrors of WWII.

Europa, Europa

In the intimate, suspenseful *Olivier, Olivier* (1991), a French production, Holland focuses on a 15-year old street hustler, who returns to his family after a six-year absence. The question of his true identity remains in question as the desperate family strives to restore its harmony.

The artistic success of *Secret Garden* (1993), produced by Coppola's American Zoetrope, not only confirms Holland's status as the preeminent Polish director of international renown, but also as one of the key women filmmakers of our time.

Agnieszka Holland outlines her approach to contemporary international cinema:

> IF I AM MAKING A MOVIE AND I AM SENDING A MESSAGE INTO THE WORLD, I WANT IT TO BE RECEIVED BY SOMEONE OTHER THAN JUST MY IMMEDIATE FAMILY.

> A COMMERCIAL MOVIE IS A MOVIE THAT PAYS FOR ITSELF, BECAUSE PEOPLE, OUT OF THEIR FREE WILL, PAID FOR THE TICKETS. THAT'S WHAT IT'S ALL ABOUT.

Richard Bugajski's *The Interrogation* (*Przesluchanie*, 1982), remains one of the most impressive films to deal with abuse of power in Stalinist Poland—its overt denouncement of the state's intimidation practices results in the movie's withdrawal from distribution until 1990.

Krystyna Janda in *Interrogation*

Piotr Szulkin, an inventive visual stylist, directs *War of the World's—Next Century* (*Wojna swiatów —nastepne stulecie*, 1981), an allegorical depiction of totalitarian regime which has more in common with Orwell's *1984*, a definite Index title, than with the H.G. Wells original. The film is banned on political grounds.

After the political amnesty of 1984 and the loosening of censorship, Polish filmmakers enjoy more creative freedom, which results in such work as *Lake Constance* (*Jezioro Bodenskie*, Janusz Zaorski, 1986) or *Hero of the Year* (*Bohater roku*, Feliks Falk, 1987), while some repressed titles are released with minor cuts (e.g. *Custody*/ *Nadzor*, Wieslaw Saniewski, 1981, *Mother of Kings*/*Matka Krolow*, J. Zaorski, 1982).

In 1989, **Krzysztof Kieslowski** completes his ten-part TV series, *Dekalog*, a loose, informal interpretation of the Ten Commandments. Two episodes are released in extended versions as *A Short Film About Killing* (*Krotki film o zabijaniu*) and *A Short Film About Love* (*Krotki film o milosci*), marking the beginning of Kieslowski's outstanding, however brief, international career.

The Double Life of Véronique (*Podwojne zycie Weroniki*, 1991), Kieslowski's first art-house hit, is an enigmatic tale of two identical women—one Polish, the other one French. Deliberately ambiguous but executed with a sure sense of artistic direction, the movie announces Kieslowski's final departure from socially-oriented cinema.

Véronique senses the presence of Weronika: Iréne Jacob in *The Double Life of Véronique*

Kieslowski's subsequent ***Three Colors*** trilogy focuses on the intricacies of interpersonal relationships. Alluding to the three colors of the French flag, ***Blue*** (*Trois couleurs: bleu*, 1993), ***White*** (*Trois couleurs: blanc*, 1993), and ***Red*** (*Trois couleurs: rouge*, 1994) display the smooth aesthetic of *cinéma du look* while their thematic maturity ranks them among the most eloquent explorations of love, coincidence, and destiny in the contemporary cinema.

Kieslowski reveals one of the secrets of cinema of poetry:

ALL THREE FILMS ARE ABOUT PEOPLE WHO POSSESS INTUITION OR SPECIAL SENSITIVITY, WHO SENSE SOMETHING SUBCONSCIOUSLY. WHICH IS NOT NECESSARILY REVEALED IN DIALOGUE. RARELY DO SCENES ADDRESS THINGS DIRECTLY. WHAT IS IMPORTANT FREQUENTLY TAKES PLACE OUTSIDE THE FRAME*.

*From Kieslowski's *About Myself*

White, the most humorous of the three, but just as complex in its narrative, paints a rather bleak portrait of contemporary Poland, now a fully independent, democratic state whose free-market economy and renegade entrepreneurship gradually (and quite naturally) replace political concerns of the 1980s.

Sensing that Polish audiences are ready for a domestic brand of Hollywood, **Waldemar Pasikowski**'s ***Pigs*** (*Psy*, 1992) applies the slick aesthetic of action cinema to the topical subject of post-communist confusion. The movie and its bloody sequel, ***Pigs II*** (*Psy 2*, 1994), become instant box-office champions.

Boguslaw Linda in *Pigs II*

POP

Meanwhile, **Roman Polanski** creates the ambiguous thriller, ***Frantic*** (1988), with Harrison Ford, and explores new depths of marital sexuality in ***Bitter Moon*** (*Lunes de fiel*, 1992). The most political film of Polanski's career, ***Death and the Maiden*** (1995), is a taut adaptation of the austere Chilean play by **Ariel Dorfman**, which inverts state-sanctioned torture, when a former victim of a South American regime (Sigourney Weaver) holds captive one of her oppressors (Ben Kingsley).

HUNGARY

Hungary of the early 1980s experiences an influx of films openly critical of the Stalinist regime: *The Match* (*Mérkőzés*, Ferenz Kósa, 1980), *The Day Before Yesterda* (*Tegnapelőtt*, Péter Bacsó, 1981), *Another Way* (*Eymásra nézve*, Károly Makk, 1982), and *Wasted Lives* (*Kettévált mennyezet*, Pál Gábor, 1984). Their influence, however, is limited, as the Hungarian authorities suppress politically oriented work and thus allowing Western style entertainment to permeate the film and video market.

In an attempt to salvage the weakening film industry of the period, Hungarian filmmakers gear their work toward international audiences. The most successful picture in this category becomes **Isztván Szabó**'s *Mephisto* (1981), co-produced with West Germany, a Faustian tale of a stage actor's rise t artistic prominence in Nazi Germany.

Klaus-Maria Brandauer in *Mephisto*

In the equally artful *Colonel Redl* (*Redl Ezredes*, 1984), also a Hungaro-Germa production, Szabó presents the tumultuous life of a notorious career officer in the Austro-Hungarian empire.

Brandauer as Redl

Szabó's recent *Sweet Emma, Darling Böbe* (*Édes Emma, drága Böbe*, 1992) is an extremely insightful presentation of Hungary's rocky transition from a communist country into a democratic state.

Peter Gothár enjoys critical acclaim for his energetic examination of the Hungarian contemporary reality in *Time Stands Still* (*Megáll az idő*, 1982).

Márta Mészáros turns to autobiographical themes in the outstanding trilogy which chronicles her childhood after WWII (***A Diary for My Children***/*Napló gyermekeimnek*, 1982), young adulthood as a film student in Moscow (***A Diary for My Loves***/*Napló szerelmeimnek*, 1987), and painful experiences in the revolutionary Budapest of 1956 (***A Diary for My Mother and Father***/*Naplo apámnak, anyámnek*, 1990). While maintaining a strong focus on the central character, Mészáros' alter ego, this moving trilogy provides a rich, frequently disturbing insight into some of the most dramatic years in postwar East European history.

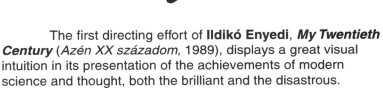

A Diary for My Mother and Father

The first directing effort of **Ildikó Enyedi**, *My Twentieth Century* (*Azén XX századom*, 1989), displays a great visual intuition in its presentation of the achievements of modern science and thought, both the brilliant and the disastrous.

Also noteworthy is the unconventional work of **Béla Tarr** (b. 1955), ***Prefabricated People*** (*Panelkapcsolat*, 1982) and ***Damnation*** (*Kárhozat*, 1988). Both experiment with cinematic styles—the first with subverting neorealism and the second with sophisticated abstraction.

BULGARIA

With the upcoming 1300th anniversary of the founding of the Bulgarian state in 681, the government invests heavily in the production of lavish epics to commemorate the most important moments of the country's history. The first of these films is **Zahari Zhdanov**'s ***Master of Boyana*** (*Boyanskiyat maistor*, 1981), a beautifully designed, fictionalized story of a 13th century fresco artist whose work quite possibly influenced the Italian Renaissance masters.

Master of Boyana

Two more epics of even greater scope follow the same year: **Georgi Djulgerov**'s *Measure for Measure* (*Mera spored mera*), a three-part account of the 1903 uprising in Greek Macedonia, and **Lyudmil Staikov**'s *Khan Asparuh*, a widescreen extravaganza which becomes Bulgaria's most popular movie ever.

In 1984, **Georgi Stoyanov** directs his monumental two-part picture, *Constantine the Philosopher* (*Konstantin Filosof*), which portrays Cyril and Methodius in their missionary activities in Moravia of the 9th century.

Constantine the Philosopher

Another exquisite superproduction, **Borislav Sharaliev**'s *Boris the First* (*Boris parvi*, 1985), chronicles the tedious process of Bulgaria's conversion to Christianity in 865.

In *The Camp* (*Lagerat*, 1989), Djulgerov examines Bulgaria's more recent past, namely the Stalinist years, as does **Ivan Nichev**'s *Ivan and Alexandra* (*Ivan i Aleksandra*, 1989), which deals with the state's despicable practice of exploiting children to obtain incriminating evidence against their parents.

The new generation of Bulgarian filmmakers, mostly graduates of **VITIS** (The Sofia Film and Theatre School), tends to focus on contemporary issues of the increasingly unbearable socialist reality (e.g. **Ljudmil Todorov**'s *Running Dogs*/*Bjagashti kucheta*, 1988 and **Chaim Cohen**'s *Protect the Small Animals*/*Zaschitete drebnite zhivotni*, 1988).

Unfortunately, the fall of Bulgarian communism in 1989-90 results in economic and political chaos. Unlike Poland and Hungary, Bulgaria seems uncertain of its direction in assimilating democratic principles. One may only hope that with proper restructurization of state funding and incentives for private investors, Bulgarian cinema will some day continue its powerful artistic legacy.

In the early 1980s, the Soviet film industry produces increasingly realistic social dramas, such as **Moscow Doesn't Believe in Tears** (*Moskva slezam ne verit*, Vladimir Menshov, 1980), while veteran directors like **Sergei Gerasimov** and **Sergei Bondarchuk** glorify Russia's historical and cultural heritage—the former directing **Lev Tolstoy** (1984) and the latter **Boris Godunov** (1986).

After being shelved for nearly a decade, **Elem Klimov**'s (b. 1933) controversial **Agony** (*Agoniya*, also known as **Rasputin**, 1975-81) is released in 1984. This portrayal of Rasputin's influence on the court of Tsar Nicholas II, the last monarch of Russia before the Revolution, features a combination of black-and-white and color photography, sometimes within the same scenes, and incorporates original stock footage of the period.

In **Come And See** (*Idi i smotri*, 1985), Klimov creates a truly apocalyptic vision of war, focusing on the horrors of the Belorussian people during the Nazi occupation of 1943. The idea for the film is suggested by Klimov's late wife, the famed director **Larissa Shepitko**, herself an ardent pacifist.

Come and See abandons the rigidity of traditional camera angles in favor of the gliding quality of Steadicam. Klimov confronts the misery of war in its most degrading moments, especially during the profoundly disturbing sequence of a village massacre. To enhance the immediacy of physical danger, the director besieges his characters with frontal close-ups and leaves them no room for escape. The forceful soundtrack thunders with outbursts of gunfire and explosions, then suddenly shuts off to an eerie silence punctuated by the croaks of hovering ravens and buzz of flies feeding on a fresh corpse. The drab, earth tones of the picture, photographed mostly with available light, further reinforce the nearly tangible atmosphere of doom. *Come and See* is one of those rare instances of moviemaking when the medium delivers the message more astutely than the plot.

Come and See

After a decade of state-imposed hiatus from filmmaking, **Sergei Paradjanov** returns with the poetic ***The Legend of Surinam Fortress*** (*Legenda o suramskoi kreposti*, 1984) and ***Ashik Kerib*** (1988), both highly reminiscent of the stylistic inventiveness of his early work.

> CINEMA IS A SYNTHETIC ART WHICH EMERGES FROM MONTAGE OF VISUAL AND MUSICAL RHYTHMS— DANCING, COLOR, AND FORM PLAY CRITICAL PART IN SHAPING THE UNIQUE PARADJANOV AESTHETIC.

Around the same time, in Italy, the greatest poet of the Russian cinema, **Andrei Tarkovsky**, creates ***Nostalghia*** (1983), an allegorical meditation on the excruciating torments of exile.

Nostalghia

Tarkovsky's final work before his untimely death of cancer in 1986, is the Swedish-produced ***Sacrifice*** (1986). A partial tribute to the cinema of Ingmar Bergman, the movie features **Erland Josephson** (*Scenes from a Marriage*) as the idealistic writer who offers his family and health to God in exchange for peace on Earth. This symbolic parable perfectly illustrates Tarkovsky's intellectual approach to cinema: his mise-en-scène is designed with utmost care and his famous long takes are executed with minute precision, allowing the audience to savor each detail and word. Photographed in muted color by Sven Nykvist, *Sacrifice* offers unforgettable experiences to those who seek thrills of the metaphysical kind.

I THINK THAT WHAT A PERSON NORMALLY GOES TO THE CINEMA FOR IS *TIME*: FOR TIME LOST OR SPENT OR NOT YET HAD. HE GOES THERE FOR LIVING EXPERIENCE; FOR CINEMA, LIKE NO OTHER ART, WIDENS, ENHANCES AND CONCENTRATES A PERSON'S EXPERIENCE, AND MAKES IT SIGNIFICANTLY LONGER. THAT IS THE POWER OF CINEMA.*

* from Tarkovsky's *Sculpting in Time*

The director, according to Tarkovsky, is a sculptor of time.

Tarkovsky on the set of *Sacrifice*

In the meantime, Tarkovsky's old classmate and colleague, **Andrei Konchalovsky**, embarks on a successful career in Hollywood, most notably directing the **Akira Kurosawa** script of *Runaway Train* (1985), a superbly paced prison escape drama with symbolic overtones. Konchalovsky's Sylvester Stallone-Kurt Russell buddy adventure yarn, *Tango and Cash* (1989), becomes the highest-grossing picture in the Soviet Union upon its release—a phenomenon as fascinating as it is disturbing.

Andrei Konchalovsky's younger brother, **Nikita Mikhalkov** (b. 1945), establishes himself as a charismatic leading actor of *Siberiad* (1979) and **Eldar Ryazanov's** *Station for Two* (*Vokzal dlya dvoikh*, 1983), before turning to directing the well crafted *Dark Eyes* (*Ochi chërnye*, 1987), loosely based on Chekhov's writings and produced by Italy, with **Marcello Mastroianni** and **Silvana Mangano** in the starring roles.

Next, Mikhalkov travels to the spectacular land of Mongolia to shoot *Close to Eden* (*Urga*, 1991), a heartwarming tale of a Caucasian man thrown into the magical wilderness of the Asian steppe and its people.

Set in the rural home of an aging hero of the Revolution, Mikhalkov's greatest international success to date, *Burnt by the Sun* (*Utomiennye solntsem*, 1994), pays homage to those who fell prey to their own idealism during the Stalinist Russia of the 1930s.

**Nadya Mikhalkov
in *Burnt by the Sun***

Nikita Mikhalkov speaks out:

THE CONTEMPORARY RUSSIAN CINEMA IS LIKE A SPONGE SUCKING ALL OF THE ONCE FORBIDDEN TOPICS. I REJECT THIS TENDENCY.

In the period when world cinema pursues visual experimentation, the work of Mikhalkov remains solidly rooted in the best schemes of traditional narration— a conscious, consistent commitment of a filmmaker assured of his strength.

One of the turning points in the cinema of *perestroika* is **Tengiz Abuladze**'s *Repentance* (*Pokjaniye, monanieba*, 1984), the Georgian-made political allegory of the evils of Stalinism. It is set in an imaginary totalitarian state ruled by the tyrannical Varlam—an embodiment of all infamous dictators of the 20th century. What sets this movie apart, besides its audacious political message, is the circular pattern of narration, which incorporates dream-within-dream sequences enhanced by surrealist imagery.

FOUR OUT OF THREE PEOPLE ARE OUR ENEMIES!

Avtandil Makharadze in *Repentance*

The futuristic science fiction genre is intelligently explored by **Konstantin Lopushansky** in ***Letters from a Dead Man*** (*Pis'ma mertvego cheloveka*, 1986), a brown-tinted contemplation on life after a nuclear holocaust, resounding with the echo of Tarkovsky's *Stalker*.

The most internationally popular movie to effectively portray the social changes of Gorbachev's perestroika is ***Little Vera*** (*Malenkaya Vera*, Vasili Pichul, 1988), whose gritty style is strongly reminiscent of the British "kitchen sink" cinema.

Pavel Lounguine's outstanding ***Taxi Blues*** (*Taksi-bliuz*, 1990), betrays stylistic influences of Scorsese in its bleak presentation of the contemporary urban reality of Russia. The story focuses on a turbulent relationship between a Moscow cab driver and his deadbeat passenger, a brilliant Jewish saxophone player.

The most devastating vision of the Soviet people's spiritual crisis belongs to ***Freeze, Die, Come to Life!*** (dir. Vitaly Kanievsky, 1990), a morality tale depicting two children caught in the barbaric reality of a remote village during WWII.

Little Vera, *Taxi Blues*, and *Freeze, Die, Come to Life!* represent the inherently Russian genre of **chernukha**, or **black film**, which is characterized by uncompromisingly sordid presentation of the human condition shaped by the communist doctrine.

Natalia Negoda
as Little Vera

Eldar Ryazanov's *A Forgotten Tune for the Flute* (*Zabytaya melodiya dlya Jeity*, 1987), becomes *glasnost*'s first comedy infused with a critique of bureaucracy.

SPARE SOME FOR A FORMER ACTIVIST

The morally uplifting, cross-cultural story of hate and forgiveness, ***The Prisoner of the Mountains*** (dir. Sergei Bodrov, 1996), suggests a shift toward a more optimistic cinema of compassion and dialogue.

CZECHOSLOVAKIA

The key figure of the Czech New Wave of the 1960s, **Jiri Menzel**, establishes himself as the leading director of the 1980s with such perceptive, humanist portrayals of socialist reality as *Cutting It Short* (*Postrizhiny*, 1980) and *The Snowdrop Festival* (*Lavosti snezenek*, 1983), both based on **Bohumil Hrabal**'s writing. Menzel's charming presentation of small community life in *My Sweet Little Village* (*Vesnicko má, stredisková*, 1985) brings him well deserved recognition in the West.

After the Velvet Revolution of 1989, which results in replacing communism with the democratically elected government of **Vaclav Havel**, Menzel directs the commercially successful *The Life and Extraordinary Adventures of Private Ivan Chonkin* (*Zivot a neobycejna dobrodruzství vojáka Ivana Conkina*, 1994), an adaptation of the famous underground Soviet novel by **Vladimir Voinovich**. Like most of Menzel's great films, *Ivan Chonkin* displays a sympathetic attitude toward small groups of individuals overcoming the hardships imposed upon them by external forces (usually communism), and his lyrical, often humorous imagery recalls the French masters of poetic realism.

The Snowdrop Festival

The veteran Slovak director **Juraj Jakubisko** continues to create visually arresting movies such as *The Millennial Bee* (*Tisicrocna vcela*, 1983), a peasant saga set in the Austro-Hungarian Empire, and, recently, *It Is Better to Be Rich and Handsome Than Poor and Ugly* (*Lepsie byt bohaty a zdravy ako chudobny a chory*, 1992), which takes a satirical look at Slovakia's nationalistic tendencies (Slovakia becomes an independent country in 1993).

The Millennial Bee

Another important but marginalized Slovak filmmaker, **Stefan Uher** (1930-93), whose ***Sunshine in a Net*** (*Slnko v sieti*, 1962) is regarded as one of the precursors of the Czech and Slovak New Wave, directs the little known ***Down to Earth*** (*Spravca skanzenu*, 1988)—an uncompromising social critique.

Some of the most interesting pictures to emerge out of the new Czech Republic are **Jan Sverák**'s ***The Elementary School*** (*Obecna skola*, 1991) and **Hynek Bocan**'s ***My Companions in the House of Anguish*** (*Prítelkyne z domu smutku*, 1993), as well as the consistently thrilling work of **Jan Svankmajer** (b. 1934), the master of surrealist puppet animation, whose ***Faust*** (*Lekce Faust*, 1994) incorporates live-action sequences.

Faust **(not a live action sequence)**

The phenomenal success of Sverák's ***Kolya*** (1996), a simple but irresistibly enchanting tale of friendship between an aging cellist and a 6-year-old boy, raises hopes for the Czech cinema to continue its long tradition of infusing reality with fairy-tale wonderment.

Zdenek Sverák and Andrei Chalimon in *Kolya*

ROMANIA

Dan Pita's ***The Contest*** (*Concurs*, 1982) and **Mircea Veroiu**'s ***To Die From Love of Life*** (*Sa mori ranit din dragoste de viata*, 1983) lead the renaissance of the Romanian cinema of the 1980s. The former is a perceptive parable on the nature of political leadership, while the latter is perhaps the best example of Eastern European film noir, spiced with a political subtext.

Mircea Daneliuc's international recognition grows with each consecutive picture: ***Glissando*** (1984) is a disquieting allegory of human depravity and ***Jacob*** (1988) denounces economic oppression of the poor in any political system.

The Oak

After the bloody overthrow of the **Ceausescu** regime in 1989, the Romanian film industry frees itself from the restraints of state censorship, but at the same time loses its chief sponsor. Some filmmakers manage to secure foreign investment, most notably **Lucian Pintilie**, whose Romanian/French production of ***The Oak*** (*Stejarul*, 1992) depicts the last stages of Romanian communism in an unflinching, frequently disturbing manner.

YUGOSLAVIA

The decade of the 1980s brings international recognition to the directors of the **Prague Group**, especially the Bosnian-born **Emir Kusturica** (b. 1955), whose debut feature ***Do You Remember Dolly Bell?*** (*Sjecas li se Dolly Bell?*, 1981), set in Sarajevo of the 1950s, instantly becomes a hit in Europe. Kusturica continues to probe his country's past in ***When Father Was Away on Business*** (*Otac na sluzbenom putu*, 1985), which takes a charming look at the rather grim post-WWII reality, shot from a perspective of a young boy. The movie remains one of Yugoslavia's most celebrated films to date and propels Kusturica to world fame.

Under the watchful eye of Tito:
When Father Was Away on Business

The Time of the Gypsies (*Dom za vesanje*, 1989) and the internationally produced **Arizona Dream** (1991) brand Kusturica's approach to cinema as oneiric—his lyrical, visually arresting style bordering on surrealism overtakes the narrative aspects of his craft. The latter stars Johnny Depp as a young New Yorker visiting Arizona, where his eccentric relatives fashion new meaning of the term "dysfunctional family."

Focusing on a pair of crooks who adapt to historical changes in the streets of Belgrade, Kusturica's recent historical epic, **Underground** (*Il était une fois un pays*, 1995), follows the identity of Yugoslavia from WWII to the moment of the country's breakup into independent states in 1992. Ironically, this powerful, symbolic movie is produced exclusively by foreign investors.

In the melancholic saga of a peasant woman, **Petrija's Wreath** (*Petrijin venal*, 1980), **Srdan Karanovic** describes the hardships of rural life; his allegorical comedy, **Something in Between** (*Nesto izmedju*, 1983) eloquently projects the duality of the Yugoslav soul suspended between Western ideals and Balkan roots.

Permeated with humor and introspection, **Hey Babu Riba** (dir. Jovan Acin, 1987) features four men reminiscing about their teenage years in the Communist 1950s. The same time period is presented from a child's point of view in **Goran Markovic**'s witty **Tito and Me** (*Tito i ja*, 1992).

The tragic effects of the civil war in Bosnia in the first half of this decade will undoubtedly influence the future outlook of creative activity in the former Yugoslavia. One of the first and certainly the most profound movies to approach the subject of ethnic conflicts in the Balkans, which lies at the very heart of the region's misery, is **Milcho Manchevski**'s **Before the Rain** (*Pred Dozdot*, 1994). Composed of three interconnected parts, the movie dissects the issues of mindless hate and vengeance which plague rural Macedonia.

Rade Serbedzija in *Before the Rain*

SOUTH AMERICA 1980-present

ARGENTINA

With its economy deteriorating at an enormous rate, Argentina's right-wing government decides to boost its public support by invading the British-held Falkland Islands in 1982. The failure of the invasion accelerates the fall of the regime, which is replaced in 1982 through democratic elections.

The first wave of movies to emerge after the end of political censorship focuses on Argentina's "dirty war" of 1976-83, during which the military repressed its opposition with the illegal arrest and murder of thousands of innocent people. This harrowing subject is bracketed by two very influential films: **Hector Olivera**'s violent farce **Funny, Dirty Little War** (*No habrá más penas ni olvido*, 1983) and **Luis Puenzo**'s social drama **The Official Story** (*La historia oficial*, 1985).

Set in a small rural town in 1974, *Funny, Dirty Little War* depicts the struggle of civilian rebel forces against the military terror, foreshadowing Argentina's upcoming reign of dictatorial regime.

For a Peronist there is nothing better than another Peronist: the Left and the Right of Peron in *Funny, Dirty Little War*

The Official Story portrays the growing political awareness of a woman who suspects that her adopted child's real parents fell prey to "death squad" atrocities.

The aftermath of oppression, namely issues of external and internal exile, are presented with great effectiveness by **Fernando Solanas** in **Tangos: The Exile of Gardel** (*Tangos —el exilo de Gardel*, 1985), which deals with political and cultural issues of Argentina as expressed through the dance

Tangos

(*tanguedia*). Solanas' **South** (*Sur*, 1988) is a moving story of a newly released political prisoner who, marred by ghoulish memories, wanders the streets of Buenos Aires' south side attempting to reunite with his family.

In *Camila* (1984), **María Luisa Bemberg** (b. 1917) uses a true 19th century love story between a young socialite and a Catholic priest to create a powerful allegory of the recent tyrannical oppression of Argentinian society as well as to outline the vulnerability of women in a patriarchal system of values.

Susú Pecoraro as Camila

Among the best apolitical films of the period is **Eliseo Subielá**'s ***Man Facing Southeast*** (*Hombre mirando al sudeste*, 1986), an unusual sci-fi picture set in a mental asylum, which deals with issues of personal alienation in a world where emotions are replaced by insensitivity and human compassion is the thing of the past.

An Unidentified Flying Patient:
Man Facing Southeast

The recent years in Argentinian cinema are marked by a string of highly popular commercial films which give a much needed boost to the ailing motion picture industry; ***The Worst of It*** (*Yo, la peor de todas*, M.L. Bemberg, 1990) and ***Funes: A Great Love*** (*Funes, un gran amor*, 1993) are among the most successful titles.

327

BRAZIL

One of the most profound Brazilian pictures to denounce the rampant poverty and desperation of common people living under the post-militaristic leadership of Gen. Figueiredo is **Hector Babenco**'s *Pixote* (1981). This unmitigatedly realistic picture exposes the deplorable social conditions which drive young children to prostitution and violent crime—the only feasible ways of urban survival. To give his movie an enhanced sense of realism, Babenco shoots on location in the Rio de Janeiro slums, and casts local homeless children in leading roles.

Fernando Ramos da Silva as Pixote

Among other memorable Brazilian titles are *Gaigin* (dir. **Tizuka Yamasaki**, 1980), which presents the experiences of the Japanese immigrant laborers in South America, and **Memories of Prison** (*Memorias do carcere*, 1984), an involving drama of political incarceration, directed by the veteran filmmaker **Nelson Pereira dos Santos**.

MEXICO

The decade of the 1980s proves to be the most disastrous period in the history of Mexican cinema. The failed attempt at privatization of the industry puts many filmmakers out of work and the largest Latin American film archives, located in Mexico City, perishes in a huge fire, while the country finds itself on a brink of economic collapse due to the slump in oil prices.

Remarkably, several directors of unswerving perseverance manage to create astonishing work despite the piling obstacles.

In *Frida* (1983), **Paul Leduc** recreates the rich life of Frida Kahlo, the famed Mexican painter whose work combined elements of folk art and modernism and whose communist beliefs and freespirited attitude caused as much controversy as admiration. Leduc disposes of traditional plot and dialogue, instead weaving a colorful tapestry of introspective vignettes whose blend of symbolism and harsh directness recall Kahlo's unique painting style.

Ofelia Medina as Frida Kahlo

In an audacious move, **Jaime Humberto Hermosillo** directs ***Doña Herlinda and Her Son*** (*Doña Erlinda y su hijo*, 1984), the very first Mexican movie to address homosexual themes openly.

Among several major international productions shot in Mexico, ***Erendira*** (1982) and ***Cabeza de Vaca*** (1990) enjoy worldwide recognition.

Directed by the Brazilian filmmaker **Ruy Guerra**, *Erendira* is a strange, nearly surrealist tale of a domineering matron, played by the great Greek actress **Irene Papas**, who exploits the charms of her pretty granddaughter in an attempt to rebuild the lost family fortune. Scripted by **Gabriel García Márquez**, *Erendira* becomes the key example of **Magical Realism** in Latin American cinema.

Nicolás Echevarria's *Cabeza de Vaca* concerns the fate of a 16th century Spanish conquistador whose ship capsizes off the coast of Florida. Exposed to most arduous experiences, the protagonist begins to question the morality of his countrymen and grows to respect the ways and values of Native American Indians. Alternately dramatic and mystical, *Cabeza de Vaca* provides a fresh perspective on the historical events that shaped the foundation of the New World.

In 1992, **Laura Esquivel** adapts her popular novel of love and cooking, ***Like Water for Chocolate*** (*Como aqua para chocolate*) into a pleasurable movie of the same name. Directed by **Alfonso Arau** (b. 1931), it becomes one of Mexico's most successful international hits in recent years.

Nicaragua's first narrative feature, ***Alsino and the Condor*** (*Alsino y el condor*, 1983), is directed by the Chilean exile **Miguel Littín**. Following the great tradition of films dealing with horrors of war through the eyes of a child, the movie focuses on an adolescent boy named Alsino (**Alan Esquivel**), whose daydreams of soaring through the skies like a free bird allow him to escape the crippling madness of the world below. Set in war-torn Nicaragua, *Alsino* is openly sympathetic toward the Sandinista rebels, while the Contras and their American advisors, represented by **Dean Stockwell**, are markedly sadistic and dispassionate.

Alan Esquivel as Alsino

Francisco José Lombardi (b. 1950) establishes himself as the key figure in **Peruvian** cinema with ***The City and the Dogs*** (*La ciudad y los perros*, 1985), a fierce exploration of military corruption and the nature of dictatorship, based on the novel by **Mario Vargas Llosa**.

Rodrigo D.: No Future (*Rodrigo D.—No Futuro*, 1986, released 1989), directed by **Victor Gaviria**, becomes the first **Colombian** movie to receive worldwide acclaim. The film's title recalls De Sica's *Umberto D.* (1952), but its street urchin theme is closer to his *Shoeshine* (1946) as well as to Buñuel's *Los Olvidados* (1951). Shot in the *cinéma-vérité* style, *Rodrigo D.* probes the reckless life-styles of Colombia's Medellín youth, whose dead-end attitude reflects the darker aspects of the country's existence, most notably drug trafficking and abuse, and mindless violence. Tragically, most of the nonprofessional young actors who perform in the movie die of street violence shortly after *Rodrigo D.*'s completion—a sad testimony to Colombia's profoundly disturbing urban reality.

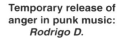

Temporary release of anger in punk music: *Rodrigo D.*

Two of the more interesting films to emerge out of **Venezuela** are made by **Fina Torres**: ***Oriana*** (*Oriane*, 1984) is a beautifully photographed art film evoking a woman's childhood memories and ***Celestial Clockwork*** (1996) presents a young Venezuelan woman on a bizarre self-discovery journey in Paris.

CUBA

In the early 1980s, the Cuban state film agency, **ICAIC** (Instituto Cubano del Arte e Industria Cinematograficos, est. 1959), undergoes a restructurization similar to Eastern European film units: each production team is headed by a renowned director and wields relative autonomy, providing that the output fits within the ideological guidelines of the revolution.

Toward the end of the 1980s, Cuban filmmakers begin to explore previously neglected or forbidden genres, such as satirical comedy, of which **Plaff!** (dir. Carlos Pablo, 1988) is the most popular and audacious one.

The collapse of Eastern European communism accelerates Cuba's economic isolation in the early 1990s. While **Fidel Castro** proudly glorifies his country as the last true bastion of Marxist-Leninist ideology, censorship of political and cultural activities intensifies.

In 1992, **Daniel Díaz Torres** (b. 1948) makes **Alice in Wonderland** (*Alicia en el pueblo de maravillas*), an updated version of the Lewis Carroll classic, set in present-day Cuba. Despite the movie's restrained satirical overtones, the state officials declare it ideologically corrupt and withdraw it from domestic distribution—a move that only reinforces *Alicia*'s international momentum.

Alice in Wonderland

A veteran of Cuban cinema, **Tomás Gutiérrez Alea** (*Memories of Underdevelopment*, 1968), breaks a strict moral taboo with **Strawberry and Chocolate** (*Fresa y chocolate*, 1993), the first Cuban film to depict homosexuality in a favorable light. Set in 1979, at the peak of political repressions, the movie calls for reevaluation of revolutionary doctrine and openness to diversity, both ideological and cultural. Withdrawn domestically shortly after its release, *Strawberry and Chocolate* quickly becomes one of the greatest worldwide hits of contemporary Cuban cinema.

331

INDIA 1980-present

While still retaining socially committed ideology, India's "parallel cinema" of the 1980s gradually moves toward mainstream production values: big stars, higher budgets, and more accessible plots. The change is most noticeable in the work of **Shyam Benegal**, whose **The Machine Age** (*Kalyug*, 1981) and **The Essence** (*Susman*, 1987) offer both entertainment and food for thought.

Aparna Sen, one of India's more prominent woman filmmakers, directs **36 Chowringhee Lane** (1981), a well acted story of disillusionment suffered by an elderly Anglo-Indian teacher's (**Jennifer Kendal**) disillusionment, shot in a subdued style reminiscent of Satyajit Ray's.

36 Chowringhee Lane

Kerala, India's heavily populated Southwest state, organizes a film cooperative devoted to independent films. One major work to emerge out of this region is **Adoor Gopalakrishnan**'s **Rat Trap** (*Elippathayam*, 1981), a stylized allegory of a man's resistance to social change.

Ketan Mehta emerges as the most innovative director of the new generation with **A Folk Tale** (*Bhavni bhavai*, 1981), which provides a new approach to traditional folk storytelling by employing alternative endings. Mehta's musical **A Touch of Spice** (*Mirch masala*, 1987) offers an entertaining blend of popular film genres in the style of old Indian cinema.

After a long hiatus, the "parallel cinema" veteran **Kumar Shahani** (*Mirror of Illusion/Maya darpan*, 1972), creates **Kasba** (1990), an introspective examination of rural life, which employs major movie stars—a characteristic shared by most of the contemporary "parallel" films.

Salaam Bombay!

The greatest crossover triumph of modern Indian cinema is **Mira Nair**'s (b. 1957) *Salaam Bombay!* (1988), co-produced with France and Britain's Channel 4. Shot from the perspective of a young impoverished boy, the movie unveils the hardships of Bombay's underbelly existence. Coming from a documentary background, Nair approaches her subject with a gripping edge of realism.

After relocating to Hollywood, Nair continues to direct movies revolving around minority themes. Her **Mississippi Masala** (1991) is an interracial romance story between a black blue collar worker (**Denzel Washington**) and an Indian woman (**Sarita Choudhury**); **The Perez Family** (1995) deals with the hectic experiences of illegal Cuban immigrants in Florida. Nair's latest effort, **Kama Sutra: A Tale of Love** (1997) is a stylish soft core erotica which focuses on a rivalry of two 16th century Indian women.

Channel 4 contributes funds to the latest international hit of Indian film, **Bandit Queen** (dir. Shakhar Kapur, 1994), a true story of the notorious Phoolan Devi, a poor, illiterate woman who overcomes tremendous amount of physical and mental abuse to become a fearsome fighter for social justice.

Seema Biswas as Phoolan Devi in Bandit Queen

Marred by ongoing political chaos, a weakening economy, and natural disasters, India cannot sustain its once magnificent cinematic production. With the proliferation of video piracy, the expansion of cable and satellite television, as well with the pressing competition from Hollywood, the future of Indian film remains at best uncertain.

JAPAN 1980-present

In 1980, the grand master of Japanese cinema, **Akira Kurosawa**, enters his fifth decade as a filmmaker with ***Kagemusha*** (*Shadow Warrior*)—a lush period drama of political intrigue set in the 16th century, whose visual splendor recalls Kurosawa's early *jidai-geki*. This story of a lookalike who assumes duties of a presumed-dead clan leader, perfectly balances human drama with elaborate battle scenes, especially spectacular in painterly color supported by thundering sound effects.

Kagemusha

It takes Kurosawa five years to get his cameras rolling again, but the wait is well worth it—***Ran*** (1985) is widely considered to be the Japanese director's greatest masterpiece since *The Seven Samurai* (1954). Returning to his beloved Shakespeare, Kurosawa transplants *King Lear* onto the feudal Japanese soil, turning Lear's daughters into three sons who vie for political power as the old patriarch, once a mighty clan chief, endures their treachery in the autumn of his life.

The extravagance of costume design and period detail, as well as the mastery of composition and camera movement make *Ran* an unforgettable visual experience, while the intricacies of the plot and subtlety of acting provide drama of the highest caliber.

Tatsuya Nakadai as Hidetora (Lear) in *Ran*

By now in his mid seventies, Kurosawa contemplates retirement from moviemaking but returns in 1990 with ***Akira Kurosawa's Dreams***, a sequential film comprised of impressionistic meditations on life, art, and the threat of a nuclear holocaust.

The *enfant terrible* of Japanese film, **Nagisa Oshima**, makes the interesting WWII drama, ***Merry Christmas, Mr. Lawrence*** (1982). Set in a Japanese POW camp in Java, the movie chronicles a rather bizarre relationship between an English officer (David Bowie) and his captor (**Ryuichi Sakamoto**).

ALMOST THERE, MA.

I SHOULD HAVE SIGNED UP FOR MEDICARE.

The Ballad of Narayama

Another veteran of the Japanese New Wave of the 1960s, **Shohei Imamura** creates ***The Ballad of Narayama*** (*Narayamabushi-ko*, 1983), a superb remake of the Keisuke Kinoshita movie from 1958. Inhabitants of a village are compelled by an ancient custom to take their elderly parents into the mountains and leave them to die in solitude once they prove useless to the community. Imamura combines harsh realism with poetic, almost mythical glorification of the forces of nature, evoking a powerful vision of life in its most primal form.

One of the most internationally recognizable Japanese auteurs of the new generation is **Yuzo Itami** (b. 1933). Heavily infused with black humor, ***The Funeral*** (*Ososhiki*, 1984) is a satire of the middle class; ***Tampopo*** (1986) becomes a parody of genre films, specifically the western, while celebrating the great benefits of food, sexual stimulation included. Itami's biggest commercial hit, ***A Taxing Woman*** (*Marusa no onna*, 1987), dissects the avaricious nature of the Japanese in a witty, well observed manner.

The Funeral

Mitsuo Yanagimachi
(b. 1950) enjoys critical acclaim for his ***Fire Festival*** (*Himatsuri*, 1985), a murder-suicide tale with ecological concerns.

Another intriguing younger director, **Kaizo Hayashi** (b. 1957), makes the ambitious ***To Sleep, So as to Dream*** (*Yume miruyoni nemuritai*, 1986), which assumes the format of a silent Japanese movie: the dialogue is communicated through intertitles, and the traditional *benshi* narrator comments on the action. The movie does, however, make use of a musical score and sound effects.

On the fertile scene of the Japanese cult filmmaking, **Shinya Tsukamoto** (b. 1960) makes his visually arresting mark with ***Tetsuo: The Iron Man*** (1989), a surreal horror fable about a man who merges with a machine, and ***Tetsuo: The Body Hammer*** (1991), a bloodie and wilder variation of the original.

Tetsuo: The Body Hammer

Finally, mention must be made of the unbelievably popular Japanese cinematic phenomenon of ***anime***—feature-length animated movies, mostly of the techno sci-fi genre, characterized by brilliant art design and inventive editing. The most accomplished *anime* to date is ***Akira*** (1987), directed by **Katsuhiro Otomo** and based on his own comic book, which revolves around a young biker subjected to scientific experimentation in futuristic Tokyo.

CHINA'S FIFTH GENERATION

Many years of the disastrous "true communist" rule of **Mao Zedong** culminate with the atrocious implementation of the Great Proletarian Cultural Revolution (1966-1976), whose chief goal is to reinstate the weakening Maoist ideology and prevent the spread of capitalism. Prominent intellectuals and artists, as well as the overwhelming majority of other professionals, are forcibly relocated to remote rural regions of the country to "learn" from the peasants.

Chinese cinema is rendered virtually nonexistent. After Mao's death in 1976 and several years of internal power struggle, a more progressive (by Chinese communist standards) government emerges under the direction of **Deng Xiaoping**.

In 1978, after over a decade of being shut down, the Beijing Film Academy opens its doors to a new group of students—the **Fifth Generation** (the previous four correspond to other tumultuous periods in China's past). Graduated in 1982, Fifth Generation becomes the first group of Chinese filmmakers to receive world recognition, most notably **Chen Kaige** (b. 1952) and **Zhang Yimou** (b. 1950).

Chen Kaige's impressive debut, *Yellow Earth* (*Huang tudi*, 1984), is a lyrical account of a communist soldier on a mission to collect folk songs from a distant region of China.

Yellow Earth

As his second feature, Kaige directs **The Big Parade** (*Da yuebing*, 1985), which focuses on the Chinese Army paratroopers training for the National Day festivities held in Tiananmen Square. Both pictures benefit from the sensational cinematography of Zhang Yimou, who saturates the image with rich, sensuous hues and allows the sunlight to radiate the filmstock.

His fame stretching well beyond China, Kaige in now allowed to make films with international money. In the poetic **Life on a String** (*Bian zhou bian chang*, 1991), Kaige abandons the typical narrative format for a meditative, Zen-like atmosphere. His greatest popular success to date, however, becomes **Farewell My Concubine** (*Bawamg boe ji*, 1993), a magnificent epic film in the tradition of David Lean, but without the obtrusive stereotyping and clichés. Following the friendship of two Peking Opera performers, the movie chronicles the history of modern China since the 1930s until the onset of the Cultural Revolution.

WE FEEL RESPONSIBLE FOR OUR GENERATION, WHO SURVIVED THE CULTURAL REVOLUTION. SO OFTEN, I FEEL THAT I'M A SOLDIER RATHER THAN A FILMMAKER.

Chen Kaige

Meanwhile, **Zhang Yimou** forgoes his booming career as China's preeminent cinematographer, and devotes himself to directing. His first movie, ***Red Sorghum*** (*Hong gaoliang*, 1988), immediately proves that Yimou's new career choice is the right one: the film astonishes with its tactile beauty, from the dramatic use of color to a perfectly balanced mise-en-scène. This moving story about a man recalling his grandparents' love affair mixes humor and tragedy, subtly asserting the natural law of the land over the imposing communist doctrine.

Red Sorghum also marks the beginning of the enduring collaboration between Yimou and **Gong Li**, his strikingly beautiful and talented leading lady.

Gong Li in *Red Sorghum*

In his great international hit, ***Ju Dou*** (1990), co-produced with Japan, Yimou tells a tragic story of vengeance inflicted by an old, impotent husband on his sensuous wife (Gong Li) and her lover. Set in a silk-dying shop in the pre-communist China, the movie manages to convey as much feeling through imagery and color as it does through the narrative. Like *Red Sorghum*, *Ju Dou* is photographed by the outstanding Chinese cinematographer, **Gu Changwei** also responsible for Kaige's *Farewell My Concubine*.

Ju Dou

In the engrossing, almost claustrophobic **Raise the Red Lantern** (*Dahong lenglong gaogao gua*, 1991), Yimou also harks back to the pre-revolutionary era, this time concentrating on the fate of a young new bride (Li), who must overcome animosity of the patriarch's other three wives. Both *Ju Dou* and *Raise the Red Lantern* are briefly banned in China on ideological grounds.

Zheng Yimou

Gong Li sheds her usual glamorous image for a down-to-earth portrayal of a pregnant peasant woman in **The Story of Qiu Ju** (*Quiju da guansi*, 1992), a gritty, low-key documentary-like account of present-day life in rural China—a complete stylistic departure for Yimou. The movie enjoys enormous critical acclaim and popularity in the West, drawing favorable comparisons with Italian neorealism.

Another notable exponent of Fifth Generation is **Tian Zhuangzhuang** (b. 1952), a great visual stylist, whose **Horse Thief** (*Daoma zei*, 1987) is less concerned with plot then providing viewers with overwhelmingly beautiful images of Buddhist rituals and the harsh life of Tibetan nomads. Zhuangzhuang's **The Blue Kite** (*Lan fengzheng*, 1993) is a devastating domestic tragedy that reflects the most dramatic episodes in China's Maoist past. Not surprisingly, the film is banned and its gifted director removed from filmmaking activities.

The Horse Thief

Echoes of the Tiananmen Square massacre of June 1989 still resounds strongly in the memory of Chinese people, as the government continues its sluggish trek toward a more moderate rule. Fortunately, China's booming economy and the influx of foreign investment indicate progress at least in some areas of life, including entertainment. More movies are being imported into the country and some of the old domestic titles released; television and video becomes widely accessible. But whether it might mean future leniency toward artistic creativity and end of censorship, it seems doubtful. The impact of the Fifth Generation is slowly dissipating, as Chinese film production veers toward cheap, empty movies designed for quick profit.

HONG KONG 1980–present

For many years identified with low-budget kung-fu movies, the cinema of Hong Kong experiences a true creative breakthrough in the 1980s with the advent of the **heroic bloodshed** genre. Initiated with **John Woo**'s (b. 1942) **A Better Tomorrow** (1986), heroic bloodshed films are visually sophisticated reinterpretations of the traditional swordplay genre, replacing historical and mythical figures with chivalrous gangsters and tormented cops. The best of the lot include Woo's **The Killer** (1989), **Bullet in the Head** (1990), and **Hard Boiled** (1992), which emulate Jean-Pierre Melville's mythical treatement of criminal underworld and elevate Sam Peckinpah's "ballet of violence" to a new aesthetic level.

Ringo Lam provides a slightly more demented twist on the genre with **City on Fire** (1987) and **Full Contact** (1992). The former serves as one of many influences for Quentin Tarantino's *Reservoir Dogs* (1992).

Chow Yun Fat, the extremely charismatic Hong Kong megastar, epitomizes best the gritty, casual intensity of a heroic bloodshed protagonist.

Shedding the blood of a hero: Chow Yun Fat in *The Killer*

The inevitable impact of heroic bloodshed on Hollywood is signified by the recent success of two **John Travolta** vehicles: **Broken Arrow** (1996) and **Face-Off** (1997), both characterized by director John Woo's fantastic sense of camera movement and editing panache.

Tsui Hark, the eclectic producer and director with a great visual flair, is responsible for creating the spectacular **Zu: Warriors from the Magic Mountain** (1982) and **A Chinese Ghost Story** (dir. Ching Sin Tung, 1987), which set new standards for the horror-fantasy genre.

Samo Hung, superstar, film director, and fight choreographer, works his acting magic in *Zu*

Trained at the famous Peking Opera Academy in Hong Kong since the age of seven, **Jackie Chan** (b. 1954) breaks into stardom with **Drunken Master** (dir. Ng See Yuen, 1978), an unbelievably energetic kung-fu adventure. Realizing early on that he should not imitate the screen persona of the late Bruce Lee, Jackie develops his unique brand of performing style which combines martial arts mastery with Keatonesque pantomime and acrobatic insanity. In the 1980s, Jackie takes the East by storm with a series of terrific action films ranging from pirate adventure, **Project A** (1984), to contemporary police thriller, **Police Story** (1986), both of which he also directs. In the 1990s, Jackie Chan's supernova shows no sign of dimming its glory—**Operation Condor** (Chan, 1991), **Supercop** (dir. Stanley Tong, 1992), **Rumble in the Bronx** (Tong, 1993), and **Jackie Chan's First Strike** (Chan, 1996) are re-edited, re-dubbed, and re-titled for successful American release—a sure sign of Jackie's well deserved and somewhat belated recognition in America (Europe has embraced his talents long ago).

> WHAT IS A BAD MOVIE? NOBODY SEES IT, THAT'S A BAD MOVIE.

Jackie Chan in action

Among the more arty Hong Kong films of recent years are **Rouge** (dir. Stanley Kwan, 1987), a toned-down romantic ghost tale produced by Jackie Chan, and **Chungking Express** (dir. Wong Kar Wai, 1994), a melancholic diptych of lovelorn urban existence.

After 99 years of British rule, in July 1997, Hong Kong is reclaimed by China. How the change will affect local film production remains uncertain; however, many prominent filmmakers plan to relocate to Taiwan, or have already done so, while others, like Woo, Hark, and Tong are already under lucrative contracts from Hollywood.

OTHER FAR EAST COUNTRIES 1980–present

Two very distinct talents stand out of the commercially oriented **Taiwanese** cinema of the 1980s: **Hou Hsiao-Hsien** (b. 1947) and **Edward Yang** (b. 1947).

Hou's big break comes with ***The Time to Live, the Time to Die*** (*Tongnian wangshi*, 1985), a nostalgic, semiautobiographical family drama of tremendous emotional strength. In the recent ***The Puppetmaster*** (*Hsimeng rensheng*, 1993), Hou tells the fascinating story of **Li Tienlu**, a great puppeteer whose experiences read like a history book of the Japanese occupation of Taiwan until 1945. Hou's cinematic style relies on refined long takes and distanced camera angles which linger on his painterly mise-en-scène.

The Time to Live, the Time to Die

Edward Yang achieves his first success with ***Taipei Story*** (*Qingmei ahuma*, 1985), followed by ***The Terrorizer*** (*Kongbu fenze*, 1987), both concerned with the chaotic urban middle-class existence. Similar milieu becomes the target of Yang's biting satire, ***The Confucian Confusion*** (1994). An avid reader of comic books, Yang endows his cinematic style with bold strokes of intense color, striking composition, and abrupt editing. Yang's greatest achievement to date is ***A Brighter Summer Day*** (*Guling jie shaonian sha ren shijan*, 1991), an very human epic film about urban life of Taiwan in the 1960s, executed with astonishing detail and care.

The Confucian Confusion

Another notable Taiwanese director is **Ang Lee** (b. 1954). Trained in the US, Lee's likable work includes ***The Wedding Banquet*** (*Xiyan*, 1993) and ***Eat Drink Man Woman*** (*Yinsh nan hu*, 1994), as well as the superb ***Sense and Sensibility*** (1995), the **Emma Thompson**-writter adaptation of **Jane Austen**'s romantic novel, co-produced by Great Britain and the US.

The most accomplished **Filipino** director is doubtlessly **Lino Brocka** (1940-91), whose **Maynila: In the Claws of Neon** *Maynila sa kuko ng liwanag*, 1975) probes the issues of social injustice in the Philippines. Brocka's **My Country: Clinging to a Knife's Edge** (*Bayan ko*, 1982) denounces President Marcos' regime, while the succeeding government of Corazón Aquino becomes the target of his **Fight for Us** (*L'Insoumis*, 1989). Tragically, the Philippines are deprived of their most outspoken filmmaker when an auto crash kills Lino Brocka in 1991.

Fight for Us

Writer-director **Tran Anh Hung** (b. 1962) creates two of the most remarkable films to emerge out of **Vietnam** in the 1990s (both are financially supported by France): **The Scent of Green Papaya** (*Mùi du du xanh*, 1993) and **Cyclo** (*Xich lo*, 1995). The former, shot with a delicate, organic style, concentrates on a young girl's experiences in 1950s Saigon; the latter, a violent urban drama, emphasizes the breakdown of old traditions under pressure from the present-day economic reality in Vietnam.

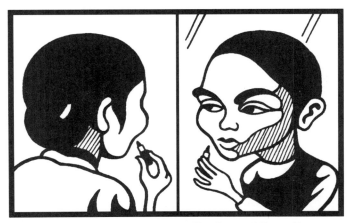

The Scent of Green Papaya

South Korea's **Why Did Bodhi-Dharma Leave for the East?** (*Dharmaga tongjoguro kan kkadalgun?*, 1989), written and directed by **Bae Yong-Kyun**, approaches the subject of Zen Buddhism with an appropriately meditative style—a loosely delineated plot line and ethereal characters become secondary to evocative imagery.

BRIEF HISTORY OF AFRICAN CINEMA

For many viewers the name **Ousmane Sembène** is synonymous with African cinema. Born in **Senegal** in 1923, Sembène receives his film training in Moscow (in the **Mark Donskoi** workshop at VGIK), and returns to Africa to embark on a prolific career as a filmmaker and novelist. His breakthrough movie, *Mandabi* ("The Money Order," 1968), is a social comedy contrasting Senegal's traditional life-style and French-influenced bureaucracy. Sembène's *Emitai* ("God of Thunder," 1971), a sharp indictment of European colonialism, presents the collective heroism of Senegalese tribesmen when drafted by the French military during WWII.

Emitai

In *Xala* ("The Curse of Impotence," 1974), Sembène attacks Senegal's indigenous *nouveau riche*, who exploit their less fortunate countrymen in much the same fashion as the French did.

The thematically controversial *Ceddo* ("Outsider," 1977), implements folk storytelling techniques in its incisive analysis of Senegal's religious makeup. Sembène's *Guelwaar* (1992) continues to probe the dynamics of the Christian–Muslim conflict, which has recently torn Senegal apart. With a fluent, economic style of filmmaking, the director manages to create a universal morality tale from material which might be otherwise inaccessible to international audiences.

Ousmane Sembène explains the ever-evolving political topicality of his work:

I LIVE AMONG MY PEOPLE. I'M LIKE A THERMOMETER.

AFRICAN CINEMA IS A FORM OF SELF-COMMUNION. THERE ARE MANY THINGS THAT WE HAVE NOT BEEN TAUGHT AND ARE IN DANGER OF LOSING: WITH CINEMA WE CAN SAFEGUARD THEM AND PEOPLE CAN SEE THEM.

Another important director to emerge out of Senegal is **Djibril Diop Mambéty** (b. 1945), the author of *Touki-Bouki* (1973)—an avant-garde picture combining African folklore aesthetic with *Nouvelle Vague* audacity of style.

Burkina Faso (formerly Upper Volta), second most potent center of African cinema after Senegal, produces *Wend Kuuni* ("God's Gift," **Gaston Kaboré**, 1982), a moving story of an abandoned child's assimilation into his adopted village community.

The overwhelming power of love is able to transcend the rigid traditions of a small African village in **Idrissa Ouedraogo**'s beautifully composed *Tilaï* ("The Law," 1990).

Ivory Coast's **Desiré Ecaré** begins his career with satires on bourgeois Africans who adopt French life-style (e.g. *À nous deux, France*, 1970) before creating one of the most effective portrayals of contemporary African life in *Faces of Women* (*Visages de femmes*, 1985). This colorful movie presents two tales: one rooted in the indigenous culture, the other in urban reality.

Faces of Women

Jean-Pierre Bekolo of **Cameroon** creates the playful *Quartier Mozart* (1992), a truly magical examination of sexual politics in a working-class neighborhood of Yaounde, told in vivid MTV style.

Kinshasa, the capital of **Zaire**, provides a vivid backdrop for ***La vie est belle*** (dir. Ngangura Mwere and Benoit Lamy, 1987), a life-affirming paean to self-reliance, which chronicles a poor village musician's rise to national fame and personal happiness.

Zimbabwe's **Michael Raeburn** writes and directs ***Jit*** (1993), a highly energetic romantic comedy with a jit-jive soundtrack which fuses traditional African rhythms with Caribbean melody.

Jit

Colonial life of **Martinique** is presented best in **Euzhan Palcy**'s ***Sugar Cane Alley*** (*Rue Cases Nègres*, 1983), which focuses on a wise grandmother's determination to save her young grandson from gruesome plantation work through education.

NORTH AFRICA

One of the most popular movies to emerge out of **Tunisia** in recent years, ***Halfaouine*** (1990), directed by **Férid Boughedir**, is daring in its approach to the subject of sexual awakening of a young Arab boy—a frequent visitor to the municipal bathhouse in Tunis.

MY MOTHER DID IT DIFFERENTLY.

Halfaouine

Moufida Tlatli, one of few female directors in the Arab world, exposes the oppressed life of women in 1950s Tunisia in her sensuous and artfully orchestrated drama, ***The Silences of the Palace*** (*Les silences du palace*, 1996).

346

SOUTH AFRICA

Place of Weeping (dir. Darrell Roodt, 1986) becomes one of the first movies made by South Africans about the woes of apartheid. Depicting a black woman's struggle to liberate herself from the oppression of the political system, this powerful movie also takes a firm stand against the internal conflicts of the indigenous people.

The plot of **Mapantsula** (dir. Oliver Schmitz, 1988) revolves around a small-time crook whose experiences on the streets of Soweto result in his growing political awareness. The movie's documentary-like treatment of life under apartheid makes for an unforgettable, frequently disturbing experience.

✳ ✳ ✳

IRAN

The most exciting director to emerge out of Iran in the past decade is **Abbas Kiarostami** (b. 1940), whose self-referential cycle of films, **Where Is the Friend's House?** (1987), **And Life Goes On** (1992), and **Through the Olive Trees** (1994), form an ever-evolving story which blends real-life and fiction.

And Life Goes On

Kiarostami writes the screenplay for **Jafar Panahi**'s critically acclaimed **White Balloon** (*Badkonake sefid*, 1995), one of the best films about children made in the past decade. For a little girl in Teheran, a simple task of buying a gold fish is rendered virtually impossible by a series of charming, unpredictable events which paint a colorful image of the city and Iranian culture.

SOMETIMES WHEN I'M IN AMERICA I SEE IMAGES FROM IRAN THAT TERRIFY ME. AND I THINK, DO I REALLY LIVE IN A COUNTRY LIKE THAT? I CAN ASSURE YOU THAT THE REAL IRANIAN SOCIETY IS MUCH CLOSER TO MY MOVIES THAN THE IMAGES YOU SEE ON TV.

Abbas Kiarostami

With the exception of digital effects (CGI), film technology as such does not undergo any dramatic changes in the 90s. The most significant development in the way movies are being in Hollywood today is the end of the studio system. Directors, writers, and actors now function as commodities contracted out to studios by omnipotent **talent agencies** such as **CAA** or **ICM**. Getting a 10% cut of their clients' fee, it is in agents' best interest to inflate the cost of making a movie; by mid 1990s, an average Hollywood film featuring an A-list star may cost between 50 and 100 million dollars, and in such extreme cases as *Waterworld* (1995) or *Titanic* (1997), reach around 150-200 million. After the release of *Jaws* in 1975, studio executives realize that the only way to make fast profit is to produce a blockbuster. Twenty years later, this horrifying mentality reaches near absurdity as Hollywood funnels its money into fewer and more costly projects of dubious merit, while neglecting modest and original work that has been the backbone of American cinema for the past three decades.

Another quick financial turnaround is provided by **product-placement strategy**, which allows studios to sell advertising space in feature films to big corporate sponsors such as soft-drink or cereal companies, blatantly displaying their product in well thought-out parts of the frame.

The media fuels this profit frenzy by providing weekly lists of top-grossing films and eagerly reporting record-breaking star salaries, equating quantity with quality. As a result, in the view of general public a good movie becomes one that lingers on a top-ten list for at least five weeks. These atrocious practices diminish interest in independent and foreign pictures, which cannot find distribution outside big metropolitan areas. Since the mid 1990s, multi-screen cineplex theatres continue to invade the country, solidifying the Great Hollywood Conglomerate of self-perpetuating mediocrity.

The dimming of inspiration is exemplified best by the material produced by American studios in the 1990s: the most financially successful pictures prove to be sequels (e.g. *Die Hard II* and *III*, *Batman Returns*, *Batman Forever*), while remakes of popular TV shows also provide a reliable source of income (e.g. *The Flintstones*, *The Brady Bunch*).

Fortunately, there are exceptions.

The tsar of Hollywood, **Steven Spielberg**, takes full advantage of his stature and financial resources to create arguably the most elaborate (but hardly the first) movie about the Jewish Holocaust during WWII, *Schindler's List* (1993). Shot on location in Poland, in and around Kraków and Auschwitz, this beautiful and uncompromisingly honest picture chronicles the real-life activities of one Oskar Schindler (**Liam Neeson**). This Austrian entrepreneur and Nazi sympathizer gradually transforms from a sly war profiteer into an ardent supporter of his Jewish employees, managing to save 1,100 of them from imminent demise. Photographed in high-contrast black-and-white by **Janusz Kaminski** and designed with utmost care for period detail by **Allan Starski** and **Ewa Braun**, famous Polish art directors, *Schindler's List* rises above the usual limitations of Hollywood aesthetic and displays a gritty, painfully realistic record of one of this century's most horrifying chapters.

Known for his technical wizardry and flashy storytelling ability, Spielberg surprises the world with the restraint and sensitivity of an ambitious, mature filmmaker; *Schindler's List* remains the most important mainstream American movie of the 1990s.

Schindler's List

After the over-the-top biopic of Jim Morrison, **The Doors** (1991), **Oliver Stone** creates his magnum opus, **JFK** (1991). This influential picture dissects investigation of the 1963 Kennedy assassination, providing few new discoveries and a lot of intriguing speculation, while pushing the envelope of moviemaking aesthetic. Stone interpolates his well-structured narrative with video and Super-8 inserts of meticulously staged documentary-like sequences which provide a dynamic counterpoint to the official version of the story. Right or wrong, *JFK's* remarkable audacity in confronting one of the most important events in American history deserves respect and admiration and proves once again that cinema is a great tool of ideological persuasion.

Oliver Stone

Stone's **Heaven and Earth** (1993) culminates his Vietnam War trilogy; this time the director exposes the aftermath of the conflict from the victim's perspective, following a Vietnamese peasant woman's experiences during and after the war, as the wife of a tormented US Marine.

In his typically controversial fashion, Stone takes the **Quentin Tarantino** story of **Natural Born Killers** (1994) for one crazy ride through the demented universe of mass murder, bloodthirsty media madness, moral corruption, and dysfunctional families that seems to comprise today's America in the eyes of the film's authors. The effect is a numbing but undeniably bold mixture of every imaginable film technique and narrative format, including mock sit-com, pseudo-documentary, road movie, and prison drama, edited with Godardesque contempt for continuity and MTV's breakneck pace that leaves viewers begging for less and shaken to the core.

Woody Harrelson and Juliette Lewis in *NBK*

Time and again, Oliver Stone confirms his status as the key innovator of mainstream American film and an impassioned social critic with an attitude.

Robert Altman returns from the lean 1980s with *The Player* (1992), the **Michael Tolkin**-written satire on Hollywood, whose lethal irony and accurate depiction of industry leaders' back-stabbing and ignorance make us understand why they continually get away with murder.

Mr. ALTMAN, IS *THE PLAYER* A PARODY OF HOLLYWOOD FORMULA FILMS?

IT'S IMPOSSIBLE TO DO A PARODY OF A PARODY.

ANY TIME YOU DO SOMETHING THAT DOESN'T HAVE A PATTERN ALREADY MADE FOR IT, IT'S VERY DIFFICULT. I'VE GOT TO BE ON THE EDGE, AND I'VE GOT TO DO SOMETHING I DON'T KNOW HOW TO DO. THAT'S THE FUN.

Robert Altman

Altman's nonchalant, episodic style of *The Player* also permeates the equally engrossing *Short Cuts* (1993), a loose adaptation of **Raymond Carver**'s short stories. Fluently crosscutting between multiple subplots that depict lives of 22 people, Altman creates a disturbing collage of contemporary urban existence, leaving little doubt about his sentiments toward Los Angeles and human depravity at large.

IN THE NAME OF ALL WRITERS I'M GOING TO KILL YOU!

Reading the fan mail:
Tim Robbins in *The Player*

While most of today's mainstream productions display a narrow emotional range, Robert Altman offers the full gamut of feelings and passions in the tradition of film's great masters and continues to surprise viewers with stylistic challenges and provoking imagery that questions the achievements of Western civilization.

Martin Scorsese enters the present decade with his greatest examination of the gangster life-style to date—***Goodfellas*** (1990). Based on an autobiographical story by **Nicholas Pileggi**, the movie chronicles an Irish-Italian man's initiation into the criminal underworld. With a peculiar flair for infusing repulsive violence with black humor, Scorsese reinforces the plot's muscular tempo with a soundtrack of great rock'n'roll tunes, dynamic editing, and swift camera work, which provide the old genre with a decisively original format.

HEY, HURRY UP, WILL YOU? MY MOTHER'S GONNA MAKE SOME FRIED PEPPERS AND SAUSAGE FOR US.

Joe Pesci in *Goodfellas*

Subsequently, Scorsese directs ***Cape Fear*** (1991), a glib remake of the 1961 noir original (directed by Jack Lee Thompson), designed to make money, and follows with ***The Age of Innocence*** (1993), an elegant but surprisingly frigid adaptation of **Edith Wharton**'s turn-of-the-century novel of sexual repression.

Scorsese's best work since *Goodfellas* is another Pileggi adaptation, ***Casino*** (1993), which probes a similar milieu, but without the former's panache.

CINEMA IS A MATTER OF WHAT'S IN THE FRAME AND WHAT'S OUT.

Martin Scorsese

A true lover of cinema, Scorsese stretches his film activities far beyond writing and directing. He is responsible for restoring and preserving numerous world cinema classics as well as for helping Eastman Kodak to develop new technologies of color film processing, which are now widely popular in the industry.

After an unfortunate attempt to imitate the German Expressionist aesthetic in *Shadows and Fog* (1992), **Woody Allen** abandons his venture into serious filmmaking for the safer territory of intelligent lightweight comedy in *Manhattan Murder Mystery* (1993).

Allen's next satirical project, *Bullets over Broadway* (1994), effortlessly recreates the jubilant mood of 1920s, focusing on backstage confusion during rehearsals for a new play. With its tongue-in-cheek pacing and hysterical humor, the movie is a directing triumph for Allen, who for the first time in years doesn't appear on screen.

Aiming for a broader audience with each consecutive film, Allen reaches for a slightly lower denomination with *Mighty Aphrodite* (1995), a sex farce involving a dim-witted hooker with a golden heart (**Mira Sorvino**) and the adopted father of her baby (Allen), who tries to do the right thing.

YOU STAND ON THE BRINK OF GREATNESS. THE WORLD WILL OPEN TO YOU LIKE AN OYSTER. NO...NOT LIKE AN OYSTER. THE WORLD WILL OPEN TO YOU LIKE A MAGNIFICENT VAGINA.

Diane Wiest and John Cusack
in *Bullets over Broadway*

Perhaps not as incisive and adventurous as in the previous decades, Woody Allen still remains one of the quintessential American auteurs, whose work possesses charm and edgy intelligence that has no equal.

The flashy neo-feminist road movie *Thelma and Louise* (1991), directed with gusto by **Ridley Scott**, becomes the first Hollywood big-budget buddy action movie to feature two female protagonists, whose adventures bring to height the bestiality of men.

Women drivers: Susan Sarandon
and Geena Davis in *Thelma and Louise*

When **James Cameron** releases his underwater sci-fi fantasy, *The Abyss*, in 1989, audiences witness something that has never been seen on the big screen before: a translucent, three-dimensional seawater creature (pseudopod) capable of mimicking any organic or artificial form in its surroundings. This special effect relies on a CGI technique called **morphing**, developed by programmers **Doug Smythe (ILM)** and **Tom Brigham (MIT)**, who independently of one another experiment with metamorphosis software in the 1980s. For ILM, the creator of *The Abyss*' visual effects, the pseudopod sequence becomes a defining moment.

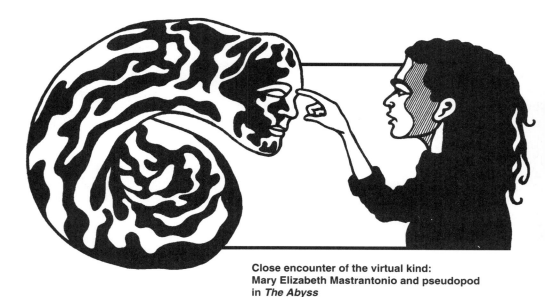

Close encounter of the virtual kind:
Mary Elizabeth Mastrantonio and pseudopod
in *The Abyss*

Supported again by ILM's ever inventive special effects team and powerful **Silicon Graphics Computers**, Cameron creates the unqualified masterpiece of modern action cinema—***Terminator 2: Judgement Day*** (1991). This terrific sci-fi adventure brings back heroes of the original ***Terminator*** (Cameron, 1984), who now battle an advanced, seemingly indestructible cyborg T-1000.

Aside from the edge-of-your-seat intensity of the plot, *Terminator 2* astonishes with its ingenious use of the morphing aesthetic: the mercurial T-1000 transforms itself into human forms or inanimate objects, liquids or solids, penetrates wall molecules and iron bars, and shatters to pieces only to pull itself back together. Conceptually, the movie recalls the surrealist paintings of Dali and Magritte and culminates with an allusion to Edvard Munch's *Scream* when the defeated T-1000 melts in a vat of pig iron.

Combining the latest technology with an engrossing narrative and breathtaking art direction, ***Terminator 2*** stands out as the single most revolutionary achievement of popular cinema of the decade.

Terminator 2's most inspiring visual effect, however, is the new role model of maternal care for the 1990s, personified by Linda Hamilton's buffed vigilance

DO I GET AN ACTION-MAMA FIGURE?

The next big challenge for ILM is provided by **Steven Spielberg** with his dinosaur adventure, **Jurassic Park** (1993). Originally conceived as a high-tech stop-motion animation project (much like the original *King-Kong*), the movie's preproduction stage reaches a real breakthrough when a test of a CGI model of a fully animated T-Rex skeleton provides a far more realistic illusion of movement than the traditional puppet techniques. Besides being a major box-office champ, *Jurassic Park* goes down in history as the first movie to feature living creatures created by computer, which seamlessly interact with real actors and environments.

I'M READY FOR MY CLOSE-UP, Señor SPIELBERGO!

The core of computer artists and animators responsible for the movie's visual triumph consists of **Dennis Murren**, **Phil Tippet**, and **Stan Winston**.

Hollywood is now convinced that computers are the most powerful tool of cinema, and with typical arrogance begins to churn-out CGI-driven movies. Unfortunately, the brilliant effects are supposed to substitute for a lack of story and cardboard cutout characters; the sequel to *Jurassic Park*, **The Lost World** (Spielberg, 1997) falls into this category, as does Cameron's disaster epic, *Titanic* (1997). Oh, yes, the latter ends up making a lot of money.

The first filmmaker to bring ILM's computer effects down to earth is **Robert Zemeckis**, whose *Forrest Gump* (1994) utilizes digital technology (under **Ken Ralston**'s supervision) to place its moronic protagonist (**Tom Hanks**) in key moments of recent American history. He also achieves such impressive illusions of reality as a floating feather, rain, or amputated legs, among numerous less noticeable details that elude viewer's attention.

Forrest Gump's ideology, however, is much less awe-inspiring.

LIFE IS LIKE A...

STOP RIGHT THERE, FORREST!

MILLIONS OF PEOPLE FELL FOR YOUR DIM-WITTED INNOCENCE, BUT YOU AIN'T GONNA FOOL OL' PROFESSOR FLICKER! YOUR CHARACTER SYMBOLIZES EVERYTHING THAT IS QUESTIONABLE ABOUT MODERN SOCIETY AT LARGE: GOING THROUGH LIFE WITHOUT ENGAGING YOUR BRAIN, FOOTBALL-PLAYING, WAR-FIGHTING, JOGGING, AND SUCCEEDING IN BUSINESS WITHOUT REALLY TRYING, WHILE THOSE AROUND YOU WHO CARE ABOUT HUMANITY LOSE THEIR LIMBS OR DIE OF AIDS, AS IF CONSCIENCE WAS A CARDINAL SIN IN TODAY'S WORLD! WHAT KIND OF A MESSAGE IS THAT?!

Forrest Gump becomes one of the top-grossing movies of all time.

In 1995, Disney releases the **Pixar**-made masterpiece of digital technology—*Toy Story*, a brain child of director **John Lasseter** (b. 1957), the pioneer of 3D computer animation. The movie becomes the first ever feature-length motion picture to rely exclusively on computer graphics, while still possessing the tempo and illusion of camera movement of a sophisticated live-action film. Moreover, *Toy Story* is a witty, intelligent tale for all ages, with more comedy, drama, and fleshed-out characters than most non-animated Hollywood features could only dream of.

Pearls before swine: Mr. Potato Head discusses principles of Cubism with Hamm the piggy bank in *Toy Story*:

LOOK AT ME! I'M A PICASSO!

I DON'T GET IT.

Another former Disney employee, **Tim Burton**, creates his neo-Gothic, Frankensteinesque paean to alienation, ***Edward Scissorhands*** (1990), which takes a charming stand against the inflexibility of suburbia.

Tim Burton recalls the dark ages of his Disney past:

I REALIZED FAIRLY EARLY ON THAT I WAS NOT CUT OUT FOR THAT, DRAWING FOXES. MY FOXES LOOKED LIKE ROADKILLS.

After his highly imaginative animated musical, ***Nightmare Before Christmas*** (1993), Burton focuses on the successful failure of Ed Wood, an obscure C-grade film director of the 1950s and a closet transvestite, whose unbelievable enthusiasm for filmmaking compensated for his profound lack of talent. Burton's wonderfully human biopic, titled simply ***Ed Wood*** (1994), approaches its effervescent subject with zeal that could only be equaled by Wood himself, shaping his story in a campy fashion reminiscent of cheaply made sci-fi and horror flicks of the period, complete with black-and-white photography and backdrop scenery that jiggles when touched. Part comedy and part drama, *Ed Wood* is Burton's heartfelt tribute to the unquenchable spirit of moviemaking—a true gem of originality from America's premier visual stylist in the 1990s.

CUT! PRINT! THAT WAS PERFECT!

Perverted optimism: Johnny Depp as Ed Wood

In his first attempt at directing, **Dances With Wolves** (1990), **Kevin Costner** (b. 1955) creates a believable, if slightly overcompensated image of Native American Indians, while portraying white men as inherently evil. Costner's handling of the Frontier theme impresses with sweeping vistas, colorful detail, and a firm grip on the human aspects of the story, which is told from the perspective of a Calvary officer (Costner) adopted into a Sioux community.

Kevin Costner and Graham Greene in *Dances With Wolves*

Another revisionist western, **Clint Eastwood**'s ***Unforgiven*** (1992), is a superb study of senseless violence, shot in a dark, moody style which recalls the noir aesthetic. Eastwood's pensive treatment of professional killer's ethic subverts some of the stereotypes he once helped to establish with his ultra-violent movies of the 1970s, as he finally decides to ask himself the essential question: what does it mean to take a man's life?

Billy Bob Thornton and Cynda Williams in *One False Move*

Another popular American genre to receive a strong boost of energy in the present decade is film noir. The best neonoirs to emerge in recent years come from lesser known directors working on modest budgets and without major stars.

After Dark My Sweet (dir. James Foley, 1991), based on a novel by Jim Thompson, puts a fresh spin on the classic drifter-meets-*femme fatale* gimmick.

Delusion (dir. Carl Colpaert, 1991) and ***One False Move*** (dir. Carl Franklin, 1992) combine noir themes with a road movie format. The former weaves an intricate tale of multiple betrayals set against desert landscapes, while the latter probes issues of racism and interpersonal relationships in a dynamic, suspenseful fashion.

John Dahl establishes himself as the key contemporary noir auteur with several variations on traditional schemes of the genre—***Kill Me Again*** (1990), ***Red Rock West*** (1993), and ***The Last Seduction*** (1994), while **Peter Medak**'s ***Romeo Is Bleeding*** (1994) utilizes a *cinéma du look* format to deliver one of the more visually stimulating neonoirs in recent memory, complete with over-the-top acting and improbable plot twists that somehow make perfect sense in the movie's hip post-modern context.

SO, YOU'RE THE BIG HOODLUM? PERSONALLY, I DON'T SEE IT.

KEEP LOOKIN'.

Lena Olin in *Romeo is Bleeding*

The allure of noir proves irresistible even for the British thespian *extraordinaire*, **Kenneth Branagh**, who directs and acts (with his leading lady **Emma Thompson**) in the stylish ***Dead Again*** (1991), an intelligent suspense thriller that owes much to Alfred Hitchcock.

Abel Ferarra enters the spotlight of controversy with ***Bad Lieutenant*** (1992), a hard-core live-action cartoon of the utter corruption of mind, body, and soul that is single-handedly raised to a new artistic level by **Harvey Keitel**'s no-hold-barred performance as a New York cop who is, well, no good at all.

Full frontal Harvey:
Keitel as Bad Lieutenant prepares for take-off

No other filmmaker in this decade has more impact on popular cinema than **Quentin Tarantino** (b. 1963), a self-taught writer-director who infuses the long forgotten term *cinéphile* with multiple new meanings. With his mind-blowing knowledge of world cinema (with emphasis on obscure trashy titles), Tarantino manages to transgress the traditions of gangster film to create easily the most unique crime movie of recent years—***Reservoir Dogs*** (1991). Openly lifting ideas from various classics of the genre from Kubrick's *The Killing* (1956) to Ringo Lam's *City on Fire* (1987), Tarantino's film is, nonetheless, a work of great originality, most notably in its subversive nonlinear narrative structure, which juggles the action between past, present, and future without breaking the story's continuity.

♪...STUCK IN THE MIDDLE WITH YOU... ♫

Tarantino's follow-up, ***Pulp Fiction*** (1994), co-written with **Roger Avary** (b. 1965), is a supremely entertaining pastiche of the gangster genre, composed of four interlocking stories told out of sequence.

Reservoir Dogs

Widely praised for its glossy surface of shrewd pop-cultural references, the movie's real merit lies in its reversal of old cinematic formulas. Rejecting pyrotechnic displays and special effects, *Pulp Fiction* becomes the first action movie in history where key scenes rely on witty conversation between full-blooded characters discussing insignificant details of life. Not unlike Antonioni, Tarantino celebrates the quieter moments of his story, marginalizing the plot's big turning points.

Last-minute career rescue:
John Travolta returns to spotlight in *Pulp Fiction*

I OWE YOU ONE, QUENTIN.

BIG TIME.

Formally, *Reservoir Dogs* and *Pulp Fiction* rely on long takes and minimal editing benefiting from the radiant photography of the Polish-born cinematographer **Andrzej Sekula**, who favors a warm yellow-orange palette and strange organic shadows that emerge from the backgrounds.

Among the best movies to expose the problems of the contemporary urban existence of minorities are **Boyz N the Hood** (1991) and **American Me** (1992), both set in Los Angeles.

In *Boyz*, writer-director **John Singleton** (b. 1968) takes a careful, human look at the dynamics of a black community, focusing on several young men from dysfunctional families torn between very few positive options and the self-destructive pressures of gang violence.

YOU'LL NEVER AMOUNT TO ANYTHING!

YOU'LL NEVER AMOUNT TO ANYTHING!

YOU'LL NEVER AMOUNT TO ANYTHING!

Ice Cube in *Boyz N the Hood*

Edward James Olmos' *American Me* dissects the Latino experience from the perspective of a middle-aged man (Olmos), who tries to piece his life together after spending 18 years in jail. In contrast to *Boyz N the Hood*, Olmos' film contains no uplifting message, as it relies on shocking depictions of the self-perpetuating street and prison violence that blossoms among the underprivileged in American society.

After leaping into a conventional mainstream format with **Mo' Better Blues** (1990) and **Jungle Fever** (1991), Spike Lee creates an ambitious big-budget biopic, **Malcolm X** (1992). Surprisingly tame for its controversial topic, the movie emphasizes the possibility of rising from a seemingly dead-end life-style into a position of great influence through hard work and religious dedication.

Denzel Washington as Malcolm X

Later in the decade, Lee enters Martin Scorsese's territory of the criminal New York underworld with **Clockers** (1995), a poignant analysis of contemporary urban subculture that pits black people against one another and entraps even those who try to rise above the vicious cycle of drugs and violence.

With his breakneck pace of one movie per year in the past ten years, Spike Lee's creative energy fluctuates from one project to another, yet he remains one of the most socially committed filmmakers of his time—a sensitive artist with a conscience and great flair for the medium of cinema.

THE INDEPENDENTS

or how the future of American film is shaped today

The big-budget Hollywood aesthetic, with its perfectly exposed color, postcard composition, and music over-accentuating each turn of the action, is well suited to action or comedy genres, but in movies dealing with realistic aspects of life it is plainly ridiculous.

Growing in prominence since the mid 1980s, American independent film continues to provide a healthy alternative to mainstream entertainment with boundless energy and originality of styles.

Some of the independently produced movies like *Boyz N the Hood*, *Reservoir Dogs*, or *Bad Lieutenant* are shot with professional crews on modest budgets, while others—**The Ultimate Fringe Films** (**TUFF**s)—emerge out of kitchen-table editing suits, leaving their authors deeply in debt.

Slacker

In the case of **Richard Linklater** (b. 1962) the max-out-your-credit-card budget of $23.000 produces the quintessential counterculture masterwork of its time, *Slacker* (1991).

The movie's fascinating structure relies on short, intense, emotional scenes which allow each of the nearly 100 eccentric characters to appear on screen only once, then pass the torch of continuity onto the next person. **Lee Daniel**'s fluid camera work provides an offhand connection between the pieces of Linklater's mosaic, unobtrusively probing the hot summer day environment of lost souls, conspiracy freaks, and coffee-shop types who form a collective hero of great eloquence and charisma.

> YO, HEY DUDE...MAN, I'M FREAKING OUT SO SEVERELY.

Other notable no-budget TUFFs include **Robert Rodriguez**' (b. 1969) *El Mariachi* (1992), a dynamic offbeat action film shot in Mexico in the heroic bloodshed mode; *Clerks* (1994), **Kevin Smith**'s (b. 1970) foulmouthed portrayal of young suburban dwellers that brims with irreverent humor and dead-on observations of life on the edge of society; and **Edward Burns**' (b. 1968) gripping family drama, *The Brothers McMullen* (1995), which recalls Woody Allen's sensitivity for character-driven plots and boldly defies the norms of commercial cinema.

El Mariachi

One of decade's best coming-of-age stories comes from **Todd Solondz**, the author of **_Welcome to the Dollhouse_** (1995), an unusually perceptive probe into the cruel universe of an 11-year-old girl whose ugly duckling experience goes well beyond traumatic. Supported by deliberately tacky art direction and a bleak New Jersey landscape, the movie makes a disturbing commentary on the dynamics of a homogenous suburban community, where love is a four-letter word on a plastic earring and compassion—a crime.

> I DON'T WANT TO GO TO DISNEYWORLD.

Wiener Sucks ↑ BIG TIME

LOVE

Heather Matarazzo in _Welcome to the Dollhouse_

Brooklyn and its colorful natives become the center of **_Smoke_** and its companion piece, **_Blue in the Face_** (both 1995), a pair of uniquely constructed movies that emerge out of the collaboration between independent director **Wayne Wang** and novelist **Paul Auster**. The latter film is comprised of improvised anecdotes unified by their common location—a corner cigar store, whose patrons engage in strange but illuminating conversations.

> WE LIT THEM UP... WE STARTED INHALING... COUGHING. COUPLE OF MINUTES LATER, WE'RE SICK, NAUSEOUS...DIZZY. BUT WE FELT SO COOL. LIKE, REAL BAD-ASS TEN-YEAR-OLD KIDS.

> GOT A LIGHT?

Jim Jarmusch fondly remembers his first smoke in _Blue in the Face_

Appearing in many independent projects in cameo roles, **Jim Jarmusch** continues to direct such original films as **_Mystery Train_** (1989), **_Night on Earth_** (1992), and **_Dead Man_** (1995), which study individual quirkiness of their characters rather than tell traditionally structured stories.

In recent years, **Tim Robbins** (b. 1958) has established himself not only as a versatile actor (*The Player*, *Shawshank Redemption*), but also as a prominent filmmaker with a decisively independent vision. His writing-directing debut, ***Bob Roberts*** (1992), is a wicked satire on American politics and media, who work shoulder to shoulder in manipulating voters' perception of reality.

Robbins' unsentimental ***Dead Man Walking*** (1995), based on the autobiographical book by **Sister Helen Prejean** (**Susan Sarandon**), portrays a strong-willed Catholic nun who helps a Death Row murderer (**Sean Penn**) find remorse for his senseless crimes.

Just when you thought Method Acting was dead:
Susan Sarandon and Sean Penn discuss their craft on the set of *Dead Man Walking*

The fatalistic story of ***Leaving Las Vegas***, based on **John O'Brien**'s book, exemplifies the darker direction of contemporary American film. Following the downward spiral of a has-been Hollywood writer who decides to drink himself to death in the human circus of Las Vegas, the movie manages to reach levels of emotion rarely seen in today's domestic cinema.

The fact that its writer-director **Mike Figgis** (b. 1950) is British is significant, but it is the outstanding performances of **Nicolas Cage** and **Elisabeth Shue** that provide the film with its edge.

Ready to pass out for a permanent stretch of time: Nicolas Cage in *Leaving Las Vegas*

One of the most exciting independent directors of recent years to receive studio backing is **Gus Van Sant**, who follows *Drugstore Cowboy* with *My Own Private Idaho* (1991), a flamboyant treatment of loneliness and male teen prostitution with a hint of Shakespeare. Despite its stylistic excess, this film has more to offer than most major releases of the time.

In his brilliant satire *To Die For* (1995), Van Sant denounces the corruptive nature of mass media, focusing on an obsessive young woman's (**Nicole Kidman**) dream of television stardom. Told in flashbacks from multiple points of view, the movie oscillates between docudrama, "hard-hitting" news reporting, and straight narrative, evoking a paranoid mood that reflects the protagonist's dementia and, by extension, the mentality of fame-obsessed America.

> YOU AREN'T REALLY ANYBODY IN AMERICA IF YOU'RE NOT ON TV.

Nicole Kidman delivers the news in *To Die For*

Out of the Long Island wasteland hails **Hal Hartley** (b. 1959), a director of cool perception and minimalist style, who celebrates the slow-paced passions of suburban existence in *Trust* (1991) and follows two brothers on a father-searching road trip in *Simple Men* (1992). Set in New York, Hartley's *Amateur* (1994) is an off-kilter thriller which involves an amnesiac, a former nun who writes erotica novels, and an ex-porn star. With its restrained editing and leisurely pace, the movie combines elements of suspense with moodiness of an art film.

Martin Donovan and Elina Lowensöhn in *Amateur*

The new master of verbal nuance, writer-director **Whit Stillman** (b. 1952), creates the witty nocturne *Metropolitan* (1990), a scathing mockery of the aspiring young intellectual elite of New York's high society. His driven by droll conversation *Barcelona* (1994) is a charming, relentlessly derisive story of Ted and Fred, two young Americans who search for cerebral and carnal fulfillment in the post-Franco Spain of the early 1980s.

After the brilliant stylistic exercise in the gangster genre, *Miller's Crossing* (1990), **Joel** and **Ethan Coen** create *Barton Fink* (1991), one of the most artistically accomplished independent movies of recent years. Inspired by the desperate career turns of Clifford Odets and William Faulkner, the movie satirizes Golden Age Hollywood for its indiscriminate exploitation of great writing talents and reaches for hellishly abstract metaphors to denounce the paranoia of studio system.

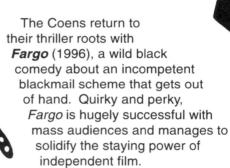

A writer behind his block John Torturro in *Barton Fink*

The Coens return to their thriller roots with *Fargo* (1996), a wild black comedy about an incompetent blackmail scheme that gets out of hand. Quirky and perky, *Fargo* is hugely successful with mass audiences and manages to solidify the staying power of independent film.

I THINK I'M GONNA BARF NOW.

Move over Clint, there's a new sheriff in town: Frances McDormand in *Fargo*

David Lynch creates the over-the-top love story, *Wild at Heart* (1990), which subverts the road movie genre in a perversely humorous, erotic, and, of course, deranged manner that is just as entertaining as it seems devoid of emotions. After a long hiatus, Lynch returns with *Lost Highway* (1997), a dark probe into the moist subconscious mind, which can be clumsily summarized as an enigmatic but nonetheless persuasive study of paranoid male jealousy. Both features are based on the intriguing writings of **Barry Gifford**, a great Northern California writer.

Ang Lee's *The Ice Storm* (1997), based on a novel by **Rick Moody**, dissects he dynamics of an affluent but heavily dysfunctional suburban community in New Canaan, Connecticut. To reinforce the theme of emotional and spiritual breakdown of he protagonists, Lee chooses an eerie, detached aesthetic reminiscent of the Photorealist art of the 1970s. The brilliant cinematographer **Fred Elmes**, a long-time collaborator of John Cassavetes and David Lynch, creates an appropriate atmosphere with washed-out pastel hues and clinically crisp detail. In a time of blockbusting sequels, *The Ice Storm* stands tall as one of the most challenging and artistically accomplished American films of the decade.

The seminal independent auteur of the 1980s, **Steven Soderbergh**, fuses biography of **Franz Kafka** with the twisted world of the writer's novels in *Kafka* (1991), a gripping exercise in form, and creates a moving portrayal of the Depression in *King of the Hill* (1993), shot from a child's point of view.

After exploring different visual approaches in each consecutive film, Soderbergh comes full circle with his recent low-budget independent adventure *Schizopolis* (1997)— he freshest, most inspired, and possibly groundbreaking movie to emerge out of America in years.

Self-reflexive beyond measure, *Schizopolis* is a deliberate cinematic aberration in the best sense of the word. Soderbergh synthesizes all possible modes of narration and subverts them with a delightful perversity. As a social satire, the movie manages to savage a wide spectrum of contemporary topics, including cinema itself, but at its core it laments the loss of our ability to communicate feelings and thoughts.

LADIES AND GENTLEMEN, YOUNG AND OLD, TALL AND SHORT! THE MOVIE YOU'RE ABOUT TO SEE IS THE MOST IMPORTANT MOVIE OF YOUR LIFE.

Soderbergh introduces his film in the opening shot of *Schizopolis*

The sheer fact that *Schizopolis* is financed by a major studio (Universal), albeit for pocket change, fortifies the impression that American film stands at the brink of a very bright future. No longer able to ignore the power of independent work, mainstream cinema begins to shyly explore some of the structural and conceptual innovations of smaller films, as fringe filmmakers are now becoming a hot commodity in the industry. Before this trend blows over, we should be able to witness some very interesting work.

Little Epilogue

WHAT IS CINEMA? WHAT MAKES IT SO POPULAR?

SOME CALL IT THE SYNTHESIS OF ALL ARTS.

BUT CINEMA TRANSCENDS ITS MANY COMPONENTS TO EMERGE AS AN INDEPENDENT FORM OF CREATIVITY. IT HAS A LIFE OF ITS OWN.

TO MANY PEOPLE, FILM IS NOTHING BUT A TOOL OF MECHANICAL REPRODUCTION OF REALITY.

TO OTHERS, IT IS A MEDIUM OF GREAT SENSITIVITY, CAPABLE OF EVOKING A NEARLY SPIRITUAL EXPERIENCE.

PLATO

IS WATCHING SHADOWS PROJECTED ONTO A MOVIE SCREEN COMPARABLE TO PLATO'S CAVE ALLEGORY, WHERE ILLUSION SUBSTITUTES FOR THE REAL WORLD?

If so, perhaps we, the spectators, are drawn to the celluloid illusion as a replacement for our unfulfilled expectations of life.

Week after week, we return almost religiously to the dim auditorium of a movie theatre. We sit there in silence and awe, surrounded by strangers, as the little beam of flickering light lures us into a self-contained universe of dreams, passions, and fears—a place of suspended disbelief and possibilities without limits.

THE END

anamorphic lens—(*Greek* "form anew") mounted on the camera, an anamorphic lens compresses the width of an image to fit it into the film's frame (the height of the image remains constant). During projection, an anamorphic lens "de-squeezes" the image into its original size to produce a widescreen effect. When used with a 35mm film stock, widescreen projection aspect ratio is 2.35:1 (CinemaScope); a 70mm stock yields a 2.75:1 ratio (Panavision 70)

angle, camera angle—position of the camera in relation to the photographed image; high angle—camera above the subject; low angle—camera below the subject; dutch angle—camera tilted to one side to deviate from the horizontal and vertical axis of the image

aspect ratio—standardized ratio of a projected image's width to its height (Academy—1.33:1; widescreen—1.66:1 European, 1.85:1 American; 70mm—2.2:1; CinemaScope—2.35:1; Panavision 70—2.75:1)

asynchronous sound, **contrapuntal sound**—any sound whose source cannot be seen within the frame of the film

auteur—(*French* "author") a term applied to a filmmaker with a unique visual style and thematic commitment that permeate his or her body of work. *La Politique des auteurs* (Politics of the Authors) was originated by François Truffaut in the film journal *Cahiers du cinéma* in 1954 and popularized by the American critic Andrew Sarris, who coined the phrase "The Auteur Theory" in the early 1960s

available light—a natural source of light illuminating a scene which doesn't involve any artificial lighting by the cinematographer (i.e. sunlight)

benshi—the traditional live narrator of a Japanese silent film

biopic—a biographical motion picture

block booking—the distributor-enforced practice of leasing a group of inferior films together with successful titles

blockbuster—a film which generates a huge financial profit; most commonly refers to extremely expensive Hollywood productions

blocking—the arrangement of actors' movements within each shot

blue screen process—a special effects process which involves photographing a person or an object against a bright blue screen and adding to the image any desired background through **optical printing** ("green screen" is the recent digital variation of it)

CGI—computer generated imagery

cinéaste—a French term applied to an enthusiastic and knowledgeable filmmaker with a great admiration for cinema

cinematography—film photography

cinéma vérité—(*French* "cinema truth") a confrontational style of documentary filmmaking which relies on lightweight portable equipment and small, mobile crews

cinéphile—a film lover

close-up—tight framing of an object or a person which allows for greater descriptiveness than a medium shot

concept art—any artwork which visualizes a specific style of a movie (e.g. futuristic architecture or costumes for a sci-fi movie)

continuity editing—an editing principle which maintains a smooth and chronological flow of the action

crane shot—a high-angle shot obtained with the camera mounted on a hydraulic arm (crane) or other device high above the ground

crosscutting or **parallel editing**—an editing technique that tells several stories simultaneously by juxtaposing scenes from each distinct story line

day-for-night—cinematographic technique which allows for shooting night scenes in daylight either with the help of a lens filter or by means of exposure manipulation

deep focus—cinematographic technique which presents all elements within a shot in focus regardless of their distance to the camera

depth of field—distance between the closest and farthest elements within a shot which remain in sharp focus; varies according to the lens' **focal length**, amount of light, and sensitivity (speed) of the film stock

dissolve—a fading-in image replaces the fading-out image

dollying—a moving shot in which the camera travels on tracks or wheels

dubbing—the process of recording dialogue or sound effects after the film has been sho

establishing shot—an overview shot which introduces the environment of a particular scene

expressionist film—a motion picture whose aesthetic relies mainly on a subjective distortion of reality as opposed to striving for realism

fade-in—an image gradually appears on film

fade-out—an image slowly fades away into white or black background or is gradually replaced by another image

fast stock, fast film—film stock that is very sensitive to light and does not require much illumination for proper exposure; yields more grainy and less detailed images than **slow stock**

film noir—(*French* "black film") a gloomy, stylized American urban thriller or detective picture of the 1940s and 1950s. Contemporary film noir pictures are referred to as "neonoir"

flashback—a film sequence describing the previous events of the narrative

flashforward—a film sequence which suggests future events of the plot

focal length—distance between the optical center of the lens and the film plane inside the camera where the farthermost image achieves sharp focus (fish-eye lens—extremely short focal length; wide-angle lens—short focal length; telephoto lens—long focal length)

focus puller—assistant cameraman responsible for maintenance of the camera equipment and adjusting focus

formalistic film—a film concerned more with its artistry than ideology

freeze-frame—a still image obtained through multiple repetition of the same frame

front projection—in this special effect, live action is filmed against a reflective screen while background imagery is projected at a 90° angle onto the screen through a semi-transparent mirror aligned with the camera

gage—the width of film; 8mm and Super 8 are mostly used by amateurs, 16mm and Super 16 are preferred in documentary, television, and low-budget work; 35mm is the standard commercial gage; 65mm and 70mm are chiefly the domain of big-budget epics; IMAX gage (frame area 3 times larger than 70mm) is being explored for super high-definition theme park attraction films

hand-held—any shot obtained with a camera held by its operator without any support; originally utilized in war and *cinéma vérité* documentaries, hand-held shots are used in narrative film to enhance the realism of action

hand-tinting—manual coloration of film strip which produces a desired mood for the projected image (e.g. a blue tint for nighttime)

high-key lighting—a cinematographic term for a high ratio of the primary (key) light to secondary (fill) lights; produces low-contrast, brightly lit images

independent film—a motion picture produced outside of the studio system; mostly, but not exclusively, of limited commercial appeal

irising—a circular expansion or contraction of the image

jump-cut—an editing technique which deliberately breaks up the continuity of a scene by "jumping" ahead in the action

Kammerspielfilm—(*German* "chamber-theatre film") the type of silent German film which deals with a small number of characters in psychologically complex situations

key light—the main artificial light source on a movie set

kino-glaz—(*Russian* "cinema eye") a documentary film aesthetic popularized by Dziga Vertov in 1920s which stressed the self-reflexive technical inventiveness of the director

lens—a transparent optical device mounted on a camera which transfers a live image onto film stock by means of light beam refraction

location shoot—shooting performed in a real environment as opposed to a studio sound stage or back lot

long shot—a shot which presents a wide perspective of the scene's environment and is usually obtained with a **wide-angle lens**

long take—an extended shot uninterrupted by editing which allows for a detailed exposition of the **mise-en-scène**

low key lighting—a cinematographic term for a low ratio of the key light to fill lights; typical of film noir, low-key lighting yields dramatic, high-contrast shadows

Magic Lantern—a 17th century apparatus designed to project images from glass plates

masking—reshaping the filmed image by blocking off parts of the camera view

matte painting—a highly realistic painting which is composed into a shot to create a specific background or foreground

medium shot—a manner of framing which presents an object or a character in a closer perspective than the establishing shot but not as tight as a close-up

mind screen—presenting the perspective of a character's mind (e.g. dreams, thoughts)

minimalism—film aesthetic characterized by a sparse, economical amount of information contained within each scene

mise-en-scène—(*French* "to put in a scene") a film directing principle which considers all elements involved in creating a particular scene (acting, lighting, camera movement, etc.

montage—(*French* "to assemble") a term that refers to the art of editing in general; also, film editing principles developed by Soviet filmmakers in 1920s which emphasized rapid juxtaposition of short, often colliding shots; montage can additionally mean any sequence of elaborately edited shots

multiple exposure—repeated exposure of the negative resulting in overlapping imagery

neorealism—film movement which originated in Italy during the last stages of WWII characterized by realistic, socially committed plots, nonprofessional acting, and location shooting

Nouvelle Vague—(*French* "new wave") French film movement initiated in the late 1950s by filmmakers associated with the film journal *Cahiers du cinéma*

nickelodeon—the first movie theatre in America built exclusively for presentation of film programs; "nickel"—admission price, "odeon"—Greek for "theatre"

off-screen space—the invisible space outside of the movie's frame where part of the action takes place unseen

optical printer—cinematographic device composed of a camera interlocked with a projector which allows for the **superimposition** of separate elements into a single frame (i.e. actors or objects placed on desired backgrounds); optical printer is also used for **dissolves**, **fades**, **wipes**, **optical zoom effects**, and **blue screen process**

optical zoom effect—a zoom-in or -out effect obtained in postproduction through **optical printing** as opposed to zoom effects achieved with a camera and **zoom lens**

panning—horizontal movement of the camera around its vertical axis

parallel action—telling several stories simultaneously through **crosscutting**

postproduction—the part of moviemaking process that follows the shooting: editing, postsynchronization, special effects, etc.

postsynchronization—recording sound after the shooting and synchronizing it with the image

rack focus—changing focus from one element of a shot to another; also known as **selective focusing**

ratings—the current classification of film content imposed by MPAA is divided into five categories: G—general, PG—parental guidance, PG-13—parental guidance for children under 13, R—restricted to children under 17 unless accompanied by an adult, NC-17—no persons under 17

reaction shot—a shot which presents the character's response to depicted or implied action

rear projection—in this special effect, live action is filmed against a translucent screen; background imagery is projected onto the screen from behind

rough cut—a tentative draft of the movie after the initial editing is completed

rushes or **dailies**—quickly processed footage from the previous day's shooting viewed before the next working day

scene—any length of film unified by a common theme; it may consist of one shot or a series of edited shots

score—a film's musical accompaniment

screenplay—the movie's action and dialogue presented in a written form

sequence—a unit of continuous dramatic action composed of related shots and scenes

sequence shot—a single, uninterrupted shot of significant duration, frequently involving elaborate camera movement; see also **long take**

shallow focus—camera is focused on one element within a shot while other planes of action remain out of focus

shooting script—a copy of the movie's screenplay which includes precise directions for camera movement, lighting, blocking, and other technical information

shot—a basic unit of film structure in which the action appears to be continuous

slapstick—a style of film comedy rooted in vaudeville, burlesque, and circus

slow motion—the camera runs at a speed higher than the standard 24 frames per second; when projected at normal speed, the filmed action appears to be slower (fast motion is achieved by reversing the procedure)

slow stock, **slow film**—film stock that is not very sensitive to light and requires more careful illumination; yields images of greater clarity and sharpness than **fast stock**

snuff film—an illegal film depicting real torture and death intended to sexually stimulate the viewer

sound stage—soundproof studio designed for shooting film and recording sound

sound track—the narrow strip of film located next to the image on which all sound information is encoded optically or magnetically

sprocket holes—perforations on one or both sides of the film strip which allow for a steady movement of film through the camera, projector, or printer

stock—unprocessed film

stock footage—film footage available for rent or purchase, usually of documentary origin, which is inserted into a motion picture

stop motion—cinematographic technique involving continuous stopping and starting of the camera; in animation, each movement of the subject (a cartoon, a puppet) is photographed one or more frames at a time

storyboarding—sketching individual shots on paper for production reference

subjective camera—a camera angle presenting the perspective (point of view) of a character in the film

subjective sound—deliberate emphasis of a particular sound within a scene

superimposition—a visual effect in which several images overlap one another

synchronous sound or **naturalistic sound**—any sound whose source is immediately visible in the **shot**

take—uninterrupted coverage of a single **shot**; each shot is covered by multiple takes from which the best take is chosen for the final cut of the film

telephoto lens, long lens—a telescopic lens with a long **focal length** which typically yields shallow depth of field; used primarily for filming distant objects in close-up

tilting—vertical movement of the camera around its horizontal axis

time-lapse photography—cinematic technique allowing for filming action that normally would be either too slow or too fast for the human eye to register (e.g. growth of a flower or a bullet coming out of a gun's barrel)

tracking shot—any shot when the camera travels horizontally on a dolly or a vehicle

travelling matte—a special effect technique used in **optical printing** which combines parts of different images to create a new composite image

voice-over—a voice heard over the action which is not synchronized with any characters appearing on screen

wide-angle lens, short lens—any lens with a short focal length providing a great **depth of field** and a wide perspective of view

widescreen—term applied to any film format with an **aspect ratio** greater than the Academy (1.33:1)

wipe—special effect in which one image appears to be pushed out of the frame by another

zoom lens—a lens with adjustable **focal length** varying form **wide-angle** to **telephoto**

zoom shot—any shot obtained with a **zoom lens** which includes a noticeable change of perspective; zooming from **wide-angle** to **telephoto** is called "zoom-in"; the reverse is called "zoom-out"

David A. Cook's third edition of **A History of Narrative Film** (New York: W.W. Norton & Company, 1996) is doubtlessly the most comprehensive and accessible English-language text on cinema history.

Bruce F. Kawin's revision of the classic cinema history textbook, **A Short History of the Movies**, by the late Gerald Mast (New York: Macmillan, 1992), outlines the history of cinema in a fluent, uncomplicated fashion that makes it a college favorite. The book also contains an outstanding general index of important films and related bibliography.

Louis D. Gianetti's **Understanding Movies** (New Jersey: Prentice-Hall, Inc., 1990) breaks down the mystery of film into enjoyable, informative chapters on individual components of the moviemaking process (i.e. photography, mise-en-scène, editing, etc.).

Adam Garbicz and Jacek Klinowski present the greatest achievements of world cinema in the compact, eloquent, and highly informative series, **Cinema, The Magic Vehicle**, vol. I and II (New York: Schocken Books, 1983).

Jerry Vermilye's comprehensive **The Great British Films** (Secaucus, N.J.: The Citadel Press, 1978) is a terrific first step for becoming familiar with the multifaceted British cinema.

James Reid Paris's **The Great French Films** (Secaucus, N.J.: The Citadel Press, 1983) will satisfy any budding film lover's thirst for basic information on French cinema.

Joseph L. Anderson and Donald Richie provide a thorough analysis of Japanese cinema from historical and social perspectives in **The Japanese Film** (Princeton, N.J.: Princeton University Press, 1982).

Nicholas Galichenko outlines the directions and sensitivities of contemporary Soviet film in **Glasnost—Soviet Cinema Responds** (University of Texas Press, 1991).

Film India: The New Generation 1960-1980 (Umada Cunha, Ed., New Delhi: The Directorate of Film Festivals, 1981) reviews the key films of *parallel cinema* and profiles its most accomplished directors.

Aleksander Kwiatkowski's **Scandinavian Film** is the greatest introductory text on cinema of Sweden, Norway, Denmark, and Finland.

The Great Spanish Films: 1950-1990 by Ronald Schwartz (Metuchen, N.J. & London: The Scarecrow Press, Inc., 1991) provides a well structured introduction to Spanish cinema.

Black African Cinema by Nwachukwn Frank Ukadike (Berkeley: University of California Press, 1994) is an indispensable text for anyone interested in this continent's film production.

The beautifully illustrated **Bulgarian Cinema** by Ronald Holloway (Associated University Press, Inc., 1986) does great justice to Eastern Europe's most underrated cinema.

Peter Bondanella's *Italian Cinema: From Neorealism to the Present* (New York: Continuum, 1990) is an eloquent, very fluent study on Italian film that will satisfy beginners as well as more advanced film lovers.

The recently published *Australian Cinema* (Scott Murray, ed., St Leonards, Australia: Australian Film Commission, 1994) is a richly illustrated, thorough glossary of cinema Down Under and includes a fantastically detailed index of its best films and directors.

John Sandford's *The New German Cinema* (New York: Da Capo Press, 1980) must be regarded as the essential English-language text on postwar German cinema's most fascinating period of creativity (c. 1965-82).

The relatively new phenomenon of American independent cinema is presented in the competent, highly entertaining pocket-size *Independent Visions* by Donald Lyons (New York: Ballantine Books, 1994).

Film Theory and Criticism (Gerald Mast and Marshall Cohen, Eds., Oxford University Press, 1985) contains an excellent selection of introductory readings by the world's most respected and astute film theoreticians and critics.

A great collection of introductory readings on cinema's most influential pioneer, *Focus On D.W. Griffith* (Harry M. Geduld, ed., Englewood Cliffs, N.J.: Spectrum, 1973) contains short nostalgic essays by Lillian Gish, Erich von Stroheim, and Griffith himself, as well as critical accounts by renowned film scholars.

Sergei Eisenstein's *Film Form* (Jay Leyda, ed., Harvest/HBJ, 1977) provides a great insight into the art of Soviet montage and dialectical filmmaking.

Kino-Eye—The Writings of Dziga Vertov (Berkeley: University of California Press, 1984) is an eye-opening collection of essays by cinema's first great experimentalist and hotheaded revolutionary.

The inconspicuous little book, *The Making of Citizen Kane*, by Robert L. Carringer (Berkeley: University of California Press, 1985) delivers a surprisingly rich and detailed account of cinema's most beloved masterpiece.

The Book of Film Noir (Ian Cameron, ed., New York: Continuum, 1993) contains an enlightening collection of critical essays on noir cinema and its most prominent figures and discusses some of the most notable contemporary examples of the genre.

Those interested in the art of cinematography will find Brian Coe's richly illustrated *The History of Movie Photography* (Westfield, N.J.: Eastview Editions, 1981) to be as informative as it is entertaining.

The author also recomeds the following English-language film magazines and periodicals: *Cineaste*, *Film Comment*, *Film Quarterly*, *Filmmaker*, *East-West Film Journal*, *Sight and Sound*, *American Film*.

ACKNOWLEDGMENTS

David A. Cook's *A History of Narrative Film* and **Bruce F. Kawin**'s revision of **Gerald Mast**'s *A Short History of the Movies* provided structural inspiration for *Cinema fo Beginners*.

A fantastic digital workstation was custom-designed for me by my friend and computer guru **Kevin Murray Page**. Without his generous help and invaluable advice this book would have looked like a note on a napkin.

Elaine Kaufmann's expert editorial suggestions and proofreading effectively disguised the strange ESL syntax of the first draft. Her friendship and presence in the darkest hour were a pure blessing.

The **J. Paul Leonard Library** at San Francisco State University deserves highest praise for its outstanding selection of film literature and strategically located water fountains.

I also want to thank Chris Page and Dana Levy for numerous yummies and caffeine-rich beverages as well as their tolerance.

Special *gracias* goes to Przemek Thiele for the ongoing immoral support.

About the author and illustrator

Jarek Kupść, the author, has been interested in cinema since the age of 5, when his cousin Malgorzata Thiele allowed him to browse through her collection of old film magazines. He then embarked on a long and arduous journey as a filmgoer, nearly flunking his senior year in high school due to a Coppola revival in his native Warsaw, Poland. His formal training includes a degree in film studies from the Community College of San Francisco and a BA in film writing and directing from San Francisco State University. He has been reviewing American films for the Polish radio and collaborated on cinema-related multimedia endeavors. In addition to writing about film, Señor Kupść is also a filmmaker. He has completed two red-lighted screenplays and shot numerous short films of which his latest, *Dog*, received an obscure Rosebud Award in best drama category.

He is also a published writer in the field of short fiction.

Jarek Kupść, the illustrator, quit art school at 16 and began his professional career as a graphic artist three years later in Athens, Greece, where he drew cartoons for local publications, solicited his skills as a street portraitist, and attempted to survive as a fine artist. After exhibiting his paintings and drawings in Philadelphia, PA, he relocated to California in 1989 and had his first solo show in San Francisco at 23. He boasts to be the first painter in history to have his work traded for a root canal job. Simultaneously with honing his fine art skills, Jarek became a commercial designer in the fine field of T-Shirt art. The long list of his clients includes The Bob Marley Estate, The National Museum of Natural History, New York, The Field Museum, Chicago, San Francisco's MOMA, The Nature Company, Imaginarium, NASA, and virtually every major zoo in the country.

He won his first and last art competition at 12, shortly before realizing that art should not be a competitive sport.

Jarek Kupść
(ya'rek coopshch)

after Andrzej Konstantinow